FEDERAL INCOME TAXATION OF INDIVIDUALS

IN A NUTSHELL

Seventh Edition

By

JOHN K. McNULTY

Roger J. Traynor Professor of Law, Emeritus
University of California, Berkeley

DANIEL J. LATHROPE

Professor of Law
University of California, Hastings

Mat #40244409

COPYRIGHT © 1972, 1978, 1983, 1988, 1995 WEST PUBLISHING CO.
COPYRIGHT © 1999 WEST GROUP
© 2004 West, a Thomson business
       610 Opperman Drive
       P.O. Box 64526
       St. Paul, MN 55164–0526
       1–800–328–9352
Printed in the United States of America

ISBN 0–314–15270–9

For my dear grandchildren,
Shea, Kyle, Conner, Kiara, and Trevor

J.K.M.

For my loving and supportive parents,
Robert and Wanda Lathrope

D.J.L.

*

PREFACE

This book, now in its seventh edition, is designed to serve as an introduction to the U.S. law of Federal Income Taxation of individuals. It thus stands as a companion to McNulty and McCouch, "Federal Estate and Gift Taxation in a Nutshell" now in its sixth edition (2003). It is written for use by law students as a supplement to usual law school courses and materials, by foreign lawyers or scholars, and perhaps as a refresher (or an introduction) for members of the bar. It summarizes the law and inquires occasionally into the policy and purposes of, and alternatives to, existing legal rules. It does not attempt a thorough critical evaluation or an adequate history or justification of the law.

The Federal Income Tax law is immensely complicated, sometimes subtle or obscure and often puzzling. Legislation during the years since the publication of the early editions of this book in the 1970s has accentuated all these characteristics. Nevertheless, a conceptual basis and structure, principles susceptible of logical and orderly analysis and presentation, can be discerned amidst the complications. It is the discovering and laying bare of that conceptual framework that forms the principal aim of this book. The extreme textual richness and the sweeping scope of the law and the problems with which it attempts to deal force this short book, even more than most such efforts, to serve as a bare beginning and a capsule review of the subject.

This edition contains new material that reflects the important developments since the sixth edition, including legislative changes in the areas of cost recovery and capital gains. New sections are also included on the taxation of the costs of education and the reduced tax rates for dividends.

The Federal Income Tax statute (the Internal Revenue Code §§ 1–1563 in particular) forms such a focus of the subject matter that a copy almost must be kept open by the side of this book. Frequent references are necessary inasmuch as the Code provisions could not be spelled out in full. Citations to statutes are to sections of the Internal Revenue Code as amended through early 2004. Such citations are usually made in the form "I.R.C. §§ _____ ", to distinguish them from cross references to other sections of this book, generally cited as "§§ _____ , *infra*." Section numbers of the Internal Revenue Code, as cited, correspond to section numbers of Title 26, U.S.C. and Title 26 U.S.C.A. Treasury Income Tax Regulations are cited as "Regs. § 1.61–(a)." Such citations conform to sections of Title 26—Internal Revenue—of the Code of Federal Regulations. Internal Revenue Service Revenue Rulings are cited to volume and page of the Cumulative Bulletin, abbreviated "C.B."

Citations are provided to only a few leading cases, statutory sections, revenue rulings and regulations. These citations aim to offer access to some central areas of authority, not to cover the entire waterfront. Further references as well as much more extensive textual analysis can be sought in other sources.

Little or nothing is given to procedure, administration, compliance, forms or tax returns, taxation of foreign income, economics, deep policy analysis or tax reform, among other important aspects of the study of Federal Income Taxation that could not be included within the confines of this volume. Also, as the title indicates, the book limits itself to the taxation of individuals; it does not cover taxation of organizations such as corporations, partnerships, limited-liability companies or exempt organizations. Nor does it do much to cover the special taxation of individuals as they are involved in such organizations, though many of the general principles of individual income taxation apply in that context as well.

We are very grateful to Hak Lee, a 2004 graduate of Hastings College of the Law, for his work in checking, updating, revising and preparing this seventh edition. We also want to acknowledge the work of Anthony Wang, a member of the Class of 2005 at Hastings, for his work in proofreading the pages. And we want to thank Ted V. Jang at Hastings for his valuable work in preparing the manuscript.

We hope this short book will prove useful to introduce or to review the subject matter of Federal Income Taxation and to afford an overview of the subject matter. It cannot substitute for, it can only supplement, a thoroughgoing examination and analysis of the Code, Regulations, Cases and Rulings which are the sources of our income tax law, and which must be emphasized in the study of that law by law students in law school courses.

JOHN K. MCNULTY
DANIEL J. LATHROPE

July, 2004

I'm very pleased that Prof. Daniel J. Lathrope of the Hastings College of the Law accepted my invitation to join me as co-author on this Seventh Edition of the income tax Nutshell, the first edition of which came out in 1972. Dan is a knowledgeable, experienced and skilled author and teacher and a most agreeable colleague. He has done most of the updating and revising to reflect changes in the law since the Sixth Edition appeared in 1999, and it's been good to depend on him so heavily. Welcome aboard, Dan!

J.K.M.

OUTLINE

OUTLINE

TABLE OF CASES

References are to Pages

A

B

C

D

E

H

I

J

K

L

O

P

R

U

V

W

*

TABLE OF INTERNAL REVENUE CODE SECTIONS

UNITED STATES

UNITED STATES CODE ANNOTATED
26 U.S.C.A.—Internal Revenue Code

UNITED STATES CODE ANNOTATED
26 U.S.C.A.—Internal Revenue Code

UNITED STATES CODE ANNOTATED
26 U.S.C.A.—Internal Revenue Code

UNITED STATES CODE ANNOTATED
26 U.S.C.A.—Internal Revenue Code

UNITED STATES CODE ANNOTATED
26 U.S.C.A.—Internal Revenue Code

UNITED STATES CODE ANNOTATED
26 U.S.C.A.—Internal Revenue Code

TABLE OF INTERNAL REVENUE CODE SECTIONS

UNITED STATES CODE ANNOTATED
26 U.S.C.A.—Internal Revenue Code

XXXIII

UNITED STATES CODE ANNOTATED
26 U.S.C.A.—Internal Revenue Code

UNITED STATES CODE ANNOTATED
26 U.S.C.A.—Internal Revenue Code

UNITED STATES CODE ANNOTATED
26 U.S.C.A.—Internal Revenue Code

XXXVI

UNITED STATES CODE ANNOTATED
26 U.S.C.A.—Internal Revenue Code

TABLE OF INTERNAL REVENUE CODE SECTIONS

UNITED STATES CODE ANNOTATED
26 U.S.C.A.—Internal Revenue Code

UNITED STATES CODE ANNOTATED
26 U.S.C.A.—Internal Revenue Code

UNITED STATES CODE ANNOTATED
26 U.S.C.A.—Internal Revenue Code

UNITED STATES CODE ANNOTATED
26 U.S.C.A.—Internal Revenue Code

UNITED STATES CODE ANNOTATED
26 U.S.C.A.—Internal Revenue Code

XLII

UNITED STATES CODE ANNOTATED
26 U.S.C.A.—Internal Revenue Code

XLIII

TABLE OF INTERNAL REVENUE CODE SECTIONS

UNITED STATES CODE ANNOTATED
26 U.S.C.A.—Internal Revenue Code

UNITED STATES CODE ANNOTATED
26 U.S.C.A.—Internal Revenue Code

TABLE OF INTERNAL REVENUE CODE SECTIONS

UNITED STATES CODE ANNOTATED
26 U.S.C.A.—Internal Revenue Code

UNITED STATES CODE ANNOTATED
26 U.S.C.A.—Internal Revenue Code

UNITED STATES CODE ANNOTATED
26 U.S.C.A.—Internal Revenue Code

UNITED STATES CODE ANNOTATED
26 U.S.C.A.—Internal Revenue Code

UNITED STATES CODE ANNOTATED
26 U.S.C.A.—Internal Revenue Code

L

UNITED STATES CODE ANNOTATED
26 U.S.C.A.—Internal Revenue Code

LI

TABLE OF INTERNAL REVENUE CODE SECTIONS

UNITED STATES CODE ANNOTATED
26 U.S.C.A.—Internal Revenue Code

UNITED STATES CODE ANNOTATED
26 U.S.C.A.—Internal Revenue Code

UNITED STATES CODE ANNOTATED
26 U.S.C.A.—Internal Revenue Code

UNITED STATES CODE ANNOTATED
26 U.S.C.A.—Internal Revenue Code

UNITED STATES CODE ANNOTATED
26 U.S.C.A.—Internal Revenue Code

TABLE OF INTERNAL REVENUE CODE SECTIONS

UNITED STATES CODE ANNOTATED
26 U.S.C.A.—Internal Revenue Code

LVII

TABLE OF INTERNAL REVENUE CODE SECTIONS

UNITED STATES CODE ANNOTATED
26 U.S.C.A.—Internal Revenue Code

TABLE OF INTERNAL REVENUE CODE SECTIONS

UNITED STATES CODE ANNOTATED
26 U.S.C.A.—Internal Revenue Code

UNITED STATES CODE ANNOTATED
26 U.S.C.A.—Internal Revenue Code

LXI

UNITED STATES CODE ANNOTATED
26 U.S.C.A.—Internal Revenue Code

UNITED STATES CODE ANNOTATED
26 U.S.C.A.—Internal Revenue Code

UNITED STATES CODE ANNOTATED
26 U.S.C.A.—Internal Revenue Code

UNITED STATES CODE ANNOTATED
26 U.S.C.A.—Internal Revenue Code

UNITED STATES CODE ANNOTATED
26 U.S.C.A.—Internal Revenue Code

TABLE OF INTERNAL REVENUE CODE SECTIONS

UNITED STATES CODE ANNOTATED
26 U.S.C.A.—Internal Revenue Code

TABLE OF INTERNAL REVENUE CODE SECTIONS

UNITED STATES CODE ANNOTATED
26 U.S.C.A.—Internal Revenue Code

LXVIII

TABLE OF INTERNAL REVENUE CODE SECTIONS

UNITED STATES CODE ANNOTATED
26 U.S.C.A.—Internal Revenue Code

*

TABLE OF TREASURY REGULATIONS

TABLE OF TREASURY REGULATIONS

TREASURY REGULATIONS

TREASURY REGULATIONS

TABLE OF TREASURY REGULATIONS

TREASURY REGULATIONS

TABLE OF TREASURY REGULATIONS

TREASURY REGULATIONS

*

TABLE OF REVENUE RULINGS

REVENUE PROCEDURES

REVENUE RULINGS

TABLE OF REVENUE RULINGS

REVENUE RULINGS

FEDERAL INCOME TAXATION OF INDIVIDUALS

IN A NUTSHELL

*

CHAPTER I

INTRODUCTION

§ 1. Role of the Income Tax

The Federal Income Tax serves a number of purposes. Of course, it is first viewed as a revenue collector, the largest in the Federal budget. In 2002, for example, the Federal government received total "income" of $1,853 billion. Of the 2002 receipts, $858 billion (43%) were taken from the private sector of the economy, for disposition by the public sector, by the Federal Income Tax on individuals, compared to $737 billion in 1997. Another $148 billion (7%) were raised in 2002 by the Federal Income Tax on corporations, compared to $182 billion in 1997. Social security and other insurance and retirement contributions raised $701 billion (35%). Excise taxes raised $67 billion (3%). The remaining $79 billion of receipts (4%) in 2002 came from customs duties, estate and gift taxes, Federal Reserve deposits, and other miscellaneous receipts. Since 2002 federal spending totaled $2,011 billion, the Government was left with a deficit of $158 billion, an amount the Government was forced to borrow. Figure 1 shows the sources from which the Government's 2002 receipts derived. Figure 2 shows how the Government spent the money.

1

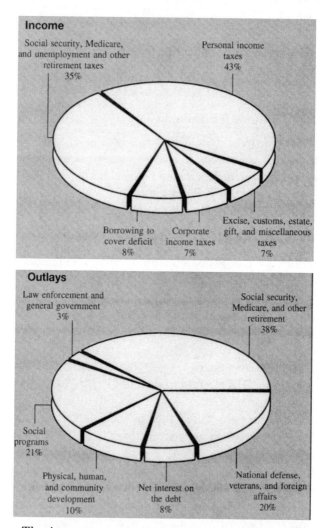

Income

Social security, Medicare, and unemployment and other retirement taxes
35%

Personal income taxes
43%

Borrowing to cover deficit
8%

Corporate income taxes
7%

Excise, customs, estate, gift, and miscellaneous taxes
7%

Outlays

Law enforcement and general government
3%

Social security, Medicare, and other retirement
38%

Social programs
21%

Physical, human, and community development
10%

Net interest on the debt
8%

National defense, veterans, and foreign affairs
20%

The income tax serves several functions in addition to financing federal government expenditures.

It also allocates resources, subsidizes some persons or activities, encourages or discourages certain kinds of economic and social behavior, redistributes wealth, stimulates or stabilizes economic growth, helps maintain our federalism, and helps solve some specific social problems such as pollution and urban decay. Further, the income tax shapes and preserves the fundamental influences that a free market economy presupposes.

§ 2. Taxpayers and Tax Returns

The Federal Income Tax applies to all residents and all citizens of the United States. Not everyone must file a return, however. The requirements for filing are found in I.R.C. §§ 6011–17.[1] Filing requirements generally have been keyed to the amounts of income a taxpayer can receive without having to pay any income tax. Each taxpayer is allowed to receive, tax free, an amount equal to a "personal exemption,"[2] [set by the statute at $2,000, an amount that is indexed after 1988 for inflation; *see* I.R.C. § 151(d)(4)]. The 2004 amount is $3,100.

A taxpayer who does not "itemize" deductions also is entitled to a "standard deduction." The statutory amount of standard deduction is $3,000 for a single, unmarried taxpayer and $4,400 for a

1. The Federal Income Tax is part of the Internal Revenue Code, embedded in the United States Code (U.S.C.) and the United States Code Annotated (U.S.C.A.). Section numbers of the Internal Revenue Code (I.R.C.) cited in this book correspond to sections of Title 26, U.S.C. and Title 26, U.S.C.A.

2. The benefits of the personal exemption are phased out for taxpayers with adjusted gross income exceeding certain amounts. *See* I.R.C. § 151(d)(3).

head of a household, also indexed for inflation. In 2004, a married couple filing jointly or a surviving spouse is allowed a standard deduction equal to twice the amount of the standard deduction for a single taxpayer. After 2004 and before 2009, a married couple filing jointly is allowed less than twice the standard deduction for a single taxpayer. See I.R.C. § 63(c)(7). A married taxpayer who files separately is allowed a standard deduction equal to one-half of the standard deduction for a married couple filing jointly. However, if the individual may be claimed as a dependent on another taxpayer's return (such as a parent's return), the standard deduction shall not exceed the greater of $800 (in 2004) or the sum of $250 plus the individual's earned income. *See* I.R.C. § 63(c)(5). In addition, such an individual cannot also take a personal exemption. *See* I.R.C. § 151(d)(2).

An additional standard deduction is granted to elderly (aged 65 or older) or blind taxpayers who do not "itemize" their deductions. The additional standard deduction amount specified in the Code for a married individual or surviving spouse is $600 ($1,200 if both elderly and blind). (The 2004 amount is $950, or $1,900 if both elderly and blind.) An elderly or blind head of household or single individual is entitled to an additional standard deduction amount of $750 ($1,500 if both elderly and blind). I.R.C. § 63(f). (The 2004 amount is $1,200, or $2,400 if both elderly and blind.) *These* additional standard deductions will not be reduced even if the elderly or blind person may be claimed as a dependent on another taxpayer's return.

In general, every individual who has gross income in excess of the applicable standard deduction plus personal exemption of $2,000 per taxpayer (indexed for inflation) must file an annual tax return (form 1040) in which he or she makes a self-assessment of income tax. In addition, an individual may also be subject to the alternative minimum tax. See § 108, *infra*.

The sum (in 2004) of the indexed standard deduction plus the indexed personal exemptions for each filing status is as follows:

	Single	Head of Household	Joint Return	Surviving Spouse	Married Filing Separately
(1) Standard Deduction	$4,850	$7,150	$9,700	$9,700	$4,850
(2) Personal Exemption	$3,100	$3,100	$6,200	$3,100	$3,100
(3) Total (maximum Taxable Income for which no tax liability is incurred)	$7,950	$10,250	$15,900	$12,800	$7,950

(All amounts are subject to change due to adjustments for inflation.)

A married couple who are both 65 or older may have as much as $17,800 in taxable income in 2004 before incurring any tax liability. They could claim two personal exemptions of $3,100 each, the basic $9,700 standard deduction and two $950 additional standard deductions (for being elderly.)

For many taxpayers, much of the income tax has been collected in advance. Employers withhold specified amounts from employees' salaries or wages, and self-employed taxpayers make quarterly prepayments of tax computed on an estimate of income for the year. For some taxpayers, the law also requires withholding of tax on dividends and interest. The tax return, filed on April 15 by most individual taxpayers, makes a final report and reconciles earlier withholding or estimated tax payments with the actual liability; taxpayers may receive a refund or may have to make an additional payment with the final return. In 2002, approximately 131 million individual income tax returns were filed.

§ 3. History

A federal income tax was used briefly during the Civil War, from 1862–1871. Its rates were graduated up to 10 percent, and it was collected at the source on wages, salaries, interest, and dividends. When the urgent need for revenue disappeared in 1872, this tax was allowed to lapse. In 1894 a flat 2% income tax was reenacted, but it was declared unconstitutional by the U.S. Supreme Court in 1895, because it was a direct tax not apportioned among the states according to population, as the Constitution requires. In 1909 Congress enacted an excise tax on corporations; the measure of tax liability was 1% of income. This tax was held to be constitutional on the ground that it was not a direct tax on income but an excise tax on the privilege of doing business in corporate form.

In 1913 the States ratified the Sixteenth Amendment to the U.S. Constitution and thus empowered the Congress to tax "incomes, from whatever source derived, without apportionment among the several States, and without regard to any census or enumeration." The present federal income tax is a lineal descendent of the income tax act passed in 1913, following ratification of the Sixteenth Amendment.

The 1913 tax applied to wages, salaries, interest, dividends, rents, incomes from entrepreneurship, and capital gains. Deductions were allowed for business expenses, personal interest, and taxes paid. Some forms of income were exempt: salaries of state and local governmental employees, interest from federal, state and local bonds, etc. Each single person enjoyed an exemption of $3,000; the exemption for married couples was $4,000. Income above those amounts was subject to a 1% normal tax and a surtax ranging from 1% to 6%. Dividends were exempt from the surtax.

Since 1913 a great many changes have been made in the income tax, as subsequent chapters of this book will relate. Rates and exemptions have shifted frequently over the years. Marginal rates went as high as 94% during World War II. For 2004, the top normal rate was 35%. Bottom rates have been as low as 1% in 1913. For 2004, the bottom rate was 10%. Personal and dependency exemptions fell to $500 during World War II but rose to $750 in 1972, $1,000 in 1979, and $2,000 in 1989; the $2,000 amount is indexed annually for inflation, putting it at $3,100 for 2004.

§ 4. The Corporation Income Tax

This book does not treat the Federal Income Tax on corporations, though corporations are taxpayers and subject to many of the same rules and doctrines as are individual taxpayers. In addition, they are covered by an intricate body of rules addressed to the peculiar problems of corporations.

The corporate income tax is a very significant revenue producer: the tax produced $148 billion in 2002, or about 7% of total federal receipts. Corporate-tax rates are 15% on the first $50,000 of taxable income, 25% on the next $25,000, 34% on income from $75,000 to $10,000,000, and 35% on income above $10,000,000. For corporations with taxable income in excess of $100,000, the amount of tax determined under these rates will be increased by the lesser of (1) 5% of the excess over $100,000 or (2) $11,750, to recapture the benefit of the lower tax brackets as to higher-income corporations. Corporations with taxable income over $15,000,000 are subject to an additional surcharge equal to the lesser of (1) 3% of the excess over $15,000,000 or (2) $100,000. And every corporation with "modified alternative minimum taxable income" over $2,000,000 is subject to a special "Environmental Tax" at the rate of 0.12 percent. *See* I.R.C. § 59A. There is also an Alternative Minimum Tax applicable to corporations. *See* I.R.C. § 55(b)(1)(B).

The taxation of corporations as separate entities and the failure of any systematic plan to integrate the corporate and individual taxes have created a number of problems and complications. For example, corporate profits are subject to "double taxation"—the corporation must pay income tax on its profits, and its shareholders must also pay tax when these profits are distributed to them as dividends. At various times, slight relief has been afforded in the form of an exclusion for small amounts of dividends received. Under I.R.C. § 116, repealed in 1986, the amount excluded was $100. At one time, a 4% shareholder credit was allowed. Currently, most types of corporate dividends received by individuals are taxed at a maximum rate of 15%, a lower rate that provides some relief from the pure double tax. See § 106, *infra*.

§ 5. Tax Legislation and Administration

Congressional tax legislation must be initiated in the House of Representatives, where hearings on tax proposals are held by the House Ways and Means Committee. After passage by the House, proposed tax laws go to the Senate and its Finance Committee. After the bill has been amended and passed by the Senate, it goes to a Conference Committee of the House and Senate to adjust and compromise differences between the two houses. The Conference Committee's action takes the form of a "conference report," which then is acted upon, and usually approved, by the House and Senate, after which the law is sent to the President for his action.

After enactment, revenue laws are administered (under the Treasury Department) by the Internal Revenue Service (I.R.S.), headed by the Commissioner of Internal Revenue. The principal office of the I.R.S. is in Washington, D.C., but the I.R.S. has an office in most large cities throughout the country. In recent years, the I.R.S. has decentralized, and as a result the local and regional offices exercise more authority. Taxpayers whose tax returns are questioned confer with an I.R.S. revenue agent or examiner in a field or office audit or other inquiry. They may later confer with superior officers called group chiefs and conferees and eventually with Appeals Office representatives. If the dispute has not been settled by then, it is necessary to "go to law." (*See* Judicial Procedure, § 6, *infra.*)

The Treasury issues Income Tax Regulations through the I.R.S. Congressional authority for such regulations lies in I.R.C. § 7805. Treasury Regulations are presumed to be valid; only rarely does a court invalidate a regulation. These Regulations appear in publications entitled "Internal Revenue Bulletin," or—when compiled for the year—"Cumulative Bulletin." Other authoritative and informative pronouncements on tax law also appear in several forms in the Cumulative Bulletin (cited as "C.B.")—Revenue Rulings, Treasury Decisions, and Revenue Procedures. The Cumulative Bulletin also publishes Senate and House Committee reports on revenue bills.

Previously, not all rulings were published; however, now private "letter-rulings" or "determination letters" are published after they have been "sanitized" by deleting all identifying references to the private parties involved in the transaction. The I.R.S. will not rule on some issues. *See* Rev.Proc. 2004–3, 2004–1 I.R.B. 114.

In practice, rulings occupy an exceedingly important role and are wisely sought in doubtful areas. Often a transaction will be made contingent upon a favorable ruling. Published rulings (called "Revenue Rulings") are applied retroactively unless they explicitly state to the contrary, and they can be revoked retroactively, unless doing so is an abuse of discretion. A letter ruling ordinarily will not be revoked or modified retroactively as to the taxpayer to whom it was issued or someone else directly involved. However, published private "letter rulings" or "determination letters" have no precedential effect, except as determined by the Internal Revenue Service. The Service also publishes an "acquiescence" or a "non-acquiescence" when it loses a case in the Tax Court to indicate whether the Service will accept that case as authority in the future or not. Also, in some rulings the Service lets it be known whether a decision or line of cases in a Federal Circuit Court of Appeals will be followed or not by the I.R.S. as to other taxpayers or other years.

Obligations of taxpayers, and penalties for breach, are set out in the Internal Revenue Code and the Regulations thereunder, in a myriad of sections, including I.R.C. §§ 6651(a) *et seq.,* §§ 7201 *et seq.,* §§ 6501 *et seq.,* and §§ 6601 *et seq.* The professional responsibilities of tax advisors are also the subject of some treatment in the Code and Regulations (such as those governing practice before the I.R.S.) and in other Treasury Department promulgations, such as Treasury Department Circular 230, issued pursuant to the authority of 31 U.S.C.A. § 1026, and also A.B.A. Formal Opinions, such as No. 85–352 (1985).

§ 6. Judicial Procedure

If proceedings are carried beyond the administrative stage and into the courts, the taxpayer has a choice of tribunals. He or she may choose not to pay the tax deficiency (in which event interest will accrue) and to petition the United States Tax Court. Or, a taxpayer may pay the tax, file a claim for refund and, after adverse action on that claim, sue for refund in the Federal District Court or the United States Claims Court. In District Court a taxpayer may request trial by jury; in Tax Court or the Court of Federal Claims, the claim will be heard by a judge without a jury. From the Tax Court or the District Court, a taxpayer may appeal his case to the U. S. Court of Appeals for the appropriate federal Circuit Court of Appeals and from there to the Supreme Court. From the Claims Court, the case can first go to the U. S. Court of Appeals for the Federal Circuit, and from there it can proceed to the Supreme Court.

§ 7. Tax Terms

Income tax law has its own terms of art, not to speak of its jargon. One of the most basic concepts is that of *gross income.* Gross income is defined by the statute (I.R.C. § 61(a)) as "all income from whatever source derived.... " The statute goes on to list fifteen items that *are* included in gross income. The list includes such things as compensation for services, gains derived from dealings in property, interest and dividends. The statute makes it clear that the list is not exhaustive. Also, § 61(a) expressly acknowledges that something fitting the definition of "income from whatever source derived" may not be "gross income" because the statute, in the same subtitle, expressly provides otherwise. Statutory exclusions from gross income are made by the Code in I.R.C. §§ 101–140; statutory inclusions and exclusions are also found in I.R.C. §§ 71–90. What fits the definition of gross income has been a rich source of litigation; cases, regulations and rulings must be consulted to begin to understand and apply § 61(a) and its helpers.

In order to arrive at "taxable income," or "taxtable income," (the amount that really matters to a taxpayer because tax rates are applied against that amount) the individual taxpayer must first determine "adjusted gross income." *Adjusted gross income* is defined in I.R.C. § 62 as gross income minus: trade and business deductions, certain trade and business deductions of employees, deductions for losses from the sale or exchange of property and fifteen other categories. These categories are mainly, though not exclusively, business or profit-related deductions for the costs of producing income. Adjusted gross income is then an intermediate figure whose closest corollary in common speech is "net income," though the two concepts do not exactly correspond.

Adjusted gross income is further reduced to yield "taxable income," to which the tax rates will be applied. For *corporate* taxpayers, *taxable income* is simply defined by I.R.C. § 63(a) as gross income minus all the deductions allowed by chapter 1 of the Code (§§ 1–1400L) other than the standard deduction. In the case of an *individual* taxpayer, *taxable income* is adjusted gross income reduced by the sum of deductions for personal exemptions provided by I.R.C. § 151 and either itemized deductions or the standard deduction provided by § 63(c) for individuals who do not itemize. However, a dependent who can be claimed on someone else's return cannot subtract the personal exemption from his own taxable income.

The taxpayer determines the tax payable by computing either "taxable income" or "tax-table income." Taxable income, if it is the appropriate computation, is multiplied by the tax rates found in I.R.C. § 1. For non-itemizing taxpayers with incomes not exceeding specified amounts, however, tax tables rather than the rates of § 1 must be used, and so "tax-table income" must be computed. *See* I.R.C. § 3. Section 3(a)(3) gives the Secretary of the Treasury the authority to apply the tables to itemizers as well.

Whether a taxpayer must use the tax-table method of computing tax rather than the taxable income method can be determined by the rules of § 3(a). To do so, a taxpayer must ascertain whether tax-table income exceeds "the ceiling amount," set by regulations but at a level not less than $100,000 (in 2003). If the taxpayer's tax-table income falls below the ceiling amount, the tax-table method applies. For higher-income taxpayers, the § 1 taxable income method will still be used.

If a tax *surcharge* is in effect, it is computed as a percentage of the income tax payable and is determined by multiplying tax payable by the surcharge rate. When the surcharge is added to tax previously determined, the result is the tax liability of the taxpayer; but the amount the taxpayer owes in fact can be reduced by any tax *credit* to which the taxpayer is entitled (for tax previously withheld, estimated tax pre-payments, foreign taxes paid, qualified expenditures, etc.).

A credit against tax is a sort of "negative tax"— an amount subtracted from tax liability to determine the actual amount payable on the due date or, in some instances, to be refunded to the taxpayer if it exceeds tax liability. A "negative income tax" is a "tax" that would require the government to pay to the citizen an amount, probably consisting of some percentage of the difference between the citizen's actual income and some standard of guaranteed annual income or subsistence.

The income tax differs from a gross receipts tax. For example, if a taxpayer sells property, he/she need not pay income tax on the entire purchase price but instead may subtract the cost of the investment in the property. The return of capital is tax free. The tax term for such unrecovered cost is *basis*, and it serves to separate gain from return of capital when property is sold. Generally, a taxpayer's basis is the cost of the property, or "cost basis." If the owner adds various improvements, he can add their cost to compute "adjusted basis." The adjustments to basis may be downward as well as upward. For example, if deductions for depreciation (or an uninsured casualty loss) are taken, the basis must be reduced by the amount of such deductions (since they allow him to recover his capital out of current income, tax free). Instead of a cost basis, a taxpayer may have a *carryover* or *substituted basis*; that is, a basis carried over from another taxpayer (as with a gift) or transferred from another property (in the case of a non-recognition transaction).

For a taxpayer engaged in manufacturing, merchandising, or mining, a cost-recovery concept like "basis" is used when gross income is defined as receipts from sales less the "cost of goods sold." *See* Regs. § 1.61–3(a).

The term *depreciation* refers to the amount by which the value of an asset diminishes, or is thought to diminish, over time. Deductions for *depreciation* of assets used in gain-seeking activities of the taxpayer were allowed in tax years beginning before 1981. Thus each year the taxpayer was given an allowance, in the form of a deduction, that (theoretically) equaled the amount of his capital that was used up to produce receipts taxable as income during the year. Over the span of years during which the asset was used and depreciation deductions were taken (the "useful life" of the property), the taxpayer would recover his cost, his investment in the asset. He then could buy a new one only if he had actually set aside the income each year and if costs remained unchanged. Special depreciation deductions have also been allowed, in the form of "accelerated depreciation," or "accelerated cost recovery," to permit a taxpayer to recover most of his costs long before the useful life of the property is over. Recovery of the cost of an asset before expiration of its useful life is advantageous to the taxpayer because of the time value of money. The taxpayer is allowed large deductions in the early years and they reduce his/her taxes. These early and large tax savings can be invested to produce further income until they are paid as taxes in later years when the depreciation deductions have shrunk. Congress provided taxpayers with this advantage in order to encourage modernization or investment in business assets and thus to stimulate production of goods, reduce unemployment, and perhaps to accomplish other economic and social goals.

In 1981 the Accelerated Cost Recovery System (A.C.R.S.) was introduced as a method to recover capital costs for most tangible depreciable property. A.C.R.S. uses accelerated methods applied over predetermined recovery periods shorter than, but generally unrelated to, assets' useful lives. A.C.R.S. (I.R.C. § 168) replaces depreciation (I.R.C. § 167) for property placed in service after 1980. More technically, the § 168 allowance becomes the "reasonable allowance" specified in § 167(a), in the case of "recovery property" entitled to A.C.R.S. *See* I.R.C. § 168(a).

§ 8. Graduated Rates; Progressive Tax

The Federal Income Tax employs a graduated rate structure, with several brackets. This graduated rate structure means that as a taxpayer's taxable income rises, the rate of tax on the *marginal* amounts of income is increased. I.R.C. § 1 contains the full rate schedules for married individuals filing joint returns, heads of households, unmarried individuals, and married individuals filing separate returns. See I.R.C. § 1(i) for rate reductions after 2000. The rates in I.R.C. § 1 are indexed each year for inflation. *See* I.R.C. § 1(f). For example, in 2004 the rates applicable to unmarried individuals are:

If taxable income is: ...The tax is:

Not over $7,150 .... 10% of taxable income.

Over $7,150 but not
   over $29,050 .... $715, plus 15% of taxable income over $7,150.

Over $29,050 but not
   over $70,350 .... $4,000, plus 25% of the excess over $29,050.

Over $70,350 but not
   over $146,750 .... $14,325, plus 28% of the excess over $70,350.

Over $146,750 but not
   over $319,100 .... $35,717, plus 33% of the excess over $146,750.

Over $319,100 .... $92,592.50, plus 35% of the excess over $319,100.

Compare the taxation of an unmarried taxpayer having $7,150 of taxable income with the taxation of an unmarried taxpayer having $20,000 of taxable income. Under I.R.C. § 1(c), taxable income not over $7,150 is taxed at 10%. The tax on total taxable income over $7,150 but not over $29,050 is $715 ($7,150 × 10%) plus 15% of the excess over $7,150. Thus, the taxpayer with taxable income of $20,000 is taxed at a rate of 10% on his first $7,150 of income ($715) and 15% on the remaining $12,850 ($1,927.50), for a total tax of $2,642.50. The taxpayer having $7,150 of taxable income is taxed at a rate of 10%, for a total tax of $715. While the taxpayer earning $7,150 is taxed at 10% on all his income, the *average* tax rate, or *effective* tax rate, confronting the taxpayer earning $20,000 is 13.2% ($2,642.50 ÷ $20,000 = 13.2%).

Because the rates on marginal income (the extra dollar earned) increase as income reaches higher levels, as the previous example demonstrates, the tax system is *progressive:* higher income is taxed at a higher average rate. Note, however, that a high-income taxpayer will never pay an *average* rate higher than (or quite as high as) his *marginal* rate because he still pays only 10% on his first $7,150 of income, 15% on income above $7,150 but not over $29,050, etc. For example, an unmarried taxpayer having $1,000,000 of taxable income will pay marginal rates of 10%, 15%, 25%, 28%, 33%, and 35% on various portions of his $1,000,000 total income (*see* the table above), for a total tax of $330,907.50.

While this taxpayer pays a marginal rate of 35% on every dollar of income over $319,100, his average rate is only 33%. Note that although higher-income taxpayers pay higher rates, they still have an incentive to earn those extra dollars of income as long as the sum of their federal, state, and local income tax rates does not equal or exceed 100%: even if $1 earned nets only $0.65 after-tax dollars, the taxpayer comes out ahead and will want to earn that extra dollar.

Rates vary somewhat among different types of taxpayers (single, married, etc.) and different kinds of income (ordinary income, dividends, capital gains, tax-preference income, etc.).

Notice the different effects of deductions, credits, exclusions, standard deductions, and exemptions under a regime of graduated rates. The tax-saving value of a $1,000 deduction is greater for a taxpayer with high income than for a low-income taxpayer; the deduction comes "off the top" and saves each taxpayer the tax otherwise owing on another $1,000 on top of his taxable income. This tax might be $250 for a 25% marginal tax rate taxpayer but only $150 for a 15% marginal tax rate taxpayer or $0 for a taxpayer whose income is less than other allowances. In contrast, a credit of $1,000 would afford equal tax savings to each taxpayer if each would otherwise owe at least $1,000 in tax, or if the credit were refundable to the extent that it exceeded tax liability. An exclusion, like a deduction, provides income-variant benefits.

A standard deduction (fixed in amount), like any other deduction, gives income-variant benefits. For that reason, the standard deduction and low-income allowance were converted, in 1977, into a "zero-bracket amount" ZBA (or zero-income bracket) and built into the tax tables. One result was that this allowance came "off the bottom" for each taxpayer and thus saved the same amount (11% or so), regardless of how much income the taxpayer may have had stacked above the zero bracket amount. This structural revision also made tax rate reduction or increase convenient, since enlarging or shrinking the zero-bracket amount could accomplish the task, with equal impact on all taxpayers having sufficient income, without any revision of the tax rates themselves. Nevertheless, in 1986 Congress returned to the standard deduction system, partly for "simplification" since, "unlike the ZBA, the standard deduction enables the taxpayer to know directly how much income is subject to tax and to understand more clearly that taxable income is the base for determining the tax." Also, because post–1986 T.R.A. tax rates are flatter, the income-variant effect of a deduction versus a ZBA is not so great.

§ 9. Payroll Taxes and Withholding

Employers are required to withhold taxes from their employees' paychecks. *See generally* I.R.C. §§ 3401–06. Employers withhold income taxes from each paycheck in accordance with tables or computational procedures prescribed by the I.R.S. The purpose of withholding in accordance with these tables is to withhold enough tax periodically, throughout the year, so that, at the end of the year, the employee will already have "paid" a total amount of tax that closely approximates his or her tax liability for the year. This method provides revenue to the government throughout the year and avoids a lump-sum tax bill for the taxpayer at the end of the year. If the taxpayer's only source of income is one job, the withholding should approximate the tax liability closely. If, however, he has outside income, he may need to ask his employer to withhold more than the tables prescribe so that he does not significantly underpay his tax during the year. Alternatively, he may be required to make "estimated tax" payments quarterly throughout the year. Like taxes withheld, these payments are credited toward final tax liability. *See* I.R.C. §§ 6654, 6315, 6402(b).

Almost all employees and employers also pay Social Security and Medicare taxes. *See generally* I.R.C. §§ 3101–28. These taxes arise under the Federal Insurance Contributions Act (F.I.C.A.) and consist of the Old–Age, Survivors, and Disability Insurance (O.A.S.D.I.) ("social security") tax and the hospital insurance ("Medicare") tax. The employee and employer each pay 6.2% social security tax on income up to $87,900 (as of 2004) and 1.45% hospital insurance (Medicare) tax (with no income cap), for a total of 7.65%. *See* I.R.C. §§ 3101 and 3111 and 68 Fed.Reg. 60,437–01 (2003). Some exceptions to these taxes are listed in § 3121(b), including the wages of student employees at a college or university. *See* I.R.C. § 3121(b)(10) and Regs. §§ 31.3121(b)(10)–2.

Self-employed individuals must pay self-employment tax on all self-employment income above $400. *See* I.R.C. §§ 1401–03. The self-employment tax consists of 12.4% for social security (in 2004, on income up to $87,900) and 2.9% for medicare (without a cap), for a total of 15.3%. *See* I.R.C. § 1401 and 68 Fed.Reg. 60,437–01 (2003). Self-employment tax is simply the sum of the employer and employee's contribution to social security and medicare—which makes sense since, in the case of a self-employed individual, the employer and employee are the same person. Section 164(f) grants the self-employed taxpayer a deduction from income of one-half of the self-employment taxes paid. This deduction is the counterpart of the non-inclusion in an employee's income of the social security and medicare tax paid by an employer of a taxpayer who is an employee.

§ 10. Annual Tax Periods and Accounting

The Federal Income Tax is based on an *annual system* of reporting. The year for which a taxpayer's income is determined may be either a calendar year (one that ends on the last day of December) or a fiscal year (one that ends on the last day of any month other than December). Although in general a taxpayer can choose whether to use a calendar year or fiscal year, non-business taxpayers almost invariably report on a calendar-year basis. *See* generally I.R.C. § 441.

In order to ascertain what income is to be included and what deductions are to be taken, a taxpayer must use an *accounting method*. The two most common methods are the *cash method* and the *accrual method*. Under the cash method, items of income and disbursements are reported in the year actually (or constructively) received or made. In contrast, the accrual method requires inclusion of income items in the year when all the events have occurred that fix the right to receive them (and when the amount thereof can be determined with reasonable accuracy), and deductions for disbursements are taken when the obligation to pay has become unconditional. *See* Regs. § 1.451–1(a).

Allocation of income to later periods and deductions to earlier periods gives rise to a deferral of tax. The more distant the deferred tax, the lower its present cost. A dollar of tax that is deferred one year costs less than a dollar of tax that is due today, because the deferred dollar of tax can be invested for a year before it is paid to the government. At an interest rate of six percent, the dollar will earn six cents for that year. Thus, the dollar of tax that is deferred costs 94 cents (one dollar less the six cents of earnings on that dollar, a six-cent "discount") as opposed to the full one-dollar cost of the tax due today. Over a period of time, compounded interest will magnify the effect. This utility of delay of a tax payment (or any payment) or utility of early receipt of income is referred to as the "time value of money."

§ 11. The Time Value of Money; Compound Interest; Discounting to Present Value

In making investment decisions, taxpayers and investors should consider the benefits of compounded interest and deferral of taxation. The discussion and examples below demonstrate the importance of these concepts.

Consider Taxpayer T, who is planning for her retirement and intends to invest $10,000 in an interest-earning bank account. Suppose T invests the $10,000, the principal, in an account that earns 10% interest. And suppose this particular account earns *simple interest*—that is, each year the bank pays T 10% interest on her principal, or $1,000 in interest each year. Thus, at the end of year 1, T will have $11,000 in her account; at the end of year 2, T will have $12,000 in her account; at the end of year 3, T will have $13,000 in her account; and so on. At the end of 10 years, T will have $20,000—her $10,000 principal plus $1,000 interest for each of the 10 years. The year 1 account of $10,000 will be worth $20,000 at the end of 10 years. That account is worth $10,000 now.

Now suppose T invests her $10,000 in another bank account that earns *compound interest* at the rate of 10%, compounded yearly. Compounded interest works as follows. In year 1, the bank pays T $1,000 interest (10% of $10,000), so at the end of year 1, T will have $11,000 in her account. At the end of year 2, the bank will pay 10% interest on $11,000—her original principal *plus* the interest paid in year 1. In other words, the bank will pay interest on the interest already earned. Thus, interest for year 2 will be $1,100, and the total balance in the account at the end of year 2 will be $12,100 (compared to $12,000 with simple interest). At the end of year 3, T will have $13,310 (compared to $13,000 with simple interest). After 10 years, T will have $25,937, compared to $20,000 in the case of simple interest.[3]

Because the bank is paying interest on the interest, and because the account will contain more interest in later years, the effects of compounded interest become quite dramatic as time passes.[4] For example, with simple interest, T will have $30,000 after 20 years, while compounded interest will generate $67,275—a difference of $37,275. In reality, many banks compound interest daily or monthly, as opposed to annually as in the examples above, thereby increasing even further the exponential effect of compounded interest. (The higher the interest rate is, the larger the effect of compounding.) The table below demonstrates the effect of compounded interest:

3. To determine the future value, *FV,* of an amount *PV* that is invested for *y* years at interest rate *r,* use the following formula:

$$FV = PV (1 + r)^y$$

4. *See* Appendix to this book.

BALANCE

Year	Simple Interest	Compounded Yearly
1	$11,000	$ 11,000
5	$15,000	$ 16,105
10	$20,000	$ 25,937
20	$30,000	$ 67,275
30	$40,000	$174,494

Principal	=	$10,000
Interest Rate	=	10%

The "rule of 72" provides an easy method for determining, at a given interest rate, roughly how many years must pass before the original account balance will double. Under that rule, the number of years required for the balance to double is approximately equal to 72 divided by the interest rate expressed as an integer. Thus, if the interest rate is 10 percent, the balance will double in about 7.2 years (72 ÷ 10 = 7.2). If the interest rate is 5 percent, the balance will double in about 14.4 years.

To see how these concepts can be applied, suppose T wins a sweepstakes and is offered a choice of two prizes: $10,000 today or $25,937 ten years from today. Suppose further that interest rates are expected to be constant at 10% and T places no particular value on liquidity—that is, she does not need the security of having the cash on hand for the next 10 years. T would be indifferent between the two prizes because $10,000 invested at 10% interest would generate $25,937 ten years from now. If the sweepstakes sponsor offered T only $20,000 ten years from now, T would prefer to receive $10,000 now. Similarly, returning to the first two choices, if

T expected interest rates to fall below 10% during the next 10 years, she would prefer the $25,937.

Another way of thinking about T's choices is to see that $25,937 received 10 years from now is worth only $10,000 in today's dollars, since the $10,000 can be invested at 10% and will grow to $25,937. Thus, as long as the interest rate is greater than zero, a dollar today is worth more than a dollar tomorrow (wholly apart from inflation). Specifically, at an interest rate of 10%, the *discounted present value* of $1 next year is only $0.909 today.[5]

Since the present value of $1 of *tax* paid in year 2 also is only $0.909, a taxpayer clearly has an incentive to defer tax into the future (assuming tax rates remain constant).

To comprehend the value of deferring tax, assume that T (facing a tax rate of 35%) has two choices: (1) paying tax today on $10,000 income ($3,500) and placing the remainder ($6,500) in an account earning 10% compounded interest for 10 years, paying tax on the interest each year as it is earned; or (2) placing the full $10,000 income in a tax-deferred account earning 10% compounded interest for 10 years, paying tax on the interest and principal only when the account balance is withdrawn 10 years later. In option (1), T's investment will have increased to $12,201 after 10 years. In option (2), T's investment will have grown to $25,937 before-tax dollars after 10 years, minus $9,078 in tax, for a

5. To determine the present value, *PV*, of an amount *FV* that is received *y* years in the future, when the interest rate is *r*, use the following formula:

$$PV = \frac{FV}{(1 + r)^y}$$

total of $16,859 after-tax dollars. Thus, by investing the full $10,000 in a tax-deferred account, T earned an additional $4,658—by virtue of compounded interest on tax she deferred on the principal and interest over the 10–year period. She benefited from deferring tax ($3,500) on receipt of the initial $10,000 and she benefited further from deferring tax, until withdrawal, on the interest on her investment of $10,000.

As the foregoing examples demonstrate, the value of money depends on when it is received—hence, the term "time value of money." Taxpayers usually have a strong incentive to accelerate income and to defer taxation. This incentive will become particularly apparent with the Individual Retirement Account (I.R.A.), which operates similarly to option 2 in the preceding paragraph and is discussed in § 74, *infra, and see* the appendix in this book.

§ 12. Five Basic Questions

Income taxation is a complex, dense and broad subject. Its intricacies can better be understood (and survived) if they are seen in a simple conceptual framework; fortunately, a clear framework can be constructed.

All of the substantive law of income tax breaks down into a few basic questions:

1. *What* is included in income, and what is deductible (or creditable)?

2. *When* is an item includible in income or deductible (or creditable)?

3. *Whose* income or deduction (or credit) is it?

4. *What* kind of income or deduction (or other allowance) is it? (How is the income taxed or how is the deduction allowed?)

5. What *basis* or other collateral consequences (such as holding period, carryovers, etc.) follow from the earlier determinations?

The following chapters of this text have been organized around these five basic questions.

CHAPTER II

WHAT IS INCOME?

§ 13. Income and Gross Income

Gross income is the starting point in determining the "base" of the federal income tax, i.e. that which is taxed. Section 61(a) defines "gross income" as all "income" from whatever source derived, which leads the inquiry to what is "income"? Also, the Sixteenth Amendment, on whose authority the federal income tax relies, speaks of a tax on "incomes." Income, while apparently an obvious concept, turns out to be both subtle and complex at times.

Clearly income or gross income includes *gain* whether generated by business activities, personal services or capital. Under our "global" system all income is lumped together; with very few exceptions, the source of income—business, services or personal investment—does not affect its taxability the way it would in a so-called "scheduler" system. While "income" and "gross income" do not comprehend all receipts, it is also true that gain received or enjoyed by the taxpayer need not be in the form of cash to constitute gross income to the taxpayer.

Income in kind (property, services or other benefits) is nevertheless income. So, if an employer pays his employees' taxes or discharges their debts, they realize income. *See* Old Colony Trust Co. v. Comm. (S.Ct.1929); U.S. v. Kirby Lumber Co. (S.Ct.1931); Regs. § 1.61–1(a); Regs. § 1.61–2(d)(1). (*But see* I.R.C. § 108.) A donor who makes a gift of property on the condition that the donee pay the resulting gift tax receives taxable income to the extent that the gift tax paid by the donee exceeds the donor's basis in the property transferred. *See* Diedrich v. Comm. (S.Ct.1982). A free vacation or convention trip can be compensation and hence income to an employee. *See, e.g.,* Rudolph v. U. S. (S.Ct.1961).

Income can be an irregular or unexpected receipt; it need not be periodic as wages, interest or dividends often are. Nor need the gain be compensatory, given for services rendered or the use or purchase of property. More than just wages or interest or rents can be income—treasure trove and other windfalls, gratuitous benefits and fellowships or prizes that do not qualify for exclusions such as I.R.C. §§ 74, 102, or 117, alimony (§ 71), annuity gains (§ 72), recoveries of bad debts or prior taxes or other items deducted in a prior year (§ 111), and meals or lodging (if not excluded under § 119), all are income. Regs. §§ 1.61–7 to 1.61–14. Thus nearly anything received that increases a taxpayer's net worth would seem to constitute income.

Income is computed, and taxed, in monetary, dollar terms. Nominal dollar units may not correspond to true economic income or real purchasing power, due to inflation or exchange rate fluctuations. The result may be to tax income when the taxpayer has actually suffered a loss—for example, when property bought many years before is sold for a nominal gain. Inflation shrinks the actual size of tax allowances that are set in fixed dollar terms. And inflation gradually pushes taxpayers higher in the graduated rate structure if their nominal incomes increase, even if their real incomes remain the same or fall. This phenomenon has been labeled "bracket-creep." Bracket-creep has diminished as a problem, thanks to fewer (and wider) rate brackets and because indexing of rates and allowances has been enacted. *See* I.R.C. § 1(f), § 63(c)(4), § 151(d)(4).

§ 14. Gross Receipts; Return of Capital

In ascertaining what income *is,* one useful approach drives at what income is *not.* Despite the literal meaning of "income," and the broad sweep of some accompanying language, income does *not* include everything that comes in.

Income is not the same as gross receipts, the total amount received as for the sale of goods. In a manufacturing, merchandising or mining business, gross income means total sales less the cost of goods sold. So, if Ms. A buys 1,000 pencils from a manufacturer for $10.00, and resells them for $50.00, her income (or gross income) is $40.00, not $50.00. *See* Regs. § 1.61–3. Similarly, if Mr. B buys Blackacre for $15,000 and resells it (at a gain) for $18,000, he has income of $3,000, not $18,000. *See* Regs. § 1.61–6. If he had resold Blackacre for $13,000, he would not have had $13,000 income but rather a loss of $2,000.

Income, then, means a receipt that is, or to the extent it is, a gain to the recipient. So, if Sam loans $100 to Harry at 6% simple interest, and a year later Harry pays $106 to Sam, Sam has $6 income, not $106. The $100 is a return of capital to Sam, not gain and not income. A return of capital is not income. *See, e.g.,* Doyle v. Mitchell Bros. Co. (S.Ct. 1918). The term "income" in the Sixteenth Amendment and I.R.C. § 61(a) by implication excludes capital receipts or a return of capital.

What is a return of capital in borderline cases, however, may not be easily determined. For example, income does not include some payments received as damages for a personal physical injury. However, damages for defamation, breach of contract to marry, breach of contract for personal services, for loss of business profits, or for employment discrimination have been held taxable. The question sometimes seems to be whether the damages were awarded *in lieu of* a taxable receipt or amounted to a substitution in money value for an asset or for some other non-taxable item of value that was lost or destroyed. More on this topic later; *see* § 31, *infra,* and I.R.C. § 186. So far, the conception of income as an increase in net worth (or "realized gains" or "net gain") appears to hold water; to test this hypothesis further, one must turn to the cases, after one more brief note.

§ 15. Return of Capital and Prior Years

Generally, "capital" is a concept akin to a fund of "after-tax dollars." A taxpayer's savings out of salary, after taxes, are capital. So is his inheritance or an amount received tax free as a gift.

What is capital and when a receipt is a return of capital for tax purposes may, however, present special questions. For example, whether a receipt is a return of capital may depend on the tax treatment of related events in prior years. To illustrate, a taxpayer who received from a charity the very same property he had donated to it in an earlier year was taxed as having income, because he had taken a deduction, which had given him a tax benefit, in the earlier year. *See* Perry v. U.S. (Ct.Cl.1958); Alice Phelan Sullivan Corp. v. U.S. (Ct.Cl.1967). Thus, although a return of a taxpayer's own property that was borrowed, stolen, or used by another would ordinarily be treated as a return of capital, not as income, the result may be otherwise because of a prior tax benefit. *See generally* I.R.C. § 111 and Regs. § 1.111–1; Hillsboro Nat. Bank v. Comm. (S.Ct.1983).

§ 16.   Judicial Definitions of Income

The Supreme Court once defined income as "the gain derived from capital, from labor, or from both combined, provided it be understood to include profit gained through a sale or conversion of capital assets. . . . " (Eisner v. Macomber (S.Ct.1920)). This definition does cover many or most of the things one thinks of as income: salaries, fees, wages, interest, rents, dividends, business profits and investment profits. By referring to gain, the Court's definition excludes returns of capital. But by suggesting that income had to be compensatory (for work or the use of capital) or from purposive activity (investment, labor), it seemed to leave out some other gains that might be income.

Later the Supreme Court made it plain that the Eisner v. Macomber language would be taken as offering some guidance but not a limiting rule. Thus, in Comm. v. Glenshaw Glass Co. (S.Ct.1955), the Court ruled that windfalls, such as exemplary damages for fraud and the punitive two-thirds portion of a treble-damage anti-trust recovery, are income to the recipient. In Hort v. Comm. (S.Ct.1941) the Court held that money paid to a lessor, in return for cancellation of a lease that the lessee found very unprofitable to continue, was income to the lessor. Still, the Court in *Glenshaw* approached the question of what is income on a case-by-case basis, not by a capsule definition. So, some receipts may still not be income, even though they represent a gain to the taxpayer. For example, in Edwards v. Cuba Railroad Co. (S.Ct.1925), the Supreme Court held that a subsidy paid by the Cuban government to a railroad company to aid and induce it to develop a system in Cuba was not income but rather a reimbursement for capital expenditures or a contribution to capital assets. Hence, the Court said, the payments were not income under the Sixteenth Amendment—a rare (and gratuitous) holding.

In fact, Edwards v. Cuba Railroad and Eisner v. Macomber are the only two Supreme Court cases directly holding items not to be "income" within the meaning of the Sixteenth Amendment. The

Cuba Railroad rule about contributions to capital of a corporation was codified in I.R.C. § 118(a), with significant modifications in § 118(b). A few other case authorities stand for the proposition that some receipts that do increase the taxpayer's net worth are not taxable as income.

§ 17. Significance of Definition of Income

If a purported item of income is not gross income under § 61(a), it cannot give rise to taxable income or tax liability under the Federal Income Tax. Congress could, however, later change the definition of "gross income" to include such an item. However, if an item is not "income" within the meaning of the Sixteenth Amendment, it cannot be taxed under the income tax no matter what Congress may try to do. So, the holding in *Cuba Railroad* (§ 16, *supra*) seemingly put such items beyond the reach of Congress to tax, unless Congress were to comply with both Article I, Section 9, Clause 4 of the U.S. Constitution by taxing in proportion to population and with Article I, Section 2, Clause 3 by apportioning direct taxes among the several states according to their respective numbers.

Accordingly, the question "What is income?" for Sixteenth Amendment purposes differs from the question "What is gross income?" for purposes of I.R.C. § 61(a). However, in *Glenshaw Glass Co.* there is some language to the effect that in § 61(a) Congress attempted to exercise its powers to tax income to the limits imposed by the Constitution. (Remember the broad language of § 61(a).) If so, then gross income (except as otherwise provided) in § 61(a) is identical to "income" in the Sixteenth Amendment.[1] Anything that is "income" within the meaning of the Amendment, Congress intends to tax under § 61(a), except as Congress has otherwise specifically provided.

In turn, other language in *Glenshaw* would take on constitutional, not merely legislative, stature. Even if only as a definition of the legislative term, or as a guideline, the language bears quoting. In *Glenshaw* the Court said: "Here we have instances of undeniable accessions to wealth, clearly realized, and over which the taxpayers have complete dominion."[2] Perhaps this language is the best and most authoritative non-legislative definition of income with which the modern student can work.

§ 18. Income as Gain

Income can be received in many forms, as the "definition" of income given in *Glenshaw Glass* implicitly recognizes. It may consist of money, property, or services. Therefore it can include services, meals, accommodations, cash, stock, or other property. *See* Regs. § 1.61–1(a). It includes such things as treasure trove, illegal gains, punitive damages,

1.   Possibly gross income, not merely net income, is potentially taxable by Congress. *See* Helvering v. Independent Life Ins. Co. (S.Ct.1934). In that event, deductions for costs of producing income would truly be a matter of legislative grace, as often said (*see* New Colonial Ice Co., Inc. v. Helvering (S.Ct.1934)), and only items constituting direct costs of goods sold would have to be subtracted from gross receipts, à la Regs. § 1.61–3, to arrive at the base of this tax. *See* § 39, *infra.*

2.   On the dimension of dominion and control, *see* I.R.C. § 83, *infra* § 74.

and another person's payment of the taxpayer's income taxes. *See* Regs. § 1.61–14(a). It may arise as compensation for services [Regs. § 1.61–2(a)], or from business [Regs. § 1.61–3(a)], farming [Regs. § 1.61–4(a)], from dealings in property [Regs. § 1.61–6(a)], interest [Regs. § 1.61–7(a)], rents and royalties [Regs. § 1.61–8(a)], dividends [Regs. § 1.61–9(a)], alimony, separate maintenance payments, income from life insurance and endowment contracts [Regs. § 1.61–10(a)], pensions [Regs. § 1.61–11(a)], and discharge of indebtedness [Regs. § 1.61–12(a)], among other things. Many other items could constitute gross income if Congress had not otherwise provided, though some among them arguably are not "income" at all; for example, consider gifts, prizes and awards, damages for personal physical injury or sickness, scholarship and fellowship grants, and others (to be treated more fully in the next chapter).

In other words, under contemporary thinking, income in its broadest sense—as used in the Sixteenth Amendment and, *Glenshaw Glass* says, in § 61(a)—includes almost everything that is received or "realized" (*see* § 19, next) and represents a gain to the recipient. And, actual receipt of the "income" is not a requirement. For example, if A borrows $10 from B and, later, C pays off A's debt as compensation for A's services to C, A will have $10 income as a result. Indeed, if A borrows from B and, later, in an arm's-length transaction, B agrees to discharge or sell back A's debt for less than the amount borrowed, A may have income. *See* U.S. v. Kirby

Lumber Co. (S.Ct.1931) (borrowing and discharge in same year); Comm. v. Jacobson (1949) (debt repurchased in tax years different from year of borrowing). *See* Regs. § 1.61–12 (Income from discharge of indebtedness). *And see* I.R.C. §§ 108 and 1017. Section 108 may provide one avenue of relief for A. That section allows bankrupt or insolvent taxpayers to elect to have the discharge of an indebtedness not taxed as part of gross income at the time so long as taxpayer agrees to reduce his/her basis in property or other tax attributes in ways established by the Regulations. The effect of those reductions will be to bring an amount equal to the discharge into income at some later time—for example, when taxpayer sells property or uses it in the production of income—and the amount of depreciation deductions he/she can take is reduced by the amount of the debt discharged. Congress, by these two sections, has not so much altered the definition of *what* is income as it has determined *when* the income is to be taken into account. *See also* I.R.C. § 109 and § 1019 (improvements by lessee on lessor's property excluded, and basis not affected).

§ 19. Realization

Notwithstanding the broad approach to the "receipt" of gain, not all gain is taxable income when it happens. For example, suppose A buys Blackacre for $10,000 and later, over a period of years, the most reliable evidence shows that Blackacre has become worth $15,000 (bidders make offers of that amount and more, and A feels that much richer).

Still, A will not have income for tax purposes until A sells or otherwise disposes of Blackacre. The moment A sells Blackacre for $15,000, A will "realize" the income.

This requirement of a *realization* is firmly embedded in non-statutory tax law, but it eludes a precise statement. In one case, Eisner v. Macomber (S.Ct. 1920), the Supreme Court held that gain had not been realized when a corporation declared and issued a stock dividend to its shareholders. *A fortiori,* the case indicates, income had not been realized by the shareholders earlier when the corporation—a separate taxable entity—earned and received the money. (Of course, the *corporation* realized income earlier; Eisner v. Macomber was concerned only with realization of gain by the shareholders.) In the course of its opinion holding that the stock dividend was not income, the Court said:

> "Here we have the essential matter: *not* a gain accruing to capital; not a *growth* or *increment* of value *in* the investment; but a gain, a profit, *proceeding* from the property, *severed* from the capital however invested or employed, and *coming in*, being *'derived,'* that is, *received* or *drawn* by the recipient (the taxpayer) for his *separate* use, benefit and disposal—that is income derived from property. Nothing else answers the description."

Section 305 has now legislated the rule of the *Macomber* case.

Similarly, unrealized appreciation in the market value of stocks or bonds will not, by itself, constitute a realization. However, in another case, a Federal Circuit Court said that capitalization of past-due salary obligations of a corporation to its two employees (who also were 50–50 shareholders) was a realization as to them, just as if they had been paid the salaries and used the money to purchase more stock in the corporation in equal proportions. Comm. v. Fender Sales, Inc. (9th Cir.1964).

The requirement of a realization does not mean that property must be sold for cash before income is realized. An exchange of property for other property (not cash) can constitute a realization, as might a mere gift or other disposition of property, under some special circumstances. *See, e.g.,* Helvering v. Horst (S.Ct.1940); U.S. v. General Shoe Corp. (S.Ct. 1960); U.S. v. Davis (S.Ct.1962). As the Supreme Court once said, "Where the taxpayer does not receive payment of income in money or property realization may occur when the last step is taken by which he obtains the fruition of the economic gain which has already accrued to him." Helvering v. Horst (S.Ct.1940). Nevertheless, a taxpayer who gives appreciated property to a donee usually is not deemed to have realized the gain; instead the donee takes the donor's basis and the donee, not the donor, eventually realizes the income. *See* Taft v. Bowers (S.Ct.1929); I.R.C. § 1015. *But see* I.R.C. § 84, a special rule that makes the transferor of appreciated property to a political party taxable as if he or she had sold the property and donated the proceeds. The Court has even resorted to horticultural analogies to convey its meaning: income must be separated from capital as "the fruit from the tree." Eisner v. Macomber, *supra,* §§ 16, 18.

The U.S. Supreme Court has held that there is a "disposition of property," and hence a realization, when property is exchanged for other property (so long as the exchanged properties are "materially different" from each other). *See* Cottage Savings Association v. Commissioner (S.Ct.1991) and § 93 *infra.*

Added to this notion of separation is the concept of possession or enjoyment by the taxpayer. For example, improvements made by a tenant on leased property have been held not to be income to the landlord during the term of the lease. *See* M.E. Blatt Co. v. U.S. (S.Ct.1938). But (before I.R.C. § 109 was enacted), when a landlord regained possession of his land whose value was enhanced by the lessee's improvements, he was held taxable. *See* Helvering v. Bruun (S.Ct.1940). Now *see* I.R.C. § 109 and § 1019.

Usually a division of property among co-owners is not an event of realization so as to invoke tax on inherent gain or loss. But if a co-owner's interest is transferred in discharge of his obligation, gain must be realized unless a special non-recognition rule such as I.R.C. § 1041 applies. *See* U.S. v. Davis (S.Ct.1962).

The requirement of a realization plays not only a conceptual but also a practical role. A hard-core realization event such as a sale of Blackacre for cash provides the tax system with a determination once and for all (i) whether the taxpayer has enjoyed any gain or not and (ii) what the amount of that gain is. The realization requirement also usually defers taxation until the taxpayer has the wherewithal to pay the tax. Moreover, since the occurrence of a realization is generally in a taxpayer's control (but not always—consider a condemnation of taxpayer's property or a dividend paid to him by a corporation whose dividend policies he does not control), its requirement prevents many taxpayer hardships.

The requirement of a realization is partly statutory. For example, I.R.C. § 1001 refers to "the sale or other disposition of property," (former) § 1002 referred to "the sale or exchange of property," and § 61(a)(3) mentions "dealings" in property, as though to indicate that without such events, the gain in property is not to be taxed. Of course, if the realization requirement is a constitutional rule, unrealized gain cannot be taxed under § 61(a) no matter how Congress might amend it. In Eisner v. Macomber, the Supreme Court found the requirement of a realization in the Constitution. Whether the Court would still do so, and what the outlines of such a modern constitutional rule might be, is not so clear. Some think that Helvering v. Bruun, *supra,* virtually overruled *Macomber;* others are not so sure.

In any event, the realization rule usually involves a "now or later" timing question about taxing income, not a "once and for all", "whether or not", "now or never" question.

§ 20. Imputed Income

Imputed income is a form of non-cash income, income in kind. It consists of the flow of benefits or satisfactions that result from the use and enjoyment of property (such as a house or consumer durable) owned by the taxpayer, or from goods produced and consumed or used by him, or from services performed by others or by him on his own behalf. More broadly, it includes any gain, benefit or satisfaction from a non-market transaction or event. Thus, the rental value of an owner-occupied home is imputed income to the owner-occupant. The value of the services of one's spouse or children is imputed income. When a farmer eats his homegrown produce, he is relieved of the necessity (and thus the expense) of buying groceries in the marketplace; it is as if he sold his crops and used the proceeds to buy food for himself and his family. He enjoys a benefit whose value is imputed income to him. The benefits that a college or law student receives in excess of the price he pays in tuition and fees constitute imputed income, as do the services of police, firefighters and public schools to taxpayers in the community. Leisure itself, enjoyed by the taxpayer, is consumption of something of value—the taxpayer consumes his time instead of working to earn market-type income. When a bank gives a free checking account to a depositor so long as she keeps a minimum balance of $500 in it, the depositor receives imputed interest on her money. When a doctor treats her own (or her child's) disease, she relieves herself of the expense of hiring a doctor. Similarly, an attorney who draws her own will, or who does her own tax planning, has imputed income.

Nowhere does the statute say that imputed income shall not be taxed; nowhere is imputed income excluded from the broad sweep of I.R.C. § 61(a) or the judicial (*see Glenshaw Glass, supra*) interpretations of § 61(a). Nevertheless, such income generally is *not* taxed, partly because of the administrative and compliance problems involved. An "unstated exclusion" shelters it from tax. For reasons that may be more or less obvious, the Commissioner has not sought to tax the owner-occupant of a house on its rental value (though it might be feasible to assess such values by comparing market rentals on equivalent facilities, and some other countries do tax such income). Even harder would be the task of valuing the income from owning one's own washing machine, auto, or TV set. Still tougher would be the valuation of a spouse's services or the value of a dentist's leisure when he takes Wednesdays off. To be sure, such excess productive capacity—of the dentist, or of the law professor who surrenders a lucrative practice to teach law for a modest salary— might be measured by the prices paid in the market for such services when they are sold at arm's length. But, administrative and compliance problems abound. Moreover, the unstated exclusion is so well entrenched that most layperson would be slow to agree that imputed income is income at all. But income it is.

Apart from the administrative and practical problems, by no means is it entirely clear that Congress constitutionally could tax imputed income. Not to do so, however, raises some serious questions about the economic effects and equity of the federal income tax. Propertied taxpayers, or those with valuable skills, may be able to enjoy non-market gains free of tax, while a higher proportion of the total income of other taxpayers takes market form and thus raises their tax liability. Also, to exempt leisure or self-service from tax may distort the work-leisure choice of some taxpayers, especially those in high marginal brackets. By the same token, a carpenter who builds his own house instead of building another man's house for pay, and the farmer who makes his children eat home-grown turnips rather than Good Humor ice-cream bars, may escape tax on gains from their work while an assembly-line factory worker must pay tax on all of his wages.

These problems of equity and incentives are thorny. Even were they simpler, no one would expect a serious effort to include most imputed income in the tax base in the near future. In a very few areas the I.R.S. has moved toward inclusion of some near-market benefits that involve imputed income of a fringe-benefit or compensatory variety. For example, I.R.C. § 132 excludes only certain fringe benefits from an employee's gross income. Generally any fringe benefit that qualifies as a (1) no-additional-cost service, (2) qualified employee discount, (3) working condition fringe, (4) *de minimis* fringe, (5) qualified transportation fringe, (6) qualified moving expense reimbursement, (7) qualified retirement planning services, or (8) qualified military base realignment and closure fringe shall be excluded. An insurance salesman was taxed on insurance commissions either paid to him on policies written on his own life or credited to him so as to reduce the net price he had to pay for them. Comm. v. Minzer (5th Cir.1960). A real estate broker's salesman (an employee) who bought property through his employer to get a reduced price was taxed on the amount of the commission he would have received for procuring a buyer for the property. Comm. v. Daehler (5th Cir.1960). *See also* I.R.C. § 483 (imputed interest) and § 482 ("creation of income" by reallocation). But a partner's share of partnership profits attributable to brokerage commissions he paid to the firm for transactions of his own went untaxed, although some employee bargain purchases do give rise to income. *See* Regs. § 1.61–2(d)(2)(i).

If the realization requirement retains constitutional dignity, and if it requires severance of income from capital, it would be possible to argue that taxing the value of a person's use of his own property would be precluded; but consumption or use might come to be viewed as satisfying the realization requirement even as voiced in Eisner v. Macomber, *supra* § 16, despite contrary judicial language in Helvering v. Independent Life Ins. Co. (S.Ct.1934). Economists have not finished debating the virtues or validity of accretion, as distinguished from consumption, as the basic concept of income.

§ 21. Gifts and Employee Fringe Benefits

Gifts are excluded from taxable income by I.R.C. § 102 (*see* § 26, *infra*). If they were not, would a gift constitute "income" as that term is used in the Sixteenth Amendment and in § 61(a)? May an item that does not fit the definition of "gift" in § 102 perhaps still not be gross income under § 61(a)? The Supreme Court has reserved decision on these points. *See* U.S. v. Kaiser (S.Ct.1960). Since § 102 encompasses most "gifts," the question of their taxability under § 61(a), etc., is rarely presented. And when something argued to be a gift is not given § 102 protection, the result usually has been taxability as income. *See* Comm. v. Duberstein (S.Ct. 1960). Gift or not is largely a question of fact, or inferences from fact, and appellate courts are instructed to honor the decision of a jury (unless reasonable persons could not have reached the jury's decision on the question) or of a trial judge (unless it is clearly erroneous).

However, a gift made by an employer to or for the benefit of an employee will not qualify as a gift for income tax purposes unless it qualifies as an employee achievement award under § 74(c) or as a *de minimis* fringe benefit under § 132(e). I.R.C. § 102(c). Congress concluded that a "gift" from an employer to an employee generally constitutes compensation. Nevertheless, Congress realized there was no serious potential for avoiding taxation on compensation for certain employee awards for safety or length of service, or for gifts of minimal value. Cf. Rev.Rul. 59–58, 1959–1 C.B. 17. (I.R.C. § 274(b) provides limits on the donor's business expense deductions for gifts under §§ 162 & 212.) Prior to enactment of § 102(c), if an employer made a contribution to a charity of an employee's choice or matched the employee's own contribution under a plan, it had been ruled that employee did not have income. *See* Rev.Rul. 67–137, 1967–1 C.B. 63.

Employee fringe benefits—a combination of gifts and imputed income and, sometimes, working conditions—also sometimes escape tax. Thus a company car used for business purposes or a convention trip within North America or the group insurance or the free recreation facilities or a cheap plant cafeteria enjoyed by the employee may not be taxed to him or her. But if such items rise to a high level of value and amount to payment in kind, the Commissioner will bear down. And generally on fringe benefits, *see* I.R.C. §§ 79, 83, 107, 119, 120, 125, 127, 129, 132, 421. *See also* Regs. § 1.61–21.

§ 22. Illegal Receipts and Claim of Right

Illegal income is included in gross income, the cases now say. Moreover, the fact that the criminal may be subject to an obligation to return the money or property to someone such as the victim of his extortion, blackmail, or embezzlement will not alter his taxability. The story was not always so simple.

The developing case law began when the Supreme Court ruled that a taxpayer did have income when he held property under a "claim of right" that was disputed by others. North American Oil Consolidated v. Burnet (S.Ct.1932). In U.S. v. Lewis (S.Ct.

1951), the Court held that a bonus an employee was paid in 1944 was income to him then, because he held it under a claim of right, even though he later had to repay it when it was determined to have been erroneously computed. (On repayment, he was entitled to a deduction.) In Comm. v. Wilcox (S.Ct. 1946), the claim-of-right doctrine was used to conclude that an embezzler did *not* have income since he had no claim of right to the money he took—he either lacked title to the funds or perhaps had a voidable title, but he did not have a "bona-fide claim-of-right." Then, in Rutkin v. U.S. (S.Ct.1952), the Court decided that an extortionist was taxable on the money he received—and (somewhat disingenuously) distinguished rather than overruled *Wilcox*. Perhaps the Court's theory was that the extortionist secures his funds with the consent, in a way, of the victim, while the victim of an embezzler doesn't know of, much less in any way consent to, the transfer. Perhaps as a practical matter too, the embezzlement victim is more likely to chase his wrongdoer and, possibly, recover the funds.

The tenuous distinction between an embezzler in *Wilcox* and the extortionist in *Rutkin* was laid to rest in James v. U.S. (S.Ct.1961). *James* overruled *Wilcox* expressly and held that an embezzler does realize income. More generally, the court said that illegality of the receipt is irrelevant. Further, it said as to the claim-of-right doctrine, "When a taxpayer acquires earnings, lawfully or unlawfully, without the consensual recognition, express or implied, of an obligation to repay and without restriction as to their disposition,'' he has received income that he must report, even though it may still be claimed that he is not entitled to retain the money, and even though he may still be adjudged liable to restore its equivalent. As the Court said, this standard brings wrongful or mistaken appropriations within the sweep of gross income, but it excludes loans. If and to the extent that the victim recovers the misappropriated funds (if any are left after the tax liens are satisfied) from the embezzler, the embezzler may deduct his repayment from his income at that time.

The hard case remained—what of a purported loan that the ''borrower'' (a swindler or ''con man'') secretly intended not to repay? In U.S. v. Rochelle (5th Cir.1967), the court disposed of the case under the *James* standard—piercing form (loan) to substance (swindle), the Court held the swindler to have income. After all, he did not genuinely and consensually recognize an obligation to repay the ''borrowed'' funds.

Another case, Wood v. U.S. (5th Cir.1989), held that the proceeds of illegal drug sales are taxable income, even if they are forfeited to the federal government. In Collins v. Commissioner (2d Cir. 1993), a betting-parlor employee's theft of racing tickets for the purpose of placing personal bets gave rise to gross income. Over the course of a single day at work, the employee used his computer to issue himself $80,280 worth of racing tickets, for which he did not pay. At the end of the day, his bets had won only $42,175, for a net loss of $38,105. The court found that the taxpayer had income in the amount of $80,280 because he received an economic benefit or enrichment: the pleasure of betting on horses, a benefit for which other patrons had to pay. He was allowed a restitution deduction of the $42,175 he won, so his net taxable income for the day was $38,105—although he, of course, may not have viewed the $38,105 difference as income! In Zarin v. Comm. (3rd Cir. 1990), a casino loaned a taxpayer $3,435,000 for gambling after he had lost significant amounts of his own funds. The taxpayer was a compulsive gambler who was considered a "high roller" by the casino and given complimentary services and privileges. He lost all the borrowed money at the casino. The debt was subsequently settled for $500,000 and I.R.S. contended that the taxpayer had $2,935,000 of income from discharge of the debt. In an opinion that has been criticized by commentators, the court held that the taxpayer had no gross income, in part, because the loan was not enforceable under state regulations intended to protect compulsive gamblers. Additionally, the court concluded that the loan could be viewed as a disputed debt or contested liability that was settled for $500,000 and produced no tax consequences to the taxpayer.

Section 1341 (sometimes) allows an adjustment through a special deduction in a later year if an amount previously held under a claim of right, and consequently included in income, is returned or repaid.

§ 23. Accretion or Consumption Models of What Is "Income"?

A classic and very broad definition of income by two economists (R.M. Haig and H. Simons, incorporating the work of G. von Schanz) states that "Personal income may be defined as the algebraic sum of (1) the market value of rights exercised in consumption and (2) the change in the value of the store of property rights between the beginning and end of the period in question." This conception can be broadened by adding (3) the market value of goods and services given to other persons during the year (gifts). This is an "accretion model" of income, and generally it is an accretion model that the U.S. income tax employs, although it does not go so far as the Haig–Simons conceptualization in taxing all of a person's economic income. Unrealized gain, gifts made, imputed income from self-service and many other economic gains are not included in the U.S. income tax base, as a practical matter.

In contrast to an accretion model, a "consumption model" of an income tax can be constructed and has been suggested as a better model for income tax purposes. It would tax income that is consumed and other consumption—such as from the withdrawal of savings—but would not tax income that was saved. Consumption would be taxed; savings would not be taxed. One approach would be to ask each taxpayer to report all of his or her consumption during the year, and to pay tax on it. Another approach would be to ask for a report of income (and, perhaps, net worth) and tax the taxpayer on all income less any increase in savings (out of the income), and to tax any reduction in savings that paid for current consumption. Putting aside consumption from prior savings, the income tax would apply to all income except the income that was saved (for future consumption). By taxing the expenditure of income rather than receipt, accrual or accretion of income, this proposed income tax would reduce the tax burden on income that is saved for later consumption, reduce the over-taxation of income that is saved, create an incentive for increased saving and, some theorists argue, more fairly tax people with equal values of income but different lifetime timing patterns of receipt or expenditure of income.

A thoroughgoing examination of whether the main U.S. federal tax on individuals should be a consumption-type income tax rather than an accretion-type income tax may go beyond the usual scope of a basic income tax course. However, the possibility that income should be conceived in such a way as largely to comprehend consumption, or whether many allowances for savings should be installed in the income tax in order to "correctly" tax saved income or to discourage consumption, has directly to do with the attempts by courts, scholars and others to define "income." Moreover, the objection to the so-called "overtaxation" of savings under an income tax that does not contain exemptions for savings is freighted with considerations important for an understanding of the income tax in general.

The overtaxation argument has to do, at its roots, with the value of deferring the payment of tax and with the disadvantage of having to pay tax earlier, rather than later. Suppose, for example, that a person has wages of $20,000 and under an income tax is deemed to have $20,000 of income (even if he saves $1,000 out of his income). He will pay tax at the established rate or rates on $20,000, if that is the amount of his "taxable" income. Suppose for the moment that the tax law chose to say that the amount of his so-called income that was used for savings would not be taxed, until such time as he chose to end the savings and use the saved amounts for consumption. In that case, the taxpayer who saved $1,000 would not have to pay tax on that $1,000 until a later time. Even if rates and all other events were constant and thus tax to be paid on that $1,000 at a later time would be the same number of dollars, of constant purchasing power, as the number of dollars in tax that would have been required in year one, the second taxpayer has an advantage. That advantage consists of his or her ability to use the amount of the tax that did not have to be paid in year one for investment.

Until the tax must be paid, an amount equal to that tax can be put to work in a savings account or other investment for the benefit of the taxpayer, and thus it would generate additional income. To be sure, that additional income presumably would itself be subject to tax, but so long as the tax is less than 100%, the taxpayer will have a net benefit from the deferral of the tax payment to the time of consumption.

If the deferral were as long as 10 years and if interest rates were about 7½%, the amount of deferred tax could be put in a savings account at compound interest and would double by the end of the 10–year period. There would then be enough dollars in the account to pay the tax on the original deposit and accumulated interest and still have an additional amount left over. The taxpayer may have to pay tax on the interest as it accrues over the years, and therefore the net benefit would be somewhat less than the computations suggested. Nevertheless, there would be very significant net benefits. This benefit of deferral shows the advantage of an income tax that postpones tax on income until it is used for consumption. The concept of deferral has much to do with tax planning as well as the principles of taxation.

The same principles show the advantage of deferral under an income tax system, deferral of any kind. It is much more valuable not to have to pay the tax in year one and to have to pay tax on an equivalent amount (plus interest later) than the reverse.

If the meaning of "income" is taken to be a conception that stresses expenditure, consumption or net disposable command over resources, the result will be to "tilt" the income tax in the direction of a tax on consumption, with the resulting deferral benefits. If that conception is used as the model against which to compare the current U.S. income tax, an income tax that is not "tilted" in the direction of a consumption tax, that is to say a Haig–Simons accretion-type income tax, the present U.S. tax will be observed to produce higher taxation, by way of taxation sooner, on income that is used for savings or investment, compared to the consumption model tax.

§ 24. Summary and Overview

To shorten the long story, the Supreme Court seems to have acknowledged the futility of trying to capture the concept of income and confine it in a definition. Instead, the cases show the Court's descriptions and generalizations about income changing as the Court's attitude toward the income tax itself has changed. In Eisner v. Macomber, the Court described income as gain derived from capital or labor or both, including sales of capital assets. Such a standard might well exclude cancellation of indebtedness, found money, prizes and awards, and embezzled funds. These items would be reached by the far more expansive language in *Glenshaw Glass* about realized accessions to wealth under the taxpayer's dominion. Moreover, in *James,* the Court talked as though only a consensual recognition, express or implied, of an obligation to repay, or a material restriction as to disposition of the money or property, would prevent almost any value coming into the taxpayer's possession from taxability as income.

Although judicial notions of what is income have broadened, they have not gone so far as the economists' definitions. The famous Haig–Simons definition, mentioned above, would define income as the sum of (1) the market value of rights exercised in consumption and (2) the change in value of the store of property rights of the taxpayer, over time. Or, income may be defined as the money value of the net accretion to economic power between two points of time. Such a definition, while conceptually "correct" (and useful as a basis for evaluating the Internal Revenue Code), is too broad to describe existing law. It would include all forms of non-market benefits, imputed income and unrealized appreciation in assets. Thus far, Congress has not sought to define income so broadly, for tax purposes.

Thus we are left with guidelines but no self-executing standard. As Justice Holmes observed in an overstatement in *Kirby Lumber,* "We see nothing to be gained by the discussion of judicial definitions." For purposes of the Sixteenth Amendment, the Court may be anxious to avoid allowing a direct tax on property to slip through in the guise of an income tax not apportioned among the states according to population. As Justice Holmes said, words have their plain meaning—a return of capital is different from income. Nevertheless, while the borderline content of "income" must be determined case by case, it would be surprising if anything for which there was a reasonable basis to tax under the income tax, almost any accretion to wealth, were found today to be beyond Congress' constitutional competence to tax.

As a consequence, most "what is income" questions have become matters of statutory interpretation rather than constitutional adjudication. Accordingly, the next chapter turns to the more specific statutory inclusions and exclusions. Problems and authorities to be found there may illuminate further the central issue of this chapter: "What is income?" And that question will arise again in connection with deductions, those amounts that are subtracted from gross income to arrive at net income (or whatever term defines the base of the federal income tax).

CHAPTER III

STATUTORY INCLUSION AND EXCLUSION FROM GROSS INCOME

§ 25. Introduction

In the preceding chapter, the question was whether given items are "income" in the Sixteenth Amendment sense or in the I.R.C. § 61(a) sense of "income from whatever source derived ... [e]xcept as otherwise provided in this subtitle." Now we come to the statutes that do provide otherwise. In other words, in some sections of the Internal Revenue Code, Congress has expressly removed specified receipts from the reach of the tax law's definition of gross income. Some of these excluded items would be income within § 61(a) if the exclusionary sections were repealed. Other items were of doubtful status when the exclusions were enacted but probably would be considered constitutionally taxable as income today. And, they probably would be held to fall within the embrace of § 61(a) as a matter of statutory interpretation. Some of the exclusions may be constitutionally compelled, even now. Or, even if Congress could include them in gross income, § 61(a) might be construed not to comprehend them, until amended.

61

The following sections of this chapter take up the most important statutory exclusions, section by section. They differ in historical origin, policy, defensibility and economic effect. They share several characteristics, one of which is their income-variant effect. That is to say, the tax saving that an exclusion affords to a taxpayer varies with his or her marginal rate of tax, which depends on total taxable income. So, excluding $1,000 of income from a 28%-bracket taxpayer's gross income can save as much as $280 in tax, but a 15%-bracket taxpayer would save only $150. In other words, an exclusion saves the amount of tax that would be collected if the receipt were not excluded, and that amount is a function of the graduated income tax rates and the taxpayer's top rate or rates.

§ 26. Gifts and Bequests

Section 102(a) of the I.R.C. provides that gross income does not include the value of property acquired by gift, bequest, devise or inheritance. However, subsection (b) explains that subsection (a) does not exclude from gross income the income from any of the property referred to in subsection (a) or a gift or bequest that is of income (alone) from property. Consequently, if F gives property to S, S does not have income by virtue of the receipt. Later, if the property produces income to S, S will be taxed on that income.

And I.R.C. § 102(c) states that the exclusionary rule of § 102(a) shall not apply to "any amount transferred by or from an employer to, or for the benefit of, an employee." Nevertheless, an employee's gross income will not include qualified employee achievement awards or *de minimis* gifts from the employer. *See* I.R.C. § 74(c) and § 132(a)(4).

Why are gifts excluded from gross income? Several effects and possible purposes of § 102 suggest themselves. Perhaps Congress was in doubt whether gifts are income, as the term is used in the Sixteenth Amendment or in common understanding. Perhaps Congress merely wanted to keep the income tax auditor away from the Christmas tree and birthday cake—to relieve intra-family, affectionate gifts from any tax cost or tax compliance flavor. Perhaps Congress wanted to encourage, or at least not to discourage, gifts and the redistribution of wealth they often entail; usually the richer give to the poorer, rather than vice versa. More simply, Congress may have concluded that a reallocation of wealth by gift is not an appropriate occasion to impose an income tax. Still other reasons occur to justify or explain § 102. It may be hard for a donee to pay an income tax on a gift, especially when the gift is in kind, not in cash. Also, another federal tax, the gift tax, is imposed on the donor of some gifts amounting to more than $11,000 (in 2004) per donee, per year. And, the estate tax will apply to some bequests. Although the transfer taxes are different from income tax in application, rate, and impact, perhaps some members of Congress think the one tax is enough. And, the income tax itself will apply to income from the gift property in the hands of the donee. The assignment-of-income rules (to be encountered later) should serve to prevent evasion of high tax rates by gifts of income only, or anticipatory assignments of income. Finally, the steeply graduated income tax rates may have been thought unsuitable to tax large, non-periodic receipts lumped in a single tax year.

According to I.R.C. § 102 and basic income principles for "who is taxable" on income from property, after a donor makes a gift of property, the subsequent income from the property is taxable to the donee at his, her or its applicable rate. Employing this principle, high-income parents were able to save tax by transferring property to their children after which the income from the property became taxable at the child's marginal rate, typically lower than the parents', leaving more after-tax income for the child, perhaps for college expenses. Congress has now largely closed this planning opportunity by requiring that such a donee, if a child under 14, must pay tax at the parents' applicable rate (the rate at which the income would have been taxed if taxable to them). This is affectionately called the "kiddie tax," and it applies above a low exemption level, of a maximum of (a statutory amount of) $1,000 (the $500 standard deduction plus a kiddie-tax exemption of $500), indexed for inflation (so as to total $1,600 for 2004). *See* I.R.C. § 1(g) and Temp. Regs. § 1.1(i)–1T.

Whatever the original reason for enactment of § 102 and its forerunners, and whatever the reasons for its continued presence in the Code, the exclusion for gifts and bequests is an important one.

It permits some individuals to receive substantial additions to their economic power, repeatedly or occasionally, without paying tax as they would if the addition came in earned, windfall or other taxable form. Accordingly, the redistributive power of the income tax is perhaps reduced, and questions of its equity are raised. Substantial revenue is foregone.

Marginal interpretive questions are presented in applying § 102. What is a gift? Does the concept include tips? Strike benefits? Business gifts? Bonuses to employees? Does a bequest include an amount willed to a faithful family retainer who has served the decedent at low pay for many years? Such questions are largely questions of fact or of inferences to be drawn from facts, under the test laid down by the Supreme Court in Comm. v. Duberstein (S.Ct.1960). In that case the Court refused to adopt some rules, suggested by the Government, for determining whether or not something was a gift, as a matter of legal categories. The Government suggested that gifts should be defined as transfers for personal, as distinguished from business, reasons. The Government added several corollaries. For example, voluntary transfers from employer to employee would almost always be taxable and would not be gifts. [*See* recently enacted § 102(c).] If a payment were deducted by the donor as a business expense, it would not be a gift to the donee. A business corporation, in the Government's view, could not make a gift.

The Court opted instead for a more general standard to be applied on a case-by-case basis. A gift, it said, proceeds from a "detached and disinterested generosity," "out of affection, respect, admiration, charity or like impulses," not from "the constraining force of any moral or legal duty" or from "the incentive of anticipated benefit." The key inquiry is the donor's intention, but that intention is different from the "donative intent" of the common law. And the donor's own characterization of his action is not determinative—there is to be an objective inquiry into the dominant reason that explains his action. Mere absence of a legal or moral obligation to make a transfer does not suffice to establish that it is a gift.

Under *Duberstein,* appellate courts are to defer to the fact-finding tribunal's determination after it has applied its experience with the "mainsprings of human conduct" to the facts of each case. A jury's decision must therefore stand unless reasonable people could not have come to the jury's announced conclusion. If trial were before a judge alone, his conclusion remains unless it is "clearly erroneous." Applying this standard, the Court held that Duberstein was taxable on an expensive automobile given to him by a business acquaintance in appreciation for business advice (as the Tax Court had found). On remand of an accompanying case, the lower court held that a cash payment by an employer to an employee upon termination of that employee's service was a nontaxable gift. *See* Stanton v. U.S. (D.C.N.Y.1960). [*But see* I.R.C. § 102(c), enacted since.] Strike benefits given by a union to a non-union striking employee were held to be non-taxable gifts (as the jury had found) in U.S. v. Kaiser (S.Ct.1960). Compare Gregory v. U.S. (E.D.N.C. 1986), in which the Court held that strike benefits received by union members constituted taxable income, not excludable gifts, and distinguished *Kaiser*, where the recipients were not union members and the union had no obligation to make payments to these non-members.

The plethora of cases that have followed are not subject to easy generalization; the court's case-by-case, trier-of-fact-to-decide approach has continued. For example, tips (called "tokes," from "tokens") given by gambling casino patrons to craps dealers were first held to be tax-free gifts by a District Court, but later ruled taxable income, like tips generally. Olk v. U.S. (9th Cir.1976).

The I.R.S. at first ruled that books gratuitously received from a publisher by a professional book reviewer constituted gross income. Rev. Rul. 70–330, 1970–1 C.B. 14. Soon the Service thought better of it and ruled that they must be included in income only if and when the reviewer sought a tax benefit by donating them to a charity. Rev. Rul. 70–498, 1970–2 C.B. 6.

The Seventh Circuit came to the same conclusion in Haverly v. U.S. (7th Cir.1975), finding that when a school principal donated to charity unsolicited books he received from an educational publisher and claimed a charitable deduction for the donation, he was exercising "complete dominion" over them so as to render their value "gross income" to him at the time of donation to charity.

At this point, a few related tax consequences should be mentioned. First, § 102(a) excludes from the donee's income the value of a gift received. Possibly a *donor* will be deemed to have realized income upon making a gift of appreciated property or of income about to be realized. *See, e.g.,* Helvering v. Horst, *infra,* § 81; I.R.C. § 453B (gain or loss on disposition of installment obligations), *infra,* § 72; I.R.C. § 84 (transferor taxed on transfer of appreciated property to a political organization).

Secondly, § 102(a) excludes the gift from income at the time of its receipt. The donee may, nevertheless, have occasion to report income as a result of a gift or bequest of property that is later sold by the donee. For, as a price of tax-free receipt, the donee of a gift must take the donor's own basis as his basis in the gift property for purposes of determining *gain* on sale by the donee. *See* I.R.C. § 1015(a); Taft v. Bowers (S.Ct.1929). Consequently, if A owns Blackacre for which he paid $10,000 (his cost basis) and gives it to B when Blackacre is worth $15,000, and if B later sells Blackacre for $17,000, B will have taxable gain of $7,000. If Blackacre had been worth just $8,000 when A gave it to B, B would also have $7,000 gain when he sold it for $17,000 later.

However, for purposes of determining *loss* on subsequent sale, the donee must take as his basis the lesser of (i) the donor's own basis or (ii) fair market value (FMV) of the property at the time of the gift. Consequently, if A's basis had been $10,000 and FMV had been $8,000 at date of gift, and if B later sold the gift property for $7,000, B would have had a realized loss of only $1,000; A's loss of $2,000 would never be recognized by A or B. If, perchance, B had sold Blackacre for $9,000 (an amount in between A's basis—$10,000—and FMV—$8,000—at the time of gift), B would realize neither gain nor loss, a strange result that follows from selling the property in the "gray" area between the two bases and the basis rules of I.R.C. § 1015(a). *See* Regs. § 1.1015–1. (The rule for determining loss is irrelevant because if it applied, donor would be seen to have gained; if the rule for computing gain is used, the result shows a loss.)

In contrast, when property is transferred between spouses or between former spouses incident to divorce, neither gain nor loss will be recognized, and the basis to the transferee will be the same as it was in the hands of the transferor, for gain or loss purposes. *See* I.R.C. §§ 1041(a) & (b).

Somewhat different rules apply to bequests (or lifetime transfers included in the estate of the decedent). The legatee's basis is the fair market value of the property at date of death (or the alternative valuation date elected for estate tax purposes). I.R.C. § 1014(a). Thus if A bequeaths Blackacre, which cost him $10,000, to B, and if Blackacre was worth $12,000 at the date of death, or alternate valuation date, B's basis in Blackacre is $12,000. If the FMV at death had been $9,000, B's basis will be $9,000. Thus, in the gift situation, the donor's gain would later be taxed to the donee if and when the donee sold the property and realized a price in excess of the donor's basis, but in the bequest situation the donor's gain (or loss) goes untaxed (or undeducted), and the legatee begins with a new basis equal to valuation of the property for federal estate tax purposes—"fresh-start basis." The general "stepped-up" basis rule of I.R.C. § 1014(a) does not apply to appreciated property acquired by the decedent through gift within one year of death if the property passes to the donor or donor's spouse upon the donee's death. I.R.C. § 1014(e). This exception prevents a prospective heir from giving property to a decedent immediately prior to death only to regain ownership of the property with a higher basis.

The fresh-start basis rule of § 1014 is scheduled to terminate with respect to decedents dying after December 31, 2009. I.R.C. § 1014(f). Beginning in 2010, the estate tax (but not the gift tax) is repealed and § 1014 is replaced by § 1022 which provides that property acquired from a decedent after December 31, 2009 is treated as transferred by gift and the basis of the person acquiring such property is the lesser of (a) the decedent's basis, or (b) the fair market value of the property at the decedent's death. I.R.C. § 1022(a). The carryover basis rule in § 1022 is modified by provisions that generally allow a $1.3 million basis increase (up to fair market value) for property left to anyone and an extra $3 million basis increase (again, up to fair market value) for property left to a spouse. I.R.C.

§ 1022(b), (c), (d)(2). However, the repeal of the estate tax and § 1022 are now both scheduled to be repealed beginning in 2011 so in 2011 the estate tax and § 1014 are scheduled to be back in place. There can be little doubt that future legislation will decide the ultimate fate of the fresh-start basis rule in § 1014.

Once before, in the mid–1970s, Congress sought drastically to change the basis rule for some property transferred at death. In general, for bequests or lifetime transfers, a recipient's basis under that rule (§ 1023) was to be the transferor's adjusted basis of the property immediately before the death of the transferor, adjusted for transfer taxes paid. I.R.C. § 1023. That provision was short-lived, however, due to the serious administrative and compliance problems it created. These included ascertaining the decedent's cost basis, upon later sale by the donee, of property (passing at death) which was acquired by the decedent years earlier, perhaps affected by depreciation or capital adjustment. Another problem was to ensure a fair distribution of assets with bases different from their respective fair market values to recipients in different tax brackets. Section 1023 eventually was repealed (retroactively) but taxpayers were allowed to elect its basis rules for the period § 1023 would have been in effect but for the many postponements of its effective date. Congress cited the significant increase in the time, and therefore the costs, required to administer an estate and the unduly complicated rules as reasons for the repeal. One advantage of the rule of I.R.C.

§ 1014(a) is that fair market value at death is easier to ascertain than the decedent's basis, and it is particularly easy if it has been established for estate tax purposes.

The carryover basis rule of § 1023 was enacted largely for reasons of equity and economics. Under § 1014 the income tax does not reach pre-death appreciation in the hands of the decedent or the heir, an escape from tax thought to be unacceptable as a matter of tax equity. And the resulting incentive to retain appreciated property until death but to sell loss property to realize the tax deduction before death creates a skewing of investment incentives and, at least in terms of price level increase, a serious lock-in effect. To be sure, the estate tax law would include property held at death at its fair market value, but that did not justify failure to tax the unrealized income since the estate tax also would apply to the proceeds of sale, or property in which those proceeds were invested, in the case of a taxpayer who sold before death. Thus, it is not surprising that Congress linked the repeal of the estate tax in 2010 with the modified-carryover basis rule in I.R.C. § 1022. However, the generous basis increases available under that section will still permit substantial amounts of gains to escape the income tax.

One alternative for maintaining the "fresh-start" basis rule at death while closing the escape route for unrealized appreciation would be to make death a deemed (constructive) realization event. Constructive realization, however, is thought by many to involve undue liquidity problems; assets often would have to be sold to pay income tax at a time when there has not been a voluntary disposition, such as a sale or exchange, which makes invocation of a tax bill suitable. Small businesses, farms, and estates consisting mainly of a family residence or other illiquid assets would be especially hard hit by constructive realization at death.

Again note that § 102(a) excludes from the donee's gross income only the property itself. Income *from* the property—dividends, rents, interest, etc.— will be taxed to the donee under the usual rules applicable to such items. Thus, if A gives stock worth $10,000 to B, receipt of the stock itself will not produce immediately recognized income to B, but dividends later received will be taxable to B. The Code also provides that if a gift or bequest consists of income only, the gift itself will be income to the donee. I.R.C. § 102(b). See § 84, *infra*, regarding the tax treatment of income in respect of a decedent.

If a donor transfers property, in trust or otherwise, so that one donee receives the income from it for life or a period of years, and another donee gets the property outright, as a remainder interest, after the term, how will the two donees be taxed? Will each get the benefit of the exclusion, completely or in part, or will it apply only to one? If the excludable amount is to be the fair market value of the property at time of transfer, a pro-ration would be necessary in most instances. This is true because the nominal value, in dollars, of the income received over years by the term beneficiary and then the value of the property itself when it goes to the remainderman will exceed the static value at time of transfer. So the value at transfer could be apportioned according to relative values of term and remainder interest, and the income beneficiary could be given a basis in that interest, to be received tax-free.

The law has been settled on this point, and it goes against apportionment. The income beneficiary will not be able to exclude anything, and the remainderman will exclude everything. *See* Irwin v. Gavit (S.Ct.1925). *And see* § 102(b)(1). The income beneficiary holding a life or terminable interest acquired by gift or bequest may not take any deduction for shrinkage or expiration of his interest due to lapse of time. I.R.C. § 273. Section 102(b) contains two rules for determining whether a gift is a gift of property or income, in doubtful cases. In general, when payment of the gift is to be made at intervals, not in a lump sum, the transfer is to be treated as a gift of income to the extent paid out of income. Also, any amount included in the gross income of a beneficiary of an estate or trust is to be treated as a gift of income from property.

As explained in this § 26 above, the § 1(g) "kiddie tax" adds a twist to the previous rule as well. If the property is transferred to a minor (below the age of 14), the income from the transferred property must be taxed at the parents' marginal tax rate, over the two small exemptions.

At one time, former I.R.C. § 101(b) provided that the first $5,000 of amounts received by the beneficiaries or the estate of an employee, from or on behalf of an employer and paid by reason of the death of the employee, would not be included in gross income, a quasi-gift exclusion. The repeal of that section and the enactment of § 102(c)(1) (no exclusion on "gift" transfers, by or for an employer, to or for the benefit of an employee) make it no longer possible to contend that such amounts are excluded even under a general § 102 gift theory. Also, I.R.C. § 274(b) limits an employee's corporation to a $25 deduction; that limitation will tend to discourage employee gifts.

§ 27. Prizes and Awards

Formerly there was some question whether any or all prizes were income. The answer depended on whether they could be shown to be gifts. Prior to enactment of I.R.C. § 74, most prizes were held to be income, although awards for public service or achievement managed to qualify as gifts and thus to escape tax. Some random or windfall prizes were excluded as "gifts." Now the gift exclusion has been broken down into three separate exclusions—§ 102 for ordinary gifts, § 117 for scholarship and fellowship grants and § 74 for prizes and awards.

Since enactment of the 1986 TRA, the fair market value of almost all prizes and awards is included in the recipient's gross income. I.R.C. § 74. However, there are several exceptions to this general rule. The most notable exception is for certain prizes and awards transferred to charities. Under this exception, a prize or award will be excluded if (1) it was given in recognition of religious, charitable, scientific, educational, artistic, literary, or civic achievement; (2) the recipient did not take any action to enter the contest or proceeding; (3) the recipient is not required to render future services as a condition of receiving the prize or award; and (4) the recipient assigns the prize or award to a governmental unit or tax-exempt charitable organization. The taxpayer's assignment of the prize or award must be made before the taxpayer uses the awarded item. This last requirement, which came into being in 1986, practically precludes the exclusion of most prizes and awards from income—unless the winner will part with the prize.

Certain employee achievement awards for length of service or safety will also be excluded from the recipient's gross income. The award must consist of tangible personal property (not cash) awarded as part of a meaningful presentation under conditions that do not create a significant likelihood that the payment is disguised compensation. I.R.C. § 274(j)(3)(A). The fair market value of an achievement award is fully excludable from the recipient's gross income only if the cost of the award is fully deductible by the employer. I.R.C. § 74(c); see I.R.C. § 274(j)(2) for limitations on the employer's deduction. If part of the employer's cost is not deductible, the employee must include in her gross income the greater of (1) the amount of the employer's cost that is not deductible (but not in excess of the value of the award), or (2) the amount by which the value of the award exceeds the employer's deduction. I.R.C. § 74(c).

An employee award will also be excluded from the recipient's gross income if it qualifies as a *de minimis* fringe benefit under I.R.C. § 132(e). Under this exception the award must have a small value, and the employee must not have received many such awards.

Before 1986, when the requirement of assignment to either a government or charitable organization entered the law, imaginative taxpayers tested the limits of § 74. Athletes argued that their accomplishments were civic achievements. A lucky fisherman argued that his was a civic achievement when he caught a tagged fish entitling him to a $25,000 cash prize paid by a beer company to advertise its wares. *See* Simmons v. U.S. (4th Cir.1962). (Both taxpayers lost their cases.)

The purposes of the pre–1986 § 74(b) exclusion were varied. Congress may have wanted to subsidize recognition of meritorious achievement (while sidestepping games of chance or contests of skill), to put such awards on a par with gifts and scholarships, to reflect doubt about whether a prize is income, or to relieve these once-in-a-lifetime receipts from the impact of graduated rates applied on an annual basis and designed mainly to tax a fairly even flow of income. Not everyone agreed with these policies or with the outlines of the § 74(b) exclusion, which accounts for the major change, or reversal, in 1986.

If a taxable prize is awarded in a form other than cash, the fair market value of the prize—if not excludable—must be determined and included in income.

§ 28. Scholarships and Fellowships

More obvious and agreeable, perhaps, are the policies behind § 117's exclusion from gross income of qualified scholarships received by an individual who is a degree candidate at an educational institution. The policies probably involved are to aid and subsidize education and scholarly activities, to put scholarship recipients on a par with students and fellows supported by tax-free gifts and, perhaps, to avoid any hard question about whether a scholarship is income. Congress may also have sought to equalize (tax-wise) students paying low or no tuition at state universities or colleges with those paying high tuition at private schools. The students at the low-tuition schools, of course, receive a tax-free subsidy much like a scholarship. Even before § 117, most scholarships were excludable as gifts, unless the recipient was required to render services for the payment.

To be excluded under § 117, the amount (including the value of contributed services and accommodations) received as a scholarship or fellowship must not exceed the individual's "qualified tuition and related expenses." Qualified tuition and related expenses are limited to (a) tuition and fees required for the enrollment or attendance at an educational organization as defined in I.R.C. § 170(b)(1)(A)(ii), and (b) fees, books, supplies, and equipment required for the courses of instruction at such an educational organization. *See* I.R.C. § 117(b)(2). To the extent that the amount of scholarship or fellowship grant received by an individual exceeds his qualified tuition and related expenses, the excess must be included in his/her gross income.

Not all amounts that support a student or scholar are excluded. The exclusion generally will not cover payment for teaching, research, or other services required as a condition of the grant. I.R.C. § 117(c). Many cases have held, under the general rule, that a physician, resident or intern who treats patients in a training hospital for a stipend may not exclude the pay for services rendered. And amounts paid to an employee on "education leave" have, on the facts (including required further employment), been held taxable as compensation. *See* Bingler v. Johnson (S.Ct.1969); Regs. § 1.117–4(c).

A case-by-case approach must be made despite the apparent clarity of § 117. To qualify as a scholarship or fellowship, a grant must be made for the primary purpose of aiding a degree candidate in pursuit of his studies or in research. *See* Regs. § 1.117–3(a) and (c). Awards for other purposes will not qualify for exclusion under § 117.

Sometimes hard questions are raised by the terms of § 117 and by facts that may be ambiguous about just who the donor really is (when a wealthy alumnus channels his gift through an institution whose awards tend to follow the alumnus' wishes), or whether a scholarship is given as compensation by an employer (in which case the "scholarship" is taxable as income). Extensive regulations attempt to cope with many of these problems, as well as the potential overlap of §§ 117, 102, and 74. In general, a grant that is a scholarship or fellowship, as defined in the Regulations, must seek exclusion under § 117 and nowhere else. But if a grant fails under § 117 because it is not a scholarship or fellowship, shelter can be sought for it under § 102 or § 74, wherever it can fit.

By way of reflection on public policy considerations, one can note that the exclusion for scholarships, like other exclusions, benefits most those members of society who enjoy receipts (income) that fit the definition of the excluded receipt. And, among recipients, those who receive the largest amounts enjoy the greatest tax benefit. And among recipients of equal amounts, those who derive the greatest tax benefit from an exclusion are those with the largest taxable incomes from other sources. As to them, if the excluded receipt were not excluded and thus were taxable as gross income, the receipt would be taxed at a higher rate than it would be taxed to their brethren with lower incomes that fit into correspondingly lower marginal income tax rates.

§ 29. Life Insurance and Other Death Benefits

Section 101(a)(1) of the I.R.C. excludes from gross income amounts received under a life insurance contract paid by reason of the death of the insured (with a few exceptions). As a result, no income is realized in the common case of a man who has paid, for example, $30,000 in life insurance premiums who dies, and then the policy's face amount, say $50,000, is paid to his widow or other designated beneficiary. (The federal estate tax may apply if the decedent retained incidents of ownership in the policies; state estate or inheritance or even income taxes may apply, according to their own rules.) "Mortality gains" are not taxed.

This exclusion may rest in part on the notion that at least part of the proceeds paid at death are akin to a return of capital or to a gift. By way of comparison, the man who self-insures by saving out of his income can bequeath his savings to his widow or children without income tax to the recipients. To some extent, life insurance proceeds are the equivalent of such savings since they arise from lifetime premium payments by the insured. Undoubtedly also the life insurance companies have been effective in lobbying for § 101(a). And, the income tax, with its annual system and graduated rates, may be regarded as ill suited to taxing relatively large amounts of money transferred all at once upon the extraordinary event of death. Moreover, sound social policy may recommend not taxing (under an income tax) funds that often are needed for the support of dependent survivors. While other and perhaps more limited rules might equally or better accomplish any one of these aims singly,[1] taken

1. For example, proceeds of insurance could be excluded to the extent of premiums paid. Or the exclusion of § 101 could be repealed and a deduction installed for insurance premiums paid.

together such policies may add up to strong support for this exclusion.

The § 101(a) exclusion applies only to payments that properly may be called proceeds of life insurance. Life insurance must, therefore, be distinguished from annuity payments, pensions, other social security or retirement plans, or survivor benefits, joint savings accounts and the like. The basic question is whether the arrangement involved an actuarial risk on the part of the insurance company or other payor.

The exclusion of § 101(a)(1) does not apply if the life insurance policy has been transferred for a valuable consideration, except to the extent of the consideration given and any premiums paid afterwards by the transferee. I.R.C. § 101(a)(2). In other words, a transferee/purchaser of such a policy on another's life can receive only his cost as a tax-free return of capital. An exception to that exception is made for a transfer of a life insurance policy if the transferee's basis in the policy is determined in part or wholly by reference to its basis in the hands of the transferor, or if the transfer is to a partnership or corporation in which the insured is a member. So, someone who receives such a policy in a tax-free transfer or exchange (often such a holder is the alter ego of the transferor or a donee who is a close family member) will be treated like the transferor. Regs. § 1.101–1 contains some helpful illustrations.

The § 101(a)(1) exclusion also does not apply to interest paid by the insurance company if the excluded proceeds of the policy are held after death and paid out over a period of time. I.R.C. § 101(c). If proceeds are paid out over intervals after death, a pro-ration between the proceeds themselves and interest on them is called for by § 101(d). However, the 1986 T.R.A. repealed the special provision that enabled a surviving spouse to receive up to $1,000 per year without the necessity of pro-rating. *See* I.R.C. § 101(d)(1).

The § 101(a) exclusion applies to "flexible premium" life insurance policies issued before 1985 (with special rules applying to policies issued before 1983) only if certain requirements are met. A flexible premium policy is similar to whole life insurance except that the policyholder has the option of paying substantial sums into the policy's cash value fund without increasing the death benefit, thereby using it as a tax-free vehicle for investment of the additional contributions. To qualify for income exclusion, a flexible premium life insurance policy either cannot exceed a specifically computed guideline limitation and any amount payable upon the death of the insured cannot be less than the "applicable percentage" of the contract's cash value as of the date of death, or the cash value may not exceed the "net single premium" for the death benefit at such time. *See* I.R.C. § 101(f) as enacted in 1982 for the definitions of these terms and the specific rules.

An "unstated exclusion" of sorts is enjoyed by holders of some life insurance. The insured's premium payments build up a fund, reflected in the cash surrender value of straight-life insurance, the interest on which benefits him and reduces the amount of the annual premium he has to pay. Nevertheless, he is not taxed on this interest [unless he cashes in the policy and the proceeds exceed the premiums paid—*see* § 72(e)]. This interest is not realized, since it cannot be withdrawn without surrendering the insurance, yet it reduces the insured's expenditures just as much as if he earned it on money deposited in the bank that he then withdrew and used to pay part of his annual premium. If he dies without cashing in his policies, the interest will go untaxed to him (or anyone else) under the income tax. If a life insurance policy is surrendered by the owner (often the insured, but not always), and the "cash surrender value" is paid out by the company, the tax consequences are determined under I.R.C. § 72(e)(5), which provides that the excess of the cash value over the premiums paid constitutes taxable income. Rarely will there be such an excess, since the premiums reflect a cost of insurance over the years and the risk attached, and the cash surrender value will consist of the excess of premiums paid, plus earnings on those amounts in the hands of the company, over the cost of insurance. However, following the enactment of I.R.C. § 72(e)(5)(C) in 1982, giving the Treasury authority to issue guidelines as to when the amount of risk under a life insurance contract is sufficiently minimal to treat the contract as an annuity (*see* § 30, *infra*) thereby changing the income tax consequences, the taxpayer may have to act cautiously when surrendering a life insurance policy.

Section 101(g) also provides an important exclusion where a terminally ill or chronically ill individual receives an amount under a life insurance contract while still alive. Under § 101(g) such amounts may be treated as "amounts paid by reason of the death of the insured" that are excluded under § 101(a). A "terminally ill" individual is defined as an individual who has been certified by a physician as having an illness or physical condition that can reasonably be expected to result in death in 24 months or less. I.R.C. § 101(g)(4)(A). A "chronically ill" individual is defined as an individual (a) who has been certified as unable to perform at least two activities of daily living for a period of at least 90 days due to a loss of functional capacity, or (b) requiring substantial supervision to protect such individual from threats to health and safety due to severe cognitive impairment. I.R.C. §§ 101(g)(4)(B), 7702B(c)(2). The amounts excluded under § 101(g) may be received from the insurer or may be from a sale or assignment to a viatical settlement provider, generally a person regularly engaged in the trade or business of purchasing or taking assignments of life insurance contracts. I.R.C. § 101(g)(2). There is no limit on the amount that may be excluded by a terminally ill individual under § 101(g). A chronically ill individual may exclude payments for costs of qualified long-term care service (less other reimbursements) but the exclusion may not exceed a per diem limitation of $230 (in 2004). I.R.C. §§ 101(g)(3), 7702B(d). For purposes of the § 101(g) exclusion, an individual who is both terminally ill and chronically ill is treated as terminally ill. I.R.C. § 101(g)(4)(B).

No deduction is allowed for insurance premiums paid by a person for insurance on his or her life. If those premiums are paid by someone else, such as an employer, they may be partly or wholly exempt from taxation, and this gives a tax benefit akin to a deduction. I.R.C. § 79 taxes an employee on the premiums for group-term life insurance paid by the employer, but only to the extent that the death benefits of insurance so provided exceed $50,000; so, premiums paid for insurance up to $50,000 are not taxed to the employee, an important exclusion in itself. However, for tax years beginning after 1983, such group-term life plans must be non-discriminatory in order for key employees to obtain the $50,000 exclusion. *See* I.R.C. § 79(d) for the non-discriminatory provisions. A key employee is defined in I.R.C. § 416(i) as (i) an officer of the employer having an annual compensation greater than $130,000, (ii) a five-percent owner of the employer, or (iii) a one-percent owner of the employer having an annual compensation from the employer of over $150,000. Section 416(i)(B) defines (ii) and (iii) above and provides constructive ownership rules.

When death benefits under a life insurance policy are paid, they consist in part of the interest earned by the premiums collected by the company and invested. That interest was not taxed to the insured during life and it also will not be taxable when paid out as part of the death benefit, which makes the "tax shelter" of life insurance all the more generous.

The exclusion from income of the "investment gains" in insurance, where death benefits pay out more than premiums have cost, can be likened to the fresh start basis rule of § 1014, which on death removes from income tax the lifetime appreciation in assets.

To prevent taxpayers from converting non-deductible life insurance premiums into deductible payments cast in the form of interest, and some other excesses associated with life insurance, § 264 disallows a deduction for certain interest on loans to purchase or carry life insurance and on some premiums that otherwise would be deducted as business costs.

A life insurance policy purchased together with an annuity contract may deprive the recipient of the § 101 exclusion, since the I.R.S. says that the package lacks the essential characteristics of insurance. Insurance consists of risk-shifting or risk-spreading. The package of two policies can mean that there is no shifting of risk, since if the purchaser lives long he will "win" in the annuity but "lose" in the insurance, and vice-versa if he dies early. If the plan does not qualify for § 101, the proceeds of the life insurance contract will be includable to the extent they exceed net premiums paid for that contract.

All in all, life insurance enjoys a favored position under the income tax and serves as an important technique for tax planning.

§ 30. Annuities

Amounts received as an annuity (whether for a specified period of years or for the duration of one or more lives) under an annuity, endowment or life insurance contract are included in or excluded from gross income according to a formula called an "exclusion ratio." The exclusion ratio is a fraction. The numerator is the taxpayer's investment in the annuity contract and the denominator is the taxpayer's expected return over the annuity period. *See* I.R.C. §§ 72(a), (b), (c)(1), & (c)(3). Generally the period is for someone's life or for a fixed term. This ratio is applied to each payment to fix the amount to be excluded. The rest of each payment is taxable as income. This rule can best be understood by applying it to a fact situation.

Consider, by way of simple illustration, a single man of sixty-five years of age who has saved $100,000. Unsure of how long he will live and unable to support himself on the 5% interest his savings produce each year on deposit in the bank, he enters into an annuity contract with an annuity company. He will pay to the company a single premium of $100,000. In return the company will pay $10,000 to him each year for life. The company calculates that a man of sixty-five will probably live to age 80 and that his single premium plus earnings on it when invested by the company will equal approximately the $150,000 it will pay out over 15 years, plus some profit for the company. Of the $10,000 yearly annuity payment, he may exclude the exclusion ratio of two-thirds or $6,666.67. (The two-thirds exclusion ratio was determined by dividing the $100,000 investment in the annuity contract, defined in § 72(c)(1), by the $150,000 expected return, defined in § 72(c)(3).)

Of course, if this annuitant lives to be 100, the company will lose money on his contract. If he dies at age 70, the company will gain. On the average, over many such contracts, it figures to make a fair profit. Each annuitant gambles too, but gains the security of a steady income for as long as he may live. If he lives the expected time, he will receive annual payments that add up to his investment (capital) plus some interest on that investment. The task for the law is to tax each annuitant fairly on the interest but not the return of capital he receives from the annuity company in annual or other installments.

Once the amount of annuity payments that have been excluded from the annuitant's gross income equals the amount of his investment in the contract, all additional annuity payments will be included in his gross income, under I.R.C. § 72(b)(2). Thus, in the previous example, if the annuitant lives to be 81, he must include in his gross income the entire $10,000 payment received in his 81st year, because he already has excluded his $100,000 "investment in the contract" in prior years. (This restriction does not apply to an annuity with a starting date before January 1, 1987. The annuity starting date is the date on which the first payment under the contract is made.)

If annuity payments cease before the taxpayer's investment is recovered for tax purposes, the taxpayer is granted an itemized deduction for the amount of the "unrecovered investment." *See* I.R.C. § 72(b)(3). The "unrecovered investment" is the difference between the amount of investment in the annuity contract, as of the annuity starting date, and the aggregate amount of distributions made under the contract that were excluded from the taxpayer's gross income. Thus, if the annuitant in the previous example lives to be only 79, he will have an itemized deduction (on the tax return for his last taxable year) for his unrecovered investment of $6,666.67 (the difference between his $100,000 investment in the annuity contract and the $93,333.33 ($\frac{2}{3}$ x $140,000) of distributions made under the contract that were excluded from his gross income).

The theory of § 72(b) seems rooted deeply in return-of-capital notions. The annuitant will be taxed on none of his "capital" and on all of his "gain."

So, the exclusion ratio separates capital from income. It permits an annuitant to receive a level flow of after-tax dollars for the term of his annuity, until he has recovered his capital without tax. In contrast, other possible rules, such as one allowing tax-free return of capital (10 years at $10,000 in the example), and thus full taxability of remaining payments as gain, would often produce a more drastic drop in after-tax income in an annuitant's later years, a difficult consequence for many annuitants to plan for or to bear. Instead of allowing an annuitant to receive each payment tax-free until all capital investment has been returned or using an exclusion ratio based on predictions, the law could impute income to each payment on some standard rate-of-return formula, or using a fixed percentage, or it could tax the transaction without a deduction for loss in the event of premature death, or without a tax on mortality gains when an annuitant outlives the mortality tables. In fact, the income tax has tried almost every conceivable method at one time or another and seems to have settled upon the present treatment as the best solution.

The Regulations under I.R.C. § 72 provide mortality tables to use in determining the life expectancy of an annuitant and thus the expected return on an annuity for life. The rules of § 72 apply both to commercial and private annuities (the latter a contract between private individuals, often family members, calling for periodic (annuity) payments by one to another in return for a transfer of cash or property). As to private annuities purchased with appreciated property, there arises the question of realized gain at the time of transfer. *See* 212 Corp. v. Comm. (Tax Court 1978), which held that the gain resulting from the transfer of appreciated real property in exchange for an annuity was taxable to the transferors in the year of exchange.

§ 31. Compensation for Personal Injury and Sickness, Accident and Health Plan Benefits, and Disability Payments

Gross income does not include many benefits received by a taxpayer such as disability pay, health or accident insurance, damages for personal physical injury, workers' compensation, and the like. The theory behind many of these rules is that the taxpayer has received a return of capital or a replacement of capital lost, not income or gain. Specifically, a nest of provisions in I.R.C. §§ 104–106 serve to exclude from gross income many payments that are in the nature of damages received for physical injury to the person [§ 104(a)(2)], under workers' compensation [§ 104(a)(1)], or amounts received through accident or health insurance for personal injuries or sickness (other than amounts paid by an employer or by insurance carried by the employer whose contributions were not includable in the employee's gross income) [§ 104(a)(3)].

For accident and health plans, § 105(a) provides the general rule that "amounts received by an employee through accident or health insurance for personal injuries or sickness shall be *included* in gross income to the extent such amounts (1) are attributable to contributions by the employer which were not includible in the gross income of the employee, or (2) are paid by the employer." However, under § 105(b), gross income does *not* include "amounts referred to in subsection (a) if such amounts are paid, directly or indirectly, to the taxpayer to reimburse the taxpayer for expenses incurred by him for the medical care (as defined in section 213(d)) of the taxpayer, his spouse, and his dependents (as defined in section 152)," as long as he did not deduct those expenses under § 213 in a prior taxable year. This last qualification prevents a double tax benefit, as discussed below.

Lastly, § 106(a) contains the general rule that an employee's gross income does not include coverage provided by his employer under accident or health plans. Hence *payments* under such plans that are not for as yet un-deducted medical care expenses are *not* excludable by the employee under the rules of § 105(a) or § 104(a)(3), and their receipt must be included in gross income by the taxpayer unless rescued by § 105(b).

The exclusionary rule of I.R.C. § 105(b) swallows up and countermands much of the inclusionary rule of § 105(a). What is left of § 105(a) is a rule including in income payments, for example, through accident and health insurance for personal injuries or sickness that are not for medical care expenses. An example would be amounts payable to someone who has lost an eye or a hand or foot that exceed, or are in addition to, expenses for medical care to cure, heal or ameliorate the injury.

In some cases, the exclusion of accident and health benefits from gross income might threaten to give a taxpayer a double tax benefit. This could arise because under I.R.C. § 213, medical expenses in excess of 7½ percent of a taxpayer's adjusted gross income are deductible. Hence, a taxpayer might deduct his payment of doctors' bills in Year 1 and attempt to exclude amounts he received in Year 2 under accident or health insurance to reimburse him for his medical costs. To prevent such a double tax benefit, §§ 104 and 105 provide that accident and health benefits are *not* to be excluded from gross income to the extent a prior deduction has been taken. And § 213 allows a deduction only for medical expenses not compensated for by insurance or otherwise.

A similar problem would be presented by an employee taxpayer who was given free medical insurance by his employer if the employee were not taxed on the insurance coverage as compensation (under § 106) and if he also could exclude benefits payments from the insurance when he received them even if they were not reimbursements for expenses that would be deductible under § 213 if borne solely by the taxpayer. To block this doubling of tax benefits, § 105 requires the insurance payments to be included in gross income if they are paid by the employer or result from insurance carried by the employer when the coverage was not taxed to the employee because of the § 106 exclusion, unless they fit the § 213 category.

Before its repeal, former § 105(d) permitted wages, or payments in lieu of wages, made during a period when the employee was absent from work on account of a permanent and total disability, to be excluded from gross income, up to specified limits. Previously, § 105(d) had permitted wages continued during an employee's illness (sick pay) to be excluded from gross income up to specified limits, set in terms of amounts and duration, e.g. $100 per week. This sick-pay exclusion was converted and narrowed into the permanent disability provision as of 1977, but all of § 105(d) was repealed in 1983. As a consequence, such payments now must be included in income (unless elsewhere provided otherwise).

The exclusions afforded by §§ 104–106 apply to those benefits named or described in the statutes. Such benefits must therefore be distinguished from taxable salary, pension or retirement payments and from annuities, gifts, and other receipts whose taxability is governed by other rules. Thus, if a taxpayer who has reached retirement age is also disabled or ill and entitled to payments on account of injury or illness, a determination must be made, on the facts, whether or not he is receiving a payment that fits §§ 104–106.

Extensive regulations under the statutory rules, and case law, should be consulted for further guidance. Noteworthy, however, is the fact that litigated cases in this area often disagree with the I.R.S. application of the Regulations.

Sections 104–106 and the overall pattern of exclusion for damages for personal injury or illness historically have rested at least partly on return-of-capital notions as well as on a social policy to refrain from imposing the income tax upon benefits resembling private social welfare—as a subsidy, an incentive or an act of governmental charity. Some background is needed to understand the evolution of § 104(a)(2) and the current tax treatment of recoveries for personal injuries. Before 1997, § 104(a)(2) excluded "the amount of any damages received ... on account of personal injuries or sickness." In a 1986 decision, the Tax Court adopted the view that the proper test for determining the taxability of damages under § 104 was to determine the nature of the injury rather than to focus on the consequences of that injury. *See* Threlkeld v. Comm. (Tax Court 1986). The Supreme Court concurred, holding that the § 104(a)(2) exclusion applied to compensation for "tort-like" personal injuries. U.S. v. Burke (S.Ct.1992). In *Burke*, the Court declined to exclude from the taxpayer's income a back-pay award resulting from the taxpayer's Title VII sex-discrimination settlement agreement. In another case, the Court followed its reasoning in *Burke* in holding that liquidated damages, provided for by statute, from an award for a willful violation of the Age Discrimination in Employment Act were not excludable from income. Comm. v. Schleier (S.Ct.1995).

Before 1997 the tax treatment of recoveries of *punitive* damage for personal injuries was also an issue. Before 1996, § 104(a)(2) required inclusion in gross income of punitive damages from *nonphysical* personal injuries but it was unclear whether punitive damages for *physical* personal injuries escaped taxation under the § 104(a)(2) exclusion for "any" damages. The Supreme Court eventually resolved the issue by agreeing with the I.R.S. that such punitive damages were gross income under the pre–1997 version of § 104(a)(2). O'Gilvie v. U.S. (S.Ct. 1996).

In 1996, Congress acted both to limit the scope of the exclusion under § 104(a)(2) and to clarify the treatment of punitive damages. Section 104(a)(2) now provides an exclusion only for any damages (other than punitive damages) received on account of personal "physical" injuries or "physical" sickness. Thus, any recovery for a personal physical injury (including a claim for lost wages but not punitive damages) may be excluded from gross income. In contrast, recoveries for nonphysical injuries, such as defamation, injury to reputation, or sex and age discrimination claims, are taxable. The statute specifically provides that emotional distress alone is not to be treated as a physical injury or physical sickness so recoveries for emotional distress, other than damages received for medical care attributable to emotional distress, are gross income. But if damages are received for emotional distress attributable to physical injury or physical sickness, such damages are within the protection of § 104(a)(2). Section 104(a)(2) also contains one special exception to the rule that all punitive damages are taxable. An exclusion is permitted for punitive damages received in a wrongful-death action if state law (in effect on September 13, 1995) provides that *only* punitive damages can be awarded in a wrongful-death action. See I.R.C. § 104(c).

In determining whether payment of a judgment or settlement in an action for personal injuries, lost income and pain and suffering is income or not, great weight is given to the pleadings, settlement agreement or, of course, a special verdict of the jury, if any. Generally, tax treatment of damages or other recoveries will follow the tax treatment that would have been accorded the underlying claim.

Interest on an award for and damages received for lost business profits, or in lieu of an item which would be taxable, are income. If the damages are paid for injury to or loss of property, including business goodwill in which taxpayer has a basis, they are a return of capital, not gross income, up to the amount of basis.

Section 186 enacted a special rule for taxing the recovery of damages for anti-trust violations, patent law infringement, and breach of contract or fiduciary duty obligations. It provides that if a "compensatory amount," (defined in § 186(c) as an amount paid for a compensable injury, which in turn is defined in § 186(b)) is included in income, a deduction will be allowed for the lesser of that amount or unrecovered losses sustained as a result of the injury. So that portion of the original loss that did not give rise to a tax benefit reduces the inclusion in income.

§ 32. Interest on Governmental Obligations

Another receipt excluded from income by statute is interest payments made to the holder of state and local government obligations (bonds) other than arbitrage bonds or certain private activity bonds. *See* I.R.C. § 103(a). (In contrast, interest paid on most Federal Government obligations is fully taxable.) Grounded historically in notions of federalism, the independent sovereignty of the states, and in doubts about the constitutional power of the Federal Government to tax such interest (the doctrine of intergovernmental immunity), the § 103 exclusion serves now to provide a substantial subsidy from the Federal Government to states and municipalities. Their costs of government, and hence their taxes, are lower because they can borrow funds at lower interest rates. Lenders will accept such rates because the interest is tax free to them, by virtue of the § 103 exclusion, and hence yields an equal or higher after-tax rate of return than private bonds paying a higher (pre-tax) interest rate. Since the exclusion is income-variant, high income-tax bracket taxpayers are especially keen to invest in state bonds. For example, suppose a taxpayer in the 35% bracket invests $10,000 in a taxable bond paying 5% interest. The bond will pay $500 interest, but the taxpayer will pay $175 in taxes. Thus, the taxpayer will be left with $325 after taxes, for an after-tax return of only 3.25%. This taxpayer will prefer to invest in a tax-exempt bond if it pays any interest rate higher than 3.25% (his "indifference point"), since his return will not be reduced by an income tax. While a low-bracket taxpayer still will prefer tax-exempt bonds in general, his indifference point will be closer to the interest rate of the taxable bond. Returning to the previous example, a taxpayer in the 15% bracket will pay only $75 tax on the $500 interest, leaving him with an after-tax return of 4.25%. This taxpayer will prefer tax-exempt bonds if they pay an interest rate higher than 4.25%. To a tax-exempt lender, the § 103 exclusion will provide no value; it will prefer whichever bond pays the highest before-tax interest, because for a tax-exempt "taxpayer," before- and after-tax rates of return are the same.

Not all income from investing in state and local bonds escapes tax; sale of such a bond at a gain produces investment income that is not "interest" and hence not excluded by § 103. Section 103(b) denies an exemption for interest paid on private activity bonds as defined in § 141 and on arbitrage bonds as defined in § 148. *Also see* Regs. § 1.150–1 for definitions that apply to § 103.

All obligations generally must be put in "registered form" to qualify for tax-exempt status. *See* I.R.C. § § 103(b)(3), 149.

Viewed as a subsidy or as implicit revenue sharing, the exclusion and incentive of § 103 should be evaluated in terms of efficiency. How much dollar gain is obtained by the state and local governments for each dollar of revenue foregone by the federal government under § 103? Compared to a subsidy in the form of cash if § 103 were repealed and all federal income tax revenues from state and local bonds were paid over to the states, § 103 may be inefficient, since some of the foregone revenue will be captured by lenders (especially those in high tax brackets) to induce them to loan their money to state and local governments rather than to other borrowers.

Despite this financial inefficiency, however, arguments can be made to retain § 103 rather than to repeal it and turn over the increased federal tax revenues to the states. For example, such turnover might more likely be reduced periodically by Congress or made to depend on a surrender of local autonomy more than is the tax subsidy.

Proposals to repeal the interest exclusion of § 103 often are accompanied by suggestions about how the extra revenue could be used. The federal government could use the revenue gained from such repeal (and more) to make direct grants (or "subventions") of fixed amounts to state governments. Or, it could be used to pay amounts estimated to equal the higher interest each government must pay in order to sell its taxable bonds (*i.e.*, borrow money and pay interest that is taxable to the lender/bondholders), such as 30–35% of the borrowing cost (a proposal that might be offered as a "taxable bond option" without repealing § 103). Alternatively, the Federal Government could loan money to state governments at present rates (established in the non-taxable bond market) and finance such massive financing by selling Federal bonds (*i.e.*, borrowing money) with taxable interest.

Because interest on state and municipal bonds is exempt from tax, a taxpayer who borrows money to invest in such bonds may not deduct the interest he pays on his loan, since the interest is at best a cost of producing tax-free income. *See* I.R.C. § 265.

§ 33. Meals and Lodging

Section 119 of the Internal Revenue Code exempts from gross income of an employee certain meals and lodging furnished to him, his spouse, or his dependents, by his employer, under specified conditions.

The purpose of § 119 is to separate meals and lodging that are given as a form of compensation from those given because without them the employee could hardly do his job. Hotel managers, forest rangers, doctors on 24–hour duty in a hospital, and jailors in a prison facility illustrate the latter category of taxpayers. The § 119 exclusion applies only if several tests are met. First, the meals or lodging must be furnished for the convenience of the employer (as distinguished from the convenience, or compensation, of the employee). *All* meals furnished on the premises of an employer for its employees are treated as furnished for the convenience of the employer *if more than half* of the meals furnished to employees on the employer's premises are furnished "for the convenience of the employer". I.R.C. § 119(b)(4). Second, any meals must be furnished on the business premises of the employer and, in the case of lodging, the employee must be required to accept the lodging as a condition of his employment. I.R.C. § 119(a).

The specific standards of § 119 were designed to provide greater certainty and predictability than former law, which had simply inquired whether the meals or lodging were furnished as compensation (in which event they were income) or not (as a gift or simply as employment conditions). Although § 119 was designed to dispense with this compensatory test, that test has crept back in. Section 119(b)(1), following the business-premises and condition-of-employment clauses, strangely goes on to say that in determining whether meals or lodging are furnished for the convenience of the employer, the terms of an employment contract or a state statute fixing terms of employment shall not be determinative of whether the meals or lodging are intended "as compensation." The best reading this language can be given suggests an either/or test: meals or lodging are furnished either for the convenience of the employer or for compensation (never for both reasons or for some third purpose). Such an approach presents problems inasmuch as the facts of many cases show that meals and lodging are often furnished for the mutual convenience of employer and employee, or for compensatory purposes as well as for the employer's convenience.

In addition, § 119 speaks to some interpretive issues and contains some operative rules. Section 119(b)(2) states that, in determining whether meals are furnished "for the convenience of the employer," the fact that a charge is made and the fact that the employee may accept or decline such meals shall not be taken into account. Subsection (3) says (A) that if an employee is required to pay on a periodic basis a fixed charge for his meals, and if such meals are furnished by the employer for the convenience of the employer, an amount equal to such fixed charge shall be excluded from the employee's gross income, and (B) the rule of (A) applies whether the employee pays the fixed charge out of his stated compensation or out of his own funds, and only if the employee is required to make the payment whether he accepts or declines the meals. Section 119(c) contains a special rule for lodging furnished to an individual in a camp located in a foreign country, by or on behalf of his employer—the camp, if it qualifies, will be considered part of the business premises of the employer.

Congress has carved out a specific lodging provision for employees of educational institutions and "academic health centers." Under § 119(d), gross income does not include the value of "qualified campus lodging" except to the extent provided in § 119(d)(2).

The purposes of the § 119 exclusion may be to avoid trying to place a value on many benefits that are small or in any event difficult to value, to avoid taxing some employees on what amounts to conditions of employment rather than bargained-for and sought-after compensation, or perhaps even to encourage and subsidize employer provision of meals and lodging. Correspondingly, under the 1986 T.R.A., a statutory exclusion is granted for an employer's operation of an eating facility for employees if the benefits to the employees qualify as a *de minimus* fringe benefit under § 132(e)(2). In any event, the statute is unclear in its scope and in its underlying theory. If meals are intended as compensation though they are also for the employer's convenience, are they excluded? Is a primary-purpose test to apply? What are the employer's premises, and why is that rule used? Why the condition-of-employment test as to lodging and not as to meals? Why is an "all-or-nothing" test used rather than a rule prorating the value of meals and lodging according to compensation and employer's convenience? What if the employer furnishes lavish meals or lodging—but the minimum, at least, is for his convenience? Can the lavish excess be income? The Regulations attempt to answer some but not all of these questions. If § 119 were repealed, some question might remain whether all employer-furnished meals and lodging would be includable in gross income, even apart from the *de minimis* fringe benefit rule of § 132(e). To the extent that lodging, or meals going beyond the § 132(e) *de minimis* rule, are not compensatory, they resemble imputed income or the untaxed benefits an employee gets when he works in an air-conditioned, well-lighted and pleasing office or plant. And, like many fringe benefits that are not taxed as a practical matter now even though not expressly excluded (*e.g.,* a ping-pong table in the employee locker room), administrative convenience might require that some meals and lodging go untaxed even without § 119.

Cases have tested the meaning of § 119. In some, state policemen were held not to be taxable on the cash reimbursement given them for lunches at roadside diners during lunch hours while on highway patrol. (Other cases have ruled the opposite on similar facts.) Motel managers and their families have escaped tax, as have some hospital residents (medical doctors), university presidents living on campus, and brewery executives living at the plant. Interpretive questions have included whether "meals" includes groceries to be cooked in the employees' home on the employer's business premises [yes, Jacob v. U.S. (3d Cir.1974)] and whether the employer's business premises include a rented house located across the street from a motel and occupied by its manager (yes).

More than mere shelter and sustenance have been sheltered from tax by the terms "meals" and "lodging." Section 119 has removed some, but far from all, of the uncertainty in the area.

In the continuing case law, some judges have suggested that a non-statutory exclusion based on "convenience of the employer" can make non-taxable some benefits that fail to meet the standards of § 119. Thus a cash allowance to state troopers might have been excluded not by interpreting § 119 to allow it, but by holding that § 119 does not preempt the field. *See, e.g.,* Kowalski v. Comm. (3d Cir.1976). This analysis often seems to rest on notions of horizontal equity: An employee who receives a small cash payment to use at a nearby restaurant may seem to deserve identical treatment as that given to an employee whose employer builds a cafeteria.

The U.S. Supreme Court took a state trooper meal allowance case in order to settle the conflict in the Circuit Courts and to try to quiet the uneasy state of the law. In a case having implications far broader than those affecting state troopers, Comm. v. Kowalski (S.Ct.1977), the Court held that cash meal allowances were includable in a New Jersey state trooper's gross income. The troopers involved were allowed to eat mid-shift meals wherever they wanted, so long as they remained on call in their assigned duty areas. They were not required to account for their "meal allowances." The Commissioner claimed that the lower-court decision, holding the allowances excludable, invited employers on a wide scale to provide tax-free compensation to employees in the form of defraying the costs of meals or other living expenses. The majority of the Court viewed the allowances as income because they were clearly realized accessions to wealth over which the taxpayer had dominion and control; they were not excludable under I.R.C. § 119 since the employer had not furnished the meals; and § 119 modified the pre-existing "convenience of the employer" doctrine. Two dissenters would have excluded the payments under § 119 by rejecting a distinction between cash allowances and in-kind provision. They called attention to the differential tax treatment the Court's rule would give to paramilitary troopers in New Jersey and to federal military employees.

The questions of excluding an employer's provision of meals or lodging in kind or giving the employee a cash allowance have a counterpart on the deduction side. Ordinarily an employee's out-of-pocket expenditures for food and lodging are not deductible because they amount to "personal" expenses. However, in a few cases, an employee such as a firefighter has been permitted to deduct a mandatory payment for participation in a racially non-exclusionary organized mess at which he was required to eat (at his fire station) as an ordinary and necessary business expense under § 162. *See, e.g.,* Cooper v. Comm. (Tax Court 1977); Sibla v. Comm. (Tax Court 1977). *But see* Duggan v. Comm. (Tax Court 1981), which held that a fireman could not deduct his contributions to an organized mess at the fire station, where it was optional and organized by employees rather than required by the employer. Cf. Regs. § 1.119–1(a)(3). If the expenditure can be deducted, a case can be made for excluding provision-in-kind or reimbursement, on equal-treatment-of-equals grounds. But in reverse that principle might require a deduction for all employee lunches, even voluntary ones, something the law does not allow. Reasoning backward from that denial of deduction, one may become doubtful about the deduction for mandatory mess payments except for § 119(b)(3), *supra,* and thence about cash reimbursements, and thence about provision in kind that does not fall within the main target area of § 119.

Not excludable under § 119 is the value of lodgings furnished by an employer at a discount when the other tests of § 119 were not met; the value of the lodgings taxable to the employee is the arm's-length rental paid by the employer to the owner of the property. *See* McDonald v. Comm. (Tax Court 1976). (However, *see* § 119(d) excluding all or a part of lodging provided to employees of an educational institution.)

Section 107 contains a specific exclusion for housing or rental allowances furnished to a minister of the gospel even when furnished as compensation.

§ 34. Employee Fringe Benefits

A great variety of cash and non-cash fringe benefits at one time or another have been provided by employers to their employees. Such benefits include payment of moving expenses to an employee transferred from one business location to another, interest-free loans, employee discounts on purchases from the employer, free medical treatment, free use of recreational facilities, educational benefits, gifts, meals, clothing allowances, free or discount travel, legal services, and low-cost life insurance. With respect to all such benefits, the question is whether or not the employee must treat them as income. Some benefits fall under, or near to, express statutory exclusions.

Sections 82, 132(a)(6), 132(g) and 217 operate to exclude from gross income a "qualified moving expense reimbursement" paid by an employer to an employee to reimburse the employee for moving expenses that are attributable to the commencement of work at a new location. Section 82 includes such reimbursements except as § 132(a)(6) excludes them. In turn, § 132(a)(6) and § 132(g) allow such reimbursements to be excluded if and to the extent § 217 would allow the taxpayer to deduct the expense if directly paid or incurred by the individual (employee or self-employed person). Section 217 provides the detailed tests the taxpayer must meet in order to qualify for the deduction or exclusion (*e.g.*, the taxpayer's new principal place of work must be at least 50 miles further from the former residence than was his former principal place of work). Under § 217, moving expenses include only the reasonable expenses of moving household goods and personal effects from the former residence to the new residence and of traveling (including lodging) from the former residence to the new residence. Expenses for meals are not deductible as moving expenses. Section 217 also provides a deduction for such expenses borne by self-employed individuals.

If an employee sells his old residence at a loss and is reimbursed by the employer, most authorities now require that the existing or new employee treat the loss reimbursement as additional compensation, rather than as part of the proceeds of sale.

Section 125 states that benefits received by an employee under an employer's qualified "cafeteria plan" of benefits (one giving the employee a choice among a number of employee fringe benefits, possibly some qualified (excludable) and others, such as cash, taxable) will not be included in the employee's gross income solely because the employee may choose among the "menu" of benefits. Such a plan may include cash or qualified benefits but cannot contain most forms of deferred compensation. However, it can include a profit-sharing or stock bonus plan involving a qualified cash or deferred-compensation arrangement. The cafeteria plan will not qualify if it discriminates in favor of highly compensated or key employees.

Section 127 excludes from an employee's income the benefits of an employer's qualified non-discriminatory educational assistance program. The major impact of the rule is to eliminate the distinction between job-related and non-job-related programs. The requirements of a qualified educational assistance program are found in § 127(b).

Section 129, excludes from an employee's income each year up to $5,000 of payments made, or expenses incurred by, employers for dependent care if pursuant to a written non-discriminatory plan.

Section 132 excludes from the income of employees certain fringe benefits provided by an employer. The excluded fringe benefits are those benefits that qualify under one of the following: (1) a no-additional-cost service, (2) a qualified employee discount, (3) a working condition fringe, (4) a *de minimis* fringe, (5) a qualified transportation fringe (relating to commuting or parking), (6) a qualified moving expense reimbursement, (7) qualified retirement planning services or, (8) qualified military base realignment and closure fringe. [Some of the exclusions cover benefits provided to the spouse and dependent children of a current employee or to retired former employees. *See* § 132(h).] Services provided to, or on behalf of, an employee by his employer may qualify as no-additional-cost services if two requirements are met: (1) The services provided must be of the type offered by the employer to customers in the ordinary course of the line of business in which the employee works; (2) The employer must not incur a substantial additional cost by providing the benefit. *See* I.R.C. § 132(b). Free occupancy of empty seats on an airline by off-duty airline employees is an example of a situation that may qualify under this rule.

Some or all of the value of an employee discount will be excluded from the gross income of the employee if the discount is offered on qualified property or services. *See* I.R.C. § 132(c). Property or services are qualified if they are offered for sale to customers in the ordinary course of the line of business in which the employee works (not including personal property held for investment or any real property). *See* I.R.C. § 132(c)(4). An employee discount is excluded from the employee's gross income only to the extent that the discount does not exceed the gross profit percentage of the price charged to customers.

No-additional-cost services and qualified employee discounts will be excluded from the gross income of highly compensated employees only if they are offered to other employees on substantially the same terms. *See* I.R.C. § 132(j)(1).

An excludable working condition fringe benefit is property or services offered to an employee to the extent that the employee would be allowed a deduction for such items, under I.R.C. §§ 162 or 167, if the employee had paid for them himself. I.R.C. § 132(d). A *de minimis* fringe benefit includes property or services of such a small value that accounting for it would be unreasonable or administratively impracticable. I.R.C. § 132(e).

A very general section that deals with many in-kind benefits has a particular bearing upon the timing of taxing forfeitable or contingent compensatory items such as employee stock options, and also contains some important principles for all such compensation. Suppose a corporate employer transfers stock in itself, or options to buy stock at a fixed price, to an employee (or to his spouse or child) as a bonus for his hard work. Section 83(a) says that property transferred, in connection with the performance of services, to any person other than the person for whom such services are performed shall be included in the gross income of the person who performed such services in the first taxable year in which the rights of the person having the beneficial interest in such property are transferable or are not subject to a substantial risk of forfeiture. The amount to be included must be the excess of fair market value of the property (at the specified time) over the amount, if any, paid for the property. The Regulations define "property" in this section as not including cash. Regs. § 1.83–3(e).

Section 83(b) gives the performer of services an option to include, in the year the property is transferred, the excess of fair market value (without regard to any temporary restriction) over the amount, if any, paid for the property. This option can be used only if the property has a readily ascertainable fair market value at the time of receipt.

Obviously, § 83 may apply to transfers of property that are intended to be compensatory—stock options, bonus stock, and other in-kind transfers, possibly subject to some contingency or risk of forfeiture having to do with continued employment or performance. Also, § 83 may apply to other fringe benefits having some compensatory components. An example includes educational benefit trusts formed for the children of corporate executives. *See* Rev. Rul. 75–448, 1975–42 I.R.B. 6. Compare I.R.C. § 117(d) which may allow an exclusion for a qualified tuition reduction provided by an educational institution to the children of employees.

Many other employee fringe benefits—such as gifts, free medical, educational or recreational services, purchase discounts, low cost loans, etc.—escape taxation often because they are small in amount and difficult to value. (Statutory *de minimis* fringe benefits were discussed above.) Some are regarded as gifts (*see* Rev. Rul. 59–58, 1959–1 C.B. 17, ruling no inclusion for a turkey or ham distributed generally to each employee at Christmas; *but see* § 102(c) on employee gifts), or as conditions of employment, not as compensation for services. Severe administrative difficulties stand in the way of taxing many of these benefits. However, free use of a company car for personal purposes or free occupancy of an employer-owned residence is likely to be includable in gross income, if it comes to the attention of the I.R.S. Administrative policy has tightened somewhat: some interest-free loans (as in split-dollar life insurance programs) and free holiday or vacation "convention" trips for employees and their spouses or families have been the subject of adverse ruling or enforcement action. As to some benefits, Congress has taken action. For example, § 79 requires inclusion of some employer-provided life insurance.

See Regs. § 1.61–21 and the regulations under I.R.C. § 132 for more detail on the taxation of fringe benefits. *See also* § 21, *supra,* on Gifts and Employee Fringe Benefits.

§ 35. Tax Preference Income And The Alternative Minimum Tax

An important and different set of rules, resembling rules of inclusion in gross income, lie in the Alternative Minimum Tax system found in I.R.C. §§ 55–59. Section 57 defines "items of tax preference," items which are treated as income and subjected to a special tax, under § 55. (*See* § 108, *infra,* Ch. IX.) To be sure, not all the items to be included as tax preference income are described in terms of receipts or additions to net worth. Some tax preference items are receipts that escape taxation under the normal definition of taxable income because of exclusions or deductions. As to them, § 57 acts like a usual inclusion rule. Some tax preference items or adjustments, however, are defined in terms of expenditures, or costs, or are related to special deduction allowances. But they too increase income as if by a new rule of inclusion. See I.R.C. §§ 56, 58.

When a minimum tax on tax preference items was first enacted in 1969, Congress felt that some taxpayers were overly benefiting from some of the deductions and allowances in the Code and thus escaping a fair burden of tax on their incomes, particularly investment income. The minimum tax rate and exemption have been amended several times, and the respective roles of the (former) add-on and alternative minimum taxes have also changed over the years. These reforms may have been politically feasible alternatives to repealing special allowances or steepening the graduation of the basic rate schedule. The minimum tax approach differs from more direct reforms in that it attempts to reach taxpayers who individually are thought to have "abused" or overused allowances that in principle should remain in the Code, and remain separately without ceilings on their use, or that reformers cannot muster a sufficient coalition to repeal.

In computing alternative minimum taxable income (A.M.T.I.) under I.R.C. §§ 55–59, a taxpayer is required to redetermine the base for his alternative minimum income tax, starting with "taxable income" as computed under the "regular" income tax. The redetermination involves separate calculations to be made for certain items for which the

I.R.C. provides favorable tax treatment. A.M.T.I. is determined by (a) adjusting the amount of certain items that are taken into account in determining taxable income (a specially computed item is substituted for the amount used in computing regular taxable income), I.R.C. §§ 56 & 58, and (b) adding the amount of certain tax benefits which are deemed to be items of tax preference. *See* I.R.C. § 57.

With respect to some of these adjustments and tax preference items, such as depreciation, a taxpayer may be required to recompute a deduction in a manner that is less favorable than that allowed in determining the taxpayer's regular tax. For other preference items, such as intangible drilling costs, a portion of the deduction allowable for regular tax purposes must be added back to adjusted gross income to arrive at alternative minimum taxable income.

Section 56 specifies the adjustment items. Examples of adjustments include: depreciation allowances for any tangible property, mining exploration and development costs, alternative-tax net operating loss deductions; medical expense deductions; and itemized deductions for individuals.

Section 57 specifies tax preference items to be added back to recompute the taxable income for individual taxpayers. These tax preference items include: some depletion allowances, part of § 1202 excludable gains, and certain tax-exempt interest. Once the figure for alternative minimum taxable income is found, a fixed rate of 26% (28% for amounts over $175,000) for individual taxpayers (20% for corporations) is applied to so much of the taxpayer's A.M.T.I. for the taxable year as exceeds the exemption amount, to compute tentative minimum tax. The taxpayer's alternative minimum tax is the excess of tentative minimum tax over regular tax for the year. I.R.C. § 55(a). The taxpayer's total tax for the year is the regular tax plus the alternative minimum tax. The exemption amount depends on the taxpayer's filing status. For example, in 2004 it is $40,250 for a single taxpayer and $58,000 in the case of a married couple filing a joint return. *See* I.R.C. § 55(d)(1). If the A.M.T.I. exceeds a certain amount, the taxpayer's exemption amount is phased out altogether. *See* I.R.C. § 55(d)(3).

§ 36. Miscellaneous Exclusions and Related Allowances

Internal Revenue Code §§ 71–84, 101–129, & 132 contain a number of other statutory rules for inclusion in and exclusion from gross income—such as those for payments for the services of a child and combat pay to soldiers. In addition, some important exclusions are authorized by other statutes—such as those for veterans' benefits, a portion of railroad retirement annuities § 86(d), and welfare benefits. Amounts received as pensions or annuities under the Social Security Act are partially excluded from gross income. *See* I.R.C. § 86. The theory may have been that employees, on the average, have paid for these benefits with their contributions (which were not deductible). No showing must be made in each case, however, and the theory may even prove false on the averages, if other revenues are used to finance social security benefits, or when payroll tax revenues from the current work-force finance benefits to the prior generation of workers, now retired or disabled. Other amounts paid from a general welfare fund in the interest of the general public, such as payments from a Crime Victim's Compensation Board, also can be received without tax (to the extent no prior deduction has been taken). *See* the "tax benefit rule"; Cf. § 111 and Regs.

A credit for the elderly and for the permanently and totally disabled (not an exclusion or a deduction) is granted by I.R.C. § 22. This credit attempts to approximate the tax treatment of retired individuals who receive taxable pensions with retired taxpayers who live on (now partially) tax-exempt social security benefits. Thus it performed a function like that of an exclusion for retirement income, but with an income-constant, and limited, effect. Section 22 allows a credit of 15% on specified amounts (the "initial amount"), reduced by excludable Social Security, Railroad Retirement or Veterans' benefits received.

Section 73 grants an exclusion, in a sense, when it states that the income of a child for services shall be taxed to the child and not to the parent, even if the amounts are not received by the child. It thus excludes the income from the parents' income and reflects a decision not to treat the entire family with minor children as a taxable unit. (However, enactment of the "kiddie tax" in I.R.C. § 1(g) qualifies the broad principle reflected by § 73 since it will tax *unearned* (investment) income of a child under 14 to the child but at the parents' rate.)

Section 121 completely excludes from gross income gain from the sale or exchange of property if the taxpayer had used the property as his principal residence for at least two of the past five years. The exclusion is limited to $250,000 for individuals and $500,000 for spouses filing jointly, provided that they meet the requirements of I.R.C. § 121(b). Benefits of the exclusion are prorated in some instances in which the basic requirements have not fully been met. *See* § 121(c). Generally, the exclusion is available for one sale or exchange every two years.

Section 134 excludes "qualified military benefits"—those benefits that are received by a member or former member (or dependent thereof) of the United States uniformed services and were excludable from gross income on September 9, 1986.

Section 135 excludes amounts attributable to the redemption of a qualified United States savings bond if the proceeds are, in effect, used to pay higher-education expenses (i.e., tuition and fees). The full exclusion is available only to taxpayers whose income does not exceed $59,850 (in 2004) ($89,750 in the case of a joint return in 2004). The exclusion is reduced for higher income amounts, and the exclusion is completely eliminated when the taxpayer's income reaches $74,850 (again, in 2004) ($119,750 in the case of a joint return in 2004).

Section 136 excludes from gross income (with some limitations) the value of a subsidy provided by a public utility to a customer for the purchase or installation of any "energy conservation measure," defined as "any installation or modification primarily designed to reduce consumption of electricity or natural gas or to improve the management of energy demand."

Section 137 excludes from gross income of an employee up to $10,390 (in 2004) for amounts paid or expenses incurred by an employer for qualified adoption expenses in connection with the adoption of a child by an employee if such amounts are furnished pursuant to an adoption assistance program. In the case of an adoption of a child with special needs, the qualified adoption expenses are increased by the excess (if any) of $10,390 over the actual aggregate qualified expenses. I.R.C. § 137(a)(2). The exclusion is phased out for taxpayers with adjusted gross income (as defined in I.R.C. § 137(b)(3)) between $115,860 and $195,860 (in 2004). I.R.C. § 137(b).

Section 139 excludes any amount received by an individual as a qualified disaster relief payment under § 139(b).

Many other exclusions are authorized by nonstatutory sources: Medicare benefits by Rev. Rul. 70–341, 1970–1 C.B. 31; anti-recidivism stipends to probationers by Rev. Rul. 72–340, 1972–2 C.B. 31; political funds used for campaign expenses by Rev. Proc. 68–19, 1968–1 C.B. 810 and Rev. Rul. 71–449, 1971–2 C.B. 77.

CHAPTER IV

WHAT IS DEDUCTIBLE: PROFIT–RELATED DEDUCTIONS AND OTHER ALLOWANCES

§ 37. Introduction

Deductions in the income tax are amounts subtracted from gross income to determine taxable income, the tax base. Deductions are allowed only if specific statutory authorization can be found. Unlike gross income, which is broadly defined in § 61(a) and expansively interpreted by the courts, deductions are cast in narrow statutory language which, in turn, is construed strictly against the taxpayer. Deductions in arriving at taxable income fall into three categories: (a) profit-related, (b) mixed, and (c) personal. This chapter will deal with the first category; the other two categories will be discussed in the next two chapters.[1]

The so-called profit-related deductions are those allowed for costs of producing income. As such they are demanded by the logic of a tax on (net) income or "gain." They may be required as well by the Constitution if "income" in the Sixteenth Amendment is used in the sense of gain or *net* profit,

1. Along with deductions, these chapters will treat some other "allowances," such as *credits* against tax.

rather than in the sense of gross profit, gross receipts, or something else.

In our income tax, "costs of goods sold" are deducted from "gross receipts" to determine "gross income." *See* Regs. § 1.61–3(a). Other costs, expenses, and losses that serve to reduce a taxpayer's net gain from profit-oriented (or profit-producing) activities are to be deducted from gross income (or from adjusted gross income in a few instances) to work toward adjusted gross income or "net income" (a term not actually used in the Internal Revenue Code) and eventually to "taxable income." Such expenses, deductible as costs of producing income, include wages to employees, rent for business premises, advertising expenses, property or license taxes, postage, and all the other expenses of doing business or otherwise earning income.

The logic of an income tax also suggests that expenditures *other* than those that are costs of producing income must *not* be deducted. If non-income-producing expenditures were deductible, the income tax would—in the extreme—become a tax on savings, a tax on receipts less all expenditures. Somehow, most or all personal consumption expenditures and payments into savings must be ruled out as deductions. (A few, perhaps, may be allowed for reasons of social welfare, equity, incentive, subsidy, or other reasons.) Thus the line between profit-seeking or business expenditures on the one hand and expenditures for personal consumption or saving on the other hand becomes a crucial one. Some items are easy to categorize as costs of producing income, some are easy to see as personal, and others stand in an ambiguous or unclear status, or differ in status from one taxpayer to another.

The basic code sections that carve out the lines indicated by this analysis are I.R.C. §§ 162, 212, 262 and 263. Perhaps the starting point is I.R.C. § 262. It states that (except as otherwise expressly provided) no deduction shall be allowed for personal, living, or family expenses. The purpose and effect of § 262 are obvious but its application sometimes is more difficult. Clearly, § 262 and the Regulations (Regs. § 1.262–1) bar any deduction for rent of a family's home, basic telephone service, bills for food, clothing, personal life insurance, vacations, a personal automobile, non-business legal fees, commuting, much non-business education, and other purely personal consumption expenditures. But some instances are harder to decide. For example, is the cost of a businessperson's luncheon with clients, customers, or business associates personal or deductible? What is the nature of an employee's expenditures on work clothing, tools, education, commuting, eyeglasses? These questions must be settled one way or the other, or prorations must be made, under § 262 and the other key provisions.

Section 263 of the I.R.C. denies a deduction for "capital expenditures" such as payments for new buildings, permanent improvements, restorations, etc., even if made for business or profit-seeking reasons. Thus a taxpayer cannot gain a deduction just by turning money into property by buying an asset, even a business asset. However, depreciation and amortization or "cost-recovery" deductions will be allowed to him or her later for many business and investment capital expenditures, as we shall soon see. These deductions treat such business capital expenditures as costs of producing income but spread the deductions over a period of time.

The two remaining statutory sections mentioned (§§ 162 and 212) authorize the deductions for business or profit-seeking expenditures that a true income tax requires. Section 162(a) allows a deduction for all the ordinary and necessary expenses paid or incurred during the taxable year in carrying on any trade or business. Section 162 goes on to mention three particular examples. Deductions are allowed for reasonable salaries or other compensation paid for personal services, taxpayer's traveling expenses (including meals and lodging) while away from home in pursuing a trade or business, and rentals or other payments for occupancy or use of property for purposes of a trade or business. Notably, all of the § 162(a) deductions are for expenses in a "trade or business."

Not every profit-seeking activity, however, is properly called a "trade or business." Handling one's own investments in the stock market or in real estate, for example, would not fit the usual meaning of trade or business, nor would other profit-directed activities such as speculative investments, occasional services for pay, creative activities rewarded by royalties or other remuneration, etc. *See, e.g.,* Higgins v. Comm. (S.Ct.1941). Accordingly, § 212 was enacted to authorize the deduction of costs of producing income in gain-seeking activities even if they do not amount to a trade or business.

I.R.C. § 212 allows, in the case of an individual, a deduction for all the ordinary and necessary expenses paid or incurred during the taxable year in three ranges of activity: (1) expenses for the production or collection of income; (2) expenses for the management, conservation, or maintenance of property held for the production of income; or (3) expenses in the determination, collection, or refund of any tax. Section 212 applies only to individuals. Corporations and other business entities are regarded as falling within the trade or business category of I.R.C. § 162 in all their profit-oriented activities, at least as a general matter.

To add one last important rule, to be elaborated later, I.R.C. §§ 165(a) and (c) allow a deduction for losses sustained in a trade or business, or in any transaction entered into for profit though not connected with a trade or business. So, losses that amount to costs of producing income are, in principle, deductible in computing "net" or taxable income.

However, the deductibility of losses under § 165 is limited by I.R.C. §§ 465 and 469. Section 465 dictates that the taxpayer can deduct a loss incurred in a profit-making activity from income only up to the extent of the aggregate amount for which the taxpayer is "at risk" for such activity. And, the section goes on to define the amounts considered "at risk." Generally, the amount at risk is the sum of the amount of money and adjusted basis of the property contributed by the taxpayer for the activity and the amount borrowed with respect to the activity, if borrowed with personal liability or with other security. In addition, § 469 provides that if a taxpayer incurs a loss from a passive activity, the amount of the loss from such activity cannot be deducted from the income of other non-passive activities (such as an active trade or business or an investment portfolio); instead, it may be set off only against income from other passive activities.

A variety of situations have tested the limits of which expenses are sufficiently profit-directed or trade or business-connected to be deductible under § 162 or § 212. For example, commuting fares are not deductible. *See* Regs. § 1.162–2(e); Comm. v. Flowers (S.Ct.1946). But costs of business travel out of town are deductible. *See* I.R.C. § 162(a)(2); § 162(h). Temporary living expenses while seeking permanent housing at a new place of work have been held not to be deductible under §§ 162 and 212. The cost and expenses of settling a personal injury suit arising out of an accident that occurred en route from taxpayer's place of employment to an office where his partnership did business were held to be personal, not deductible. Freedman v. Comm. (5th Cir.1962). But, in another case a deduction was allowed for such costs of an accident because it occurred en route from one site to another of the same business. *See* Harold Dancer v. Comm. (Tax Court 1980). And in another opinion, the legal fees paid by an irate husband to divorce his wife and protect his business property and job from her claims for alimony and property settlement were held to be too personal in their origin and nature to justify a deduction. *See* U.S. v. Gilmore (S.Ct.1963). The fact that his legal expenses had the consequence of preserving his property, his job, and hence his income was held to be insufficient to warrant a deduction for those expenses as costs of producing income under I.R.C. § 162 or § 212. The Court said that the *origin* and nature of the expenditure, not its *effect*, motive, purpose, intent, or other characteristics, are to govern deductibility.

Section 162 also permits deductions to be taken for expenditures for education (as ordinary and necessary business expenses) only if the education maintains or improves the taxpayer's skills in the area in which he or she is employed, or meets express requirements for retention of established employment or rate of compensation. This allowance does not include expenses for education required as a minimum for qualification in a trade or business, regardless of whether the taxpayer is already employed in that profession. *See* Regs. § 1.162–5. Contrast I.R.C. § 127 (exclusion for benefits of employer's educational assistance plan), I.R.C. § 222 (deduction for qualified tuition and related expenses effective through 2005), I.R.C. § 529 (qualified tuition programs), I.R.C. § 530 (Coverdell education savings accounts), and I.R.C. § 25A (credits for certain educational expenses).

Section 174 allows a taxpayer to take a deduction for research or experimental expenditures incurred in connection with his trade or business. The Supreme Court held in Snow v. Comm. (S.Ct.1974) that Congress' purpose in enacting this section was to counteract the suggestion that a trade or business was to be so narrowly conceived as to mean only an activity that involves holding oneself out to others as engaged in the selling of goods or services. The Court pointed out that the words "trade or business" are used in about 60 different sections of the Code, with somewhat different shades of context and meaning in some of them. Thus, the Court allowed a deduction to a limited partner for expenses incurred in developing a special-purpose incinerator, even though no sales were reported during the taxable year.

A taxpayer may have more than one trade or business. To illustrate, an actively practicing lawyer or doctor may have an additional trade or business as a real estate developer, or as a photographer, or as an employee of a foundation. An employee has a trade or business as such and may have trade and business deductions as an employee. *See* I.R.C. § 62(a)(2)(A). Having two trades or businesses must be distinguished from having one (the practicing lawyer) and also engaging in investment or speculative activities (such as investing in stocks or old masters) that are income-producing § 212 activities but fall short of amounting to a trade or business. In the event a person has more than a single "hat" as a taxpayer, it can become important to determine to which role or activity an expenditure is to be attributed.

The lines between a taxpayer's trade or business and (a) his personal life and (b) his other income-seeking or income-producing life carry important tax consequences for the deduction of expenses, losses and bad debts, the taxation of capital and quasi-capital gains, and more. For present purposes, the lines are drawn mainly to determine the scope of § 162 and § 212 gain-seeking activities. To illustrate this point, a person who actively practices law and also owns an apartment house or office building (managed by another firm for a fee) probably would be deemed to have a § 162 trade or business in law and § 212 investment property in the form of the building. But if the lawyer discharges the management firm and spends a lot of time and energy in seeking tenants, managing and maintaining the premises, collecting rents, etc., she or he may then be deemed also to be actively engaged in the trade or business of rental property, not just investing in it. This crossing over a line may or may not make a practical difference for deduction purposes under § 162 and § 212; it will be more likely to carry consequences in other respects. It also may be that expenses will have to be allocated or differentiated between one trade or business or investment activity and a second one that is deemed to be a hobby or activity not engaged in for profit and subject to I.R.C. § 183 (hobby losses) or § 280A (disallowance of expenses for business use of home or rental of vacation home). And, as mentioned above, §§ 465 and 469 may limit the deductibility of a loss incurred in a rental activity. If the taxpayer participates in such activity only passively, or if the rental activity can qualify only as "passive" under § 469(c)(2), § 469 prohibits him from deducting a loss incurred in that activity from active or portfolio income.

On the other hand, even if the taxpayer actively participates for § 469 purposes, the at-risk limitation of § 465 is still applicable, and he can deduct a loss incurred in the activity only to the extent of the amount at risk.

§ 38. Ordinary and Necessary Expenses

Both §§ 162 and 212 authorize deductions only to the extent business or profit-directed expenditures are *ordinary* and *necessary*. The term "necessary" does not mean that a payment must be compelled by a legally enforceable obligation. It need not even be as indispensable in the business as the payment of rents or some similar cost might be. Rather "necessary" has been taken to mean "appropriate and helpful." *See* Welch v. Helvering (S.Ct.1933). If a taxpayer chooses to spend his money in a business context or to produce income the courts will be slow to override his judgment that the expenditure is necessary, however "unnecessary" others might think the expenditure to be.

The term "ordinary" has proven more difficult to interpret. If a deduction were denied for all business expenses that are "extraordinary" in the sense of unusual in general or unique in the experience of a given taxpayer, innovation would be discouraged and new or infrequently incurred expenses, however business related, would be disallowed. As a result, something more than net income or profit would be taxed. Consequently, it was early held that "ordinary" does not mean that the expenses must be habitual or normal in the sense that the same taxpayer will often have to make them. For example, the expenses of a lawsuit affecting the safety of a business may happen once in a lifetime and be so heavy that repetition is unlikely or impossible. Nevertheless, the expense is "ordinary" for tax purposes because, from experience, it is known that payments for such a purpose, large or small, are the common, accepted, and appropriate means of defense. Although the situation is unique in the life of the individual affected, it is not unique in the life of the group of which he is a part. Norms of conduct inform the judgment; though the instance is erratic, it is of a known and familiar type. *See* Welch v. Helvering, *supra*. Similarly, payment for a novel and innovative form of advertising will not be denied deduction, even though no one has used that means before; if it falls within that familiar category "business advertising," it will be deductible— particularly if no personal-consumption, non-business element can be seen in it.

If a taxpayer makes a payment that in character and circumstance so departs from accepted standards and expected conduct as to suggest some aberration or some other influence behind the payment (gift, bribe, reparations, purchase of an asset), a deduction will be denied because the payment is not "ordinary." Thus "ordinary" serves as an emphasis on the requirement that the expenditure really be in pursuit of a trade or business or profit seeking venture, not for some other (non-business) reason, and that it not be a capital expenditure.

The upshot of I.R.C. §§ 162, 212, 262 and 263 in general is to allow as deductions in arriving at taxable income those expenditures that are made to produce gross income—that is, the costs of engaging in a trade or business or other profit-seeking activities. No simple rules can be given to describe the lines between those expenditures made in a business or gain-seeking context that will be deemed ordinary and necessary and other non-deductible items. Generally, the expense will be deductible if it is closely or causally related to attempts to produce income, if it is common in the industry, or if it seems logically designed to increase or preserve the flow of receipts. Indeed, the Supreme Court affirmed precedent recently when it ruled that taxpayer activities fall within the scope of § 162 only if the taxpayer intended to profit from the activities. *See* Portland Golf Club v. Comm. (S.Ct.1990). If the expense is seen to be a gift, dividend, or personal payment in disguise, it will not be allowed as a business deduction. In determining whether an action is engaged in "for profit," greater weight is given to objective facts than to the taxpayer's mere statement of intent. *See* Regs. § 1.183–2(a).

Even if an expenditure is sufficiently related to the taxpayer's trade or business or profit-seeking activity to qualify under I.R.C. §§ 162 or 212, deduction of the item may be disallowed by a statutory, judicial, or administrative prohibition. Some of the most important of these limiting doctrines are examined in the following pages.

§ 39. Public Policy Exception

One important judge-made rule disallowing deductions for business expenses is the so-called public policy exception or limitation. Under this doctrine, a payment that amounts to a cost of doing business may be disallowed as a deduction because to allow the deduction would frustrate a sharply defined national or state policy proscribing a particular type of conduct. *See, e.g.,* Tank Truck Rentals, Inc. v. Comm. (S.Ct.1958). Some courts have indicated that the finding of "necessity" cannot in such event be made. *See, e.g.,* United Draperies, Inc. v. Comm. (7th Cir.1964). Fines paid by a trucking company for deliberately overloading its trucks to ship their contents in economical quantities were disallowed as deductions in the *Tank Truck* case. The Court in *Tank Truck* reasoned that taking the sting out of a state's penalty by allowing a federal tax deduction would frustrate the state's policy of deterring the criminal conduct.

When a governmental policy will or will not be decreed to be frustrated or violated by a tax deduction is a hazardous judgment to make since clear rules are lacking. For example, in one case the Supreme Court refused to disallow a deduction for improper kickback payments by opticians to eyedoctors. *See* Lilly v. Comm. (S.Ct.1952). However, kickback payments were disallowed in another case, United Draperies, Inc. v. Comm. (7th Cir.1964). When the taxpayer's expenditure itself is illegal (not the lawful payment of a penalty for an illegal act as in *Tank Truck*), frustration of public policy is most likely to be found. Nevertheless, wages and rental costs incurred by an illegal bookmaking business were allowed as deductions in Comm. v. Sullivan (S.Ct.1958), to avoid taxing the business on gross receipts rather than on "income."

Congress has denied deductions for some specified business costs on a public policy basis similar to the judicial doctrine. Section 162(f) denies a deduction under § 162(a) for any fine or similar penalty paid to a government for the violation of any law; it thus codifies the *Tank Truck* rule. Section 162(c) prohibits deduction under § 162(a) of some bribes and kickbacks, but it preserves the deductibility of payments made to foreign government officials or employees after September 3, 1982, unless illegal under the Foreign Corrupt Practices Act of 1977. *But see* § 280E, enacted in 1982, which prohibits the deduction of business expenses paid or incurred in the trafficking of drugs that are illegal under federal or state law. (Note that § 212 is *not* similarly inhibited.) *See also* I.R.C. § 162(e) (denial of deduction for lobbying and some campaign expenses of a business) and § 162(g) (treble damages in a civil antitrust suit not deductible if defendant convicted or pleaded guilty or *nolo contendere* in related criminal proceeding.)

Lawyers' fees and other legal expenses arising out of business activities are deductible, even if incurred in the unsuccessful defense of criminal charges or in an illegal business. *See* Comm. v. Tellier (S.Ct.1966). No public policy is affronted by allowing a deduction to a person who hires a lawyer to defend himself, even if later it be determined that the accused was guilty. Similarly, if a wrongdoer repays amounts wrongfully received he may take a deduction, and the form of deduction (capital or ordinary) will be keyed to the form of taxation of the earlier receipt. *See, e.g.,* Mitchell v. Comm. (6th Cir.1970) and Stephens v. Comm. (2nd Cir.1990).

In the public policy cases, the Supreme Court has repeatedly remarked that deductions are a matter of legislative grace and, thus, the intent of Congress is to be divined as to whether an otherwise deductible expense shall be disallowed. Also, the courts have said, if gross receipts or gross income rather than net income is to be taxed, it is for Congress to say so. Such statements have led some commentators to the conclusion that "income" as used in the Sixteenth Amendment cannot strictly be taken to mean net income, defined as gain with allowances for all costs of producing it. For if income has that meaning, deductions for costs of producing income cannot be disallowed by Congress or anyone else, lest the income tax be levied on more than "income" and thus be unconstitutional. The question has not been settled by a judicial holding. Some courts have expressed reluctance to deny a deduction for a business cost for constitutional reasons.

See, e.g., Lela Sullenger (Tax Court 1948). Others seem not to have hesitated. *See, e.g.,* The Weather–Seal Mfg. Co. v. Comm. (6th Cir.1952).

The suggestion has been made that "income" in the Sixteenth Amendment means "gross income," as used in I.R.C. § 61(a)—gross receipts minus the costs of goods sold (in the accounting sense of direct factory costs, raw materials, etc.), but without subtraction of expenses, as in § 162, for expenditures for management, advertising, travel and the like. *See* Lela Sullenger, *supra.* Cf. Comm. v. Sullivan (S.Ct.1958) (Congress may be able to tax gross receipts, but it has not attempted to do so). *See also* footnote 1, § 17 *supra.*

Related to the question of disallowing deductions on public policy grounds is the possibility that *exclusions* might be circumscribed by a similar concept. Would a gift given to induce someone to violate the law or because he had done so surely qualify for § 102? Food and lodging provided to prostitutes in an illegal bordello? A fellowship to study and discover new ways to evade taxes? Little or no law has developed to indicate the path of judicial thinking vis-à-vis this problem.

§ 40. Reasonable Compensation

Another limitation on deductibility of a common business expense is implied by I.R.C. § 162(a)(1) which includes in the category of deductible ordinary and necessary trade or business expenses "a reasonable allowance for salaries or other compensation for personal services actually rendered." To qualify for such deduction, payments must be established to be genuine compensation (not gifts or other distributions to employees). Then, the amounts must be determined to be reasonable. These requirements attempt to insure that no deduction will be allowed for an expenditure that is not what it appears to be—compensation. If an employee is also a shareholder (who might be given excessive salary, etc., in lieu of dividends, because salary but not dividends is deductible from the business's gross income), or if an employee is also a relative or other natural object of the business owner's bounty (so that he might be receiving a nondeductible family gift or support in the form of deductible salary), the I.R.S. and courts will scrutinize the reasonableness of amounts paid. Likewise, it may appear that excessive (unreasonable) compensation is disguised payment of the purchase price of an asset, a bribe, or payment of extortion.

Reasonableness is determined on a case-by-case basis. The courts make reference to similar payments by similar employers, by comparing the payments with the extent and value of services rendered and considering all other facts and circumstances relevant to the purpose of the inquiry. One circuit court has applied an "independent investor" test to determine the reasonableness of compensation by focusing on the rate of return earned by investors. See Exacto Spring Corp. v. Comm. (7th Cir.1999). If contingent compensation is awarded (*e.g.,* a bonus under a percentage-of-profits formula) pursuant to a reasonable bargain made *before* the services were rendered, it will generally be deductible in full, even if the amounts when actually paid exceed the usual norms. Regs. § 1.162–7(b)(2).

The test for deducting compensation may be viewed as a two-tiered matter. First, the payment of compensation must be reasonable in amount. Second, such payment must not contain an element that is not compensation and hence not deductible. And, an "automatic dividend" rule has been suggested: in the absence of prior dividends, purported compensation payments by a profitable corporation to its shareholders *must* contain a dividend component. *See, e.g.,* McCandless Tile Service v. U.S. (Ct.Cl.1970). However, the I.R.S. has rejected this approach. *See* Rev.Rul. 79–8, 1979–1 C.B. 92.

Repayment by the employee of compensation deemed to be excessive may be deducted by him if he is compelled by law or prior agreement to pay it back, but not if he does so voluntarily or under a promise made after the date of the original payment. *See, e.g.,* Vincent E. Oswald (Tax Court 1968); George L. Blanton (Tax Court 1966).

§ 41. Traveling Expenses

Section 162(a)(2) allows a deduction for traveling expenses (including amounts expended for meals and lodging that are not lavish or extravagant) while away from home in the pursuit of a trade or business. This section has produced reams of litigation about the meaning of "away from home," "in pursuit of," and "meals and lodging."

To begin with an issue that has been solved by a label, expenses of "commuting" from the taxpayer's residence to his place of work are not deductible no matter how far he travels. *See* Comm. v. Flowers (S.Ct.1946); Regs. § 1.162–2(e). Normal commuting must be separated from deductible daily business travel (as with a traveling salesman whose fares or auto costs may be deducted) and from similar transportation that goes beyond the personal aspects of a commute or is necessary to transport tools and equipment to work. Sullivan v. Comm. (2d Cir. 1966); Tyne v. Comm. (7th Cir.1969).

Expenses of a trip made primarily in pursuit of pleasure, though with some business flavoring, will not be deductible. *See, e.g.,* Rudolph v. U.S. (5th Cir.1961). If a trip is primarily a business trip, though some personal motives or benefits coexist, the taxpayer may deduct his entire transportation cost [Regs. § 1.162–2(b)], and he will be allowed to deduct a portion of his expenses (such as hotel bills and restaurant charges) other than transportation costs that are directly related or proportionate to the business element of the trip. Section 274(c) contains special allocation rules for foreign travel "away from home." Section 274(d) imposes special verification requirements on a taxpayer who wishes to deduct any travel expenses, because travel can so easily disguise personal pleasure as business efforts.

The statutory term "away from home" has required further definition. While the Supreme Court has not squarely decided what "home" means, and whether it means residence or a business headquarters, there does seem to be a notion of "tax home" in the cases. *See* Comm. v. Stidger (S.Ct.1967) (permanent duty station in Japan of a Marine Corps captain was his home, although his family resided stateside and was prohibited from accompanying him); *see also* Comm. v. Flowers, *supra.* The I.R.S., the Tax Court, and some Circuit Courts of Appeal take the position that a taxpayer's tax home is her principal place of business. *See*, *e.g.*, Rev. Rul. 75–432. Other Circuit Courts have held that a taxpayer's home is her residence and travel expenses must be based on business necessity in order to be deducted. *See*, *e.g.*, Rosenspan v. U.S. (2d Cir.1971).

The Supreme Court affirmed the Commissioner's "sleep or rest rule" under which travel "away from home" is construed to exclude all trips requiring neither sleep nor rest, regardless of the trip's length. So, lunch on the road for a salesman who returns home each night cannot be deducted merely because he is far out of town or in a distant city. *See* U.S. v. Correll (S.Ct.1967). If such an employee is reimbursed by his employer, the question of excluding such amounts becomes crucial. *See* I.R.C. § 119 and § 33, *supra. But see* I.R.C. § 162(h), which defines state legislators who elect to treat their legislative districts as their tax homes as being "away from home" on any day in which the legislature is in session for the purpose of deducting travel expenses. And compare § 162(a)(2) which allows members of Congress to deduct the costs of living expenses while in Washington as travel expenses away from home to a maximum amount of $3,000 per year.

Travel expenses connected with, and the cost of meals and lodging at a job or assignment away from the taxpayer's home that is a *temporary* job or assignment are deductible under § 162. A taxpayer is considered to be away from home only if the job or assignment does not exceed one year. *See* I.R.C. § 162(a). If the employment away from home in a single location is realistically expected to last for more than one year or there is no realistic expectation that the employment will last for one year or less, the employment is indefinite and, thus, not temporary under § 162(a). If the employment away from home is realistically expected to last for one year or less, but at some later date the employment is realistically expected to exceed one year, the employment will be treated as temporary until the date the taxpayer's realistic expectation changes, and it is indefinite beyond that time. *See* Rev.Rul. 93–86.

In general, business-travel issues and the problems of travel and living expenses at a temporary job site are to be distinguished from moving expenses. Moving expenses, as distinguished from travel expenses, are deductible to the extent provided in I.R.C. § 217, and reimbursements of such expenses are includible in income under § 82 unless excludable by § 132(a)(6) and § 132(g). This topic is covered in § 34 of this text, above.

The "sleep or rest" rule, the away-from-home rule (defined as business or employment site), and the reasonable-expectations rule all are judicial approaches to the same problem—separating ordinary and necessary business expenses (deductible) from personal expenditures (non-deductible). While a difference in approach may sometimes affect the outcome in a case, the various approaches often lead to the same conclusion when applied to a particular fact situation.

Further restrictions on the deduction of travel and transportation costs are imposed by I.R.C. § 274. *See* § 42, *infra*.

§ 42. Limitations on Business Deductions

An expenditure that qualifies for deduction under § 162 or § 212 may nevertheless be disallowed or limited by other statutory rules. One important repository of such rules is I.R.C. § 274. Section 274 disallows deductions for some expenses in the nature of business entertainment, business gifts, and business travel. Section 274 was enacted in 1962 against a background in which taxpayers often sought to deduct, as business expenses under § 162, costs of such items as lunches with business associates, cocktail parties for potential customers, business gifts (such as gifts to elevator operators, parking-lot attendants, secretaries, court clerks, and customers), entertainment on cabin cruisers and at country or downtown clubs, and trips to conventions or meetings at tropical resorts. Section 274 was designed to tighten the rules to make taxpayers substantiate the amount and the business connection of such expenditures. In some instances, a proration of, or a flat ceiling on, the deduction was imposed.

As to entertainment, § 274(a) provides that an expenditure for an entertainment activity shall not be deductible unless it was directly related to, or associated with (in the sense of preceding or following business meetings or discussion), the active conduct of the taxpayer's trade or business. No deduction is allowed with respect to a facility (such as a boat) used in connection with an entertainment activity. I.R.C. § 274(a)(1)(B). In any event, the deduction for an entertainment or recreational activity shall not exceed the portion directly related to, or associated with, the active conduct of trade or business. So, the cost of meals or cocktails immediately following a business meeting or convention may be deducted only if proven to have been sufficiently "associated with" the business and only to the extent of that portion so associated.

Expenses for recreational, social or similar activities primarily for the benefit of employees generally are deductible. I.R.C. § 274(e)(4). However, membership fees in clubs organized for business, pleasure, recreation, or any other social purpose are not deductible. See I.R.C. § 274(a)(3).

Section 274(n) provides that the amount otherwise allowable as a deduction for business meals and entertainment expense is generally limited to 50% of such expense. This percentage reduction reflects Congress' belief that business meals and entertainment inherently involve an element of personal living expense or consumption. (From 1986 to 1993, the limit was 80% of the expenses.) In addition, in order to deduct meal expenses, either the taxpayer or an employee of the taxpayer should be present at the meal. Also, such expense must not be "lavish or extravagant" under the circumstances. *See* § 274(k).

A special rule in § 274(n) increases the percentage of meal expenses that is deductible for meals consumed away from home by individuals during or incident to the period of duty subject to the hours-of-service limitations of the Department of Transportation. Covered employees include pilots, interstate truck operators and bus drivers, and certain railroad employees and merchant mariners. The percentage for 2004 and 2005 is 70 percent. This percentage will increase by five percentage points every two years until 2008, when it will be fixed at 80 percent. Congress justified this exception by noting that these individuals often are forced to eat meals away from home in circumstances in which their choice is limited, prices are comparatively high, and the opportunity for lavish meals is remote.

Section 274 imposes further limitations on specific types of expenditures. Under § 274(b), business gifts may be deducted by the donor only up to the amount of $25 per donee each year. Section 274(c) requires certain foreign travel expenses to be prorated (between business and personal accounts) beyond the extent required of § 162 domestic business travel expenses.

Section 274(d) imposes strict substantiation requirements on a taxpayer who seeks to deduct travel expenses or expenses of business activities, facilities or business gifts under § 162 or § 212. This section overrules the so-called *Cohan* rule under which an approximation was permitted if a taxpayer's records did not fully detail the extent to which expenses were business rather than personal. *See* Cohan v. Comm. (2d Cir.1930). *See also* Regs. § 1.162–17. *But see* I.R.M. 4.10.7.4.2(7) (5–14–99) giving I.R.S. agents authority to allow some away-from-home expenses even if the taxpayer cannot provide documentary evidence, seemingly contrary to the letter of § 274(d)(1) and Regs. § 1.274–5.

Subsection (e) of § 274 exempts a number of categories of expenses from the tightened rules of § 274(a). Among these categories are some reimbursed expenses in connection with services rendered, food and beverages for employees, recreational expenses for employees [but not club memberships—*see* § 274(a)(3)], and expenses of employee and shareholder meetings. *See* § 274(n)(2) for categories exempt from the 50% limitation for food, beverages and entertainment.

Subsection 274(f) provides that the § 274 limitation is *not* applicable to deductions for costs allowable without regard to their connection to the taxpayer's trade or business (or income-producing activity).

Typical of these deductions are some items of interest, taxes, and casualty losses.

Section 274(h), which governs deductions for the expenses of attending foreign conventions, allows the taxpayer to deduct the expenses of foreign conventions only if the taxpayer establishes that the meeting is directly related to the active conduct of a trade or business (not merely a § 212 profit-seeking activity) and that after taking several specified criteria into account it is as reasonable for the meeting to be held outside the North American area as within it.

Some other statutory sections disallow deductions that otherwise might qualify under §§ 162 or 212. In addition to § 263 (capital expenditures) and others to be encountered shortly, such sections include § 275 (certain taxes), § 276 (indirect contributions to political parties), § 269 (acquisitions made to evade income tax), § 183 (hobby expenses or losses), § 267 (transactions between related taxpayers), § 265 (expenses relating to tax-exempt income), § 280A (disallowance of certain expenses in connection with business use of home, rental or vacation home, etc.), and § 262 (personal living and family expenses), as well as still others. Much the same effect results from express limitations in the deduction sections themselves; *see e.g.,* §§ 162(b), (c), (e), and 217 (moving expenses).

Section 183 deserves special mention. Under that section, individual taxpayers are prevented from taking any deduction, other than those described in

§ 183(b), in connection with any activity not engaged in for profit, *e.g.*, a hobby. The deductions § 183(b) allows are those for expenses that would be deductible regardless of whether or not the activity is engaged in for profit plus profit-seeking expenses up to but not in excess of the point at which both kinds of expenses equal gross income from the "hobby" activity. *And see* Regs. § 1.162–12(b) (expenses of farmers, if farm is operated for recreation or pleasure). Whether an activity is a profit activity or not for § 183 purposes is defined with reference to §§ 162 and 212 criteria, aided by a (positive) presumption that arises when an activity gives rise to profits in any three or more of the five preceding years. Courts generally apply an objective, rather than a subjective, inquiry into whether the taxpayer's motive behind the activity is to make a profit.

Section 280A severely curtails the opportunity for claiming utility, insurance, depreciation, and maintenance expenses for using a portion of one's residence as a home office or for other business purposes. In general, to avoid the limitations in § 280A, a deduction must be allocable to a portion of a dwelling unit which is exclusively used on a regular basis: (a) as the principal place of business for any trade or business of the taxpayer (including a place used for administrative or management activities of a business if no other fixed location is so used and such activities are substantial), (b) as a place which is used by patients, customers, or clients in meetings or dealings with the taxpayer in the normal course of a business, or (c) in the case of a separate structure not attached to the dwelling, in connection with the taxpayer's business. *See* I.R.C. § 280A(c)(1). Along with the foregoing, § 280A is also used to curb the large deductions formerly claimed by some taxpayers attributable to their vacation homes.

Other limiting rules include anti-tax-shelter provisions. The term "tax shelter," while sometimes used to refer to any tax allowance or tax favored investment, more narrowly denotes those activities in which the investors seek to deduct costs in excess of their income from the investment. By so doing, they try to use the activity to shelter other income from tax. Often tax-shelter investments use *leverage*—that is, borrowed money—and sometimes the loan is without personal liability ("non-recourse" borrowing). Often they aim to accelerate tax deductions or to *defer* taxable gain. And frequently they attempt to *convert* ordinary income to capital gains (or capital losses to ordinary losses). In 1976, a variety of rules were enacted to limit the amount of loss or other deductions from tax shelters to the amount put "at risk" by the investors. These rules, some of them highly technical, are to be found in places like § 465 (deduction for losses in an activity limited to amount "at risk"). In general, a taxpayer is considered at risk for amounts contributed to an activity and amounts borrowed where the taxpayer is personally liable for the debt or other property is pledged to secure the debt. I.R.C. § 465(b). An important exception provides that a taxpayer is considered at risk for "qualified nonrecourse financing" in connection with an activity of holding real property. I.R.C. § 465(b)(6).

Various revenue rulings have applied the "at risk" concept, introduced by the Tax Reform Act of 1976, to various forms of tax shelters. These have included leveraged investments in master recordings of songs or motion pictures to be licensed for royalties, road-building equipment, timber royalties, covenants not to compete, federal land leasing, "burned out shelters," and "tax sheltered" trusts. A common feature was that the investors used non-recourse financing, putting little of their own capital "at risk," yet seeking deductions inflated by borrowed capital. The rulings limit deductions to the amount put "at risk," either at the outset increased by any amounts later put at risk, such as by subsequent payments of principal, or undertakings to pay it or pledges of other property. *See* Rev.Rul. 77–395, and 77–397–403, 1977–44 I.R.B. 6–11.

The at-risk rules apply to partners. Another rule limits a partner's share of partnership losses to the partner's basis in the partnership interest. I.R.C. § 704(d). Other restrictions include restrictions on: prepaid interest deductions (§ 461(g)), current deductions for organization and syndication fees (§ 709), prepaid feed and certain farming expenses (§ 464), and cash accounting for some farming expenses and current expensing of pre-production expenses (§ 447). Recapture rules are applied to narrow the chances for deferring tax or for converting ordinary income into capital gain. *See* § 1250 and

§ 1254. The base of the alternative minimum tax also includes certain items related to tax shelters. *See* I.R.C. §§ 57–58. *See also* §§ 705, 706, and 709.

The passive loss limitations introduced in the 1986 T.R.A. drastically altered the way in which taxpayers presently utilize some tax shelters. Section 469, which applies to rental activities above a small exemption and to many other investments, permits losses incurred in a passive activity to be deducted only from income generated by passive activities, not from active trade or business income, wages, or from portfolio income (such as dividends, interest, royalties, and gains from selling portfolio investments). A passive activity is an activity which involves a trade of business and in which the taxpayer does not materially participate (*i.e.*, regular, continuous, and substantial participation). I.R.C. § 469(c)(1),(h)(1). Losses disallowed by § 469 generally may be deducted later when the taxpayer disposes of the entire interest in the activity. I.R.C. § 469(g)(1). At income levels below $100,000, however, up to $25,000 of active income may be offset with losses from rental activities in which the taxpayer actively participated. I.R.C. § 469(i); *see* § 56, *infra* for more detailed coverage of passive losses.

In all events, the possibility that an expense may be disallowed, though apparently qualified under § 162, § 212 or some other section, must always be kept in mind and investigated.

Specific guidance for taxpayers is afforded by regulations (such as those under §§ 162, 212, 274,

465, 469, etc.) and by other I.R.S. publications. For example, Rev.Rul. 63–144, 1963–2 C.B. 129, contains answers to a number of frequently raised practical questions about business expenditures for entertainment, travel, and gifts under § 274. The ruling announces a good deal about enforcement policy and informal practices, as well as "the law." The ruling, however, does not reflect subsequent legislative changes.

I.R.C. §§ 261–280H contain still other prohibitions or limitations on deductions, some of which will be the subject of the next sections of this book. In addition, note especially: § 262 (disallowance of personal living expenses); § 264 (expenses in connection with certain insurance contracts); § 265 (expenses and interest relating to tax-exempt income); § 266 (carrying charges); § 267 (losses, expenses and interest in transactions between related taxpayers); § 268 (disallowance of expenses attributable to production of unharvested crop which was sold along with the land); § 269 (acquisitions made to evade or avoid income tax); § 273 (holders of life or terminable interests); § 274 (disallowance of certain entertainment, etc., expenses—*see* this § 42, *supra*); § 275 (certain taxes non-deductible); § 276 (disallowance of certain indirect contributions to political parties); § 279 (interest on indebtedness incurred by corporation to acquire stock or assets of another corporation); § 280A (disallowance of certain expenses in connection with business use of home, rental of vacation home, etc.); and § 280B (demolition of certain historic structures).

Note also § 162(b) (no deduction as business expense for a charitable contribution or gift that exceeds the special requirements of § 170); § 162(c) (bribes, kickbacks and other payments); § 162(e) (lobbying); § 162(f) (fines and penalties); § 162(g) (anti-trust treble damages); § 162(h) (state legislator's travel expenses away from home); § 162(j) (certain foreign advertising expenses); § 162(k) (stock-redemption expenses); § 280E (expenses related to illegal drug trafficking); § 280F (limits on luxury autos and listed properties); and § 280G (golden parachute payments). Section 212 has not become encrusted with similar growths, but the modern meaning of trade or business in § 162 seems so broad as to leave little room to take a deduction under § 212 while escaping these § 162 limitations. Compare also legislation that denies important tax allowances to a taxpayer guilty of making foreign bribes or participating in illegal boycotts. *See* I.R.C. §§ 908, 952, 964, 995, and 999.

§ 43. Capital Expenditures

Not every *expenditure* made in actively conducting a trade or business or otherwise made in producing income is deductible as a business *expense*. Under § 263, the Regulations [Regs. § 1.263(a)] and case-law doctrine, an expenditure that is capital in nature may not be entirely deducted in the year made. *See also* Regs. § 1.162–4, § 1.212–1(k), (m) & (n). Instead it must be "capitalized"—added to basis, accounted for as a purchase price—and then given whatever tax treatment is prescribed by the

Code: possibly annual depreciation or amortization deductions, depletion deductions, or some other cost-recovery method.

A prime example of a capital expenditure is a payment made to purchase a new building or for a permanent improvement made to increase the value of property. *See* § 263(a)(1). And, rent on business property will not be deductible if the taxpayer is thereby taking or has taken title or is building up an equity, because the "rent" really amounts to payment of the purchase price in installments. *See* § 162(a)(3). The purchase price of a building must be capitalized, which means treating it as part of cost for purposes of determining basis or adjustments to basis under §§ 1012 and 1016. By adding to basis, the expenditure will affect gain or loss on sale of the asset and will increase depreciation deductions allowable if the asset is depreciable. In contrast, expenses of current upkeep and repairs on business property are deductible currently. *See* Regs. § 1.162–4.

To determine which expenditures are properly chargeable to capital account and which may be expensed as current deductions is no easy task. Section 263 mentions a few categories of expenditures for which a deduction may not be taken. In addition to payments for new buildings or for improvements, subsection (a)(2) of § 263 mentions any amount expended in restoring property or in making good the exhaustion thereof for which an allowance (such as depreciation or cost recovery) is or has been made. The Regulations [§ 1.263(a)–

1(b)] encompass amounts paid to add to the value, or substantially prolong the useful life, of property or to adapt property to a new or different use. By example, Regs. § 1.263(a)–2 include as capital expenditures payments for securing a copyright and plates, the cost of defending or perfecting title to property, and the cost of goodwill in connection with the acquisition of the assets of a going concern. Other nondeductible capital expenditures are payments for an architect's services, broker's commissions paid when stocks or bonds are purchased by private investors, a shareholder's contributions to the capital of his corporation, loans to a borrower, or the purchase price paid to acquire stocks, bonds or most other property.

The Supreme Court held in INDOPCO v. Comm. (S.Ct.1992) that realization of benefits beyond the year in which an expenditure is incurred is "undeniably important" in determining whether the appropriate tax treatment is an immediate deduction or capitalization. Thus, investment-banking fees incurred in a friendly corporate acquisition were capital in nature because they were incurred for the purpose of changing the corporate structure for the benefit of future operations. However, investment-banking fees expended to defend against a hostile takeover and preserve the status quo may be deductible as ordinary and necessary business expenses. *See* A.E. Staley Manufacturing Company and Subsidiaries v. Comm. (7th Cir.1997). The I.R.S. has issued regulations on capitalization of amounts paid to acquire, create, or enhance intangible assets. *See* Regs. § 1.263(a)–4, –5.

In Welch v. Helvering (S.Ct.1933), the Supreme Court held that payments of the debts of a defunct corporation by a former officer after bankruptcy, made for the purpose of improving his own business standing, were non-deductible capital outlays rather than ordinary and necessary business expenses. *See also* Gilmore v. U.S. (D.C.Cal.1965), which held that litigation expenses for defense of title to stock in a divorce case were not deductible currently but were capital expenditures.

In Norwest Corp. and Subsidiaries v. Comm., (Tax Court1997), the Tax Court held that the taxpayer must, under § 263, capitalize (not deduct currently) the costs of asbestos removed from a building it had constructed earlier because the costs were part of a general plan of rehabilitation and remodeling.

A particular and important problem is how a taxpayer must, or may, treat costs incurred in producing inventory, other goods held for sale to customers, or long-lived assets such as a manuscript or other composition. If an encyclopedia publisher purchases a manuscript for an unrelated person, the cost would have to be capitalized under normal principles. *See* Encyclopedia Britannica v. Comm. (7th Cir.1982). But in-house costs of creating an equivalent manuscript long were regarded as currently deductible, in part because it is difficult to apportion the salaries and time of employers and other general costs and expenses to one project or another. However Congress has enacted § 263A to help bring clarity and uniformity of treatment to taxpayers. Section 263A, which provides the so-called "uniform capitalization rules," requires that costs incurred in the production or acquisition by the taxpayer of real or tangible property for resale not be deducted but either be (1) included in the cost of inventory if the property is inventory in the hands of the taxpayer, or (2) capitalized. Exceptions are provided for small businesses and some special taxpayers (farmers, authors, photographers, artists).

The "UNICAP" (uniform capitalization) rules of § 263A require that the costs of creating an asset produced by the taxpayer, as in the case of in-house production of an encyclopedia manuscript, must be treated as part of the cost of that asset, and hence must be capitalized, rather than being deducted as ongoing trade in business expenses. Consequently, salaries of employees researching and writing the manuscript, and indirect expenses such as the salaries of administrators, supervisory and staff people, could not be deducted currently. Similarly, insurance covering a manufacturing plant must be treated as part of the cost of producing goods added to inventory and sold sometime later. Some advertising and marketing costs and some public relations and overall business planning expenses are exempted. *See* Regs. § 1.263A–1(e)(iii) and (iv).

Under special statutory sections, some taxpayers are given an election to expense certain items that otherwise would have to be capitalized. *See, e.g.,* § 173 (circulation expenditures), § 174 (research and experimental expenditures), § 175 (soil and water conservation expenditures), § 179 (certain business property purchase expenditures), § 180 (expenditures by farmers for fertilizer), § 195 (start-up expenditures), § 197 (amortization of goodwill and certain other intangibles), § 248 (organizational expenditures of a corporation), and §§ 616–617 (development and some mining exploration expenditures). Such taxpayers' elections often yield material financial benefits and are much sought after and lobbied for by special-interest groups such as farmers and the oil and gas industry.

The U.S. Supreme Court has held that some special rules, such as § 174, which allows a deduction for research and experimental expenditures, have the broad legislative objective of providing an economic incentive, especially for small and growing businesses, to engage in a search for new products and inventions and were intended to dilute the concept of ordinary and necessary business expenses. Section 174 allows a taxpayer to treat research or experimental expenditures paid in connection with a trade or business as expenses *not* chargeable to capital account and hence allowed as a deduction. So research on new computer programming or experiments with a new medical vaccine might qualify. Section 174 is independent of the

§ 41 *credit* for *increasing* research expenditures. *See* § 48 *infra.*

A few other special provisions allow a taxpayer to capitalize items of expense to enable him to avoid losing a deduction. *See, e.g.,* I.R.C. § 266 (expenses of carrying unproductive property). Some other statutory provisions require expenses that might otherwise be deducted to be capitalized. *See* § 263A(d), which provides that expenditures incurred in planting and developing citrus and almond groves through the end of the fourth tax year after planting shall be capitalized, and § 447, which requires certain farming corporations to capitalize preproduction expenses.

Capital expenditures may come in disguised forms. For example, one taxpayer entered an agreement to buy a race horse jointly with his "partner." One partner paid to purchase the horse and the other paid to board and maintain it. The court treated one-half of the costs borne by each as capital expenditures and one-half as deductible maintenance. *See* Herbert K. Stevens (Tax Court 1966). Part of the legal expenses of defending against severe threats to the business of the taxpayer in a bitter divorce suit were held to be capital in nature. *See* Gilmore v. U.S. (N.D.Cal.1965). Rent or lease payments for property the taxpayer will be entitled to buy for a nominal option price at the end of the rental term, when the property will have significant value remaining, will be held to be installment purchase payments, not rent. As such, the payments are installments of a purchase price that create a basis for depreciation (or "cost recovery") over time according to applicable rules and cannot be deducted as rent when made.

When a taxpayer such as a construction company undertakes to use equipment and machinery to build an asset it will own (or sell), such as a dam or a building, can depreciation deductions be taken on the equipment and machinery? One might think so, since deductions could be taken if the equipment were used to construct a building on contract for another owner. But the cost of using up the equipment does resemble the wage costs for workers who build the dam or building, and those costs of construction must be capitalized, not expensed (deducted currently). So must the depreciation costs, ruled the U.S. Supreme Court in Comm. v. Idaho Power Co. (S.Ct.1974). The Court read § 263 as taking priority over § 167 (which provides for depreciation deductions) and held that the use of one piece of equipment to build an asset is a cost to be capitalized as if it were payment of a purchase price or a cash expenditure for construction. Creation of a separate asset has always been one hallmark of a capital expenditure. *See* Comm. v. Lincoln Savings & Loan Ass'n (S.Ct.1971).

Section 195 denies a deduction to a taxpayer for "start-up expenditures" unless the taxpayer makes a § 195(b) election to amortize them equally over a fixed period of not less than 60 months. Otherwise such expenditures could only be capitalized and added to the taxpayer's basis in the business, which perhaps would benefit the taxpayer on the eventual sale of the business—maybe a long time in the future. "Start-up expenditures" are defined in § 195(c) to include amounts spent in investigating the creation or acquisition of an active trade or business, in creating such a business, or profit-seeking or income-producing expenditures before, but in anticipation of, the beginning of an active trade or business—but only if the expenditures would be deductible if incurred by an existing active trade or business.

§ 44.   Depreciation, Accelerated Cost Recovery, and Amortization

When a taxpayer uses income-producing assets such as machines, trucks, tools, a building or other property in business or gain-seeking activity, some of gross income is considered to be a return of capital. That is true because the machines, for example, have a limited useful life—they are wearing out and growing obsolete while generating income. (Land, in contrast, is thought to have an unlimited useful life.) The capital investment that the taxpayer made when he bought the machines is being used up to produce a flow of receipts and gross income. In effect, taxpayer is gradually selling those of his assets that have a limited useful life. Thus, part of his gross income should be seen as a return of his capital expenditure and investments, not as profit or "net income." Accordingly, the tax law (as well as financial accounting) has developed rules to separate the return of capital amounts from income. Additional rules have evolved to protect against abuses of the basic allowance or to give special tax incentives for other reasons.

Depreciation.[2] For property placed in service in a business or for the production of income prior to 1981, the rules allowing deductions for the amount deemed a return-of-capital are found in I.R.C. §§ 167 and 179. The rules applicable to post–1980 property, the Accelerated Cost Recovery System ("A.C.R.S."), are contained in § 168 and § 179, which will be discussed, *infra.*

Though depreciation appears to have been replaced by A.C.R.S., depreciation must nevertheless be understood as it (1) still applies to all property used in a trade or business or held for the production of income in tax years beginning before 1981; and (2) taxpayers may elect certain variants of "depreciation" under A.C.R.S. Also, the "cost recovery" deduction under § 168 simply has become the § 167 "reasonable allowance" provided by § 167 and thus can be viewed as a fast, stipulated depreciation method. Thus, the term "depreciation" is broadly used and sometimes refers to pre-A.C.R.S. methods alone, and sometimes to A.C.R.S. as well.

Under § 167, depreciation deductions are allowed for the exhaustion, wear and tear and obsolescence of property used in the trade or business or held for the production of income. Using up the property in the business may in fact be likened to a gradual sale

2. Now often denominated as "cost recovery." *See* this § 44 *infra,* re. A.C.R.S. The interim discussion will treat the subject of "depreciation" generically, to refer to the tax and accounting concept in general.

of the property—basis in either event is to be recovered (as a return of capital). The basis recovered as a return of capital by depreciation deductions is the adjusted basis provided in § 1011 for the purpose of determining gain or loss on the sale or other disposition of such property. I.R.C. § 167(c). In turn, the basis of depreciable property has to be adjusted downward each year for depreciation allowed or allowable (even if not actually taken). Also, basis can be adjusted upward to reflect capital additions to the property. I.R.C. § 1016(a).

Apart from § 167 deductions, a taxpayer may elect to treat the cost of some depreciable property (§ 179 property) as an expense not chargeable to capital account and hence may deduct all the cost when the property is first placed in service—up to $100,000 per year in taxable years beginning after 2002 and before 2006 ($25,000 thereafter). I.R.C. § 179(b)(1). However, that amount is reduced (but not below zero) by the amount by which the cost of § 179 property placed in service in that year, exceeds $400,000 ($200,000 after 2005). *See* I.R.C. §§ 179(a), (b)(1), (b)(2). In 2004 and 2005, the $100,000 and $400,000 figures are adjusted for inflation. I.R.C. § 179(b)(5).

Not all trade or business assets are depreciable. Land, for example, (theoretically) has an unlimited useful life. Therefore no depreciation deduction is allowed for land since nothing was being used up. So, if a taxpayer buys land with buildings or other depreciable property on it, the purchase price has to be allocated between the land and improvements to determine the basis of each. Only the basis allocated to depreciable assets can give rise to deductions for depreciation. Depreciation is also not allowed for inventory or for personal assets, for other reasons.

Under traditional depreciation principles, the basis of an asset was allowed to be recovered over its useful life through annual depreciation deductions. *See* I.R.C. § 167(c). Salvage value calculated to remain at the end of the useful life had to be subtracted in determining the amount of cost or other basis to be depreciated. Salvage value was then recovered upon sale or abandonment of the asset at the end of its useful life—taxable gain was reduced on sale or a deduction was taken for abandonment. So a new building costing $100,000 (apart from land) with a useful life of 40 years and a salvage value of $20,000 at the end would have entitled its owner to depreciation allowances totaling $80,000 over 40 years, at some appropriate rate.

Under prior law, intangible property with a *limited* life that was exhausted or diminished in value during use in generating income also gave rise to depreciation deductions. For example, deductions were allowed for a patent or copyright. *See* Regs. § 1.167(a)–3. Goodwill was not depreciable since it was thought theoretically to have an indefinite useful life. In 1993, Congress enacted new I.R.C. § 197, which provides an exclusive amortization deduction for goodwill and certain other intangibles. *See* the discussion on § 197 at the end of this section. Otherwise and in general, if the taxpayer cannot show that an intangible (capital expenditure or cost) not covered by § 197 has a finite and determinable useful life, he is not allowed to take a deduction.

The rate at which depreciable basis is allowed to be deducted or written off is called the "method of depreciation." The most basic method is the so-called straight-line method, under which an equal amount can be deducted each year, or $2,000 per year over 40 years in the foregoing example. In other words, the number of years of the asset's useful life is divided into its cost or other basis, and the result is the annual deduction. The same fraction and amount are deducted each year. So-called accelerated depreciation methods such as the "double-declining-balance method" or "sum-of-the-years-digits method" allow larger deductions in the early years of an asset's life and correspondingly lower deductions in later years, so that the total allowance is the same under any of these methods. *See* Regs. § 1.167(b)–0. Under all of them, actual cost is to be allowed—no more, no less. Nonetheless, accelerated depreciation methods are usually advantageous to taxpayers because they produce large tax benefits earlier in return for smaller ones later. The value of the quick tax reduction can be calculated arithmetically and can amount to a large sum. Accelerated depreciation was allowed by Congress and the Treasury to acknowledge the economic facts of sudden early reductions in value of new assets and to encourage investment and reinvestment in depreciable assets, for fiscal and economic reasons.

To visualize the financial benefits, in terms of increased cash flow, afforded by accelerated depreciation, compare conventional (straight-line) depreciation with faster write-offs. For example, suppose taxpayer purchased a depreciable business asset for $100 and placed it in service on July 1. It had a ten-year useful life and no salvage value. The following table shows how the three most important methods of depreciation operated and compares them with accelerated cost recovery under § 168 (as before and after the 1986 Act).

Year	STRAIGHT-LINE Annual Deduction	Cumulative Cost Recovered	DECLINING BALANCE Annual Deduction	Cumulative Cost Recovered	SUM OF DIGITS Annual Deduction	Cumulative Cost Recovered	PRE-1986 A.C.R.S. (5 yr., property) Annual Deduction	Cumulative Cost Recovered	POST-1986 A.C.R.S. (7 yr. property) Annual Deduction	Cumulative Cost Recovered
1	$ 5	$ 5	$10	$ 10	$ 9	$ 9	$15	$ 15	$14.29	$ 14.29
2	10	15	18	28	17	26	22	37	24.49	38.78
3	10	25	14.4	42.4	15.5	41.5	21	58	17.49	56.27
4	10	35	11.52	53.92	14	55.5	21	79	12.49	68.76
5	10	45	9.22	63.14	12	67.5	21	100	8.93	77.69
6	10	55	7.37	70.51	10	77.5			8.93	86.61
7	10	65	6.55	77.06	8	85.5			8.92	95.54
8	10	75	6.55	83.61	6	91.5			4.46	100.
9	10	85	6.55	90.71	4.5	96				
10	10	95	6.55	96.72	3	99				
11	5	100	3.29	100	1	100				

Observe that at the end of the third tax year, cumulative cost recovered under the straight-line method was exceeded by $17.40 under the declining balance method, $16.50 under the sum-of-digits method, $33 under the pre–1986 A.C.R.S. method, and $31.27 under the post–1986 A.C.R.S. method. After the fifth taxable year, the straight-line method permitted 45% recovery, the declining balance method permitted 63.14% recovery, the sum-of-digits method permitted 67.5% recovery, the pre–1986 A.C.R.S. method permitted 100% recovery, and the post–1986 A.C.R.S. method permitted 77.69% recovery. Of course, the total recovery under all five methods eventually totaled 100% of the depreciable cost of the asset. However, the A.C.R.S. methods provide the advantage of early recovery to the taxpayer, by assigning a useful life of less than ten years to the asset, as well as by employing rapid *rates* of recovery.

Not all assets can be depreciated at the same rate. Different assets have different useful lives and salvage values, both inherently and in different taxpayer uses. Years ago, useful life guidelines were provided for classes of tangible personal property in Revenue Procedure 62–21, 1962–2 C.B. 418.

The Procedure set forth guidelines for computing depreciation allowances on tangible personal property used in a trade or business or held for the production of income. About 75 broad classes of assets were assigned guideline lives; these instructions replaced old Bulletin F, which assigned useful lives on an item basis. The new guideline lives were estimated by the Treasury to be 30%–40% shorter than those under Bulletin F. (And, any taxpayer was free to use an even shorter useful life if his replacement policies would support that position.) Thus, administratively a change in taxability was accomplished that produced tremendous economic influences and consequences for the revenue. Industry responded to the invitation to write off assets more quickly. Demand, employment, and profits were stimulated and, together with the legislative changes of 1962, the new guidelines sparked a period of economic growth of remarkable stature and duration.

Asset Depreciation Range (A.D.R.) System. To shorten the periods over which some assets could be written off, Congress enacted what is known as the Asset Depreciation Range (ADR) system, which it later repealed in 1981, but which still serves as a reference point for current "cost recovery" depreciation.

Useful life, cost and basis. Depreciation always has to be taken over the useful life of the property in the use put to it by the particular taxpayer in his trade, business or other method of income production, not over the entire physical life of the property itself. Massey Motors, Inc. v. U.S. (S.Ct.1960). Depreciation is not tied exactly to market depreciation or appreciation. For example, depreciation deductions can be taken by a taxpayer whose property is actually rising in value on the market. Until he sells it, the law continues to presume that taxpayer's investment is being used up and will not be recovered on sale (except for salvage value, already accounted for). Even in the year of sale at a gain, depreciation can be taken for that year or portion of that year. *See* Fribourg Navigation Co., Inc. v. Comm. (S.Ct.1966).

To provide for the possibility that the market value could change at a different rate from the depreciation projections, and generally to insure that only the taxpayer's actual investment of capital or "after-tax dollars" was recovered, the Code exacts a price for depreciation. Under § 1016(a)(2), a taxpayer's basis in an asset has to be reduced for depreciation deductions *allowed or allowable*. As a consequence of basis reductions for depreciation, a taxpayer who sells his depreciated asset for more than adjusted basis at the end of its useful life in his hands has a taxable gain (amount realized over basis—adjusted downward for the earlier tax-free recovery of capital through annual deductions from income). And, if he sells it for less than adjusted basis, he has a deductible loss (adjusted basis minus amount realized). His depreciation deductions and his gain or loss computation on sale combine to allow him tax-free recovery of his investment and nothing more or less. (To be sure, this recovery may occur sooner or later and at the same or different rates depending on market facts, and depending on depreciation recapture rules such as I.R.C. §§ 1245 and 1250, discussed *infra,* Ch. IX, § 104.)

Actual (historic) cost, not replacement cost, is the basis for depreciation. No revision is made in the depreciation deductions even if inflation or rising costs make replacement of the asset much more expensive than its historic purchase price. So depreciation deductions do not necessarily enable a taxpayer to set aside, tax free, exactly the number of dollars needed in order to replace the asset he is using up in the business.

Additional first-year depreciation was allowed by pre-E.R.T.A. § 179 on certain property; now § 179 grants an election to "expense," or deduct at once, a cost that otherwise would be chargeable to capital account. Amortization allowances, akin to depreciation on tangible property, are allowed for similar costs for intangible properties "used up" in producing income; "depreciation" is the term often used interchangeably for amortizing such assets as patents and copyrights. *See* Regs. § 1.167(a)–3 (intangibles); *but see* § 169 (amortization [sic] of pollution control facilities). A change in depreciation method is permitted or required in some circumstances due to changed facts or knowledge of facts. *See* Regs. § 1.167(e)–1.

Sometimes a piece of depreciable property is owned by two or more taxpayers jointly or successively. In such an instance, depreciation deductions have to be allocated between the two joint owners or, for example, between the life tenant and remainderman or between the estate and the beneficiaries to whom the property eventually is distributed. Special rules or contractual agreements can govern these allocations. *See* I.R.C. § 167(d). When depreciable property is leased by a lessor to a lessee, the general principle requires each to take depreciation on his own investment. Accordingly, the lessor can depreciate the property he leased (the allowances thus set off against his rental income from leasing the property) and the lessee can depreciate any investment or improvement he made over the shorter of the life of the lease or the life of the depreciable property. As to costs of acquiring or renewing a lease, *see* I.R.C. § 178.

The taxpayer's basis for depreciation purposes depends on how much the property cost, prior adjustments to basis, and how the asset was acquired, if not by purchase. Property acquired by gift or bequest generally falls under the appropriate basis rules for such transactions. *See* § 26, *supra.*

Property acquired as a "contribution to capital" of a corporation is subject to another regime, but with sometimes corresponding results. I.R.C. § 362(a)(2) says that property acquired by a corporation as a contribution to capital shall have a basis the same as it would in the hands of the transferor, increased by gain (if any) recognized on the transfer. Section 362(b) contains a related rule for property acquired in corporate reorganizations. But what if the property was received in some other way? In U.S. v. Chicago, Burlington & Quincy R.R. Co. (S.Ct.1973), the U.S. Supreme Court held that grants received by a railroad from state governments to improve grade crossings with overpasses, signals, etc., did not constitute contributions to the taxpayer's capital under § 113(a)(8) of the 1939 Code and therefore created a zero basis under § 1052(c) of the 1954 Code. As a consequence, no depreciation was allowable, the effect of which is similar to saying that the corporation received income when it got the property, but with a very different practical tax cost. The prior inclusion in income would have entitled the taxpayer to a basis equal to the amount included. But depreciating that basis over time, after paying tax on receipt, would be much less advantageous than bypassing tax at the outset, foregoing depreciation deductions, and having no basis to offset the amount realized in sale. The exclusion from income at the most amounts to "instant depreciation," which is worth more than deferred depreciation.

Under A.D.R., any taxpayer who placed tangible property qualifying as § 1245 or § 1250 property into service during a taxable year could elect ADR treatment if the property fell within an established asset guideline class. Guideline classes were organized in terms of the primary use of assets in the taxpayer's business or income producing activity (*e.g.*, "manufacturing tobacco and tobacco products," "wholesale and retail trade," etc.). *See* Revenue Procedure 72–10, 1972–1 C.B. 721 and supplementing or superseding revenue procedures for a complete breakdown of the existing asset guideline classes.

A taxpayer who elected the ADR system had to assign his eligible property to "vintage accounts." A vintage account was a closed-end depreciation account consisting of one or more assets within a single guideline class, all of which were placed in service during the same taxable year (hence the term "vintage"). Within a given guideline class, a taxpayer could create as many or as few vintage accounts as he desired, subject to certain limitations on the grouping of assets. *See generally* Regs. § 1.167(a)–11(b)(3).

After the taxpayer had established his vintage accounts, he determined the useful life (or "asset depreciation period") for each account by consulting the "asset guideline periods" promulgated for each guideline class. *See* Revenue Procedure 72–10, 1972–1 C.B. 721. If no asset depreciation range was in effect for a particular class, the asset guideline period became the useful life for the taxpayer's accounts within that class. The purpose of ADR admittedly was to stimulate the economy for the sake of employment, profits and taxes rather than to conform scheduled useful lives to changed economic utilities.

Even after its repeal in 1981 and after the 1986 T.R.A., A.D.R. remains relevant. The 1986 rules reclassified certain assets based on their midpoint lives under the A.D.R. system. For example, the property whose A.D.R. midpoint was more than four and less than ten years is to be treated as five-year property. *See* I.R.C. § 168(e).

Accelerated Cost Recovery System (A.C.R.S.). The Economic Recovery Tax Act of 1981 introduced the Accelerated Cost Recovery System (A.C.R.S.) as a method to recover capital costs for most tangible depreciable property placed in service after December 31, 1980, and Congress repealed the Asset Depreciation Range A.D.R. system as of January 1, 1981, although A.D.R. remains relevant under post–

1986 law as a reference point for recovery periods. A.C.R.S. was intended to benefit small business, which made little use of A.D.R., to eliminate litigation over the useful life of an asset, and to provide an incentive for businesses to buy new equipment. To accomplish this goal, A.C.R.S. uses accelerated methods applied over pre-determined recovery periods shorter than, but generally unrelated to, assets' useful lives. The recovery periods differ for real and personal property. Under I.R.C. § 168(b)(4) salvage value is not taken into account when computing cost recovery.

A.C.R.S. deductions may be taken on "recovery property," which includes tangible personal and real property but excludes property that the taxpayer elects to depreciate according to a method not based on a term of years (*i.e.,* the unit-of-production or income-forecast methods), certain acquisitions of property from related parties, and certain property acquired in tax-free transactions. *See* I.R.C. § 168(f).

Personal Property. Before the 1986 T.R.A., tangible personal property was divided into four general cost recovery periods that were based on the nature of the asset (3–, 5–, 10– and 15–year classes). Section 168(b)(1) provided that the annual deduction was a pre-determined percentage of the unadjusted basis of the property.

The 1986 T.R.A. drastically revamped the A.C.R.S. system that was first introduced in 1981. Tangible personal property placed in service after July 31, 1986, is divided into six general cost-recovery periods that are based on the Asset Depreciation Range (A.D.R.) system in effect prior to 1981. The annual deduction permitted is that allowed by the double-declining-balance method for 3–, 5–, 7–, and 10–year property, the 150–percent declining-balance method for 15– and 20–year property, and the straight-line method for 27.5– and 39–year real property. *See* I.R.C. § 168(b). However, under I.R.C. § 50(c), before calculating the A.C.R.S. deduction, basis must be reduced by 100% of the I.R.C. § 47 rehabilitation credit taken by the taxpayer and 50% of any I.R.C. § 48 energy credit or reforestation credit taken. Congress enacted the basis-reduction requirements described above because it determined that the combined tax benefits of both a credit and A.C.R.S. were too great.

Most tangible personal property is now divided into classes, as defined by I.R.C. § 168(c) and (e). Generally, they can be described as follows:

3–year: includes any race-horse more than 2 years and less than 13 years old when placed in service, and *any other asset* with an A.D.R. midpoint ("class life") of 4 years or less, excluding autos and trucks;

5–year: includes autos, light trucks, property used in research and development activities, computers, semiconductor manufacturing equipment, and *any other assets* with an A.D.R. midpoint of more than 4 but less than 10 years;

7–year: includes railroad tracks, agricultural structures, any property which is not real property and is not otherwise classified, and *any other asset* with an A.D.R. midpoint of more than 10 but less than 16 years;

10–year: includes *any asset* with an A.D.R. midpoint of more than 16 but less than 20 years;

15–year: includes municipal wastewater treatment plants, telephone distribution plants, and *any asset* with an A.D.R. midpoint between 20 and 25 years;

20–year: any asset with an A.D.R. midpoint of 25 or more years.

Real Property. The 1986 T.R.A. lengthened the recovery period for real property by introducing a 27.5–year recovery period for residential rental real estate and a 39–year recovery period for other real property. *See* § 168(c). Only the straight-line depreciation method is allowed under A.C.R.S. for real property. *See* § 168(b)(3).

The amount of recovery for the year in which the property is placed in service generally is determined as if it were placed in service at the midpoint of the taxable year (in which the property is actually placed in service), called the half-year convention. For non-residential real property and residential rental property, the amount of recovery is determined by the mid-month convention, which, as its name suggests, treats all property placed in service during any month as placed in service at the midpoint of such month. *See* I.R.C. § 168(d)(1) and § 168(d)(2).

Under § 168(b)(3) and (5) a taxpayer (as an alternative to A.C.R.S.) can elect to take straight-line depreciation over the applicable recovery periods that, if elected, apply to all property in a particular class for that year. Also, § 168(g) requires alternative A.C.R.S. based on the straight-line method of depreciation to be used for selected property (*e.g.* any tax-exempt-use property, any tax-exempt-bond-financed property, etc.). A taxpayer may also elect to use alternative A.C.R.S. under § 168(g)(7).

So-called "anti-churning rules" are contained in § 168(f)(5) to prevent taxpayers from somehow bringing property placed in service before 1987 under the post–1986 A.C.R.S. rules by a "churning" or substitution transaction. They render the assets to which the rules apply ineligible for post–1986 treatment, but they do not apply to (1) any residential rental property or non-residential real property, or (2) any property if, for the first tax year in which the property is placed in service, the amount of depreciation allowable under the post–1986 rules would be less than that allowable under the pre–1987 A.C.R.S. rules. Also, a prior set of anti-churning rules applicable to property originally placed in service before 1981 have been retained.

Section 168(k) Special Allowance: *"Bonus Depreciation"*. Section 168(k) allows taxpayers to take additional first-year depreciation on most new depreciable personal property with a recovery period of 20 years or less. *See* I.R.C. § 168(k)(2). This "bonus depreciation" was granted as a tax incentive to increase business capital investment and thus to spur economic recovery and growth. To qualify, the property generally must be acquired after September 10, 2001 and before January 1, 2005. The § 168(k) allowance is 30% of the property's adjusted basis in the case of property acquired after September 10, 2001 and before May 6, 2003. The allowance increases to 50% of adjusted basis in the case of property acquired after May 5, 2003 and before January 1, 2005. *See* I.R.C. § 168(k)(4). The § 168(k) allowance is taken before A.C.R.S. deductions are calculated and the basis of the property is reduced by the amount of the § 168(k) allowance before A.C.R.S. deductions are calculated. I.R.C. § 168(k)(1). A taxpayer may elect to forego the benefits of § 168(k) and may elect to take 30% depreciation in lieu of 50% depreciation. *See* I.R.C. § 168(k)(2)(c)(iii), (4)(E).

Section 179 Election to Expense Certain Property. Section 179 allows taxpayers (other than trusts, estates, or certain non-corporate lessors) to elect to treat the cost of qualifying property (namely "section 179 property") as an expense rather than as a capital expenditure. Qualifying "section 179 property" generally is defined as any tangible property (to which § 168 applies) that is § 1245 property (as defined in section 1245(a)(3)) and that is acquired by purchase for use in the active conduct of a trade or business. The dollar limitations have gradually increased to a maximum of $100,000 per year in taxable years beginning after 2002 and before 2006 ($25,000 thereafter). That limit is reduced by the amount by which the cost of § 179 property placed in service in that year exceeds $400,000 ($200,000 after 2005). *See* I.R.C. §§ 179(a), (b)(1), (b)(2). In 2004 and 2005, the $100,000 and $400,000 figures are adjusted for inflation. I.R.C. § 179(b)(5). Because § 179 allows the taxpayer to *expense* the cost of qualifying property, a deduction under § 179 is taken before § 168 A.C.R.S. is calculated (including § 168(k)) and a § 179 deduction reduces the basis of the property. I.R.C. § 1016(a)(2).

Goodwill and Other Intangibles: I.R.C. § 197. In 1993, Congress enacted § 197, which allows an amortization deduction for goodwill and certain other intangibles. The amount of the deduction for an "amortizable section 197 intangible" (defined below) is determined by amortizing the adjusted basis (for purposes of determining gain) of the intangible ratably over the 15–year period beginning with the month in which the intangible was acquired. Section 197 applies to property acquired after the date of enactment of the statute, August 10, 1993, unless the taxpayer makes a special election.

Section 197 grants an amortization deduction only to "amortizable section 197 intangibles." According to § 197(d), "section 197 intangibles" include: goodwill; going-concern value; workforce in place; business books and records, operating systems, and customer lists; patents, copyrights, formulas, processes, designs, and patterns; any license, permit, or other right granted by a government unit or agency; any covenant not to compete entered into in connection with an acquisition of an interest in a trade or business; any franchise, trademark, or trade name; composition of market; market share; supplier relationships; and, in the case of financial institutions, deposit base. Section 1060 provides special allocation rules to be used to allocate the purchase price of the assets of a going business among the tangible and intangible assets, such as "goodwill" or going-concern value.

A "section 197 intangible" will not be an "amortizable § 197 intangible" unless it is held in connection with the conduct of a trade or business or an activity described in § 212. *See* § 197(c)(1). Also not amortizable are certain intangibles such as goodwill or going-concern value if these intangibles are created by the taxpayer—unless they are created in connection with a transaction involving the acquisition of assets constituting a trade or business. *See* § 197(c)(2). Property that qualifies as an "amortizable section 197 intangible" is allowed no depreciation or amortization deduction other than the one provided for by § 197; thus, § 197 is exclusive. I.R.C. § 197(b).

Certain property is specifically excluded from the reach of § 197. For example, an interest in land or in a corporation, partnership, trust, or estate is not a "section 197 intangible." Certain computer software is excluded. Also, unless the interests are acquired in an acquisition of assets constituting a trade or business, "section 197 intangibles" do not include interests in a patent or copyright or in a film, sound recording, videotape, book, or similar property. *See* § 197(d) for a complete list of property specifically included within the definition of

"§ 197 intangible," *and see* § 197(e) for a list of exclusions.

Similarly, I.R.C. § 248 allows a taxpayer to treat the organizational expenditures of forming a new corporation as deferred expenses and to deduct them ratably over a 5–year period. Section 709 provides the same treatment for amounts paid or incurred to organize a partnership. Other code sections also provide special cost-recovery rules for items that would otherwise have to be capitalized. *See, e.g.,* I.R.C. §§ 174 (research and experimental expenditures), 195 (start-up expenditures); *see* § 43, *supra.*

§ 45. Investment Credit

For some years in the 1960's, a seven-percent investment credit was allowed by I.R.C. § 38 and § 46(a) for tangible personal property used in the taxpayer's trade or business. The credit was suspended for a term and was repealed in 1969, although it continued to apply to some pre-repeal investments. In 1971 the investment credit was restored, at the seven-percent rate. The rate of the credit was raised to 10% in 1975 and remained at that level through 1986. *See* I.R.C. § 46.

The 1986 T.R.A. generally repealed the 10% regular investment tax credit ("I.T.C.") for property placed in service after December 31, 1985. Nevertheless, it remains important to understand the concept of an investment tax credit. Some specialized tax credits patterned after the I.T.C. remain in the law. *See* the "General Business Credit" of § 38, actually composed of a dozen more specific credits. *And see* § 46 and its "Investment Credit", consisting of three components. And, as experience shows, the I.T.C. may be re-instated at any time.

When in effect, the investment credit gave a credit (not a deduction) against tax liability for a statutory percentage of a taxpayer's investment in qualified assets (such as depreciable property, other than buildings, used in the trade or business). Thus, a taxpayer who bought a 10–percent credit-eligible machine for $1,000 and put it into service during the tax year would enjoy a credit of $100 against tax for that year. It was as if the price of the machine had been only $900, or as if the government simply sent him a check of $100 for that year. The credit was granted principally to encourage investment in credit-qualified property and thus stimulate the economy, increase profits, and/or reduce prices, stimulate demand and provide more jobs.

The statute contained various rules to define property eligible for the credit, to set the amount of the credit, to put a ceiling on the amount of credit any one taxpayer could receive, to determine the effect of the credit on depreciation, to recapture the credit in some instances, and to suspend, reinstate, or terminate the credit.

A tax credit differs from a deduction in that it is subtracted at its face value from tax liability, whereas a deduction reduces taxable income and hence reduces tax only by the percentage of its face value equal to the marginal rate of tax. So, with a credit of 10%, the government pays 10% of the cost of the property. The credit is like a (tax-exempt) cash subsidy.

§ 46.　Leasing and Tax Allowances

A taxpayer must be the *owner* of property used in a trade or business to be entitled to take depreciation (§ 167), A.C.R.S. (§ 168), or expense deductions (§ 179). If a user of property is considered the *lessee*, he may deduct rental payments made on the property, under I.R.C. § 162, as an ordinary and necessary business expense. Thus, if business property is being leased, the *lessor* may take the allowable depreciation or A.C.R.S. deductions. In this area of great economic significance, the administration of the tax law has long blurred the definition of property ownership by a distinction between "conditional sales" or "financing arrangements" and "leases" of primarily, but not exclusively, personal property used in a trade or business. Taxpayers have been structuring their transactions to take advantage of the deductions most favorable to them (i.e., those of an owner-lessor, owner-purchaser, or lessee), but the Internal Revenue Service has generally relied on its own criteria to determine the status of a transaction as a "true lease" or a "financing arrangement." In the former, the lessor is the owner, entitled to depreciation or ACRS deductions. In the latter, a conditional sale or loan, the user may take these tax benefits.

Prior to 1981, a number of specified requirements had to be met in order to qualify as a lease for the purpose of an I.R.S. *advance ruling*. They were not necessarily determinative of the final outcome. *See* Rev. Procs. 75–21, 1975–1 C.B. 715; 75–28, 1975–1 C.B. 752; 76–30, 1976–2 C.B. 647.

Judicial decisions did not always rely on the same factors. A notable example is Frank Lyon Co. v. United States (S.Ct.1978), involving a sale-leaseback of real property, when the Court balanced over 30 factors and finally held for the taxpayer and characterized the transaction as a lease.

With the 1981 enactment of E.R.T.A., Congress decided to make lease characterization more definitely available. The underlying purpose was not so much to clarify the state of the law but to augment and disperse the stimulus to invest in new equipment provided by A.C.R.S. and liberalized investment credit allowances. Because many companies in need of new equipment were incurring losses, A.C.R.S. and other deductions provided no investment incentive to them as they had no tax liability. So that these companies could benefit from A.C.R.S. and the increased investment credits, Congress created "safe-harbor leasing" by means of which nontaxpaying businesses could transfer tax benefits to profitable corporations in exchange for less expensive equipment financing. Thus, a profitable business would provide part of the financing on a lease of equipment to a loss company while benefiting from investment credit and A.C.R.S. deductions. The safe harbor of I.R.C. § 168(f)(8) (prior to the 1986 T.R.A.) guaranteed that the transaction would qualify as a lease rather than as a "financing arrangement" or "sale," by virtue of little more than the "lease" label on the papers. The taxpayer eligible for the benefits but not in a position to utilize them thus could "sell" them to a profitable taxpayer in return for favorable terms.

Later, a new category of leases, generally applicable to those entered into after December 31, 1983, was designated a "finance-lease." (*See* pre–1987 I.R.C. §§ 168(f)(8) and (i), as effective for property placed in service after 1983.) If the parties complied with the requirements of the statute, their transaction would be characterized as a lease for tax purposes. Aside from its tax benefits, the lease had to have economic substance, and the lessor reasonably had to expect to derive a profit from the transaction. The lessee did not need to have an investment in the property.

The foregoing statutory "finance lease" rules that determined whether a transaction was a lease or a purchase for purposes of ascertaining who was entitled to deductions for business expenses and depreciation generally were repealed by the 1986 T.R.A. for agreements entered into after 1986. So, in general, beginning in 1987, *non-statutory* rules apply to determine whether a transaction is a lease. Under these rules, the courts and the I.R.S. look to the economic substance of the transaction rather than to its form or to some artificial safe-harbors. *See, e.g.,* Rev. Proc. 2001–28; Rev. Proc. 2001–29 (on standards for advance rulings).

The equalization of investment incentives by the mechanism of leasing is highly controversial. For the argument that the law should not differentiate between "leasing" and "financing" for tax purposes, not for incentive but for reasons of simplicity, certainty and ease of compliance/administration, *see* Note, *"Safe Harbor" As Tax Reform: Taxpayer Election of Lease Treatment,* 95 Harv.L.Rev. 1648 (1982), which contains clear explanations and examples of the earlier categories of "leases" and safe-harbor leases.

§ 47. Depletion Allowances

Sections 611–613A authorize deductions for depletion of specified mineral and other natural deposits. Depletable assets include such resources as mines, oil and gas wells, other natural deposits, timber, and geothermal resources. Often the ownership of such assets is divided and the depletion deduction must be allocated between the owners. Some economic interests in depletable resources are not ownership interests; such items include leases, subleases, rights to royalty payments and income interests taken as security or as payment. Nevertheless, such interests may be entitled to depletion deductions under the concept of "economic interest" developed by the courts to determine the right to depletion allowances. This economic interest, roughly speaking, means an investment interest in the minerals in place which will provide the only resource for recovering the investment. The parties may determine this interest by the terms of their contract. Still, this problem has kept the courts busy.

Cost depletion, like depreciation, bases the allowance on historic cost of the income-producing property. *See* I.R.C. § 612. (Discovery value at one time was used as the measure of tax-free recovery.) If taxpayer buys rights to extract a pool of oil from the ground for $1,000,000, he should be allowed to recover his capital tax-free when he extracts and sells the oil. That is, the receipts from the depletable property should be regarded as containing a return of taxpayer's capital investment. A proportionate part of receipts each year should be received free of taxation as income. Treating the oil as a "wasting asset," cost depletion would allow annual deductions designed to permit him to receive $1,000,000 tax-free over the life of his pumping operations. To do so, the law allows taxpayer to divide his investment by the (estimated) number of recoverable units in the mineral or other deposit. This cost per unit is then multiplied by the number of units sold each year, and the result is the depletion deduction allowed for that year. The more units sold, the higher the depletion allowance. The process stops when the total cost has been recovered.

Percentage Depletion. In contrast to cost depletion (§§ 611–612), the *percentage depletion* deduction departs from recovery of cost as a measure of the deduction. A percentage of income, rather than cost, is deductible each year, even if all cost (or discovery value) has been received previously. Thus, percentage depletion admittedly offers an extra tax "subsidy" to discovery, development and exhaustion of eligible reserves.

Since 1969, percentage depletion for oil and gas and some other deposits has been sharply curtailed or repealed. Other deposits or energy sources such as geothermal steam remain eligible for percentage depletion.

The percentage of *gross* revenue that may be deducted as depletion depends on the kind of deposit. (The percentages range from 5% to 22%.) However, except for oil and gas properties, the deduction cannot exceed 50% of the *taxable income* from the property, computed without the depletion allowance.

Percentage depletion for natural deposits, as defined in I.R.C. § 613, offers an immensely valuable allowance as an alternative to cost depletion. Employing percentage depletion, the taxpayer computes a flat (statutory) percentage of his gross income and deducts that amount from gross income each year. He continues to do so as long as the property produces income—even after his actual cost has been recovered in full. Some taxpayers elect to use *cost depletion* in early years when they are extracting and selling a large number of units of the deposit, and then they shift to percentage depletion when cost has been recovered or otherwise when percentage depletion will give a larger deduction.

The subsidy given by percentage depletion and its departure from the recovery-of-capital principle in cost depletion and in depreciation began after World War I. Supposedly to encourage exploration for minerals, cost depletion was enlarged by allowing *discovery value* rather than cost to be the measure of tax free recovery. The problem remained, however, how to estimate the number of depletable units in advance of extraction. To solve this problem, *percentage* depletion was authorized in 1924. Since that time, it was expanded to include more minerals and other deposits and to increase rates of depletion in some instances. Later it was contracted because of undue profits and tax benefits realized by some companies. Some resources such as timber, oil and gas (in most instances), water and soil are eligible only for cost depletion, not percentage depletion.

The gross income from which percentage depletion is calculated must be limited to income from extracting and selling the deposit, not from refining, processing or manufacturing it. When a vertically integrated taxpayer uses the extracted material in later processes and does not sell it raw, an amount must be computed as the constructive gross income from mining. *See, e.g.,* U.S. v. Cannelton Sewer Pipe Co. (S.Ct.1960).

One added tax benefit for the industries that enjoy depletion allowances is the option to expense (deduct currently) exploration and development expenditures (including intangible drilling costs— I.D.C.) instead of capitalizing them. *See* I.R.C. §§ 263(c), 616–617. Such expenditures generally result in greater tax benefit if deducted at once and would never be recovered if percentage depletion were used since that depletion is based on gross income, not on the cost of the capital invested in the enterprise.

§ 48. Other Allowances

The investment tax credit gave a tax subsidy and incentive for investment in tangible equipment used in producing income. *See* § 45, *supra.* Another factor of production is human capital, labor, the employment of which can add to output and help the economy and society in myriad ways. Recent years have witnessed growing use of the tax laws to encourage employment.

Currently, the § 51 work-opportunity credit is equal to 40 percent of the first $6,000 of qualified first-year wages. However, if an employer elects to take the work-opportunity credit, the deduction taken for wages paid must be reduced by the amount of the credit (I.R.C. § 280C). The full wage deduction may be taken if the credit is not elected.

The tax credit for employment has been described as in part designed to offset the disincentive to hire that stems from the additional Social Security payroll tax the employer will have to pay if it adds another employee. And the (refundable) earned income credit, *see* § 63, *infra,* has been viewed as an offset for an employee's social security tax burden, usually thought to be regressive because of its income ceiling and lack of exemptions.

The work-opportunity credit can be viewed as something of a counterpart (for human capital) of the special incentives for investment in depreciable property (e.g., §§ 168(k) and 179). Even so, human capital is not treated quite the same, perhaps not so advantageously, by the credit (nor by the income tax law generally) as is other capital.

An incremental research credit is allowed in present I.R.C. § 41, extended at least through June 2004. The incremental credit rate is 20%. The allowable research credit is computed by taking the sum of (1) 20% of the excess (if any) of the qualified research expenses over the base period research expense, and (2) 20% of the university basic research payments.

Other important credits are to be found in I.R.C. §§ 21–45F, for tax withheld on wages, foreign income taxes paid, expenses for dependent care services, expenditures to provide access to disabled individuals, and other activities. Section 39 allows for some carryback and carryforward of unused credits.

Compare the credit form of allowance with other forms, especially the deduction or the deduction with a floor or a ceiling or a high-income phase-out, in connection with coming topics as well as with deductions covered in this chapter.

Also, take note of I.R.C. §§ 9001–9013 which establish a check-off system for contributions to political campaigns in a presidential election.

For description of other credits, such as the earned income credit, *see* § 63, *infra*.

CHAPTER V

MIXED (PERSONAL AND PROFIT SEEKING) DEDUCTIONS AND OTHER ALLOWANCES

§ 49. Introduction

The deductions (and other allowances) considered in Chapter IV were those sufficiently related to income-producing activities to be allowable as costs of producing income. As such, they had to be delineated to exclude expenditures that were personal (consumption or saving) in origin, purpose, or effect. Section 262 of the I.R.C. emphasizes that, except as otherwise provided, no deduction is allowed for personal, living, or family expenses.

The Code does occasionally "provide otherwise." That is, it allows deductions for some expenditures that are partly or wholly, sometimes or often, personal in nature. Those deductible expenses that usually or primarily are personal are treated in Chapter VI below. This Chapter covers mixed expenses; expenses that for some or most taxpayers, sometimes or usually, stem from personal as well as, or instead of, profit-seeking activities. Some of these expenses would be deductible, for some taxpayers at least, or on some occasions, as costs of producing income under I.R.C. §§ 162 or 212. Others would rarely if ever be deductible but for the special provisions made for them in the Code.

Whether an item is deductible as a "personal" or as an "income-producing" expenditure is more than merely a matter of theory. Most deductions that are profit-related are subtracted from *Gross Income* in arriving at *Adjusted Gross Income* (A.G.I.), for individuals. *See* I.R.C. § 62. (Corporations do not enjoy "personal" or "mixed" deductions and do not compute "adjusted gross income;" they compute "taxable income" directly from gross income.) Profit-related deductions, taken "above the line" of Adjusted Gross Income, reduce A.G.I. from what it otherwise would be to a smaller amount. That result is important because some other deductions, taken later in the process of computing *Taxable Income*, are allowable only up to, or (in other instances) above, a percentage of A.G.I. For example, "miscellaneous itemized deductions" for any taxable year shall be allowed only to the extent that the aggregate of such deductions exceeds 2% of adjusted gross income. *See* I.R.C. § 67.

In addition, I.R.C. § 68 imposes an overall limitation on itemized deductions for taxpayers with A.G.I. above $100,000. Section 68 reduces otherwise allowable itemized deductions by the lesser of (1) 3 percent of the excess of A.G.I. over $100,000, or (2) 80 percent of the amount of itemized deductions otherwise allowable for the taxable year. In effect, this graduated reduction of otherwise deductible amounts constitutes an effective tax rate increase, above the nominal, statutory rates, for higher-income taxpayers. Deductions for medical expenses, investment interest, and casualty and wagering losses are excluded from the definition of itemized deductions for the purpose of § 68. The $100,000 figure is adjusted for inflation after 1991 and is $142,700 in 2004. The § 68 reduction in itemized deductions is phased out in 2006–2009 (⅔ of the reduction applies in 2006 and 2007; ⅓ of the reduction applies in 2008 and 2009). Section 68 does not apply to taxable years beginning after December 31, 2009.

Non-business deductions, to the extent they exceed the taxpayer's standard deduction, are subtracted from A.G.I. in computing taxable income. Consequently they do not affect A.G.I. *See* I.R.C. § 63. If or to the extent that the non-business deductions do not exceed the standard deduction, they do not provide any benefit to the taxpayer—he or she may receive that amount of income free from tax in any event. In fact, the standard deduction partly was intended to substitute for itemized deductions for many taxpayers—for the sake of simplicity and perhaps equity as well. However, some items, such as taxes or interest, can either be deducted above the A.G.I. line or are used in computing "excess itemized deductions" (that are subtracted below the line), depending on the character of the particular item for the given taxpayer in the given year. *See, e.g.,* Brown v. U.S. (5th Cir.1970) (taxes). Deductions for expenses of producing income in an activity not engaged in for profit (*e.g.,* a hobby), unlike "business expenses," are deductible from adjusted gross income in computing taxable income and thus may be taken only if the taxpayer itemizes deductions. *See* I.R.C. §§ 62, 63, 183.

Congress, however, has decided to allow some items such as alimony (spousal support) to be deducted "above the line," from gross income to arrive at A.G.I., mainly to make certain that a taxpayer will have the advantage of the deduction even if he or she does not itemize deductions. *See* I.R.C. § 62(a)(10). Some other costs of producing income must be taken as itemized deductions, between A.G.I. and taxable income, simply because of the structure of the statute and the definitions and rules of § 62, which delineates what may be subtracted from gross income to determine A.G.I. *See, e.g.,* I.R.C. § 62(a)(1); Rev.Rul. 76–278, 1976–2 C.B. 84 (executives' premiums on liability policy concerning wrongs committed while acting as corporate employees).

By converting a deduction to a credit, as Congress has done with the dependent and child-care allowance (formerly a § 214 deduction, now a § 21 credit, *see* § 57 below), the legislators can affect the interaction between the allowance and rules for itemizing deductions or taking a standard allowance in lieu of itemizing, and between the allowance and the computation of A.G.I., which in turn may affect other deductions (such as for charitable contributions and medical expenses—*see* Ch. VI, below).

As an alternative to the I.R.C. § 1 tax rates on taxable income, § 3 conveniently imposes a tax determined by *tax tables,* using the § 1 rates, for taxpayers whose taxable income does not exceed the "ceiling amount."

To sum up the differences between individual and business taxpayers: the business taxpayer starts with gross sales or gross receipts and subtracts the cost of goods sold (beginning inventory plus additions to inventory minus closing inventory) to determine gross income. All available deductions must then be taken from gross income to derive taxable income. An individual, in contrast, must determine adjusted gross income as a step between gross income and taxable income. Adjusted gross income is gross income less the deductions outlined in I.R.C. § 62—trade or business and other cost-of-producing-income deductions and some others. From adjusted gross income, the individual taxpayer subtracts his or her allowable itemized deductions, if the amount allowed exceeds the standard deduction, and personal exemptions to determine taxable income. Again, the so-called "miscellaneous itemized deductions" are allowed only to the extent they exceed 2% of A.G.I. Since higher A.G.I. reduces the amount of deductions allowed, this rule acts to increase the effective rate of tax, above the nominal statutory rates of I.R.C. § 1, for higher income taxpayers. *See* I.R.C. § 67. Further limits on itemized deductions may be imposed by § 68, as discussed earlier in this section.

Note that no deduction may be taken by any taxpayer unless the deduction is specifically authorized by the statute. No counterpart of § 61(a) exists to serve as a "catch-all" for deductions. No unstated deductions parallel the unstated exclusions from income examined earlier. Moreover, courts often say that since deductions are a matter of legislative grace, they are to be construed strictly (against the taxpayer).

§ 50. Interest

Before 1987, I.R.C. § 163 allowed as a deduction "all interest paid or accrued within the taxable year on indebtedness." Interestingly enough, § 163 did not then restrict the deduction to business interest, *i.e.,* interest incurred on borrowings to finance income-producing activity. Accordingly, interest on personal loans (to buy a TV set or a vacation trip) was just as deductible as interest on a debt incurred to provide working capital in a business, to purchase a factory, or to pay wages. Interest on borrowing for income-producing activities probably would be deductible, under I.R.C. § 162 or § 212, even if § 163 were repealed. Interest on personal loans would not be deductible were it not for pre–1987 § 163. Personal interest was an itemized deduction, one whose benefit would be lost if taxpayer did not itemize deductions. Business interest can be deducted (above the A.G.I. line) in any event.

The 1986 T.R.A. eliminated the § 163 deduction for interest on most "personal" loans, with a big exception for qualified residence interest (on home mortgages). *See* § 163(h). Consequently, only business or profit-related interest expense is deductible now, except for the specific exceptions in § 163(h).

The deduction for interest on gain-seeking borrowing treats that interest as a cost of generating income. Interest on business borrowing no doubt is deductible so that if an individual or corporation borrows to engage in purposive, (hopefully) profitable activity, he or it shall not fare worse from an income tax standpoint than one who finances the venture with capital that otherwise would have been yielding income (and which income he therefore foregoes). The interest-paying borrower may be compared to the renter of assets and both contrasted with the owner of assets whose imputed income is excluded from the owner's tax base.

However, the deduction for interest even on gain-seeking borrowing often is limited (for noncorporate taxpayers). Where the interest is incurred in connection with a taxpayer's conduct of a trade or business in which the taxpayer materially participates (except as an employee), the interest is fully deductible. *See* I.R.C. § 163(h)(2)(A). If the interest is incurred in connection with an investment of the taxpayer or with a trade or business in which the (noncorporate) taxpayer does *not* materially participate, the deductibility of such interest is subject to several limitations. If interest is connected with a passive activity, it will be aggregated with other deductions connected with that activity and subject to the passive loss limitations. *See* I.R.C. § 469. Interest incurred in connection with portfolio investments is subject to the investment interest limitations, and it is deductible only to the extent of the taxpayer's net investment income. *See* I.R.C. § 163(d)(1).

The 1986 T.R.A. eliminated the deduction for interest of a noncorporate taxpayer that is incurred in connection with most consumer purchases. Consequently interest on a loan to finance a personal family car or vacation is no longer deductible.

Section 221 grants a special deduction for interest paid on qualified education loans. For the first 60 months in which interest payments are required on a qualified education loan (as defined in I.R.C. § 221(d)(1)), the taxpayer may deduct up to $2,500 in interest payments. The deduction is phased out for taxpayers with modified adjusted gross income (as defined in I.R.C. § 221(b)(2)(C)) between $50,000 and $65,000 ($100,000 and $130,000 for joint returns). These phaseout amounts are indexed for inflation. I.R.C. § 221(f). The deduction is not available to an individual who can be claimed as a dependent on another person's tax return. I.R.C. § 221(c).

A major exception to post–1986 nondeductibility of personal interest allows a deduction for "qualified residence interest." *See* § 163(h)(2)(D) and Temp. Regs. § 1.163–10T. "Qualified residence interest" is interest on a debt secured by the principal residence of the taxpayer and one other residence selected by the taxpayer and used as a residence (for the greater of 14 days or 10% of the number of days it was rented). However, if the taxpayer does not rent or use the selected property at all during the year, it will still be considered a qualified residence.

The amount of interest on a debt secured by a qualified residence that can constitute deductible qualified residence interest is subject to several limitations. A taxpayer may deduct interest only on "acquisition indebtedness" and "home equity indebtedness." I.R.C. § 163(h)(3). Acquisition indebtedness is defined as debt incurred to acquire, construct, or substantially rehabilitate the taxpayer's principal or secondary residence. The total amount of acquisition indebtedness that can give use to deductible residence interest is $1 million. This debt is reduced as the principal amount is paid off. The only way to *increase* acquisition debt is to make substantial improvements in the residence.

The other category of qualified residence interest, home equity indebtedness, is borrowing such as a second mortgage. Home equity indebtedness cannot exceed the difference between the taxpayer's total acquisition debt and the home's fair market value. Home equity debt is also limited to $100,000. A taxpayer's overall debt on both a principal and second home thus cannot exceed $1,100,000 (home equity plus acquisition indebtedness).

To illustrate acquisition and home equity indebtedness, suppose a taxpayer bought a home 15 years ago for $100,000, and has completely paid off her mortgage. The home is now worth $200,000. In 2004 the taxpayer obtains a $150,000 home loan, and uses $130,000 to make home improvements and

$20,000 to buy a car. Interest on the entire loan is deductible, since $130,000 is acquisition indebtedness, and the remaining $20,000 qualifies as home equity indebtedness.

Why did Congress for so many years allow interest on all personal borrowing to be deductible? The deduction for personal interest could be justified by one or more of several considerations. One practical reason for the deduction was that if interest is deductible only on business loans, it often is hard to ascertain whether a given borrowing was for business or personal uses. That would be especially true, for example, if taxpayers simply pooled their business and personal funds or took to borrowing on their business assets in order to make funds available to finance their vacations. Secondly, the personal interest deduction could stimulate the economy, profits, and employment by reducing the cost of consumer finance. Thirdly, the deduction could help equalize the borrowing taxpayer with one who uses savings or other property to finance his consumption, and who thereby forgoes income (and tax) on those savings. The fact that personal interest remains deductible for "qualified residence" indebtedness proves enormously important to many homeowners who borrow on a mortgage or "deed of trust" to buy a home. Deducting the interest (which often amounts to a large share of each monthly payment) makes home ownership much cheaper than it otherwise would be and perhaps cheaper than renting equivalent accommodations. Congress recognized that the deduction for personal interest tended to encourage people to spend rather than save. Government was subsidizing, by a tax expenditure, individual borrowing to purchase personal consumption goods or services. By eliminating the deductibility of personal interest, Congress intended to rebalance the tax law's incentive to borrow rather than save.

Some cases have tested the limits of what is "interest ... on indebtedness." Since dividends are not deductible by corporations, payments by those corporations to their shareholders are sometimes called "interest" though they be excessive in amount (given any actual indebtedness to the shareholders) or otherwise appropriately regarded as a distribution of profits. Such "interest" payments will be recast and treated as non-deductible dividends. Similarly, "interest" must be differentiated from partnership shares of profits, gifts, the purchase price of an asset, repayment of principal on a debt, and other non-deductible payments. Intra-family "interest" payments are particularly suspect.

Interest need not be denominated as such to be deductible. "Points" paid by a home purchaser on mortgage financing (a fee equal to one or more percentage points of the principal amount of the mortgage) are deductible. *See* I.R.C. § 461(g)(2). So is a prepayment charge when a mortgage loan is paid off before maturity. Interest "on indebtedness" includes interest for money borrowed, owed for services rendered, or for the purchase of goods. Under I.R.C. § 483 and § 163(b), interest will be imputed if adequate interest is not separately stated in a contract for installment payments or deferred payments in the sale and purchase of property. (Truth-in-lending laws now require separate statement of interest more often than formerly was the case.)

"Hidden" interest can arise elsewhere, too. I.R.C. § 7872 ("gift loans") provides that in the case of any loan with a below-market interest rate, the foregone interest must be treated as transferred from the lender to the borrower and retransferred by the borrower to the lender as (potentially deductible) interest. In the event of a loan with original issue discount (one "borrows" $100 but gets only $93 and must repay $100 at the due date), the amount of the discount ($7) serves as "interest." The deductible portion of the original issue discount for a taxable year is the aggregate daily discount portion of the original issue discount for the days during such taxable year. *See* I.R.C. § 163(e). *See also* §§ 1271–1275 on original issue discount or "O.I.D."

Interest generally is deductible in the period with respect to which the interest represents a charge for the use or forbearance of money. Thus, the cash-method taxpayer may not deduct prepaid interest when paid, but instead he or she must allocate the amounts not representing interest for that year to capital account; then he or she may deduct the amounts during their proper periods. *See* I.R.C. § 461(g)(1). The effect of this rule is that cash-method and accrual-method taxpayers generally treat prepaid interest in the same way.

A cash-method taxpayer generally can deduct interest only when it is "paid," and that requirement will not be met if the lender merely withholds interest, for example by lending $90 but requiring that $100 be repaid after one year.

In some situations, the Internal Revenue Code specifically denies a deduction for interest. Interest on indebtedness incurred to produce tax-exempt income (such as to purchase state or municipal bonds) may not be deducted because of I.R.C. § 265(a)(2). Since insurance proceeds are excluded from income by § 101, interest paid on a loan to buy or keep in effect a single-premium life insurance policy does not yield a deduction. *See* § 264(a)(2). Section 264(a)(3) prohibits a deduction for interest on a debt incurred to purchase or continue life insurance with a systematic borrowback plan. Section 163(d) blocks an interest deduction on investment indebtedness, with qualifications, to prevent a taxpayer from borrowing to buy an asset, paying interest only, deducting the interest, and selling the asset with gain taxed at capital gains rates. This section, in other words, was intended to discourage the acquisition of property by high-bracket taxpayers whose main aim was the interest deduction, or who sought to transmute ordinary income into capital gain. Other restrictions on the deductibility of interest are imposed by I.R.C. §§ 266 (carrying charges may be capitalized), 267(a) (interest on transactions between related taxpayers), and the general rule that one taxpayer may not deduct interest he pays on the debt of someone else. *See* Rev.Rul. 57–481, 1957–2 C.B. 48. *See also* § 249 (limitation on deduction of bond premium on repurchase); § 279(b) (corporate acquisition indebtedness); § 385 (interest vs. dividends).

In a famous line of cases, epitomized by Knetsch v. U.S. (S.Ct.1960), courts have denied a deduction for interest in schemes when the transaction was a "sham" or lacked "independent business purpose" or "economic substance." The reach of this judicial doctrine has not been fully defined. It surely does not mean that a deduction will be denied merely because a bona-fide and valid or real business/investment transaction would not be profitable enough to be undertaken if the interest payments were not deductible. But if a transaction can be profitable only by manufacturing an interest deduction in a situation where there is no "purposive activity" involving interest as an incident of the financing method, or if no real interest on a real debt is being paid at all, substance will triumph over form, and the deduction will not be allowed. Two doctrinal hurdles—sham and economic substance (or independent business purpose)—must be surmounted to gain a deduction.

Original Issue Discount and the Time Value of Money. Original issue discount is the difference between the face value of an obligation, like a promissory note or a bond, and the price at which it is sold (or the amount of money lent to the borrower, the person who "issued" the note or bond). For example, suppose B wants to borrow approximately $100 and "issues," or tries to sell, its bond or note in which B promises to pay the lender $100 plus interest at the end of 2 years (or perhaps to pay interest at this stated rate to the lender each year until the principal is paid in 2 years). Suppose the bond states the interest rate to be 7%. If that interest rate is inadequate, adjusted for risk, because the market generally offers and requires 8% interest, the issuer may have to sell the bond for, say, $98 or less. The extra $2, called "original issue discount," works economically like interest. The lender of the bond will receive 7% interest plus an extra $2 at maturity. The question is how to treat this discount paid by the borrower to the lender, for income tax purposes. It seems to be gain; should it be taxed only upon payment at maturity? Is it capital gain or ordinary income? Should the issuer be able to deduct the $2 as interest? When? Upon payment or as the obligation accrues over the years?

At one time, the Code (in 1939) treated the discount premium paid to the lender at maturity as capital gain. Later, the Supreme Court in U.S. v. Midland–Ross (S.Ct.1965) held that original issue discount (O.I.D.) was the functional equivalent of interest and not gain from selling a capital asset— the gain was ordinary income. The 1954 Internal Revenue Code enacted that principle.

This decision left open the question of (i) *when* the O.I.D. would be income—upon purchase, upon repayment, or ratably over the life of the bond as the interest was "earned," and (ii) when it could be deducted by the borrower. In 1969, Congress required the lender to accrue the O.I.D. ratably over time. Over the two-year time to maturity, the $2 discount would be taxable as income in the amount of $1 per year. Because of this inclusion, the lender's basis in the bond would be increased by $1 each year, and no further income from the O.I.D. would be taxable when the borrower paid $100 principal to the lender upon maturity. Some kind of ratable inclusion is acknowledged to be the right principle in general, but because the lender does not receive the O.I.D. cash until maturity, the lender is re-lending the O.I.D. "interest" to the borrower. So simple ratable inclusion doesn't take this compounding of interest into account.

In 1982, Congress enacted O.I.D. rules that do take this "compound interest" effect into account. These rules, now found in I.R.C. §§ 1271–1275, reduce the deduction available to the issuer (and the income includible to the lender) in the early years of an O.I.D. bond and increase the deductions (and income) in the later years, something called "back-loading," to take account of the effect of compounding. So, the lender of an O.I.D. bond must include in his income (and the issuer may deduct) a ratable portion of the original issue discount computed by referring to the yield to maturity in a way that takes compounding of interest into effect. The inclusion and upward basis increase is done, in effect, daily. *See generally* I.R.C. §§ 1271–1275. So, in the example, some amount less than $1 would be deductible in the first year and some amount greater than $1 in the second year.

§ 51. Taxes

Until 1964, I.R.C. § 164 allowed a deduction for *all* state and local taxes a taxpayer is obliged to pay and does pay or accrue. Now, § 164 limits the deduction to the many broad classes of taxes there listed (e.g., state and local real and personal property taxes, state and local income taxes, etc.) and defined in § 164(b). Despite this change, § 164 allows the deduction of most state and local taxes. The principal category of state and local taxes not deductible under § 164 is personal sales taxes. Also, *all* state, local and foreign taxes paid or accrued in carrying on a trade or business or a § 212 activity are deductible.

What is a tax, or an income tax, presents a question of scope. For example, in McGowan v. Comm. (Tax Court 1976), the Tax Court held that a compulsory contribution made by an employee to a state disability insurance fund was deductible as a state income tax. Some limitations on the deductibility of taxes are imposed by § 164(c)—for example, taxes amounting to assessments for a local benefit tending to increase the value of taxpayer's property are not deductible. So, if an owner of real property is assessed a tax to pay for a new street or sewer in front of his home, payment of the tax will not be deductible.

Section 275 specifically bars a deduction for certain taxes, whether they be gain-seeking, connected with a trade or business, or investment, or personal in nature. Examples of such non-deductible taxes include federal income and social security taxes, gift, estate and inheritance taxes, and withholding taxes. Also, the uniform capitalization rules in I.R.C. § 263A require that costs (including taxes) attributable to inventory be added to the cost of inventory and that costs attributable to producing or acquiring other property be capitalized.

Several reasons may be suggested for the I.R.C. § 164 deduction for taxes. First, constitutional shadows having to do with federalism may have fallen over suggestions that such taxes did not have to be allowed as deductions, as in the days when government salaries were exempted from tax for constitutional reasons. Secondly, many taxes amount to costs of producing income, such as when a business taxpayer pays real estate and sales taxes. Thirdly, and more importantly, the Federal deduction for payment of state taxes clearly assists states in raising revenue—at the expense of the federal treasury—by reducing the after-Federal-tax cost of paying deductible state income taxes. Fourthly, especially back in the days when Federal income tax rates went into the 90–percent range, state income taxes could possibly have extended the combined federal-state income tax rate over 100% were it not for the deduction. And, lastly, payment of state taxes does reduce the taxpayer's "ability to pay" the Federal Income Tax, whether in the business/investment or in the personal context.

State property taxes paid on a personal residence are deductible (though rent paid to occupy such premises is not), and this deduction seems to afford another important tax advantage of home ownership (over renting). However, a landlord's ability to deduct his/her/its property taxes on rental property may serve to reduce the rent charged in the market for residential rental accommodations. When a home or other real property is sold, I.R.C. § 164(d) requires an apportionment of taxes on real property between seller and purchaser (based on the customary allocation in an escrow statement) for time of occupancy. Section 1001(b) makes appropriate adjustments in the sale calculations for taxes imposed on the purchaser. Section 1012 makes similarly appropriate basis adjustments for the same taxes.

A taxpayer may also deduct all the ordinary and necessary expenses he pays or incurs during the taxable year in connection with the determination, collection, or refund of any tax. I.R.C. § 212(3). If liability for a tax on real property is contested, § 461(f) permits accrual of the contested liability in the year in which the protest of payment is made. If taxpayer gets a refund in a later year, taxability of the refund will depend on whether or not the earlier payment was deducted and produced a tax benefit. *See* I.R.C. § 111.

A credit is allowed (at the option of the taxpayer) for some foreign taxes paid, in lieu of a deduction under I.R.C. § 164, by §§ 27 and 901–908. *See* I.R.C. § 275.

§ 52. Losses, in General

Section § 165(a) states, as a general rule, that a deduction shall be allowed for any loss sustained during the taxable year and not compensated for by insurance or otherwise. Section 165(b) provides that the basis for determining loss under subsection (a) shall be the adjusted basis provided in § 1011 for determining loss from the sale or other disposition of property. Accordingly, to get a deduction, taxpayer must establish that he, she or it has a basis in the item lost. So, a failure to get an anticipated gain (that has not yet been taken into income) will not give rise to a loss deduction. *See, e.g.,* Escofil v. Comm. (3d Cir.1972). Basis generally requires an investment of cash or property, or prior inclusion in income. Generally, the basis requirement involves "property," and hence § 165 applies mainly to losses of or on property, intangible as well as tangible. Basis under § 1011 (adjusted basis) means cost of the property as determined by § 1012 (or other basis such as under §§ 1014 and 1015) adjusted as § 1016 requires for depreciation/cost recovery and other allowances.

Business and investment losses are deductible as part of the logic of taxing net income. To earn income, one must incur the risk, and therefore sometimes the actuality, of loss. It is a cost of doing business or investing. Also, of course, a loss reduces the taxpayer's ability to pay taxes. Furthermore, to tax gain but not allow an offset for losses would bias the income tax against risk. If the income tax is to remain "neutral" as to risk and investment decisions, it must allow a deduction for losses in profit-seeking activities or transactions. Otherwise, investments heavily laden with risk will go unmade or will require a much higher rate of return, if successful, to compensate for the unmitigated loss if unsuccessful.

Against this background must be reported the substantial inroads made by I.R.C. § 165(c) upon the general rule of § 165(a). Subsection (c) decrees that in the case of an individual taxpayer (not a corporation), a loss may be deductible only if it is (a) incurred in a trade or business, (b) incurred in a transaction entered into for profit, or (c) if it is a property loss (not connected with a trade or business or a transaction entered into for profit) arising from fire, storm, shipwreck, or other casualty, or from theft. The casualty and theft losses, moreover, are deductible only in excess of the first $100 for each casualty. Also, net nonbusiness casualty and theft losses are deductible only to the extent that such losses (after reduction of the $100 floor for each) in total also exceed 10 percent of an individual's adjusted gross income. *See* I.R.C. § 165(h)(2)(A). Other limitations are given in § 165(d)–(i), to be discussed shortly. Thus, for an individual taxpayer, losses that are incurred in a trade or business or in profit-seeking activity are deductible; losses arising in his personal life are deductible only if caused by a casualty or theft—and then only for the excess above $100, and only if aggregating in excess of 10 percent of adjusted gross income (and only if the taxpayer elects to itemize deductions). Hence many personal losses cannot be deducted. A taxpayer who sells a personal automobile or home or camera or painting at a loss will *realize* a loss, but the loss will not be *deductible* under § 165.

The literal language of I.R.C. § 165(a) and the limitation in § 165(c) to individuals would seem to allow non-individual taxpayers, such as corporations, to deduct all losses, whether or not incurred in business or through a casualty. Nevertheless, the Commissioner sought to deny a non-business, non-casualty loss to a corporation that sold resort property maintained primarily for the personal benefit of the shareholders and their families on the ground that a "trade or business" limitation should be read into the statute. Although the Tax Court agreed with the Commissioner, that decision was reversed on appeal. The appellate court held that the literal language of § 165 would not allow a trade or business limit to be read in. *See* International Trading Co. v. Comm. (Tax Court 1971) *rev'd* (7th Cir 1973). So, losses incurred on property used for personal, family, or living purposes will be deductible on sale by a corporation, unless (perhaps) this doctrine is employed merely to use a corporation to "front" for individuals.

A similar question is whether a corporation may deduct non-business *expenses* (versus losses), as in connection with a personal residence purchased from an officer-shareholder. Not only the "ordinary and necessary" (appropriate and helpful) limits of I.R.C. § 162, but also the anti-personal-deduction rules of § 262, will apply to deny the deduction of non-business expenses, or to treat them as the payment of (non-deductible) dividends to shareholders. *See* International Artists, Ltd. v. Comm. (Tax Court 1970); American Properties, Inc. v. Comm. (9th Cir.1958); Fred W. Amend Co. v. Comm. (Tax Court 1970). Depreciation deductions also will be disallowed on non-business property. *See* International Trading Co. v. Comm. (7th Cir.1960).

For any loss to be deductible, it must be "realized." Mere fluctuations in the market value of the piece of property are not deductible (just as they are not includible in income on the "up side"). For a loss to be deductible, a closed and completed transaction, fixed by identifiable events, bona-fide, and actually sustained during the taxable period must mark the event. Regs. § 1.165–1(b). So, if property has declined in value or even become worthless, it must be sold or abandoned, or some other event such as total destruction must occur, to provide a deduction. *See, e.g.,* Reporter Pub. Co. v. Comm. (10th Cir.1953).

In addition, losses from any activity engaged in to carry on a trade or business or to produce income are limited to the amount that the individual investor places "at risk" in the particular activity. *See* I.R.C. § 465. The reason for this "at risk" rule is to restrict some tax shelter investment benefits that rely on borrowed money (or "leverage") from non-recourse loans—for which the investor does not have personal liability—to produce artificial loss deductions in excess of the amount that the investor actually could lose in any event. An important exception to the § 465 "at-risk" loss limitation rules provides that, for real estate investments, "qualified nonrecourse financing" is considered at risk. *See* I.R.C. § 465(b)(6); *see also* § 42, *supra*.

Another limitation on the allowance of otherwise deductible losses was enacted in 1986. Section 469 states that a loss from a "passive activity" may not freely be deducted from other income—that is, income from other than passive activities. Losses from passive activities thus are deductible only against income from that same passive activity or from other passive activities, but not from income from a non-passive activity or from portfolio income (such as dividends, interest or royalties). (There are some small exceptions and carryover possibilities.) The term "passive activity" includes rental activity (*e.g.*, rental real estate), with a special $25,000 offset (exception) that phases out with modified adjusted gross income over $100,000. *See* I.R.C. § 469(c)(2) and (i). However, if certain taxpayers in the real property business (measured by objective tests) materially participate in their real property trade or business, their rental activities will no longer be considered passive activities. *See* § 469(c)(7).

Under § 165(d), losses from wagering transactions may be taken only to the extent of gains from wagering, whether by a professional gambler or an amateur. In other words, § 165(c) does not apply to gambling losses. *See* Nitzberg v. Comm. (9th Cir. 1978). The U.S. Supreme Court held, in Comm. v. Groetzinger (S.Ct.1987), that a full-time, professional gambler who bet solely for his own account was "engaged in a trade or business" under § 162, and hence his losses were not items of tax preference subject to the minimum tax. This decision did not, however, imply that his gambling losses could be deducted under § 162 or § 165 in excess of his (taxable) gambling winnings, because of the § 165(d) limitation. A professional gambler may take his losses, subject to § 165(d), from gross income in arriving at adjusted gross income; an amateur may take them only from adjusted gross income in determining taxable income, also subject to § 165(d). *See also* Boyd v. U.S. (9th Cir.1985).

§ 53. Business/Profit–Seeking Losses

Losses in business or gain-seeking activities are deductible under I.R.C. § 165(a). Deductions for losses in a trade or business or in a transaction entered into for profit depend on a showing of a profit motive or intent in the mind of the taxpayer who suffered the loss. Profit must have been the primary motive, but it need not have been the only one. An activity primarily entered into for profit but incidentally affording recreation or other non-financial rewards will, if resulting in a loss, give rise to a deduction. In contrast, a primarily personal activity such as a hobby, though offering some opportunity for gain (which is taxable if realized), does not provide a loss deduction if a net loss results. Special rules about hobbies are found in I.R.C. § 183 and in Regulations §§ 1.162–12, 1.165–6(a)(3), and 1.183 (expenses of, and losses from, farms not engaged in for profit). Regs. §§ 1.162–12 and 1.212–1(c) refer the reader to § 183 for post–1969 taxable years, as to expenses in activities not for profit.

A loss deduction will not be allowed if the transaction allegedly giving rise to the loss is a sham or if it had no economic substance other than to create a tax deduction—for it then would not be a transaction entered into for profit. Also, a loss deduction may be denied if it occurs on a so-called wash-sale of stock or securities under I.R.C. § 1091 (a sale followed shortly by a repurchase of the same or substantially similar property) which leaves the taxpayer essentially in his pre-sale position. Similarly, a loss may not give rise to a deduction if it arose on a transaction with a related taxpayer (including taxpayer's spouse and some controlled corporations, trusts, and charitable organizations), so that the asset sold is still "in the family." *See* I.R.C. § 267. Losses that exceed income can be carried backward and forward to the extent that they fit I.R.C. § 172 and its rules about net operating losses or § 1212 and its rules about capital-loss carrybacks and carryovers.

Because a loss cannot be deducted by an individual taxpayer unless it fits either the casualty/theft or the trade, business, and investment pigeonholes of I.R.C. § 165(c), he may not deduct his loss on sale of his personal residence, automobile, or other personal (non-business or profit) property. So, if taxpayer buys a house for $400,000, occupies it as his principal residence for ten years and then sells it for $250,000, the $150,000 loss cannot be deducted.

The reason for denying the loss deduction on sale of such personal assets is that the diminution in value presumably results from personal consumption of the item. Thus, taxpayer's $150,000 loss is the counterpart of rent ($15,000 per year for 10 years), which could not have been deducted, since no code provision authorizes such a deduction, and in fact § 262 bars it. Another way of viewing the problem is to observe that his loss reflects accumulated depreciation; since depreciation on one's personal residence cannot be deducted, neither can the loss.[1] To go one step further, if personal expenses or losses were deductible, the income tax would become a tax on savings—since both profit-oriented and personal expenditures would be subtracted from gross income to arrive at the tax base. Still another way of viewing the problem is to regard loss on sale (quasi-rent) as a cost of producing untaxed income (the imputed rental value of owner-occupied dwelling). Thus, by analogy to I.R.C. § 265, which denies a deduction for costs of producing tax-exempt income, § 165 denies a deduction for the loss—since it occurred in a transaction that produced tax-free income. In any event, loss on sale of a personal asset, reflecting (largely but not necessarily) personal consumption, cannot be deducted.

If a personal asset is converted to business or profit-oriented use, a deduction will be allowed on sale of that asset at a loss. But the basis for deter-

---

1. Some have proposed imputing non-deductible depreciation, in such an instance, and requiring a corresponding basis adjustment, to reduce loss and possibly produce taxable gain on sale of the residence.

mining loss in such an instance will be the lesser of cost or fair market value at the time of conversion to business use. Regs. § 1.165–9(b)(2). So, if taxpayer buys his house for $400,000 and occupies it as a residence for ten years, then when the house is worth $300,000 he converts it to business or income-producing property, uses it for a few years for which $40,000 A.C.R.S. deductions are allowed, and sells the house for $200,000, his basis will be $300,000 adjusted to $260,000 for accelerated cost recovery deductions. He will have a deductible loss of $60,000. (Similarly, his basis for depreciation or accelerated cost recovery will be the lower of cost or fair market value at time of conversion. *See* Regs. § 1.167(g)–1.) In the foregoing example, the taxpayer's basis for determining *gain* will still be original cost adjusted for depreciation. So if he sold the house for $500,000, his basis would be $400,000 adjusted to $360,000 for accelerated cost recovery deductions, for a gain of $140,000. In between the sales prices of $360,000 and $260,000 lies a "no-man's land" where sale of the residence converted to income production will produce neither taxable gain nor deductible loss. (This example presumes that the transfer of property from personal to business use does not violate the "anti-churning rules" of § 168(f)(5). *See* § 44, *supra.*)

If taxpayer converts business property to personal use, as with a residence formerly rented out and later occupied by the owner, the sale of the personal asset will not give rise to any loss deduction, since the asset is personal at time of sale. To be deducted, the loss actually occurring during business years must be realized while the asset is a business/profit asset. Conversion to personal use thus can forfeit the loss deduction. Basis, of course, will be adjusted for A.C.R.S. deductions allowable during the asset's business/profit years. No A.C.R.S. deduction is allowable for personal uses, and accordingly no basis adjustment need be made for such uses.[2] Property used partially for business and partially for non-business must be treated as two separate parcels for purposes of allocating basis, A.C.R.S., and loss deductions.

Section 165(f) states that losses from the sale or exchange of capital assets shall be allowed only to the extent permitted by I.R.C. §§ 1211 and 1212, a less advantageous allowance than that for "ordinary losses." Other Code sections, however, reconvert some capital losses into ordinary ones, which may affect their allowance as deductions under § 1211, or the tax benefit from deducting them. *See, e.g.,* § 1244 (losses on shares of stock in small businesses). *See generally,* on capital losses, Ch. IX below, §§ 94, 96–97, *et passim.*

Finally, as to losses in the business context, a net operating loss may be carried forward and backward into other tax years by virtue of I.R.C. § 172. Hence, if business expenses exceed gains so that a net loss results, the deduction will not be lost merely because it exceeds income in the year realized. Losses disallowed under § 465 and § 469 also can be carried over to the immediately following year.

2. *See* footnote 1, § 53, *supra.*

See I.R.C. § 465(a)(2) and § 469(b). *See also* I.R.C. § 1212 (capital loss carrybacks and carryovers).

§ 54. Casualty Losses

Casualty, theft, and similar losses are deductible by virtue of I.R.C. § 165(c), whether they occur to business or to personal property. In other words, casualty losses to property may be deducted whether or not related to gain-seeking activities. Hence, if lightning strikes taxpayer's $40,000 house and does $15,000 damage (not covered by insurance), the loss in value will be deductible to the extent that the loss exceeds $100 and that this excess ($14,900) exceeds 10 percent of the taxpayer's adjusted gross income. *See* § 165(h)(2)(A). So, in the example, the taxpayer must have an adjusted gross income of less than $149,000 to be entitled to any portion of the loss deduction. If taxpayer's A.G.I. is $130,000, for example, she may take a deduction of $1,900 on this $15,000 loss. If her A.G.I. is $30,000, she may take a $11,900 deduction on the $15,000 loss.

One further limitation applies: the casualty loss deduction may be taken for the amount of the loss (measured by the difference between fair market value before and after the casualty) but only up to and not in excess of the taxpayer's basis in the property. *See* I.R.C. § 165(b). This rule is consistent with the general approach that allows deductions for some losses of capital (after-tax dollars), but not for the failure to receive income and not for capital used up in personal consumption. So, for nonbusiness property, the amount of deduction is limited to the *lower* of loss in value or adjusted basis. *See* Helvering v. Owens (S.Ct.1939).

A different rule applies to business property destroyed by a casualty—in such event, if adjusted basis exceeds (pre-casualty) fair market value, the full loss up to the amount of adjusted basis may be deducted. *See* Regs. § 1.165–7(b)(1). And, a casualty loss of business property is not subject to the $100 floor applicable to casualty loss of nonbusiness property, nor to the 10%-of-adjusted-gross-income rule. *See* I.R.C. § 165(h)(2)(A). If a loss is sustained on property used partially for business purposes and partially for nonbusiness purposes, the $100 limitation applies only to the nonbusiness portion. Regs. § 1.165–7(b)(4)(iv). Presumably, the rule requiring a nonbusiness loss to exceed 10 percent of taxpayer's adjusted gross income also applies only to the nonbusiness portion of property used partially for business purposes and partially for non-business purposes.

The casualty loss deduction does not depend on an out-of-pocket loss and does not require that the damage to the property be repaired or repairable. However, cost of repairs to damaged property can be acceptable evidence of the loss of value. *See* Regs. § 1.165–7(a)(2)(ii). Congress has authorized regulations providing for use of an appraisal for the purpose of obtaining a loan of federal funds or a loan guarantee from the Federal government to establish the amount of the loss. *See* I.R.C. § 165(i)(4). The loss can consist of, or "come from," unrealized appreciation in a sense (so long as the deduction does not exceed adjusted basis in the case of personal loss). *See, e.g.,* Cox v. U.S. (9th Cir.1976).

Recognition of the loss will entail a downward adjustment in the basis of the property by the amount of the deduction. That is fair enough, since to that extent taxpayer has been allowed to replenish capital tax-free. Amounts spent rebuilding or replacing the damaged property will increase the basis, since additional capital is then being devoted to that particular asset. *See* I.R.C. § 1016.

To be deductible, the casualty must cause a loss to taxpayer's own property; damages incurred for negligent injury to another's property are not deductible as a casualty loss of the taxpayer. *See, e.g.,* Oransky v. Comm. (B.T.A.1925).

Why is a deduction allowed for a casualty loss to non-business assets when loss on their sale would not be? For one thing, the loss occasioned by casualty or theft does not reflect personal consumption, at least not in the same way that loss on sale of the asset presumably does. In fact, the change in market value before and after the casualty (up to basis) is the measure of the loss—it does not, directly at least, reflect personal, living or family costs. For another thing, a casualty produces, by definition, an unexpected, sudden and sharp loss to the taxpayer. Her ability to pay tax is impaired, she should be encouraged and perhaps even aided in restoring it, and equity or charity suggests that a tax allowance is appropriate.

The strange result produced by the Federal Income Tax allowance for a casualty loss in the form of a deduction is somewhat counteracted by the rule limiting the deduction to the excess of 10–percent of adjusted gross income (after reduction for the $100 floor on each loss). Since the benefit of a deduction is income-variant under a progressive tax rate system, greater relief is afforded to high income taxpayers than to lower ones—who, arguably, need it the most. For a 28% bracket taxpayer, the government is a co-insurer to the extent of 28% of the casualty loss. For a 15% bracket taxpayer, the government insures only a smaller portion (15%) of the loss. Yet in both instances the deduction form allows the taxpayer to replenish the loss of capital out of current income, tax-free. That simply relieves the first taxpayer of the higher tax burden the law would have placed on that income if no loss had been suffered. So the income-variant effect of the deduction merely is produced as a corollary of the reasons for choosing graduated rates in general. Under the rule imposing a 10% of A.G.I. threshold, and the flatter rate progression that currently applies, the tax relief afforded low-income and high-income taxpayers will be more nearly equal (on the same amount of loss). As the example above illustrated, a high-income taxpayer will be allowed a smaller deduction ("co-insured" to 28% of that amount), or even no deduction, if the 10% rule cuts in, whereas a low-income taxpayer will be allowed a larger deduction ("co-insured" at a lesser rate) if the 10% rule does not affect him.

What is a casualty is not always an easy question to answer. Section 165(c) mentions some: fire, storm, shipwreck, and then says "or other casualty, or from theft." "Other casualty" has been taken to mean events resembling the enumerated ones in their main characteristics, especially suddenness. So, other natural disasters or man-made catastrophes such as automobile accidents and excavation collapses are included. Ordinary wear and tear will not qualify. Termite damage is viewed by the I.R.S. as not a casualty loss (even if the building crumbles suddenly). *See* Rev.Rul. 63–232, 1963–2 C.B. 97. Some courts, however, have allowed the deduction. The courts have allowed a deduction for more sudden damages, as when a husband slammed his wife's hand in the car door and thereby dislodged the diamond from her engagement ring, never again to be found in the gravel driveway. *See* White v. Comm. (Tax Court 1967). *And see* Rev.Rul. 72–592, 1972–2 C.B. 101. But, too much human intervention by the taxpayer, especially if it rises to the level of willful negligence, will rule out a deduction, no matter how sudden the damage. *See, e.g.,* Regs. § 1.165–7(a)(3) (damage to automobiles). If taxpayer just plain loses his property and cannot find it, the requisite suddenness or intervening force is missing, and a deduction usually will not be allowed.

Theft losses, deductible under § 165(c)(3) (subject to a $100 floor and the 10–percent of A.G.I. threshold) are treated as sustained during the taxable year in which the taxpayer discovers the loss (even though the thief stole the property earlier). *See* I.R.C. § 165(e). To be deductible as a theft loss, taxpayer's loss must be proven to have been the result of theft, not mysterious unexplained disappearance or misplacement of property. "Theft" as used in the tax law includes more than just the common-law or statutory crime so named. It covers losses from embezzlement, some fraudulent misrepresentations, and the like. Even ransom payments to a kidnapper are included. *See* Rev.Rul. 72–112, 1972–1 C.B. 60.

Section 165 contains a few other rules worthy of mention. Under § 165(d), wagering losses are deductible only to the extent of wagering gains. Under § 165(f), losses deductible under § 165, but arising from sale or exchange of capital assets, are allowed only to the extent specified in §§ 1211 and 1212; in other words, capital losses are deductible as capital losses—nothing more. Section 165(h)(2)(B) contains a "hotchpot" (no longer part of § 1231) for netting personal casualty losses and gains. If the gains exceed the losses, both are treated as capital in nature. Furthermore, most losses, whether capital or ordinary, can be deducted—if at all—only under § 165. No other statutory authority for a loss deduction can be found (except for bad-debt losses under § 166 and for net operating losses carried into the tax year from other years, § 172).

Section 165(g) (on worthless securities) enables a taxpayer who owns a security such as a share of stock or a bond or note with interest coupons or in registered form, which is a capital asset and which becomes worthless during the taxable year, to treat the loss as one from the sale or exchange of a capital asset on the last day of the taxable year. *And see* I.R.C. §§ 271, 582, 1242–1244.

Lastly, I.R.C. § 165(i) puts forward a special rule for certain disaster losses. If in an area determined by the President to warrant Federal assistance, the taxpayer may elect to take the loss into account in the taxable year preceding the year in which the disaster occurs. *See also* Regs. § 1.165–11. Section 165(k) allows any loss attributable to a disaster to be treated as a casualty loss when a taxpayer is ordered to demolish or relocate his or her residence in a disaster area because of the disaster. And § 165(*l*) allows a qualified taxpayer to treat a loss of a deposit made in a qualified financial institution which became insolvent as a casualty loss. *See* I.R.C. § 165(*l*).

A public policy exception may have been engrafted even on the casualty loss deduction. In Mazzei v. Comm. (Tax Court 1974), the Tax Court denied a deduction on public policy grounds to a man who had lost $20,000 to thieves while they (his supposed future partners) demonstrated an alleged counterfeiting device to him. Dissenters thought that allowing a deduction would not encourage crime and that recent amendments to § 162 had been meant to pre-empt, or narrow, the field of public policy exceptions.

No deduction is allowed for premiums paid on insurance policies to cover casualty losses (*e.g.*, fire or earthquake) to non-business assets, presumably since such premiums constitute a cost of earning tax-free income from use of the property (or tax-free recovery of capital in the event of casualty loss).

Regs. § 1.165–1(d)(2)(iii) state that if a taxpayer later receives compensation for a casualty loss deducted in a prior year, the taxpayer is to include in income the amount of the reimbursement in the year received (rather than recomputing tax for the year of deduction). If reimbursement were to occur in the same year, of course, it would reduce or erase the loss deduction, which thus would be partly or wholly "compensated."

Special rules for the deductibility of losses that must be treated as capital losses are explained in Chapter IX below, especially in §§ 96–97.

§ 55. Bad–Debt Losses

Section 166(a) establishes the general rule that a deduction shall be allowed for a debt that becomes worthless within the taxable year. Section 166(b) provides that the basis for a bad-debt loss deduction is to be determined under § 1011. Bad-debt losses must qualify under § 166 if at all; they cannot be taken directly under § 165 (the general loss deduction section). Since § 165 restricts the deduction for losses (incurred by individual taxpayers), other than by casualty or theft, to those arising in gain-seeking activity, a non-business loss may be deducted if it results from a bad debt but not if it results from some other non-casualty or theft event. Thus the line between bad debts and other losses can be crucial to the taxpayer.

A rule that allows a deduction for bad-debt losses has obvious justifications in the case of a taxpayer who engages in the trade or business of lending money for profit or who does so in a transaction entered into for profit (though not a trade or business). For such a taxpayer, the bad-debt loss is a risk and cost of doing business. As such it should be deducted so as to tax only net income. Perhaps less than obvious is the reason why a deduction should be allowed for a loss on a personal loan, made solely out of affection, loyalty or other ties of family, friendship or goodwill. Is not such a loss personal and therefore not a cost of producing income? Perhaps, but it too is an involuntary, sudden drop in wealth and taxpaying ability, much like a casualty loss. Moreover, it would be hard—though surely not impossible—to administer a tax rule that required separating the purely personal loans (some at no interest, some with interest) from the business or profit-seeking loan. To be sure, present § 166 requires that such a line be policed, because of a difference in deductibility between business and non-business bad-debt losses.

Instead, the Code lumps both personal and profit-seeking bad-debt losses in one category (nonbusiness debts) and separates them from business debts. All are deductible, but while business bad-debt losses can be deducted fully from ordinary income, the nonbusiness bad-debt losses (personal and profit-seeking) are limited to short-term capital loss treatment. *See* I.R.C. § 166(d). This half-hearted deduction seems to be a compromise between full deductibility (which might be abused, for example by calling some gifts "bad debts" to gain a deduction) and disallowing a deduction altogether (unfair to the legitimate debt losses). Also, capital-loss treatment of investment losses on loans not made in taxpayer's trade or business puts an investor in debt instruments on a par with an investor in stock of a company that goes broke. Each can deduct his/her loss incurred in making a profit-seeking investment, but only as a *capital* loss (therefore subject to certain restrictions). As a result of this business-versus-nonbusiness categorization, the line between business and all other bad-debt losses proves to be critical; the line between personal and profit-seeking means nothing (though with other loss and expense deductions it meant a great deal—*see* I.R.C. § 165(c), § 162 and § 212). To draw this latter line may be nearly as difficult as to differentiate between business and personal bad-debt losses and to allow a deduction only for the former. At least it re-introduces a line-drawing task of the kind that allowing some deduction even for personal bad-debt losses may have been designed to avoid.

A debt evidenced by a security is restricted to I.R.C. § 165(g)(2)(C) (capital loss) treatment by § 166(e), so that the holder obtains the same treatment as a stockholder who loses his investment. In contrast, a guarantor will be treated as having suffered a bad-debt loss in the year he "makes good" by paying as he is obligated to do, and the deduction may be taken against ordinary income if the guaranty agreement arose out of the guarantor's trade or business. As to either direct or guaranteed loans, a taxpayer may take a fully deductible loss if he can show that the loan was made in his trade or business of loaning money and financing businesses. But a fully deductible business-debt loss of this kind cannot be obtained by a shareholder who loans money to one or more of his own corporations or promoted ventures, since he (usually) will not be able to show that he has a separate trade or business of lending money or promoting businesses.

A bad-debt deduction will not be allowed for an unpaid obligation in which taxpayer has no basis, I.R.C. § 166(b), or which amounts to a failure to receive income. Thus, unpaid rent does not give rise to a bad-debt loss deduction for a cash-method taxpayer who has not previously taken the rent into income. *See* Gertz v. Comm. (Tax Court 1975); Regs. § 1.166–1(e). Cf. Alsop v. Comm. (2d Cir. 1961).

Section 271 blocks any bad-debt deduction for most worthless obligations of political parties—to prevent non-deductible political contributions from being disguised as loans which then become worthless. An exception is provided for instances in which the debt arises from a bona-fide sale of goods or services in the ordinary course of the taxpayer's trade or business, under described circumstances. *See* I.R.C. § 271(c).

The deductibility of bad debts and the peculiar line-drawing between business and all other debts has led to much dispute and litigation over several factual issues. First, the question arises whether a debt or an (equity) investment or even a gift was made. Was the transaction a loan or an investment of capital? This question often arises when a shareholder puts money into his corporation and suffers a loss. Second, was the transaction a business or a non-business bad debt? The answer must be found in the "dominant motivation" of the taxpayer. *See, e.g.,* U.S. v. Generes (S.Ct.1972) (indemnification of loan to shareholder/employee's corporation); Regs. § 1.166–5(b). The form of deductibility hinges on the answer to this question. Third, was there a bad-debt loss, subject to I.R.C. § 166, or a business expense? Fourth, was a direct loan or a guaranty made? Fifth, was there a bad-debt loss or a loss on a worthless security (stock or bond) under I.R.C. § 166(e) and § 165(g)(2)(c)? All are fact questions, and extensive case law must be consulted to discern the guidelines in each sphere.

A wholly worthless debt is deductible in the year in which it becomes worthless. *See* I.R.C. § 166(a). A partially worthless debt must be charged off to the extent of its worthlessness and to that extent deducted for the year. I.R.C. § 166(a)(2). Difficult questions arise when a taxpayer attempts to determine in which year a debt became partially or entirely worthless. A debt will be considered worthless if collection seems hopeless to a reasonable person. Riss v. C.I.R. (8th Cir.1973). The normal three-year statute of limitations has therefore been extended to seven years to allow the taxpayer to file a claim for a bad-debt-loss deduction. *See* I.R.C. § 6511(d)(1).

Recovery of a bad debt in a year subsequent to that in which the debt was written off as worthless and the loss deducted will give rise to income in the later year to the extent that a tax benefit resulted from the earlier deduction. *See* I.R.C. § 111 and regulations thereunder.

§ 56. Passive Losses

After the 1986 T.R.A., the amount of "passive losses" that can be deducted is generally limited to the amount of the taxpayer's "passive income." Passive losses cannot be used to offset income from active sources such as the taxpayer's salary or a business actively carried on by the taxpayer. Moreover, passive losses may not be used to offset portfolio income, such as interest and dividends. *See* I.R.C. § 469(a).

To implement this principle, the passive loss provisions divide a taxpayer's investment and business activities into three separate categories to determine the amount of income that can be offset by passive losses. The first category, passive activities, includes activities which involve the conduct of a trade or business in which the taxpayer does *not* materially participate. *See* I.R.C. § 469(c)(1). In order to participate in an activity materially, the taxpayer must be involved in the operations of the activity on a regular, continuous and substantial basis. *See* I.R.C. § 469(h)(1) and Temp. Reg. § 1.469–5T. As a general rule, a taxpayer will not be deemed to materially participate in activities in which he or she only holds a limited partnership interest. *See* § 469(h)(2). Under I.R.C. § 469(c)(2), a rental activity is considered a passive activity unless the taxpayer meets the "material participation" requirement of § 469(c)(7)(B). However, there is an exemption for up to $25,000 of passive activity loss from rental activities. This exemption is phased out for taxpayers with adjusted gross income over $100,000. *See* I.R.C. § 469(i). The $25,000 limit is lowered by 50 percent of the excess of the taxpayer's modified adjusted gross income over $100,000. *See* I.R.C. § 469(i)(3)(A).

The second category, portfolio activities, includes investments that give rise to interest, dividends, royalties and annuities, and it also includes gains or losses attributable to the disposition of portfolio property. *See* § 469(e). The third category is comprised of trade or business activities in which the taxpayer materially participates and investment activities that are not portfolio activities. The consequence (and purpose) of this division of activities is that losses arising from passive activities can be deducted only from income generated by passive activities and not from income generated by the other categories of activities.

If passive losses cannot be utilized in a tax year, they can be carried forward indefinitely to reduce passive activity income in subsequent years. *See* § 469(b) and Regs. § 1.469–1. Passive loss carryforwards are allowed to be fully deducted against all of the taxpayer's income, of whatever nature, when the taxpayer finally disposes of this entire interest in the activity. I.R.C. § 469(g). However, when an interest in a passive activity is distributed by a trust, the basis of the interest before distribution will be increased by the amount of the passive-activity loss, and no deduction of the loss will be allowed. *See* § 469(j)(12).

§ 57. Expenses for Household and Dependent Care Services Necessary for Gainful Employment

Sometimes when parents pay someone else to care for their children or for elderly or incapacitated members of the household, the payments amount to a cost of producing income—in the sense that the child or other dependent care permits one or both parents to work or otherwise to produce income. Other times, such expenses are incurred for personal reasons—to enable a parent to engage in recreational or civic activities. Sometimes payments enabling one or both parents to work are really personal consumption expenditures, since the parent would rather work at an office or other job than work at caring for children, an incapacitated spouse or other person, apart from monetary gain. When a child-care or other care payment is made in order to enable a parent to work at gainful employment, it is not easy to decide whether the payment is a cost of producing income or a personal, living or family expense, or both and in what proportion.

The tax rules that give an allowance for dependent care services have consisted of compromises that reflect the difficulties presented by the combination of personal and business functions served by family care expenses. Previously, these expenses were deductible but only to the extent allowed by now-repealed I.R.C. § 214. In order to benefit taxpayers whose itemized deductions did not exceed the zero-bracket amount (now the standard deduction), and with the effect of eliminating the income-variant effect of the deduction form, the deduction was changed to a credit. *See* I.R.C. § 21.

Section 21 allows a credit against tax for a percentage of some of the employment-related expenses for household and dependent care. Qualifying dependents include an incapacitated spouse, or a child under the age of thirteen. *See* I.R.C. § 21(b)(1).

Expenses eligible for the credit can include costs of day care, nursery school, a housekeeper or other care in the home, or even in day camp. Expenses for overnight camp, however, are not covered. *See* I.R.C. § 21(b)(2)(A).

The amount of the credit is set at 35 percent of the employment-related expenses of taxpayers with adjusted gross incomes of up to $15,000. I.R.C. § 21(a)(2). The credit is reduced by one percent for each $2,000 of income above $15,000. The credit rate remains 20 percent for taxpayers with adjusted gross incomes over $43,000. The maximum amount of expense to be taken into account in determining the credit is $3,000 for one dependent and $6,000 for two or more dependents. Non-institutional out-of-home care, other than in non-licensed dependent-care centers, is also eligible for the credit. I.R.C. § 21(b)(2)(C),(D). (Recall I.R.C. § 129 excluding payments made or expenses incurred for dependent daycare by employers from employees' gross income if made pursuant to a written non-discriminatory plan. *See* § 34, *supra.*)

The credit is not refundable. So, any excess credit will be lost and of no advantage to the taxpayer. Expenses covered by § 21 (whether or not actually creditable or in excess of creditable levels) cannot be deducted as business expenses under § 162. There could, however, be some overlap with § 213 (medical expense deduction).

The conflicting philosophies behind § 21 can be observed in its structure and limitations. Partly rooted in an attempt to take into account the costs of producing income, the allowance takes a form—a credit as contrasted to a deduction—that seems better suited to a subsidy or incentive. And why should there be income limitations on an allowance if it is made for a cost of producing income? Similarly, why have dollar amount limitations? Perhaps the shape of the allowance suggests that its drafters were particularly mindful of two-income families, employment obstacles facing women (housewives and mothers), general employment levels, the child-care business, single parents, adults with aged and infirm parents to care for, and similar special situations, as much as in arriving at an accurate definition of net income in general. Yet the expenses must be for the purpose of gainful employment. This allowance affords one an excellent opportunity to compare the tax allowance (perhaps viewed as a "tax expenditure," to the extent of some or all of the revenue foregone) with a program of direct payments in cash to deserving recipients.

Child and dependent care tax allowances have come in for some important attacks. For example, in Nammack v. Comm. (Tax Court 1971) the court held that the dollar amount limits of § 214, the predecessor of § 21, did not constitute unconstitutional discrimination against working women with children. And former § 214 came under attack for sex discrimination when challenged because it denied the deduction to males who had never married; the court there ruled for the taxpayer but, instead of ruling § 214 invalid, decreed that the deduction should be granted to the taxpayer. *See* Moritz v. Comm. (10th Cir.1972). 1971 legislation ended the literal discriminations of § 214, and § 21 has now replaced § 214.

Section 23 provides a credit of up to $10,000 for the amount of qualified adoption expenses paid or incurred by the taxpayer. In the case of an adoption of a child with "special needs," as defined in § 23(d)(3), the taxpayer is treated as having paid $10,000 of qualified expenses (less expenses actually paid) in the year the adoption becomes final. I.R.C. § 23(a)(3). The credit is phased out for taxpayers with adjusted gross income (as defined in I.R.C. § 23(b)(2)(B)) between $150,000 and $190,000. The $150,000 and $190,000 figures are adjusted for inflation after 2002. This credit is not refundable, but after 2003 unused credits carry forward. I.R.C. § 23(c).

§ 58. A Reminder and Some Special Topics

In the area of "mixed" deductions as well as in connection with profit-seeking deductions, the rule of I.R.C. § 262, which denies any deduction for personal, family and living expenses, must be kept in mind. This blanket denial, combined with the necessity for a taxpayer to find an applicable express authorization for a deduction to be allowed, means that many unmentioned items cannot be deducted.

Sometimes a taxpayer incurs expenses in connection with combined personal and gain-seeking activities. Some of these expenditures having mixed purposes or roles are explicitly deductible, as set forth in this chapter—taxes, interest, bad debts, etc. In other situations, a pro-ration is necessary. For example, if a taxpayer uses his car or home in part for business and in part for personal pleasure, any expenses and losses incurred must be pro-rated with only the business or gain-seeking component allowed as a deduction. So, that portion of the rent, utilities, and upkeep of a home that is attributable to the office part of the house may be deducted. (*But see* the limits and rules of I.R.C. § 280A.) Business mileage and a proportionate part of repair expenses on the car may be deducted. (*See also* the limits in I.R.C. § 280F.)

Section 183 also limits the deduction of expenses incurred in a hobby activity to the extent of the excess of the income from such activity over otherwise allowable expenses. Section 274(n) also limits the deductibility of business meal expenses for most employees to 50% of the expenses actually incurred. Congress installed this limit on the ground that most business meals inherently involve some personal consumption, or a saving of non-deductible personal expense, as well as a cost of producing income.

Other possibly mixed items are given all-or-nothing treatment. For example, union dues and professional association dues are deductible. Regs. § 1.162–6. Some work clothing and uniforms are deductible, if the clothing is not suitable for off-duty wear. *See* Mimeograph 6463, 1950–1 C.B. 29. Education expenses are deductible in full if closely related to the requirements of an existing job or business, but not otherwise as *business* expenses. Regs. § 1.162–5. For other provisions dealing with the tax treatment of education expenditures, *see* § 62, *infra.*

Some mixed items have been given pro-rata or limited deductibility or some other ambivalent treatment. Contributions to political parties for a time were deductible or creditable, up to specified dollar limits. *See* former I.R.C. §§ 24, 218. Now no allowance is given for direct or indirect political contributions. *See* I.R.C. § 276. (To back up these rules, a deduction is denied for the bad debts of political parties and similar organizations, except for carefully circumscribed instances. *See* I.R.C. § 271. *And see* § 84.) An individual taxpayer can designate $3 of his income tax liability to be set aside in a special account for use by presidential candidates, the "Presidential Election Campaign Fund." I.R.C. §§ 6096(a), 9001–9013. Legal expenses in general are not deductible unless they fit the business or gain-seeking-related tests of I.R.C. §§ 162 and 212; *and see* U. S. v. Gilmore (S.Ct. 1963). *See also* § 212(3), allowing a deduction for tax law advice or services. Some legal expenses may, however, be capitalized and added to the cost basis of property. Capital expenditures, other than those which may be expensed under post-E.R.T.A. § 179, may not be deducted. I.R.C. § 263. Capital expenditures include those made to acquire property, to improve or alter it, and to defend or to perfect title to it. Travel and moving expenses are deductible only to the extent allowed by I.R.C. §§ 162, 212 and 217. Finally, I.R.C. § 183, relating to activities not engaged in for profit, must be kept in mind as a limitation on the deductibility of mixed-motive expenditures. And, along the same lines, *see* §§ 274, 280A and other miscellaneous rules found in I.R.C. §§ 261–280H.

Among the several "mixed deductions," the law has drawn lines of importance at different places. For example, with respect to bad-debt losses, the line between personal and profit-seeking—so important under § 162 and § 212—has no importance. Much depends, instead, on the line between trade or business bad debts on the one hand and all others, including "profit seeking" but not "trade or business," on the other hand. As to § 165 losses, the key line lies between the personal area and all others (profit-seeking and trade or business) or, for personal losses, between casualty and non-casualty. So, since almost all bad debts are deductible, if an ambiguous transaction must be admitted to be personal, taxpayer will prefer it to be characterized as a bad debt rather than another form of loss. If it is a trade or business transaction, either § 166 or § 165 will do. If the loss is in the investment/profit-seeking area (but not in the select trade or business category), a loss will be fully deductible but a bad debt will be limited to § 166(d) capital treatment. These lines provide incentives for recharacterization, as well as reasons for administrative and compliance friction and for litigation.

CHAPTER VI

PERSONAL DEDUCTIONS AND OTHER ALLOWANCES

§ 59. Introduction

This chapter covers deductions and some other allowances given by the Code even though no income-producing or business purpose, motive, origin, intent or effect can be found in the expenditure giving rise to the deduction, either in the circumstance of the particular taxpayer in question or of other taxpayers in general. The historical reasons and present policy justifications for the deductions must consequently be sought in other directions and in the myriad of pressures on Congress.

This chapter focuses on three personal deductions, those for charitable contributions, education expenses, and medical expenses. Also treated are personal and dependency exemptions and the standard deduction. And some allowances that are not cast in deduction form are described—the general tax credit and other credits, for example. Earlier chapters also have touched upon some deductions that are allowed without regard to their relationship to any gain-seeking activity in general: casualty and theft losses under I.R.C. § 165(c)(3) and non-business bad debts under I.R.C. § 166(d). Other deductions that are allowed, even though in a particular instance they may not be related to gain seeking, include the deduction for interest under I.R.C. § 163 (including qualified residence interest) and taxes under § 164 (including taxes on personal-use property, but no longer for state sales taxes). Another deduction, unrelated to income-producing activity, is allowed by I.R.C. §§ 71 and 215 for alimony and separate maintenance payments, *see* § 83, *infra*. Thus the contents of this chapter are not perfectly determined; they do, however, contain the prime and clearest examples of those deductions allowed without any dependence on a "cost of producing income" rationale.

Personal deductions will affect the taxpayer's taxable income only if, and to the extent that, they exceed the taxpayer's standard deduction. This result occurs because the taxpayer can elect either to itemize personal deductions or to take the standard deduction. *See* I.R.C. § 63. (Credits against tax can be taken in any event, of course.) In 2004, the standard deduction exempts from taxation $4,850 on a tax return of a single individual, $9,700 for a married couple filing a joint return, and $4,850 for a married individual filing separately. *See* I.R.C. § 63(c). The standard deduction is adjusted annually for inflation.

The I.R.C. § 67 rule that allows "miscellaneous itemized deductions" only to the extent that they aggregate more than 2% of taxpayer's A.G.I. will not affect the principal deductions covered in this Chapter VI, since "miscellaneous itemized deductions'' are defined by § 67(b) as itemized deductions other than deductions for § 170 charitable contributions or § 213 medical expenses (among others). Section 67 also will not affect the § 222 deduction for qualified tuition and related expenses because that deduction is taken in determining A.G.I. *See* I.R.C. § 62(a)(18), 63(d)(1).

Nevertheless, computing *taxable income* still is a two-step process, so the taxpayer may take most business and gain-seeking deductions whether or not other deductions are itemized. As a result of this two-tier system, some items that are lumped together in the Code may have to be separated by the taxpayer in completing his or her tax return in order to determine whether he has excess itemized deductions. For example, § 163 interest on a qualified, owner-occupied personal residence loan may be used only in computing itemized deductions (the excess of which is subtracted from Adjusted Gross Income, or A.G.I.), but § 163 interest may be deducted from *gross income*, in determining A.G.I., if it was a trade or business expense. *See* § 62(a)(1). Similar separations may have to be made between business and personal taxes, bad debts, etc.

Separating personal from profit-seeking deductions also is important in determining Adjusted Gross Income (A.G.I.). Adjusted gross income generally means gross income less trade or business expenses and the other items set forth in I.R.C. § 62. In turn, A.G.I. affects the amount of deductions allowable for charitable contributions, extraor-

dinary medical expenses, and miscellaneous itemized deductions (under § 67).

§ 60. Charitable Contributions and Gifts

The primary Code provision permitting a deduction for charitable contributions is I.R.C.
§ 170(a)(1), which permits a taxpayer to deduct any
charitable contribution, payment of which is made
within the taxable year. Payment may be made in
money or property. A pledge (or even accrual by an
accrual-method individual taxpayer) will not suffice.
Deductions of $250 or more are allowed only if they
are substantiated by a "contemporaneous written
acknowledgement" of the contribution by the donee
organization that meets the requirements of
§ 170(f)(8)(B). Presumably this deduction is allowed
to encourage and subsidize socially desirable behavior (contribution to charities) which, incidentally,
relieves government of some welfare costs it otherwise would be called upon to bear and which also
leaves the contributing taxpayer less able to pay his
tax bill. In fact, the deduction may be seen as a way
for the taxpayer to redirect a portion of his current
income (the amount of his contribution) to charity
and avoid paying tax on that portion with which he
parts.

The effect of giving the tax allowance in the form
of a deduction is to give larger tax relief to high-
bracket taxpayers than low-bracket taxpayers, per
dollar contributed. The logic of that result is that it
merely forgives the high-income taxpayer the heavier tax burden he would have had to pay had he not

contributed to charity. Nonetheless, the result is to make the after-tax cost of contributing $100 to charity just $72 for a 28% taxpayer and $85 to a poorer, 15% taxpayer (who, to begin with, had less income from which to make a donation). Of course, the degree of this income-variant effect declines as the amount of graduation of the statutory rates decreases.

In general, for tax purposes the amount of a taxpayer's charitable contribution equals the value of the money or property he gives or transfers to an eligible charity. *See* Regs. § 1.170A–1(c). This general rule, however, is subject to many very significant exceptions and limitations, some statutory and some judicial or administrative, to be elaborated in this section.

The face amount of a charitable contribution is reduced or eliminated for tax purposes if the taxpayer receives anything of value in return. So, for example, tuition paid to a parochial school cannot be deducted as a charitable contribution. *See* Rev. Rul. 83–104, 1983–2 C.B. 46. If taxpayer buys a dinner ticket to a charity ball for $100, he will not be allowed any deduction (whether or not he actually uses the ticket) unless he establishes that the dinner had a value less than the price of the ticket, and what that value was. *See* Rev.Rul. 67–246, 1967–2 C.B. 104. Similarly, if he receives a raffle ticket or admission to an entertainment event or even a token pen or decoration in return for a contribution, he may deduct only the excess of the amount of his contribution over the value he shows he received—the so-called "excess value rule."

Donations are deductible only if made to the organizations described in the statute as eligible for deductibility. If one of those organizations receives a contribution that is really a purchase of services by the donor (as in the case of transfer to a religious retirement home by a taxpayer whose parents are about to be taken in as residents, for example), the deduction will be denied. If the donor excessively limits the class of beneficiaries for whom the charity may use his gift, it will be construed as a gift (or compensation or other payment) directly to those beneficiaries, not to the charitable organization, and thus not deductible as a § 170 contribution. The Internal Revenue Service is likely to contest a contribution to any organization that it has not approved as a charitable organization by one of its rulings, especially if the organization favors its members, donors or persons somehow related to, or affiliated with, them.

Other limitations on the deduction for charitable contributions are to be found in subsections of I.R.C. § 170. Section 170(a)(3) declares that a taxpayer who donates a future interest in tangible personal property (such as a painting) may receive the deduction only when all intervening interests in and rights to the actual possession of the property have expired or are held by persons other than the donor-taxpayer and his immediate relatives or associates. So, since this section was enacted, taxpayers no longer can give their paintings to a museum, while retaining possession for life, and take an immediate charitable deduction for the value of the remainder donated to the museum. *See generally* Regs. § 1.170A–5.

Section 170(b) imposes significant percentage limitations on the amount of a gift that can be deductible under § 170(a). An individual taxpayer can deduct up to 50% of his "contribution base" which is defined by § 170(b)(1)(F) as his adjusted gross income without any net operating loss carryback, if the charity is a "public" charity as described in § 170(b)(1)(A) and not a "private" charity. In the case of a contribution to a private charity, the ceiling is 30% rather than 50% (or the excess of the contribution base over the amount of the contribution to public charities, whichever is less). *See* § 170(b)(1)(B). For a corporate donor, the percentage limitation is 10% of taxable income with some adjustments, under § 170(b)(2). Under § 170(d), the excess of a contribution that surpasses the 50% limitations of § 170(b) may be carried over to the five succeeding tax years. *See generally* Regs. § 1.170A–10. Other percentage rules may come into play in particular instances, some of which are treated below. Also relevant to large donations is I.R.C. § 162(b), which prevents a donation that exceeds the percentage limits of § 170 from qualifying for deduction as a business expense under § 162(a); *and see* § 170(b)(1)(C).

Charitable contributions by corporations must be used within the U.S. to be deductible; as to contributions by individuals the law only requires that the charity itself be organized in the U.S.; the funds may be used abroad. So, individual contributions to a fund organized here but doing all its work abroad would be deductible, but corporate contributions would not be.

What is a (potentially deductible) "charitable contribution?" Charitable contributions are defined by § 170(c). The term refers to a contribution or gift to or for the use of one of the following recipients. The first category includes governmental units [(c)(1)]. The second [(c)(2)] and most important refers to a corporation, trust, community chest, fund, or foundation (a) organized in the United States, exclusively for religious, charitable, scientific, literary or educational purposes, or to foster certain amateur sports competition, or for the prevention of cruelty to children or animals, (b) no part of the net earnings of which inures to the benefit of any private shareholder or individual, and (c) no substantial part of whose activities is carrying on propaganda or otherwise attempting to influence legislation and which does not participate or intervene in any political campaign on behalf of any candidate for public office. In other words, the recipient must not only meet the standards of § 501(c) to be exempt from tax, but it also must qualify under these rules of § 170(c). For example, a labor union may be exempt from tax, but contributions to it still will not be deductible as charitable contributions. Other eligible recipients are mentioned in § 170(c)(3)–(5).

Contributions of property other than money to a charity present special problems. Some contributed property is created by the taxpayer's own efforts (a painting, book, invention). Other property was not created by the taxpayer (stock, land, tangible personal property). As a first principle, the amount of a contribution made in property is deemed to be the fair market value of the property at the time of the gift. *See* Regs. § 1.170A–1(c)(1). Fair market value is defined as the price that a willing buyer would pay a willing seller. This definition seems fine in principle, but applying it proves more difficult. Many cases have involved disputes over whether the valuation given by taxpayer or the charity was realistic.

If the charity assumes a liability in accepting property, or takes the property subject to a liability, the deduction is reduced accordingly. In fact, if the liability exceeds taxpayer's basis in the donated property, he may realize gain on the contribution (because his liability is discharged). *And see* Regs. § 1.170A–3.

The value of taxpayer's services themselves may not be deducted, perhaps because to do so would amount to taking a deduction for foregone, untaxed income. Regs. § 1.170A–1(g). For similar reasons, by virtue of I.R.C. § 170(f)(3), a lease of taxpayer's property to a charity "for free" or at below market rental will not entitle him to a deduction.

However, if a taxpayer incurs unreimbursed out-of-pocket expenses in rendering services to a charity, he can deduct the expenses as contributions of property for the use of a charity. *See* Regs.

§ 1.170A–1(g). Thus gasoline expenses for using taxpayer's car for the United Crusade would be deductible. Associated expenses must be non-personal and directly connected with, and solely attributable to, the rendition of services for a charitable organization. *See, e.g.,* Rev.Rul. 73–597, 1973–2 C.B. 69, denying a child-care expense deduction to a taxpayer who incurred such expenses while she performed volunteer services for a charity.

Some rules were introduced as part of the 1969 Tax Reform Act to reduce the differences in tax treatment between a gift of property that has appreciated in value and a gift of cash (perhaps consisting of the proceeds of selling appreciated property). One such important rule is that of § 170(e)(1)(A), under which a charitable contribution of property is reduced by the amount of ordinary income or short-term capital gain that would have been realized if taxpayer had sold the property instead of contributing it to charity. *See generally* Regs. § 1.170A–4. Specifically, the amount of gain that would not have been long-term capital gain will reduce the contribution. So, if property donated would have produced some ordinary income or short-term capital gain on sale, because the property was not a capital asset in the hands of the taxpayer or because § 1245, or some other rule, would have recaptured some depreciation or credit as ordinary income, the deduction will be less than fair market value by the amount of inherent ordinary income or short-term capital gain. In other words, the amount of the deduction will be limited to the donor's basis in the property. By imposing this limitation, Congress intended to put the contributing taxpayer on a par with one who sold appreciated property and donated the total proceeds to the charity.

Similarly, if taxpayer donates tangible personal property to a charity whose use of it is unrelated to the purpose or function constituting the basis for the charity's exemption under § 501, or to a donee that is a private foundation, the contribution is reduced for purposes of computing the deduction also by the amount of gain that would have been long-term capital gain if the taxpayer had sold the property for its fair market value at the time of contribution. *See* I.R.C. § 170(e)(1)(B). If the donee is a public charity and uses the property in its exempt functions, a full deduction will be allowed. However, the ceiling percentage as to such gifts will be 30% rather than 50% of the taxpayer's contribution base, I.R.C. § 170(b)(1)(C), unless the donor chooses to take the unrealized appreciation into account for tax purposes by reducing the amount of his contribution by the amount that would have been long-term capital gain if the property had been sold. *See* I.R.C. § 170(b)(1)(C)(iii).

Section 170(e) Contribution Reductions. To examine the operation and planning implications of the contribution-reduction rules of § 170(e), one should begin with their scope. First, under the rule of § 170(e)(1)(A) & (B), donation to a charity of much, but not all, long-term capital-gain property will be exempt from the contribution-reduction rule. Exempt long-term capital-gain property includes tangible personal property whose use by the donee is related to the purpose or function constituting the basis for the donee's exemption under § 501, and real or intangible personal property given to a charitable institution other than a private foundation (with a few exceptions.) If the long-term capital-gain property consists of the "right kind," as these rules describe, its donation will yield a contribution deduction equal to the property's fair market value, not reduced by the contribution-reduction rules of § 170(e).

If the property is *not* long-term capital gain property, but is property whose sale would produce only ordinary income *or* short-term capital gain, the contribution reduction rule of I.R.C. § 170(e)(1)(A) will reduce the contribution deduction from fair market value to taxpayer's basis. That is, the deduction will be reduced from fair market value by all of the gain that would *not* have been long-term capital gain if the property had been sold.

The first contribution-reduction rule of I.R.C. § 170(e), that is subsection (e)(1)(A), was designed to put on a par those taxpayers who contributed cash and those who contributed property in-kind if and to the extent that that property would have generated the heavier income tax burden on ordinary income or short-term capital gain if sold. It does not affect contributors of qualified long-term capital gain property—they can donate in-kind and get a deduction of unrealized appreciation without including that gain in income. [So far as

§ 170(e)(1)(A) alone goes; another barrier may lie in § 170(e)(1)(B).] In that respect, a donor of property in-kind retains an advantage over a donor of cash. For example, suppose A has $150 in cash to donate, and B has a share of stock worth $150 but in which B has a basis of $50. If one donates the cash and the other the property, each will get a $150 deduction. But A has parted with, presumably, $150 after-tax dollars while B has parted with $50 after-tax dollars and $100 unrealized gain. B has saved the tax bill of realizing the gain inherent in the stock, yet he gets an equal deduction.

To see this result another way, imagine that B considered selling his stock and donating *all* the proceeds. If B did so, he would give $150 cash proceeds to the charity and get a $150 deduction under § 170, but B would have to pay tax on $100 gain realized upon sale, an additional tax cost he can escape, without any disadvantage, by giving the stock outright to the charity, since the gift is not deemed to constitute a realization of the gain.

Section 170(e)(1)(A) was designed to *eliminate* this advantage or differential but only as to property containing inherent ordinary income or short-term capital gain—*i.e.*, when the tax saving from donating in-kind would be the greatest. It does so by reducing the contribution deduction by all the inherent ordinary income or short-term gain. For cases where *all* the inherent gain is ordinary or short-term, this provision will reduce the contribution deduction to basis.

To see whether and how § 170(e)(1)(A) accomplishes this purpose, return to taxpayer A (with $150 cash to donate) and B (with stock worth $150 to donate), but imagine that the stock held by B has not been held long enough to qualify as *long*-term capital gain property and therefore its sale would generate *short*-term capital gain (or ordinary income if B were a dealer in stocks). Now if A contributes $150 cash, A will get a $150 deduction; if B contributes the stock, B will get a $50 (basis) deduction. Does this treat B as B would have been treated if B had sold the stock and donated the proceeds? If B had sold the stock for $150 and had contributed the cash proceeds to the charity, B would then have gotten the full $150 charitable contribution deduction but would have had an additional $100 in realized income to include in his tax base for the year. This additional income would have offset (or have been offset by) $100 of the charitable contribution deduction, leaving a net deduction of $50, equal to B's basis and equal to the deduction B would have gotten if B had merely donated the stock in kind, without first selling it. Therefore, § 170(e)(1)(A), when it applies, succeeds in putting A and B on a par and B in the same position whether B contributes property in kind or sells and contributes all the proceeds.

In the foregoing analysis, A and B, and B (in kind) and B (sales proceeds), were compared on the condition that if B sold the property B would donate all the proceeds. In other words, the charity would get the same value donation in any event. Now suppose B, having appreciated short-term capital gain or ordinary-income property, considers what will happen if he sells and pays the tax that such a sale incurs out of the proceeds of sale and donates the balance. Suppose B's composite marginal income tax rate would be 28% on the $100 gain in the property. If B sells first and realizes $100 gain ($150 amount realized less $50 basis), B will have to withhold $28 to pay B's 28% tax on $100 income. If so, he will contribute $122 to charity and will get a $122 deduction. Since he has paid tax on the gain out of the amount realized, the $122 deduction is not offset against income from the sale and can serve to offset or shelter other income (also, presumably, taxed at 28%). The $122 deduction will save B $34.16 in tax ($122 @ 28%). When B gave the property outright, § 170(e)(1)(A) reduced his deduction to $50, which saved him $14 in tax ($50 @ 28%), but it didn't generate any more income or tax. When he sold and donated *all* the proceeds, he got a bigger deduction ($150) for the bigger contribution but generated $100 income in the process, which used up $100 of the charitable contribution deduction, leaving B with a $50 net deduction, which would save B $14 ($50 @ 28%). And when B sold and paid (or withheld) tax on the gain out of the proceeds, he got a $122 deduction, which saved him $34.16 ($122 @ 28%) (compared to the $150 deduction for A, the cash donor, which saved $42 in tax and sheltered $150 of other income).

This comparison shows that a taxpayer who sells appreciated property, pays the ensuing tax out of the proceeds, and donates the remaining proceeds to charity gets a larger net benefit out of his actions (or sacrifices less) than does the taxpayer who contributes all the proceeds and pays tax on the gain out of his pocket. This should not be surprising and will always be true so long as the income tax rates do not reach or exceed 100%. The result merely follows from the fact that the taxpayer who paid tax out of the sale proceeds made a smaller gift to charity (and could take only a smaller deduction) and kept some of the proceeds for his own benefit— to pay the ensuing tax. So long as composite marginal tax rates do not reach 100%, it will always be financially more advantageous for a taxpayer to have income, pay tax on it, and retain it, than to have income and give *all* of it away, not retaining any for his/her own benefit, even if the more generous donor gets a bigger tax deduction. Taxpayer B, when planning to sell and withhold proceeds to pay tax, *could* change his mind and donate all the proceeds. If so, if B donated $28 more, B would get a correspondingly ($28) bigger deduction. But a $28 greater deduction does not save B as much as B would save by withholding the $28; a $28 deduction can only save B $28 multiplied by his composite marginal rate (28%), a total of $7.84 ($28 × 28%). Keeping the $28 means saving $28 less the tax on it, namely $20.16 ($28–$7.84=$20.16). Under income tax rates below 100% it must be more blessed to give than to receive, for it is more profitable to receive and keep than to (receive and) give away. A broader corollary of this analysis consists of the proposition that it will never be more profitable (under present tax rates) for a person to give property to a charity (and get the full § 170 deduction, which will save taxes on other income), than to sell the property and keep the proceeds of sale (and have to pay the tax, at less than 100%, on the gain realized). (Under rates in effect some years ago this entrancing possibility *did* exist in some extreme circumstances.)

The more complicated contribution-reduction rules of I.R.C. § 170(e)(1)(B), for (i) tangible personal property unrelated in use to the donee's exempt function, (ii) any property given to a private foundation, or for (iii) other capital gain property for which taxpayer did not observe the 30% limitation of § 170(b)(1)(C)(i) [*see* § 170(b)(1)(C)(iii)], make the arithmetic and analysis more complex and less apparent than under § 170(e)(1)(A), but the principles remain much the same. Section 170(e)(1)(A) and (B) together and the reduction amount, which now is equal to the *total* unrealized gain, will put a taxpayer who donates the § 170(e)(1)(B) property in-kind on a par with one who sells the property and donates all the proceeds. In sum, under the present law, when the taxpayer directly donates his or her § 170(e)(1)(B) property to a described charity, the amount of the contribution will be reduced by all of the unrealized gain that would have been taxed if the property had been sold.

Section 170(e) contains some exceptions to its contribution-reduction rules. Section 170(e)(3) has a special partial exception in the case of a corporate donation of inventory to a charity to benefit the ill, the needy, or infants. Section 170(e)(4) also contains a partial exception for certain corporate contributions of scientific research property. Section 170(e)(5) has a partial exception for contributions to a private foundation of stock for which market quotations are readily available. And, under § 170(e)(5) corporations may qualify for a partial exception for contributions of computer technology or equipment through 2003 to qualified elementary or secondary educational organizations.

If a taxpayer deducts the fair market value of property given to a charity, the costs and expenses of producing or acquiring the contributed property are not deductible and may not be counted as part of the taxpayer's "cost of goods" sold. *See* Regs. § 1.170A–1(c)(4).

Taxpayer can donate appreciated property without realizing gain even if the property's market value satisfies the dollar amount of a binding pledge formerly made. *See* Rev.Rul. 55–410, 1955–1 C.B. 297. However, the amount of the deduction will be governed by the rules of § 170(e)(1)(A) and (B) as above. A gift of property that has dropped in value to less than its basis will not bring about realization and deduction of the loss.

I.R.C. § 1011(b) contains a rule for a bargain sale to charity; it requires an allocation of basis between the interest contributed and the interest sold. *See* Regs. § 1.1001–1(e); § 1.1011–2. (*See also* I.R.C.

§ 170(e)(2) for a similar rule of basis allocation for a gift of less than taxpayer's entire interest in contributed property.) Prior to this rule, a taxpayer could sell appreciated property to a charity at his basis, a bargain price if the property were worth more. He was allowed to treat the sales price as a return of his capital (no gain, no tax) and was deemed to have made a contribution of the property to the extent of the bargain, the difference between price (and basis) and fair market value. In effect, he was allowed to allocate all his basis to the part sold. So, if his basis in a block of 10 shares of stock was $100 and its fair market value was $1,000, he could sell the 10 shares to charity for $100, realize no gain and deduct $900. Now, by the strength of § 1011(b), he must allocate basis between the part sold (one share at fair market value of $100) and the part donated (nine shares, or $900). Hence he will have $90 gain on the share sold ($100 price minus $10 basis) and a donation deduction of $900, thus "losing" $90 of his basis.

Other Limitations On § 170 Deductions. Another rule, one that can cause a surprised taxpayer to find that he inadvertently realized gain when he made a charitable contribution, is the assignment-of-income doctrine. As in the cases finding taxpayer to have realized income when he tries by an anticipatory assignment of income to cause the income to be taxed to a donee such as a family member (*see* § 80 *infra*), a taxpayer who gives imminent but theretofore unreceived income to a charity may be taxable on the income. For example, when a taxpayer gave an endowment insurance policy to a charity just two weeks before the policy matured and when the policy was worth (say) $100,000, though taxpayer's basis was $60,000, he found himself taxed as if he had collected the $100,000 and then donated it to the charity. *See* Friedman v. Comm. (6th Cir.1965). The result would mean realization of gain he had not desired, even though followed by a deduction to some extent. Likewise, if a taxpayer were to give appreciated property to a college with the agreement or understanding that the college would immediately sell the property, invest the proceeds in tax-exempt bonds and pay out the income to him for life, he would very likely be taxed on the gain realized upon sale of the property. *See* Rev.Rul. 60–370, 1960–2 C.B. 203.

A taxpayer taking a § 170 deduction for the donation of property should be able to support the value placed on the donated property by appraisal or other appropriate documentation. In the case of a contribution of property other than money, a taxpayer is to receive and maintain a receipt from the donee. Regs. § 1.170A–13(b). If the gift is of property, other than certain publicly traded securities, with a claimed value of over $5,000, the taxpayer generally must obtain a qualified appraisal and attach it to the tax return. Regs. § 1.170A–13(c). Section 6662 imposes a 20% penalty for a "substantial valuation misstatement" that can apply in the case of a charitable contribution if the understatement of tax attributable to the misstatement exceeds $5,000 and the claimed value of the property is 200% or more of the correct valuation. *See* I.R.C. § 6662(a), (b)(3), (d)(1), (e); *see also* I.R.C. § 6664(c) (reasonable cause exception based on appraisal and good faith investigation).

Under present law, a gift that consists only of income will not qualify for a deduction. A gift of income-producing property in trust or for a term will not yield a deduction because of I.R.C. § 170(f)(2)(B), unless there is a guaranteed annuity or unless the trust instrument guarantees a fixed amount or percentage of income to be received by the charity. Section 170(f) has a similar rule with regard to remainder interests in property placed in trust for charity. *See* I.R.C. § 170(f)(2)(A). The problem addressed by both rules is the presence of non-charitable beneficiaries, and the law's effort to restrict the deduction to gifts that eventually do go to charity, not to other recipients.

Section 170(f)(2)(A) disallows a charitable contribution deduction for a remainder interest in a trust unless the trust is a so-called "pooled-income fund" or a charitable-remainder trust. *See* I.R.C. §§ 642 & 664. A charitable deduction for a gift of a remainder following a legal life estate or estate for years generally will not be allowed unless the remainder meets tests applicable to pooled-income funds or charitable-remainder trusts. The effect is to make sure that the charity will receive something, and adequately to take into account the amounts that income beneficiaries are likely to receive by specifying what the income beneficiary is to receive, rather than to rely on the old and sometimes unrealistic formulas for discounting the present value of the charity's remainder interest. *See* Regs. § 1.170A–6 (Charitable contributions in trust). Section 170(f)(2)(B) disallows a deduction for a contribution of income interests and other partial interests unless there is a guaranteed annuity or fixed percentage distribution and the grantor of the trust is treated as the owner of such interest for purposes of § 671, which taxes the owner on income. Section 170(f)(3) subjects partial interests not in trust to rules that parallel the trust rules, with some exceptions. See § 1.170A–7 (Contributions not in trust of partial interests in property).

A charitable remainder annuity trust is one under which the non-charitable income beneficiary must receive a fixed dollar annuity but not less than 5% of the value of the trust corpus at the time it first is placed in the trust. A unitrust is one under which the non-charitable beneficiary is to receive income of a fixed percentage not less than 5% of the trust assets valued annually. *See* I.R.C. § 664(d). A pooled-income fund is one that is maintained by the donee charity, receives funds from a number of contributors, and pays income to the contributors or their nominees for life with the remainder to the charity. *See* I.R.C. § 642(c)(5).

The subject of exempt organizations and private charities merits a word or two in connection with the charitable contribution deduction. Although under I.R.C. § 501 a variety of non-profit organizations can achieve tax-exempt status, they are not thereby eligible for § 170 contributions, as noted earlier. That is, they are not *automatically* eligible; they must also meet the tests of § 170(c). Moreover, they are subject to tax on income from a business enterprise not related to the purpose for which they receive their exemption. *See* I.R.C. § 511(a). Almost all exempt organizations are subject to tax on their unrelated business income, except for a government instrumentality other than a college or university. I.R.C. § 511(a)(2). The tax rate is the usual corporate rate. I.R.C. § 511(b)(1). Dividends, interest, royalties, etc., are not unrelated income, but returns on investments. I.R.C. § 512(b)(1), *see also* I.R.C. § 513.

To skim the rules on tax-exempt "private foundations," a 2% tax is imposed by I.R.C. § 4940 on net investment income, self-dealing is prohibited by § 4941, a 15% penalty tax extendable to 100% is imposed by § 4942 if the foundation does not distribute an amount equal to its minimum investment return, stock ownership is limited to 20% of a single corporation by § 4943, and § 4944 imposes special taxes if the foundation invests its assets in a manner that will jeopardize its charitable purposes or if it expends money for "improper" purposes such as lobbying.

For the rules applicable to charitable deductions for qualified conservation contributions, *see* I.R.C. § 170(h).

Section 170(f)(9) denies a charitable deduction for a contribution to an organization engaging in lobbying or political activity (as defined in § 162(e)(1)) if the activities directly affect the donor's trade or business and if the purpose of the contribution is to secure a deduction for activities that would be disallowed by § 162(e) if the donor had conducted the activities directly. Thus, if a taxpayer could not deduct political expenses as trade or business expenses under § 162(e), the taxpayer cannot obtain the deduction by giving the money to an organization that will turn around and engage in the same activity for which a deduction was denied to the taxpayer under § 162(e).

Other Aspects of Charitable Contribution Deductions. The charitable contribution deduction described in the above pages may be taken only by taxpayers who itemize deductions (those who have deductions in excess of the standard deduction). At one time, non-itemizing taxpayers were allowed to deduct a percentage of charitable contributions directly from gross income and there have been proposals to revive that type of provision.

As with other tax allowances, rates, credits and rules, the charitable contribution deduction can be analyzed as a "tax expenditure." The revenue lost by virtue of the deduction is akin to direct payments by government to subsidize or encourage or reward certain behavior, or to redistribute wealth and power. Estimates of the amount of revenue foregone can be made by aggregating all the charitable deductions claimed on millions of tax returns and multiplying them by an average tax rate or by the actual rates applied in the returns showing the deductions. But that method produces at best a first impact estimate; if the deduction were repealed the revenue gained would depend on how taxpayers reacted to the repeal. If each continued to contribute exactly the same amount to charity and nothing else changed, more taxes would be collected. But everything else could not remain the same, if for no other reason than because more taxes *were* collected. And in fact taxpayers would contribute differently, almost certainly less overall, and would do something else with the uncontributed amounts— pay taxes, engage in other tax-favored investments, shelters or activities, or consume more. Charities thus would lose some contributions overall, and the sources remaining might not be scattered throughout the income and social scale in just the same distribution as before. So lost contributions could partly be made up out of government payments from revenue gains, but the two quantities would be most unlikely to balance each other. And because of sizeable secondary or behavioral effects and other uncertainties, it proves rather speculative to try to appraise the quantitative differences or similarities between a tax expenditure and direct governmental expenditures.

The parallel between tax allowances and direct government support or control has led to litigation about the constitutionality of the charitable contribution deduction (and income-tax-exempt status or state and local property-tax exemptions to some such institutions) vis-à-vis gifts to religious organizations, racially segregated schools and social clubs. Other constitutional challenges, including ones

based on the freedom of speech guarantee of the
First Amendment, have also been raised. Increasingly the courts seem to lean toward a view that
little if any difference can be found between financial aid provided by government directly and that
provided indirectly in the tax system. *See* Committee for Pub. Education and Religious Liberty v.
Nyquist (S.Ct.1973). But that interpretation has not
meant that property tax or income tax exemptions
or allowances have been held unconstitutional. *See,
e.g.,* Walz v. Tax Commission (S.Ct.1970) (establish-
ment of religion and state property tax exemptions).
But some have been struck down. *See, e.g.,* Coit v.
Green (S.Ct.1971) (income tax exemption for racially segregated private schools); Bob Jones University
v. U. S. (S.Ct.1983). Other cases have equated tax
allowances with "financial assistance" within the
meaning of the Civil Rights Act of 1964. *See, e.g.,*
McGlotten v. Connally (D.C.D.C.1972).

Other aspects of governmental control exercised
through a tax allowance in the form of the charitable contribution deduction or income tax exemption
include challenges to the legality of limitations on
the legislative and political activities of labor un-
ions, Marker v. Shultz (D.C.Cir.1973); the litigation
and fee-generating activities of public interest law
firms, Rev.Rul. 75–75, 1975–1 C.B. 154, Rev.Rul.
75–76, 1975–1 C.B. 154, Rev.Proc. 75–13, 1975–1
C.B. 662; sex discrimination by a § 501(c)(3), group,
McCoy v. Schultz (D.D.C.1973), Junior Chamber of
Commerce of Rochester v. The United States Jay-
cees (10th Cir.1974); and distinctions adumbrated

between § 501(c)(7) (diverse groups) and (e)(8) (fraternal orders) groups, McGlotten v. Connally (D.C.D.C.1972).

The income-variant effect of the deduction has led to the suggestion that a credit be substituted as the allowance for charitable contributions. For example, a 30% credit would entitle every contributor to reduce his or her tax bill by $30 for every $100 contributed, an income-constant form of allowance. A variation would be to give a constant credit, but to make that credit taxable, at taxpayer's marginal rate. The result would be a tax benefit that would diminish as income rises. (If the credit is not taxable, it is income-variant in a hidden way; it consists of a cash payment and an exemption for that payment—which varies in its value according to the marginal rate of each taxpayer.) And, to be truly income invariant, the credit should be refundable as well as taxable.

Another suggestion is for repeal of the tax allowance and substitution of matching grants from government to charity, equal to some percentage of amounts contributed by private donors.

A deduction, however, may turn out to be an efficient method for encouraging charitable donations, with the greatest benefit possibly targeted at the potential donors most responsive to such incentives. It may be equitable, despite its income-variant effect, when viewed in the setting of a graduated-rate income tax, a system that does not tax imputed incomes from services donated to charity, and one that allows a deduction for some other involuntary or semi-involuntary reductions in ability to pay. One way of viewing the problem is to consider a wealthy high-income (28%) taxpayer who has been giving $10,000 a year to charity and to ask what additional tax she should pay if she does not contribute the next year. Since she then would have $10,000 more to consume, many would say she should pay $2,800 more in tax. If she were a 15% taxpayer, the same observer would say she should pay $1,500 more if she does not contribute. Such an observer then would tend to be led to the conclusion that, in each example, the relief afforded for contributing should be 28% and 15%, the marginal rate of tax otherwise applicable.

And, an observer who relates this charitable contribution deduction to the exclusion enjoyed by taxpayers who donate services or appreciated intangible capital assets would be likely to conclude that a tax deduction, rather than a flat credit, is the proper structural form, since both the exclusion and the deduction are similarly income-variant.

§ 61. Medical and Dental Expenses

Section 213(a) allows a deduction for all medical and dental expenses paid during the taxable year for the taxpayer, his or her spouse and dependents, subject to some limitations imposed by following subsections. Only expenses not compensated for by insurance or otherwise can be deducted. Because the statutory language requires actual payment, accrual of a medical expense (even by an accrual-method taxpayer) will not yield a deduction. Payment during the year for services rendered in prior years can be deducted; advance payments for future services may not be, unless required by the provider of services. A dependent generally is defined for purposes of § 213(a) as a child, grandchild, brother, sister, parent, grandparent, stepfather or mother, niece, nephew, or cousin or any person who during the entire year lives in taxpayer's home as a member of his household (unless the relationship violates local law), supported by taxpayer. *See* § 152.

First, some limitations on the § 213(a) deduction should be noted. Under § 213(a), only extraordinary medical expenses are to be deductible and, as a consequence, Congress imposed a 7.5% threshold for medical expenses. That is, only medical expenses spent for the taxpayer, his/her spouse, and dependents exceeding 7.5% of A.G.I. will be allowed. Thus, if the taxpayer has $10,000 A.G.I., the first $750 of unreimbursed medical expenses cannot be deducted. (Congress probably considered this first $750 as an "ordinary" medical expense.) Also, expenses paid for drugs are deductible only in the case of prescription drugs (as defined in § 213(d)(3)) and insulin. I.R.C. § 213(b).

Medical care is defined in § 213(d)(1) as amounts paid for the diagnosis, cure, mitigation, treatment, or prevention of disease, for transportation primarily for and essential to medical care, for qualified long-term-care services as defined in § 7702B(c), and for medical care insurance. Most payments for services by doctors, hospitals, and dentists, obviously, are included in this definition. Under the regulations, "medical care" includes hospital, nursing, medical, laboratory, surgical, dental, diagnostic and healing services, X-rays, medicines, drugs, medical equipment, artificial teeth or limbs, and ambulance services. The term covers any expense paid for the purpose of affecting any structure or function of the body. Regs. § 1.213–1(e). However, under § 213(d)(9), cosmetic surgery, as defined in § 213(d)(9)(B), does not qualify for a deduction unless it is necessary to ameliorate a deformity arising from, or directly related to, a congenital abnormality, a personal injury resulting from an accident or trauma, or a disfiguring disease.

Marginal problems have produced litigation of considerable variety. For example, in Comm. v. Bilder (S.Ct.1962), the U.S. Supreme Court ruled that medical care does not include rent for an apartment in Florida for taxpayer and his family, even though a series of heart attacks had led his doctor to advise him to spend the winter in a warm climate. His transportation to and from Florida would have been deductible, but the rent while away from home, like meals and similar expenses, constituted a personal living expense (I.R.C. § 262), not deductible "medical care." *But see* I.R.C. § 213(d)(2) for a limited deduction for certain lodging expenses. In Ochs v. Comm. (2d Cir.1952), taxpayer was refused a deduction for expenses of a private school to which he sent his young children on a doctor's advice so that his wife might have a better chance of recovering from throat cancer and associated surgery. Similarly, the cost of a vacation taken for one's general health cannot be deducted.

Some rulings have gone in taxpayer's favor. A guide dog for a blind person is deductible. Contraceptives for a woman whose health and life would be jeopardized by pregnancy have passed muster. Amounts paid to participate in a weight-loss program to treat a disease (including obesity) diagnosed by a physician are expenses for medical care. Special medical diet foods can be deducted if they supplement taxpayer's diet or amount to treatment, but not if they substitute for normal consumption. Fluoride in the home water supply for taxpayer's teeth was ruled a deductible expense, but a vacuum cleaner for an allergic patient was not, nor were the legal expenses of a divorce recommended by taxpayer's psychiatrist.

Some decisions have gone even further. Clarinet lessons recommended by an orthodontist to help correct taxpayer's son's malocclusion were allowed to be deducted. Even a wig for a daughter who had lost her hair due to disease was allowed. Other "liberal" decisions could be itemized, as could seemingly "strict" ones. Obviously all these cases seek to draw a proper line between deductible § 213 medical expenses and § 262 non-deductible personal expenses.

Another line to be drawn lies between expenditures deductible as medical expenses (below the line—of A.G.I.—subject to percentage restrictions of § 213) and business expenses (subject to the rules of §§ 162 and 212). Some expenses of a type incurred in medical care can be deducted as business expenses but not as medical expenses. Examples include payments by a blind employee to a reader for services performed in connection with the blind person's work, Rev.Rul. 75–316, 1975–2 C.B. 54, and payments by other handicapped individuals for travel, meal and lodging expenses of related and unrelated helpers who perform services for them on business trips, Rev.Rul. 75–317, 1975–2 C.B. 57.

The costs of braille books for taxpayer's visually impaired child were held deductible to the extent they exceeded costs of regular printed material. Fees for marriage counseling by a clergyman associated with a counseling center are not deductible under § 213. In contrast, amounts paid by a couple for treatment by psychiatrists at a hospital for sexual inadequacy and incompatibility, but not for hotel expenses, were ruled deductible.

Even if the medical expense pays for an asset with a useful life exceeding one year, as for eyeglasses, artificial limbs or teeth, crutches or a seeing-eye dog, the expenditure can be deducted currently—it does not have to be capitalized and depreciated, as it would in a § 162 context.

No "reasonable" requirement can be found in § 213, but lavish or excessive expenditures might well be disallowed as not constituting medical expenses at all. A "lavish or extravagant" limitation applies to the limited exception for lodging costs in § 213(d)(2). If a taxpayer spends money on a facility such as a swimming pool or elevator or air conditioning, and if he can prove that the cost was incurred for medical reasons, as distinct from personal consumption, he can take a deduction—but only for the cost over and above the increase in value of his house (or car or other property) that the installation produces. The balance enlarges his basis in the property. *See* Regs. § 1.213–1(e)(1)(iii).

Private schooling has presented medical deduction problems when therapy or special custodial care is provided in addition to ordinary education. In general, if the primary purpose of private school expenses for an ill or handicapped child is for therapy or remedial training, the full cost will be deductible. If the primary purpose is educational, no deduction will be allowed. If the cost of a separate therapeutic program can be isolated, it will be deductible, and the amount for regular tuition will not be.

Reimbursements by insurance in the taxable year in which a medical expense is paid prevents a deduction for that expense. I.R.C. § 213(a). Reimbursement in a later year for previously deducted expenses will produce income to the taxpayer to the extent of his prior tax benefit. *See* I.R.C. §§ 105(b) & 111; Regs. § 1.213–1(g). Because of the percentage limitations on deduction of medical expenses, or for other reasons, the prior expenses may not have produced a beneficial deduction.

The deduction evidently is designed to encourage and subsidize medical care, to afford some relief to a taxpayer who has suffered extraordinary and perhaps crushing, unexpected and largely involuntary financial burdens in the form of medical expenses—like a casualty loss or some state taxes—and perhaps to relieve the government of some costs of health care and disease prevention. It also may be based on the view that medical expenditures are not made for personal consumption but to repair (human) capital, and thus they should not be included in the measure of ability to pay under an income tax. Because the tax allowance for medical care is given in the form of a deduction, it benefits a taxpayer whose income offset by the deduction would have been taxed at higher rates more than it benefits a lower-bracket taxpayer. Another way to view the same effect is to observe that the high-bracket taxpayer simply is relieved of the heavier tax burden he would have to carry were it not for the misfortune of his extraordinary medical expenses and the tax law's decision to let him pay such bills with pre-tax (untaxed) dollars.

Section 223 established "health savings accounts." Section 223 allows the taxpayer a deduction in determining adjusted gross income for contributions to a health savings account. *See* I.R.C. § 62(a)(19). Eligibility for a health savings account is limited to taxpayers who are covered by a high-deductible health plan. The maximum contribution to a health savings account generally is the annual deductible under the high-deductible health plan. Additional contributions are allowed for taxpayers who have attained age 55. The big tax advantage consists of the fact that distributions from health savings accounts (consisting of contributed amounts and untaxed appreciation or returns on contributions) are tax free if the distributions are used to pay medical expenses. The amount of a distribution used for other purposes is included in gross income. See generally I.R.C. § 223.

§ 62. Education Expenses

The expenses of higher education traditionally were not deductible unless they were sufficiently connected to the taxpayer's business activities. The cost of a college education, education to meet the minimum requirements for employment, and education qualifying the taxpayer for a new trade or business are considered personal or constitute an inseparable aggregate of personal and capital expenditures that are not deductible as ordinary and necessary business expenses under I.R.C. § 162. *See* Regs. § 1.162–5(b)(1); *see also* Welch v. Helvering (S.Ct. 1933) (dictum regarding nondeductibility of education expenses). In contrast, education that (a) maintains or improves the taxpayer's skills in employment or a trade or business, or (b) meets the requirements for retention of a job, generally may be deducted under § 162. Regs. 1.162–5(a).

The Internal Revenue Code, however, does have a number of tax advantages for education. They include the I.R.C. § 117 exclusion for scholarships and fellowships (see § 28, *supra*), the I.R.C. § 25A hope and lifetime learning credits (see § 64, *infra*), and the I.R.C. 529 rules for qualified tuition programs (*see* § 74, *infra*). And beginning after 2001, Congress decided to make the cost of higher education deductible in certain instances. Section 222 provides a deduction for qualified tuition and related expenses that is taken above the line in determining adjusted gross income. *See* I.R.C. § 62(a)(18). The § 222 deduction terminates for taxable years beginning after 2005. I.R.C. § 222(e). "Qualified tuition and related" expenses are defined as tuition and fees required for enrollment of the taxpayer, the taxpayer's spouse, or a dependent, at an eligible educational institution. I.R.C. §§ 222(d)(1), 25A(f). No deduction is allowed for the expenses of someone who is a dependent of another taxpayer and married taxpayers must file jointly to obtain a deduction. I.R.C. §§ 222(c)(3), (d)(4). Activity fees, athletic fees, insurance expenses, other expenses unrelated to the course of instruction (*e.g.*, housing), and expenses for education involving sports, games, or hobbies (if not part of the individual's degree program) do not qualify for the deduction. I.R.C. § 25A(f)(1)(A) & (B). No deduction is allowed for tuition or related expenses paid for with amounts excluded from gross income that are not gifts (*e.g.*, an excluded scholarship). I.R.C. § 25A(g)(2). Amounts excluded under §§ 135 (savings bond interest used for higher education), 529 (qualified tuition programs), and 530 (Coverdell education savings accounts), cannot be used to produce a deduction under § 222. Also, no deduction is allowed if the taxpayer elects a § 25A credit for the expense and a taxpayer cannot deduct an expense under both § 222 and another Code section. I.R.C. § 222(c)(2).

The Section 222 deduction is limited to $4,000 in 2004 and 2005 if the taxpayer's modified adjusted gross income does not exceed $65,000 ($130,000 for a joint return). If the taxpayer's adjusted gross income exceeds $65,000 ($130,000 for a joint return) but does not exceed $80,000 ($160,000 for a joint return) the § 222 deduction cannot exceed $2,000. I.R.C. § 222(b)(2)(B).

§ 63. Personal and Dependency Exemptions

Under I.R.C. § 151(d), a taxpayer is entitled to a statutory $2,000 deduction as an exemption for himself/herself and, if taxpayer and spouse do not file a joint return, the spouse has no gross income and is not the dependent of another taxpayer, another $2,000 exemption for his or her spouse. I.R.C. § 151(a), (b). These personal exemptions are adjusted annually for inflation, in a manner analogous to the adjustment of the standard deduction. *See* I.R.C. § 151(d)(4). In 2004, the amount of a personal exemption is $3,100.

The deduction for personal exemptions allows the taxpayer to reduce income subject to tax by the amount fixed; a credit for personal exemptions, in contrast, would allow each taxpayer to reduce tax by the amount fixed. The tax saving of an exemption consists of the marginal tax rate(s) otherwise applicable multiplied by the amount of the exemption. The exemption amounts or levels represent some notion of the cost of subsistence, income equal to which should not, it is thought, be taxed.

Additional standard deductions for taxpayers 65 or over and for those who are blind are allowed by the Code, thus acknowledging the increased costs of subsistence and the hardships experienced by such taxpayers. *See* §§ 63(c)(3) & (f). The additional amount of standard deduction for tax years beginning in 2004 is $950 for blindness and $950 for age over 65. Similar policies underlie the exclusion of some social security benefits and the I.R.C. § 22 credit for the elderly.

The taxpayer is also entitled to one additional exemption of $2,000 for each "dependent." I.R.C. § 151(c). This exemption amount also is adjusted annually for inflation (the amount for 2004 is $3,100). Dependent is defined in I.R.C. § 152 to include most close relatives (by blood or marriage) and any unrelated individuals who live, as their principal place of abode, in the taxpayer's household and who are supported by taxpayer. Thus children by a taxpayer's spouse's former marriage, or a lover, or a common-law wife or husband can qualify. For all dependents, the key test is whether taxpayer provides over one-half the "dependent's" support. Also, the dependent must earn less than the exemption amount for the particular year, or the dependent must be taxpayer's child *and* either (i) under age 19 or (ii) a student under age 24. In addition, the dependent must not be married and filing a joint return with his spouse.

To meet the support test, taxpayer must bear the burden of establishing facts that entitle him to the deduction. In the case of divorced parents, I.R.C. § 152(e) adds some presumptions to the effect that the taxpayer who has custody of the children for the greater portion of the year contributes more than one-half of their support. Also, under § 152(c), multiple support agreements (as among several adult children who share the support of an aged parent) may allocate the exemption among taxpayers under some circumstances.

For purposes of determining dependency status under the support test, "support" includes at least food, lodging, clothing, medical care and education. Scholarships are omitted in determining support of children who are students. *See* § 152(d). Alimony does not qualify as a support payment even if used to support a spouse or children. If members of a household pool their resources, each member will be deemed to receive an equal portion of the pooled contributions as support for him. If he receives more than he contributes, the other members will be treated as supporting him and vice versa. *See* Rev.Rul. 64–222, 1964–2 C.B. 47.

Although the personal and dependency exemptions are rooted in notions of subsistence, they are available to all taxpayers, even those with incomes far above anyone's notion of subsistence levels. The high-income taxpayer, like the low one, may thus earn his or her "subsistence" tax free. Like deductions, the exemptions are income-variant; they afford a smaller benefit to taxpayers at the lower end of the income scale. As flat exemptions, these items also add to the progressivity of the actual effective rates of the income tax, since they allow a larger proportion of a low-income taxpayer's income to be received tax free than can be received free of tax by a higher income taxpayer. The progressivity of personal and dependency exemptions has also been increased by a provision that phases out exemptions for taxpayers with certain high levels of adjusted gross income. *See* I.R.C. § 151(d)(3). The phaseout, however, is being reduced over time and beginning in 2010 the phaseout will no longer apply. *See* I.R.C. § 151(d)(3)(E).

Although the dollar amounts of allowances such as the personal and dependency exemptions (and the standard deduction) were raised from time to time largely to adjust to inflationary effects on nominal prices, proposals to index the tax laws (such allowances, rates and basis determinations) did not succeed until 1981. Consequently, between increases the dollar allowances did shrink in real value to taxpayers. Indexing them produces automatic periodic changes in their levels to correspond to changes in some selected cost-of-living or inflation index. While indexing seems theoretically desirable, it adds a little to compliance and administrative costs—and it may deprive legislators of the appreciation lavished upon them when they did make discretionary increases from time to time, often in an election year.

Deductions and exempt or excluded income. Sometimes it has been proposed to require each taxpayer to allocate his or her deductions between taxable and tax-exempt income. The theory of such proposals is that no deduction should be allowed for a cost or expense that is directly associated with income that is not taxed or for otherwise deductible items, to the extent of the proportion that untaxed income bears to total income. None of these proposals has been enacted. Narrower efforts have been made, along the same lines, to argue against the allowance of some specific deduction because of its relation to tax-exempt income. For example, deductions for mortgage interest or taxes on an owner-occupied residence have been attacked because the imputed income from such ownership and occupancy is not taxed. Costs of supporting oneself or one's dependents could be regarded as having such an association with the untaxed imputed income from self-service or familial services as to make for disallowance, but undoubtedly the subsistence allowances are given for reasons having nothing to do with their role as costs of producing any kind of income whatsoever. Their basic premise is that very low-income people have no taxpaying capacity, or at least none that it would be advisable to tap. Yet the allowances also generally are available to higher-income taxpayers. *See* discussion of phaseout of exemptions, *supra*.

If taxpayer has no income, or no income sufficient to equal the sum of deductions, personal and dependency exemptions, and other allowances (credits, etc.), the tax advantage of personal and dependency exemptions will be lost. No carryover of the unused portion of such allowances has been given. The taxpayer might be viewed as having "negative income" or an unused loss in such years, which might imply either a right to carry forward or back the unused portion of the allowance or even to receive from the Treasury a payment of some or all of the discrepancy—a "negative income tax." Whether this line of thinking proves any more fruitful than direct welfare or guaranteed annual wage or income analysis remains to be seen.

Whether an income-variant deduction or an income-constant credit should be the exclusive form for personal and dependency costs does not receive a unanimous answer and is a question subject to analysis similar to that suggested for charitable contributions, § 60 *supra,* and other non-business allowances.

§ 64. Credits Against Tax

Unlike a deduction, a tax credit saves the taxpayer its full face value in dollars, because the amount of the credit is subtracted from the actual *tax* liability, not from income subject to tax. Some credits can even provide a refund to a taxpayer who owes no tax or less tax than the credit. *See, e.g.,* I.R.C. §§ 31(a) (credit for tax withheld), 32 (earned income credit). Others are not refundable. *See, e.g.,* I.R.C. §§ 21 (credit for household and dependent care services), 22 (credit for elderly and permanently disabled). (Of course, the amount of the credit may be computed as a percentage of something else, such as an expenditure by the taxpayer; the investment tax credit, for example, amounted to 10% of "qualified investment expenditures.") To mention the most prominent, tax credits are allowed for taxes withheld (§ 31), foreign taxes paid (§§ 27 & 901), a portion of income of the elderly (§ 22), certain investments (§ 38), adoption expenses (§ 23), interest on certain home mortgages (§ 25), household and dependent care expenses (§ 21), and the Hope scholarship credit and lifetime learning credit (§ 25A). Another credit is the child-tax credit (§ 24).

The credit form does not immediately appear to be income-variant—a credit of a given amount benefits a low-bracket taxpayer (in absolute dollars saved) just as much as a high-bracket taxpayer. The credit form may be viewed to be income-variant in a way different from a deduction, and it might seem to favor the low-bracket taxpayer since every dollar of credit against tax allows him to receive more dollars (than a high-bracket taxpayer) tax-free. For example, consider the effect of $1.00 of credit on the income of a 28% taxpayer and a 15% taxpayer: the $1.00 credit allows the high-bracket taxpayer to receive $3.60 tax free (because the 28% bracket taxpayer would otherwise have to pay $1 in tax on income of $3.60), while the low-bracket taxpayer can receive $6.70 income tax free (because at 15% he would otherwise have to pay $1 in tax on $6.70 of income).[1]

1. Another way to look at it, however, is to see that the before-tax equivalent value of a non-taxable $1 credit is about $1.39 to a 28% bracket taxpayer and only about $1.18 to a 15% bracket taxpayer.

Section 32 provides a refundable "earned income credit" to certain lower-income taxpayers who are "eligible individuals." "Eligible individuals" under § 32 include any individual who has a "qualifying child"—as defined in § 32(c)(3)—and any individual who does not have a qualifying child, if (1) the individual's principal place of abode is in the United States for more than one-half of the taxable year, (2) the individual has attained age 25 but not age 65 by the close of the taxable year, and (3) the individual is not a dependent for whom a deduction is allowable under § 151 to another taxpayer during the same taxable year. Married persons must file a joint return in order to be eligible for the credit.

The amount of the § 32 earned-income credit varies depending on the taxpayer's income and on whether the taxpayer has one qualifying child, two or more qualifying children, or no qualifying children. For 2004, a taxpayer with one qualifying child is eligible for a credit equal to 34 percent of the first $7,660 of earned income (a maximum of $2,604). As the taxpayer's adjusted gross income (or, if greater, earned income) exceeds $14,040, the "phaseout amount," the credit is gradually phased out. At income levels of $30,338 and above, the credit is reduced to zero. A taxpayer with two or more qualifying children will receive a credit equal to 40 percent of the first $10,750 of earned income (a maximum of $4,300). The credit is phased out as modified adjusted gross income exceeds $10,040, until it is completely gone for income levels of $34,458 and above. A taxpayer with no qualifying children will receive a credit equal to 7.65% of the first $5,100 of income (a maximum of $390). Phase-out begins when modified adjusted gross income exceeds $6,390 and is complete at an income level of $11,490 or above. These phaseouts of the credit as income rises act much like tax-rate increases above those set in I.R.C. § 1.

Congress also has blocked taxpayers from claiming the earned-income credit if their aggregate amount of "disqualified income" exceeds $2,200. "Disqualified income" includes the sum of interest (taxable and tax-exempt), dividends, net rent and royalty income (if greater than zero), capital-gain net income, and net passive income (as defined in § 469), if greater than zero, that is not self-employment income. *See* I.R.C. § 32(i). Congress believed that individuals with substantial assets could use proceeds from the sale of those assets in place of the earned-income credit to support consumption in times of low income.

The earned-income credit was advocated to offset part of the employee's share of the payroll tax for social security and, perhaps, other (often non-deductible) costs of earning income, as distinguished from receiving it from an investment or in the form of unemployment insurance and similar government transfer payments or private charity. And it was expected to encourage people to seek and accept employment and to reduce the welfare rolls. It is unusual in that it is refundable to the extent not used to offset the taxpayer's tax liability. As such, it is a form of "negative income tax."

Section 24 provides a child-tax credit of $1,000 in 2004 for each child under the age of 17 who is a dependent of the taxpayer. In 2005 through 2008 the credit is $700 per child and in 2009 the credit is $800 per child. The total credit allowed to a taxpayer is phased out at a rate of $50 for each $1,000 by which the taxpayer's modified adjusted gross income (defined in § 24(b)(1)) exceeds the threshold amount. The threshold amount is $75,000 for an unmarried individual, $110,000 for a joint return, and $55,000 for a married individual filing separately. Thus, in 2004 the $1,000 credit for a married couple filing jointly would be phased out for income levels between $110,000 and $130,000.

A portion of the credit may be refundable. The credit is refundable to the extent of 10% (15% after 2004) of the taxpayer's earned income in excess of $10,000. The $10,000 figure is adjusted for inflation and is $10,750 in 2004. A taxpayer with three or more qualifying children may receive a larger refund. *See* I.R.C. § 24(d).

Section 22 proffers a modest non-refundable credit to elderly taxpayers and individuals who retired on disability and were permanently and totally disabled upon retirement. Only earned income is eligible for the credit. The rate of credit is 15% and that rate is applied to income up to fixed dollar amounts: $7,500 for a married couple filing jointly and $5,000 for a single individual. *See* I.R.C. § 22(c)(2). However, the tax benefits are confined to lower and middle-income taxpayers by reducing the credit by $1 for each $2 of A.G.I. over specified limits, ($10,000 for married couples filing joint returns, $7,500 for single individuals). *See* I.R.C. § 22(d).

A still different tax rule does not reduce a taxpayer's tax liability but purports to describe how a small part of his tax payment will be disbursed. (In some ways it resembles a 100% tax credit.) This is the system for "check-offs" for political campaign contributions established by I.R.C. § 6096, §§ 9001–9013. Taxpayer merely "checks off" a box on the tax return to designate whether $3 of his or her tax payment shall be paid over to the Presidential Election Campaign Fund to be disbursed to candidates in presidential elections. The tax form states that checking the "yes" box will not increase the filer's tax or reduce a refund. While that is true as a statement about liability at that time, if revenues to be raised for other purposes by taxes are in any sense fixed, apparently taxes will rise if more taxpayers designate $3 of their taxes for campaign uses.

For tax years beginning in 1998, Congress enacted two credits designed to assist low- and middle-income families and students in paying for the costs of post-secondary education. *See generally* I.R.C. § 25A.

The first credit is the "Hope Scholarship Credit." For every eligible student, the Hope credit provides a credit for the first $1,000 of qualified tuition and related expenses paid by the taxpayer during the taxable year. The taxpayer also can receive an additional credit of 50 percent of the next $1,000 of qualified expenses, for a maximum credit of $1,500. A taxpayer can claim the credit for his dependents or for himself. For each student, the credit is available for a maximum of two years to cover expenses for the student's first two years of postsecondary education. The credit is phased out for taxpayers with modified adjusted gross income between $40,000 and $50,000 ($80,000 and $100,000 for joint returns). I.R.C. § 25A(d). The credit and phaseout amounts are indexed for inflation. I.R.C. § 25A(h). This credit is not refundable.

The second credit, the "Lifetime Learning Credit," allows a credit equal to 20 percent of the first $10,000 of qualified tuition and related expenses paid by the taxpayer during the taxable year. Thus, the credit can be as high as $2,000. The Lifetime Learning Credit also is phased out for higher-income taxpayers. *See* I.R.C. § 25A(d). The credit and phaseout amounts are indexed for inflation. I.R.C. § 25A(h). This credit is not refundable. The taxpayer can claim the Lifetime Learning Credit for expenses incurred by his dependents or himself. No limit exists on the number of years during which a taxpayer can claim the Lifetime Learning Credit. In contrast to the Hope Scholarship Credit, however, the Lifetime Learning Credit is a maximum of $2,000 per year *per taxpayer*, not per student. I.R.C. § 25A(c). Thus, a father who has three dependent children in college can claim a maximum of $2,000 per year under the Lifetime Learning Credit for his entire family. However, he may be able to claim the Hope Scholarship Credit for one dependent student and the Lifetime Learning Credit for another student. In a particular year, a student can be eligible for either the Hope Scholarship Credit or the Lifetime Learning Credit, but the student cannot be eligible for both credits in one year.

Amounts eligible for the § 25A credits are reduced by qualified scholarships excludible under § 117 (but not gifts). *See* I.R.C. § 25A(g)(2). Special rules prevent a taxpayer from using both one of these credits and other tax preferences for educational expenses. *See* I.R.C. §§ 529(c)(3)(B)(v), 530(d)(2)(C).

Section 25B allows a credit for a percentage of an eligible individual's qualified retirement savings contributions. Contributions eligible for the credit cannot exceed $2,000. An eligible individual is defined as someone who is at least 18 and who is not allowed to be claimed as an exemption by another taxpayer and is not a student. The credit percentage varies based on the taxpayer's filing status and amount of income. Section 25B terminates after 2006.

§ 65. The Standard Deduction

The standard deduction amount establishes a threshold for the imposition of the income tax, and it represents a standardized level of the amount of the average taxpayer's personal deductions. However, it is a bit more than that, since most taxpayers are entitled to its benefits whether or not their personal deductions add up to the given amount. Previously, the zero-bracket amount (an amount in the rate tables subject to a zero rate) was used to serve the above functions. The zero-bracket amount system was adopted to simplify the computation of the tax owed and to remove the income-variant impact of the allowance.

The 1986 T.R.A. reinstated the "standard deduction." Under this system, each individual who does not itemize certain deductions (as specified in I.R.C. § 63(b)) will be entitled to take, in lieu of them, a standard deduction. *See* I.R.C. § 63(e). The standard deduction will apply, along with the taxpayer's personal and dependency exemptions, to reduce adjusted gross income in arriving at taxable income.

The standard deduction is set by the Code at $3,000 for most individual taxpayers. The standard deduction for a married couple filing a joint return is the "applicable percentage" (200% in 2004, lower percentages in 2005–2008, and 200% in 2009—*see* I.R.C. § 63(c)(7)) of the $3,000 standard deduction and the standard deduction for a married taxpayer filing separately is one-half of the standard deduction for joint filers. *See* I.R.C. § 63(c). These amounts vary from year to year as they are indexed for inflation. I.R.C. § 63(c)(4). In 2004, the standard deduction for a single taxpayer is $4,850, the standard deduction for married taxpayers filing jointly is $9,700, and the standard deduction for a married taxpayer filing a separate return is $4,850.

A special rule limits the standard deduction of a taxpayer that is a dependent of another taxpayer to the greater of $500 (adjusted for inflation to $800 in

2004) or the sum of $250 and the individual's earned income. I.R.C. § 63(c)(5). Elderly (65 or older) and blind taxpayers are entitled to an additional standard deduction of $600 (adjusted for inflation to $950 in 2004). I.R.C. § 63(f). A taxpayer may qualify for two additional standard deductions if the taxpayer is both elderly and blind. The additional standard deduction is increased to $750 (adjusted for inflation to $1,200) if the taxpayer is unmarried and not a surviving spouse. I.R.C. § 63(f)(3).

If a taxpayer has no income at all, the standard deduction, like the zero-bracket amount, will not benefit him at all; if his income is less than the available allowances, he will lose its benefits to the extent of this difference.

The procedural purpose of the standard deduction amount is to enable millions of taxpayers to avoid the difficult business of itemizing, thus to simplify compliance for them, to reduce administrative costs, and to substitute a roughly equivalent lump sum tax allowance for taxpayers who could not prove that they had made deductible expenditures equal in aggregate to this lump sum. To get the benefit of the standard deduction, the taxpayer need not, in fact *may* not, itemize. Hence, he or she need not substantiate those deductible expenditures, keep records, and otherwise go through the effort necessary for the increased benefits of excess itemized deductions. The taxpayer will choose to seek these benefits if his itemized deductions exceed the standard deduction. Whether or not the taxpayer is entitled to, or chooses to, itemize deductions, he may deduct most business and profit-seeking expenses under § 162 (unless they are "employee expenses") in computing A.G.I. from G.I. *See* I.R.C. §§ 62, 63.

Some deductions (such as interest) may occur as business deductions or as personal deductions. If deductible as business items, they will reduce A.G.I., which in turn will increase the amount of the available medical-expense, miscellaneous-itemized, and nonbusiness casualty-loss deductions, which are inversely dependent on the amount of A.G.I. (by reducing the respective 7.5%, 2% and 10% of A.G.I. thresholds of those deductions) if itemized separately. It will possibly also decrease the amount of itemized charitable contributions deductible for the year since charitable contributions are limited to a percentage (usually 50% or 30%) of A.G.I. If taxpayer does not itemize his or her deductions, these effects will not be felt.

A substantive result of previously installing the predecessor standard deduction in the tax tables as the zero-bracket amount was to construct the allowance so that it gave the same tax benefits to all taxpayers (who had incomes at least equal to the allowance) by making the allowance offset income taxed at the bottom rates (equal for all such taxpayers) rather than the top rates which, of course, vary from one taxpayer to another according to the amount of taxable income he or she has for the year in question. The legislative history, however, does not give any evidence that this result was the purpose or anticipated effect of the change. Each taxpayer's taxable income taxed at positive rates was stacked on top of the zero-bracket amount and ascended to its own height. However, the reversion to the standard deduction form recreates the income-variant result; the standard deduction in effect offsets income at the top.

Even though the zero-bracket amount established a flat allowance that did not vary with income, it could nevertheless be viewed to be progressive, since a flat allowance forms a declining percentage of income as income rises. Despite this fact, some flat-amount allowances, such as the $2,000 personal exemption, when placed against the graduated tax rates, provide a greater saving to high-bracket taxpayers than to others. (The former zero-bracket amount, however, offset income in the bottom brackets for all taxpayers alike.)

Like its predecessors and like the personal and dependency exemptions, the standard deduction also contributes to reducing administrative and compliance costs by removing many persons from the tax rolls, because the tax return filing requirements are partly linked to the amount of the standard deduction. *See* I.R.C. § 6012.

Unlike the zero-bracket amount, the standard deduction must be taken into account in computing taxable income when the taxpayer uses the tax tables under §§ 1 and 3 of the Code. Section 3 tables also incorporate the personal exemptions. Those taxpayers not eligible to use the tables under § 3 must compute their taxable income under § 63 and then find the tax applicable to that amount in the tables under § 1.

§ 66.   Other Personal Allowances

The income tax law often has been used for purposes other than raising revenue or redistributing economic resources solely on the basis of "income" defined in that law and sometimes equated to ability to pay. Some proposals to use the tax for social, economic, political and miscellaneous other goals have been enacted into law; others have failed in the attempt. Among those allowances in the former category might be mentioned those given for political contributions [I.R.C. § 24 credit for up to $50 contributed (repealed for tax years beginning after 12/31/86); former § 218 deduction for political contributions up to $100 (repealed as of 12/31/78)], for retirement savings in Individual Retirement Accounts (IRA's) (I.R.C. § 219), and a raft of others. (*See, e.g.*, § 25A, the Hope Scholarship Credit and Lifetime Learning Credit for qualified tuition and related expenses, § 30, credit for qualified electric vehicles, § 132, exclusion for mass transit passes, § 190, expenditures to remove architectural and transportation barriers to the handicapped and elderly, former § 191, amortization of certain rehabilitation expenditures for certified historic structures, and former § 23, the residential energy credit for expenditures on energy conservation property for a principal residence.)

Among those proposed but not enacted could be counted ones for a deduction or credit for legal expenses,[2] for some portion of the cost of purchasing a new personal residence (such an allowance was made in the form of a 5% credit, in I.R.C. § 44, for a period between March 12, 1975 and December 31, 1976), for home repairs, for employment of domestic (household) help, and other socially or commercially desirable activities or for necessitous circumstances such as disability.

2. Note that I.R.C. § 120 excludes from an employee's income the benefits of an employer's qualified non-discriminatory legal services plan.

CHAPTER VII

ANNUAL ACCOUNTING: WHEN IS INCOME TAXABLE?

§ 67. Introduction

The Federal Income Tax employs a periodic system for reporting and taxing income. The particular period used is the 12–month year, either a calendar or a fiscal year. This annual system, combined with the graduated rate structure, makes the timing of income (and deductions, credits, or other allowances) important. The timing is important partly because deferring tax payments provides the taxpayer with use of the tax money in the interim. Timing is also important because the same total amount of income received and taxed will involve higher tax liability (due to graduated, annual rates) if it is lumped in a few years rather than spread evenly over a greater number of years. Consequently, taxpayers often strive to delay receiving or reporting their income, to accelerate reporting their deductions, and to arrange matters so as to spread their taxable income as evenly as possible over the years. Also, applicable rates sometimes change, either when Congress legislates such changes or when a taxpayer's income rises or falls (as it often does upon retirement), or when a taxpayer's status changes (as upon marriage or divorce). So taxpayers may seek to shift income into low-rate years. The Government, on the other side, needs to assure itself of a steady and predictable flow of revenue and wants to prevent taxpayers from manipulating and distorting their income reporting, not only for revenue purposes and to protect the integrity of the law, but also to prevent some taxpayers from enjoying inequitable advantages compared to others less able to escape the consequences of annual reporting under graduated rates.

Much legislation, litigation and administrative work addresses itself to timing problems. Some exceptions to the strict annual concept must be made for reasons of equity or practicability. Elsewhere taxpayer thrusts must be met with administrative or legislative or judicial parries.

§ 68. Annual Accounting for Income—§ 441

The Federal Income Tax uses an annual (12–month) computation of income. *See* I.R.C. § 441. This annual system distinguishes itself from one using a shorter period—such as six months—or a longer period—such as five years. It also is to be differentiated from a period governed by other than calendar events, such as a cumulative lifetime averaging system. Also, the annual approach differs from a "transactional" approach or other non-periodic or non-temporal methods.

As a result of the annual system, the amount of tax to be paid may vary according to the year in which income is reportable not only because the graduated rate schedule taxes different amounts of income differently at the margin but also because rates, other tax rules, or even the taxpayer's status may be altered from time to time. Also, the statute of limitations may have run on an early year, thus preventing liability from being assessed for that year. Taxing income in annual slices may mean taxing a receipt as income in one year even though the transaction of which it is a part results in an overall loss to the taxpayer, or vice versa. *See, e.g.,* Burnet v. Sanford & Brooks Co. (S.Ct.1931).

In some areas the law does not blind itself to events in other years; however, reporting income remains basically an annual affair. Thus, a person who receives funds in one year, with every reason to claim them as a matter of right and to exercise complete dominion and control over them, must pay tax on them for that year even though it later turns out that they must be returned—because of error, theft, rules of restitution, etc. *See, e.g.,* U.S. v. Lewis (S.Ct.1951). Even though claims against the funds are outstanding when taxpayer receives them, the "claim of right" doctrine gives finality to the annual period and requires that the taxpayer report them as income until and unless compelled to part with them or their equivalent. *See* North American Oil Consolidated v. Burnet (S.Ct.1932). Later, when restitution is made, the earlier tax treatment of the receipt may influence the treatment of the subsequent payment. *See* U.S. v. Skelly Oil Co. (S.Ct. 1969) (percentage depletion calculated in year of receipt of income must reduce deductibility and tax benefit of repayment in later year). Similarly, if a charitable contribution made and deducted in year one is returned to the taxpayer in year two, the tax treatment of the receipt in year two will be geared in some way to whether a tax benefit was obtained in year one; but the tax rates and rules applicable in year two will govern all other questions. *See* Alice Phelan Sullivan Corp. v. U.S. (Ct.Cl.1967). Statutory rules offer further guidance about and modification of the purely annual system. *See, e.g.,* I.R.C. §§ 111, 186, 1341.

Occasionally, but very rarely, taxpayers have succeeded in convincing the tax authorities to depart from a strict annual approach to reporting income and losses. For two illustrative cases adopting a "transactional approach," *see* Bowers v. Kerbaugh–Empire Co. (S.Ct.1926) and Bradford v. Comm. (6th Cir.1956). Other cases have allowed the taxpayer to depart from pure annual accounting in order to conform his tax reporting with his non-tax bookkeeping, so long as he does not overdo it to gain an unfair advantage. Still, the annual approach, which looks only to the events that take place in one tax year, has prevailed. In turn, some exceptions have been granted by legislation to soften the sometimes cruel disadvantages of a strict annual system. Such legislation includes: former I.R.C. §§ 1301–1305 (income averaging, *see* § 77 below); I.R.C. § 1341 (taxpayer restores a substantial amount held under a claim of right and previously included in his income); I.R.C. § 111 and Regs. § 1.111–1(a) (the tax-benefit rule applicable when deduction in the prior year of an amount recovered later did not give taxpayer any tax benefit in the earlier year); I.R.C. § 186 (damages received for breach of contract or fiduciary duty, anti-trust injury or patent infringement).

A departure from the strict annual approach, and adoption of a transactional view, sometimes is made to determine the character, not the time of reporting, of gain or loss—*e.g.*, capital or ordinary. For example, prior-year events can be taken into account in characterizing a receipt or payment in a later, taxable, year. *See, e.g.,* Arrowsmith v. Comm. (S.Ct.1952); § 100 *infra.*

The usual period of limitations for correction of a tax return runs after three years. To prevent an injustice to a taxpayer whose current taxability is related to prior mistreatment that can no longer be corrected by amending the earlier return, the courts have sometimes applied doctrines of equitable estoppel and recoupment, which have now been codified in part in the form of I.R.C. §§ 1311–1314.

§ 69. Methods of Accounting—§ 446

To make the periodic (annual) system work, the income tax needs some principles in order to allocate items of income or deduction to particular annual tax periods. For example, will wages paid after the year end for work done before then be taxable in the year of work or the year of payment? These principles or rules make up methods of accounting—for income, expenses, or losses. *See* I.R.C. § 446. The most commonly known methods are the "cash receipts and disbursements method" and the "accrual method." Most individual taxpayers, especially those not in business, use the cash method. Most of us do so without thinking of it as a method of accounting at all.

Section 451 requires that the taxpayer include income items in the year he receives them unless his method of accounting requires inclusion in a different year. Section 461 states that a deduction or credit must be taken in the tax year that is proper under the method of accounting used to determine taxable income. Some other Code sections override these general rules as to specific items.

Generally speaking, the taxpayer may adopt any of the permissible methods of accounting he chooses—so long as, in the opinion of the Commissioner, it clearly reflects income. I.R.C. § 446(b) and (c). The method chosen must then, above all, be applied consistently. Also, the method chosen must correspond to that used by the taxpayer in keeping his own (non-tax) books. § 446(a). The "books" of an individual taxpayer need not be, and usually are not, ledgers and balance sheets, but merely his checkbook or receipts and contracts. If inventories are used in the business, the accrual method must be employed unless the Commissioner authorizes otherwise. Regs. §§ 1.446–1(c)(2)(i) and (ii), 1.471–1. Taxpayer may not change from one accounting method to another without the consent of the Commissioner, who will require taxpayer to show a business purpose for the change and may require adjustments to accomplish the transition. *See* I.R.C. §§ 446(e), 481.

I.R.C. § 446(c) specifies several permissible methods of accounting. Section 446(d) allows a taxpayer who is engaged in more than one trade or business to use a different accounting method for each trade or business. He may use one accounting method for his business and another for his personal affairs. *See* Regs. § 1.446–1(c)(1)(iv)(b). He must, however, use the same taxable year for all his activities. Section 7701(a)(25) specifies that the terms "paid or incurred" and "paid or accrued" (as they appear in various substantive Code sections, such as those allowing deductions) shall be construed according to the method of accounting used by the taxpayer to compute taxable income.

The accounting period that the taxpayer chooses must be either the calendar year (applicable if chosen or if no explicit choice is made) or the fiscal year (any year beginning with some month other than January 1), or the 52–53 week year available in some instances. I.R.C. § 441. The year chosen must agree with the taxpayer's non-tax bookkeeping. I.R.C. § 441. After choosing one period, taxpayer may not lightly change to another. I.R.C. § 442; Regs. § 1.441–1(e).

§ 70. The Cash (Receipts and Disbursements) Method of Accounting— § 446(c)(1)

The cash method is used by most individuals and small businesses and must be used if taxpayer does not keep any books. This apparently simple method of attributing income and expenses to tax years generally requires that taxpayer include income items when received and deduct expenses when paid or borne. Since income need not be received in the form of cash to be taxable, the cash method entails reporting cash *or its equivalent,* including the fair market value of property. No effort is made systematically to correlate receipts with payments to which they are economically connected. *See generally* Regs. § 1.446–1(c)(1).

Not only are cash and receipts in kind reportable when *actually* received, but they also are reportable when *constructively* received. The doctrine of constructive receipt decrees that when a cash-method taxpayer has the power to receive income but voluntarily does not receive it, the item shall be considered as having been received. So if income is credited to the taxpayer's account, set apart for him, or otherwise made available so that he may draw upon it at any time, or so that he could have drawn upon it during the taxable year if notice of intention to withdraw had been given, the income is constructively received. Regs. § 1.451–2. Not every opportunity to receive payment or other gain is treated as constructive receipt, to be sure. A taxpayer who sells his property in return for a promise to pay the price next year need not report the gain or loss this year merely because the purchaser would have been willing to agree to pay him sooner. Cf. J.D. Amend (Tax Court 1949). And, a contract that provides for payment in one year may be revised in good faith to provide for payment in the next year without taxation in the first year. *See* Howard Veit (Tax Court 1947). But if payment is offered to the taxpayer and he asks the offeror to wait until next year, the taxpayer will be treated as if he had received it in the earlier time. Taxpayer's control over the timing of receipt is the touchstone for applying the doctrine. So, interest credited to a depositor's savings account will be taxed to him whether or not withdrawn or even entered in the passbook during the year.

A doctrine of constructive *payment* has not developed very far, perhaps because so many statutory rules on deductions require that the expense be "paid," a term that has discouraged anything more than an inquiry into whether payment in fact had been made.

Some receipts present problems similar to, but distinguishable from, those of constructive receipt. Suppose, for example, a cash-method taxpayer takes a check or promissory note in payment for goods or services. Has he actually received cash? Not really. Has he constructively received cash? No, not really, unless he was offered cash and declined it. But has he received the equivalent of cash? Has he received property sufficiently susceptible of valuation to be appropriately taxable? Perhaps. Surely if the promissory note were negotiable, were made by a solvent maker having good credit, and were accepted in full payment of the price, the recipient would have a cash equivalent and such receipt, the cases hold, would be taxable, but note that he would then be taxable on the fair market value of the note (face value minus a discount, probably), not on the cash amount it states on its face. *See* Warren Jones Co. v. Comm. (9th Cir.1975) (contracts or promissory notes readily marketable in taxpayer's area). This is the key difference between the doctrine of constructive receipt (taxpayer taxable on the actual value of what he could have received) and the doctrine of cash equivalence (fair market value of what is actually received is taxable). Further, a non-negotiable note, or a mere contractual promise to pay, generally is not treated as the equivalent of cash; its receipt will not produce realization of gain or loss to a cash method taxpayer according to other cases. But see Cowden v. Comm. (5th Cir. 1961) (agreements for payment assigned to a bank were cash equivalents; court said negotiability is not the test of taxability).

An approach resembling the doctrines of constructive receipt and cash equivalence sometimes uses language of "economic benefit." Though dangerously vague in outline, the concept conveys some meaning—perhaps best conveyed by example—as it bears on the timing of taxing income. Thus if an employer compensates an employee by buying a vested (non-forfeitable), non-assignable annuity contract for him but keeps the contract in its possession, the compensation will be income to the employee in the year the annuity was purchased, not later when it pays out or when the employer hands over the contract. *See* U.S. v. Drescher (2d

Cir.1950); Rev.Rul. 62–74, 1962–1 C.B. 68 (prize money placed in escrow account is income then).

Application of the cash method to two cash-method taxpayers was illustrated in Rev.Rul. 76–135, 1976–1 C.B. 114. There a client paid a lawyer for legal services by means of a negotiable promissory note. The lawyer at once discounted the note at a bank, to which the client subsequently made payments. The lawyer was taxable on the discounted value of the note in the year it was received. The client became entitled to a deduction only when payments on the note were made to the bank.

In general, a check received by a cash-method taxpayer during the taxable year (even after banking hours) is deemed available to the taxpayer for his/her unrestricted use, and the income is actually or constructively received in that year if the check is later paid upon presentation to the drawee (even if not until sometime during the following year). The check is a conditional payment but it becomes an absolute payment if honored by the drawee. *See* M.J. Spiegel (Tax Court 1949); C.F. Kahler (Tax Court 1952). If the check is dishonored upon presentation to the drawee in the year after delivery, it would not be a taxable receipt in the prior year. In addition, the I.R.S. has ruled that at least some payments by credit card are deductible in the year the charge is made, regardless of when the bank is repaid. *See* Rev.Rul. 78–38, 1978–1 C.B. 67 (charitable contribution).

The cash-method taxpayer is taxable on a payment he receives under a claim of right even if he later may have to return some or all of it or even if there is some restriction placed on his use of the receipts. However, severe restrictions placed on its use, or other terms and facts surrounding the receipt, may indicate that he is not entitled to the money or property as his own but is merely a custodian or deposit holder. In that event, he will not be taxable unless the restrictions expire or the terms change. So, a cash-method landlord who receives advance rentals must report them as income when he receives them. But, if he receives a security deposit that he is obligated to hold and that is not to be applied on rent, he will not be taxable on that amount at that time.

On the other hand, if a cash-method taxpayer received a partial payment (or "prepayment") agreed to be retained as liquidated damages in the event that full payment is not made, the taxpayer must report income when the payment is received. *See* Martin v. U.S. (8th Cir.1969).

Just as advance receipts have created some problems for cash-method taxpayers, prepayments by them of estimated expenses require special attention. The acceleration of expense deductions gives a tax benefit by permitting taxpayer to reduce present taxes and thus to defer some taxes to later periods. Usually, a cash-method taxpayer takes a deduction in the year the expense is actually paid. However, to prevent taxpayers from distorting their income reporting, some limits have to be placed on the deductibility of prepayments. Sometimes taxpayer will be required to allocate prepayments to the years to which they relate and thus to spread the deductions over more years on a pro-rata basis. This pro-ration or amortization requirement closely resembles the rule against immediate deduction of a capital expenditure. I.R.C. § 263. So, some advance payments of rent and bonuses or commissions paid to acquire or cancel leases have to be amortized over the term of the lease. Similarly, prepaid insurance may be treated as if premiums were spread over several years. So, these pre-payments yield deductions only to the extent that the asset or service is exhausted during the current year. *And see* I.R.C. § 461(g), which requires cash method taxpayers to deduct prepaid interest over the life of the loan.

The policies behind allowing taxpayers to use the cash method seem to consist mainly of its simplicity and avoidance of complex recordkeeping and computations. Also, it allows a taxpayer to associate cash inflows with tax payment elevations and cash outflows with reduced tax payments. However, in many instances these policies are outweighed by the need properly to allocate expenses and related income to the same, and an appropriate, tax year, a task better performed by the accrual method of accounting, next.

§ 71. The Accrual Method of Accounting— § 446(c)(2)

The accrual method differs from the cash method in that it makes taxability turn not on actual receipt or payment but on the fixing of the right to receipt or the maturing of the obligation to pay. As one court put it, under the accrual method the tax returns "shall immediately reflect obligations and expenses definitely incurred and income definitely earned without regard to whether payment has been made or whether payment is due." When the right to receive an amount becomes fixed, the right accrues. Similarly when all conditions or contingencies on an obligation to pay are removed, it must be accrued as if paid. Generally speaking, then, accrual accounting requires that income earned during a tax period be charged with the expenses incurred in and properly attributable to earning that income. Moreover, accrual-method accounting seeks to allocate both income and deductions to the tax year in which the taxpayer's economic activity produced them. To do this, the accrual method refers to the year in which the right to receive payment arises and to the year an obligation to pay arises as the year when income or a deduction is to be reported. It thus differs from the cash method which, broadly speaking, refers to time of receipt and time of payment to fix the tax year in which both will be reported. Consequently, unlike an accrual taxpayer, a cash-method taxpayer can more often pay his expenses, deduct them currently, and defer tax on income by arranging for payment in a later tax period. In order to prevent manipulation of this sort and generally to relate tax reporting to business activity, the accrual method is required for any taxpayer whose income arises from the purchase and sale of goods if inventories are necessary, and it is used by most large businesses.

As stated above, § 451 of the I.R.C. states that any item of gross income must be included in the taxable year in which it is received by the taxpayer unless, under the method of accounting used in computing taxable income, such amount is properly to be accounted for as of a different period. The accrual method is such a method of accounting, but it leaves room for dispute about to which year an item is properly to be attributed, and the rules to make such allocations for tax purposes do not afford precise guidance.

In general, a taxpayer must accrue an item when the right or obligation becomes fixed, when the amount in question can reasonably be determined and when no substantial uncertainty about collection exists. On the income side, income becomes reportable when all events have occurred that fix the right to receive it and the amount can be determined with reasonable accuracy. On the deduction side, a parallel statement may be made. *See* Regs. § 1.451–1(a); § 1.461–1(a)(2). In shorthand, these two standards are referred to as the "all events" and "reasonable accuracy" tests. Applying these general maxims can give rise to troublesome questions, and the law on the subject has not fully evolved.

With the accrual method, the exact amount of an incurred liability or receipt does not need to be accurately ascertained for it to be accruable. If it can be estimated with reasonable certainty, it is accruable. Likewise, the actual payment or collection need not be free of *all* uncertainty to be accruable. A claim against a corporation, for example, may have to be accrued as income even though there is some doubt about the corporation's ability to pay it, or even if insolvency of the corporation appears as a possibility. At some point, however, if non-payment has become very likely or a virtual certainty, accrual of the income need not be made, or accrual of a bad debt may be taken if income has earlier been accrued. If the taxpayer, or someone who owes him money, is actually contesting the liability, the right to payment is not deemed to be fixed. However, I.R.C. § 461(f) allows an accrual-method taxpayer to accrue a deduction in the year he pays it even if he is still contesting his liability thereafter. If a liability is contingent, it should not be accrued until all events that determine liability have occurred. Under the accrual method, taxpayer may avoid accruing an item simply by contracting (in good faith) to defer the right to payment.

Prepayments of income and estimated expenses have presented troublesome questions for accrual-method taxpayers. The taxpayer who receives payment in advance may seek to defer accrual; the taxpayer who prepays an estimated expense may by doing so seek to advance the accrual of his deduction before his liability has become ripe. Suppose, for example, an accrual basis landlord is paid rent before it is due. Or, suppose a dance studio or auto club or furnace servicing business receives payment

for services before the services are rendered or due
to be rendered. The accrual-method taxpayer has
actually received the amounts before he had the
right to receive them. Is the right to receive them a
necessary condition for accrual as well as a sufficient condition? Can accrual of advance receipts be
deferred until future activity makes final his right
to receive the amounts? That is, can taxation of
amounts already received be deferred until some
later time?

After some vacillation, the cases have settled on *pay for future service*
an approach which makes the accrual-method tax-
payer taxable on prepayments he receives much as
if he were on the cash method. An exception to this
rule is available so that a taxpayer can defer taxation on amounts actually received if a reserve is
created to reflect a definite deferral in the services
or deliveries that the recipient is obliged to make in
order to earn the income. In such event, a proportionate amount of the prepayment may be attributed to years other than the taxable year of receipt.
A great deal turns on whether the Commissioner
concludes that such a reserve and attribution will
clearly reflect taxpayer's income, and whether a
court will conclude that the Commissioner abused
his discretion if he overruled taxpayer's system.

While an accrual-method taxpayer often must report an income item before receiving it, because he
has earned it and has a right to receive it, he cannot
so often use the "right to receive it" rule to *postpone* tax on something already received. Deferral of
advance receipts remains possible only in special

situations such as those, for example, when the costs of rendering future services for the income can reliably be predicted with a statistical basis for estimating when the services or deliveries or other expenditures will take place, and when deferral of the advance receipts will correlate them with the expenses of earning them. *See, e.g.,* Artnell Co. v. Comm. (7th Cir.1968); *see also* Tampa Bay Devil Rays Ltd. v. Comm. (Tax Ct. Memo. 2002). But courts may limit the doctrine of *Artnell* to its facts. *See, e.g.,* Johnson v. Comm. (Tax Court 1997). *And see* Rev.Rul. 71–21, 1971–2 C.B. 549 (limited deferral allowed for payments in one year for services to be rendered before the end of the following year). The claim-of-right doctrine has been used by the courts to counter the efforts of taxpayers to defer accruing advance receipts. For example, when a cash- or accrual-method taxpayer receives a prepayment to which the taxpayer has an unrestricted right, the taxpayer must include the income upon receipt of the pre-payment. *See* Martin v. U.S. (8th Cir.1969). Special statutory rules permit deferral by some taxpayers. *See, e.g.,* I.R.C. § 455 (prepaid subscription income of a publisher) and § 456 (prepaid dues of membership organizations such as automobile clubs).

Similarly, the accrual-method taxpayer will have difficulty deducting (as if paid) an expense not actually paid and one he is not yet obligated to pay, but for the payment of which he has set up a reserve and has segregated funds. If he actually makes a payment in advance, he may be permitted or even required to defer the deduction to later years. Specifically, § 461(c) allows accrual-method taxpayers to elect to attribute taxes on real property to the years to which they relate. But more difficulty is encountered if the taxpayer seeks to take a deduction early by prepaying his estimated expenses or creating and adding to a reserve account for anticipated losses.

For accrual-method taxpayers, an "economic performance" rule modifies the "all events" test. Section 461(h) provides that, in determining whether an amount (of a liability or cost) has been incurred with respect to any item during the taxable year, the "all events test" shall not be treated as met (so as to allow the accrual of a deductible expense) any earlier than when "economic performance" with respect to such items occurs. The "all events test" treats a liability as incurred in the year in which all events have occurred that determine the fact of the liability, and the amount of the liability can be determined with reasonable accuracy. *See* I.R.C. § 461(h)(4) and Reg. § 1.461–4. The Code goes on to state various principles for determining when economic performance occurs. Generally, economic performance occurs when the taxpayer is provided with services or property, if the liability arises from the receipt of such services or property. I.R.C. § 461(h)(2)(A). If the liability requires the taxpayer to provide services or property, economic performance occurs when the taxpayer provides the services or property. I.R.C. § 461(h)(2)(B).

The nature of a prepayment or advance receipt may affect the requirement that an accrual-method taxpayer include it in income or defer his deduction. A prepayment of rent, received and held without any restriction on its use or control, will have to be included in income by an accrual-basis landlord. But a similar amount received as a security deposit to be held or escrowed until the rights to it are determined on termination of a lease or as security for performance may not be accruable until and unless the recipient becomes entitled to it without encumbrance.

At some points in the Code, the statutory terms used in granting a deduction override general accounting principles. For example, a statutory section may say that a deduction is allowed for an amount (such as a charitable contribution or a medical expense or alimony) actually "paid" during the year. When such a rule is applied to an accrual-method taxpayer, the result is to put him on the cash method for those items—they are deductible when, and only when, he actually pays them. Occasionally the accrual-method taxpayer is virtually put on the cash basis for income items too. For example, he need not accrue dividends when they are declared by a corporation in which he owns stock. He may wait until the corporation actually pays them to him, for complicated reasons having to do with uniform substantive treatment of all shareholders, both those on the cash method and accrual method.

If purchases and sales of merchandise are a material income-producing factor so that inventories must be used, the accrual method must be applied to such purchases and sales unless the Commissioner authorizes otherwise. *See* Regs. § 1.446–1(c)(2)(i). *And see* § 73 below.

Section 267(a)(2) contemplates an accrual-method taxpayer who accrues an expense for a payment due to a cash-method taxpayer before payment and receipt and thus before the time that the cash-method taxpayer need report the income. For example, an employer might accrue salary to an employee, especially one who also is a shareholder, but pay later and seek to defer tax through this disparity. Section 267(a)(2) blocks the deduction to some accrual-method taxpayers who bear specified relationships to cash-method payees until the cash-method taxpayer must include the income; *i.e.*, when payment is made.

§ 72. Other Accounting Methods

Section 446(c) contemplates not only the cash and accrual methods of accounting, but also "any other method permitted by this chapter", and any combination of the foregoing methods permitted under regulations. Other, somewhat less important and less common, methods of accounting for income include the installment-sale method (*see* I.R.C. §§ 453, 453A, 453B), some hybrid methods (*see* Regs. § 1.446–1(c)(1)(iv)), the percentage-of-completion method (for long-term contracts), and the net-worth method (for reconstructing a taxpayer's income).

The Installment Method. I.R.C. §§ 453, 453A, and 453B provide a special method of accounting for the gain from certain transactions involving real or personal property. They seek to provide a measure of relief from the harsh impact of the annual accounting concept when applied to a sale involving a purchase price to be paid over a period of years. To do so, they allow the gain from some sales of property to be reported over the number of years in which the taxpayer is paid the proceeds of the sale (in cash or the equivalent of cash).

Section 453 states that a seller (who fits the description given in that section) shall return as income that proportion of each installment payment actually received each year that the gross profit, realized or to be realized when payment is completed, bears to the total contract price. To illustrate, suppose that a car is sold for a price of $10,000, to be paid in the amounts of $2,500 per year, for four years, plus interest, without any down payment. If the auto seller's basis in the property is $8,000, the gain eventually to be realized will be $2,000. If the installment method applies to a seller in this situation, four fifths of each annual payment of principal, or $2,000, will be considered to be return of capital and one fifth ($500) will be reported as income. The result is that all the gain does not have to be reported in the year of sale, either by an accrual-method taxpayer or by a cash-method taxpayer, when the installment sale method rules apply. Consequently tax need not be paid before payments of the price roll in, and the rate of tax on gain will be altered, probably reduced, by spreading taxation over several years.

The installment sale rules are contained in three basic sections: § 453 (applicable to all sales of real property and casual sales of personal property); § 453A (providing the rules for certain non-dealer transactions in real or personal property); and § 453B (concerning the disposition of installment obligations). Note that only gains, and not losses, may be spread over years under the installment sale method.

Section 453. The installment sale method of reporting income is automatic as to sales of real estate by someone who is not a dealer and as to *casual* sales of personal property, if at least one payment is received by the taxpayer after the close of the tax year in which the sale occurs. A taxpayer may use the installment sale method even if full payment is made in one "installment," provided it is after the tax year of sale. This rule has become even more attractive now that the rate structure is indexed for inflation. *See* § 1(f). A taxpayer may elect *not* to use the installment sale method by reporting the entire gain from the sale in gross income for the tax year in which the sale was made. I.R.C. § 453(d).

Section 453 generally applies to non-inventoriable personal property and real property. Gain from the sale of intangibles (trademarks, contract rights, goodwill, etc.) also qualifies for installment method treatment.

Under the installment sale method, the gross profit on a sale is pro-rated over the period in which payments are received. I.R.C. § 453(c). "Gross profit" is the selling price less the adjusted basis determined under I.R.C. § 1011, reduced by commissions and other selling expenses.

The term "payments" refers to cash or other property, marketable securities, specified assumptions of liabilities, evidences of indebtedness of the buyer that are payable on demand, and evidences of indebtedness of a corporation or government that are readily tradeable. *See* I.R.C. § 453(f)(3) & (4).

Section 453(e) contains special rules ("resale rules") for taxing sales to related parties if the buyer resells or otherwise disposes of the property (even by gift) within two years of purchase. Under these rules, if a taxpayer sells property to a related person on the installment plan, and the related person, in turn, disposes of the property within two years of the first disposition, then the amount realized upon the second disposition shall be treated as received at the time of the second disposition by the *seller* who made the *first* disposition.

Also, § 453(i) prohibits the use of installment accounting to the extent that the seller's gain is subject to the recapture rules. Recapture income must be recognized by the seller in the year of sale regardless of when the seller receives payments. The normal installment account rules of § 453(a) apply to the excess of the sales price, if any, over the recapture income. Recapture rules are found in I.R.C. §§ 1245 and 1250 and discussed in § 104, below.

Section 453(k) imposes one important limitation on the use of installment accounting. The use of the installment method is completely eliminated for sales made pursuant to a revolving credit plan and for sales of certain publicly traded property (*e.g.*, stocks or securities traded on an established market).

Section 453A. Section 453A provides special rules for the payment of interest on a deferred tax liability when a taxpayer sells any property for over $150,000, if the obligation to pay is outstanding at the end of the year and the taxpayer holds at least $5,000,000 of obligations that arose during the year and are still outstanding at the end of the year. Section 453A provides specific rules for calculating the interest on the deferred tax liability.

Prior to the Revenue Act of 1987, I.R.C. § 453A allowed dealers of *personal* property to *elect* the installment sale method to report income from sales on the installment plan. Personal property included under this section consisted *only* of inventory property. Sales of real estate, whether or not by a dealer, were covered by § 453, *supra.* The Revenue Act of 1987 repealed the installment method for dispositions of property by dealers. Generally, all payments to be received from a "dealer disposition" of property are treated as received in the year of disposition. A "dealer disposition" is defined as any disposition of personal property by a person who regularly sells or otherwise disposes of property on the installment plan. *See* I.R.C. § 453(*l*)(1). A dealer disposition also includes any disposition of real property that is held by the taxpayer for sale to customers in the ordinary course of the taxpayer's trade or business. A dealer disposition does not include certain dispositions of residential lots or timeshares *if* the taxpayer elects to pay interest on the amount of deferred tax attributable to the use of the installment method. Moreover, a dealer disposition does not include a disposition of property used or produced in the trade or business of farming.

The repeal of the installment method for dealer dispositions is effective for dispositions occurring after December 31, 1987. The reason for the repeal lay in the fact that dealer sales of property for notes or accounts receivable do not create the significant cash-flow problems solved by the installment method, because dealers can finance receivables.

Section 453B. When the taxpayer disposes of an *installment obligation* on which tax is deferred under either § 453 or § 453A, the privilege of deferral comes to an end, and taxable income generally results. The amount of income depends on the type of transaction—sale, exchange, settlement, or gift.

If an installment obligation is satisfied for an amount other than face value, or is sold, or exchanged, the gain or loss is the difference between the "basis" of the obligation (the excess of the face value of the obligation over an amount equal to the income that would be returnable if it were paid in full) and the "amount realized" by the holder of the obligation (including the cash paid or credited to the account of the seller and market value of property received). I.R.C. § 453B(a)(1), (b).

If an installment obligation is transferred as a gift or in trust or disposed of in any manner *other than* by sale, exchange, or death, the gain or loss is the difference between the fair market value of the obligation at the time of the disposition and its "basis," as defined above. I.R.C. § 453B(a)(2).

Prior to the Installment Sales Revision Act of 1980, a few dispositions by gift were deemed not to be dispositions which triggered gain. For example, when a father sold property to his son and elected the installment method of reporting, but later cancelled the balance due on the installment obligation by gift, this cancellation was held to be a "satisfaction" rather than a "disposition" so that the father-seller-donor did not have to recognize gain in the year of the gift. Miller v. Usry (D.C.La.1958). Now, § 435B(f) treats the cancellation or unenforceability of an installment obligation as a disposition other than sale or exchange such that gain or loss therefrom is calculated under § 453B(a)(2). There is a special rule in § 453B(f)(2) to the effect that in a disposition between related persons, the fair market value of the obligation will be no less than its face amount. Section 453B(g) also explicitly provides that § 453B(a) will not apply to installment obligations transferred from one spouse to the other as alimony or as part of a property settlement in divorce under § 1041.

§ 73. Inventories

Inventory accounting can become a very complex business, but it has a simple purpose. That purpose has to do with accurately determining the cost of goods sold, which cost is to be subtracted from gross receipts in order to arrive at gross income. Regs. § 1.61–3.

As noted earlier, I.R.C. § 471 authorizes the Commissioner to require the use of inventories wherever their use is necessary in order clearly to determine the income of any taxpayer. In Regs. § 1.471–1, the Commissioner has stated that inventories at the beginning and end of each taxable year are necessary any time the production, purchase or sale of merchandise is an income producing factor. Regs. § 1.446–1(a)(4)(i) demands that merchandise on hand (including finished goods, work in process, raw materials and supplies) at the beginning and end of the year shall be taken into account in computing the taxable income of the year in all cases where the production of merchandise is an income-producing factor. By these requirements, the law attempts to prevent expenditures made to acquire goods still on hand and unsold at the end of the year from being added to "cost of goods sold" and thus being subtracted from gross receipts for the year in determining gross income. Note that Regs. § 1.61–3(a) provides that in a manufacturing, merchandising, or mining business, gross income means total sales less the cost of goods sold, plus other income.

The cost of goods sold shall be determined in accordance with the method of accounting consistently used by the taxpayer and including the uniform capitalization rules of I.R.C. § 263A. The physical taking of inventories and the inventory method of accounting are merely for the purpose of assigning a figure to the category "cost of goods sold." "Cost of goods sold" amounts to the following: cost of goods in the opening inventory plus cost of goods purchased and manufactured, minus cost of goods in the closing inventory. Detailed rules about what inventories should include and how they should be valued are afforded by the Regulations. Regs. §§ 1.471–1.472.

If inventories were not taken, and if all business expenditures were deductible, a taxpayer could charge off and deduct all his costs of buying or producing *all* goods during the year against his receipts from selling *some* of them. By building up his supply of goods in inventory over the years, he could indefinitely postpone recognition of any taxable income, or he could manipulate its recognition to suit his purposes, apart from the real gains from his business activities. Inventory accounting blocks this opportunity by limiting the subtraction for cost of goods sold to the cost of those goods that were *actually* sold during the tax year in question.

Rather than determining the cost of goods sold by tracing each item, the inventorying taxpayer makes his determination on an aggregate basis. He counts what he has in inventory at the beginning of the year and values it (determines its cost) according to some proper procedure. Then, at the end of the year, he counts and values what is left (which may be more or less than, or the same as, what he had at the outset). The difference, plus his purchases during the year and his additions from manufacture, is his cost of goods sold.

Properly applying an inventory method involves two steps or procedures, as indicated. The first is to choose a way by which to determine the goods in the closing inventory and how much they cost. He must do this exercise because the cost of those goods, unsold at the year end, must not be treated as part of the cost of goods sold—since they are still in hand.

To attribute a cost to closing inventories, the items in stock may either be specifically identified or identified more generally by presumptive rules, two of which are called LIFO (last in, first out) and FIFO (first in, first out). Under LIFO, the items last (most recently) purchased or manufactured are presumed to have been sold first; under FIFO, the cost of closing inventory is determined as if the specific items first purchased or manufactured were first to be sold. FIFO is the most common method, but I.R.C. § 472 authorizes LIFO as well.

The second step in accounting for inventories is to apply a rule by which an overall cost/value is assigned to the goods in inventory (actually or presumptively) at the beginning and at the end of the year. The rule must be employed consistently and it must be a proper accounting rule, says I.R.C. § 472. Two rules are the most common: Inventory is valued at either (1) cost or (2) the lower of cost or fair market value. Both the year's opening inventory (which is the same as the prior year's closing inventory) and closing inventory must be valued by the same method.

So, an inventory method might use FIFO in determining the items presumed to be those in the closing inventory and then use lower of cost or market to value that inventory. Applying those methods, the taxpayer can ascertain two of the three figures he needs to determine cost of goods sold—dollar cost (or value) of opening inventory and dollar cost (or value) of closing inventory. The difference between the two, plus cost of goods purchased and manufactured during the year, determines the cost of goods sold.

A simple example of the purpose and result of the inventory concept may be helpful. Suppose a taxpayer sells 1,000 widgets in 2004 at a total price of $1,000, or $1 each. His expenditures for raw materials, direct labor in the widget factory, etc. total $500. (Evidently it costs him $.50 to produce each widget.) In addition, he had other business expenses (advertising, legal and accounting fees, etc.) of $200. If he were required to go no further, he presumably would subtract $500 as the cost of goods sold from gross receipts to arrive at $500 gross income. His other expenses of $200, deducted under § 162, would determine taxable income to be just $300. But, what if he had actually produced 1,500 widgets that year and 500 of them remain in his storeroom at the year's end? Now we see that his direct costs amounted to $.30 per widget produced, not $.50. Had he sold all 1,500 widgets for a total of $1,500, his gross income would have been $1,000 ($1,500 less $500) and his taxable income would have been $800. But because he has not sold 500 of his widgets he is not yet taxable on that much income, whether he is an accrual or cash-method taxpayer. His income will be more clearly reflected, accountants and the I.R.S. would say, if he is not allowed to subtract $500 as the cost of goods sold in this year, since only $333 were costs of goods actually sold this year (⅔ of $500 for materials and labor). Next year, if he sells the remaining 500 widgets for $500, he may deduct $167 (the remaining ⅓ of materials and direct labor) from gross receipts as the cost of producing them. He may even be pleased that year that the inventory method forced him to defer subtracting the $167, for without deferral his entire receipts from selling the widgets sold in the second year, but manufactured in an earlier year, would be included in gross income during the later year. So the accrual method of accounting, supplemented by inventories where required, attempts to attribute costs to the same year in which income, realized as a result of those costs, is taxed.

The lower-of-cost-or-market method of assigning value to inventory may be used only if FIFO is the method of identifying inventory; with LIFO, only the cost method of valuation may be employed. *See* I.R.C. § 472(b)(2).

During times of pronounced inflation, suggestions multiply for accounting adjustments that will take account of rapidly increasing costs as measured in dollars (of diminishing purchasing power). One such adjustment is a switch from FIFO to LIFO as a method for inventory evaluation. LIFO (last-in, first-out) gives an advantage because it attributes higher costs to goods sold and thus reduces reportable income. In a time of decreasing costs, LIFO evaluation would produce the opposite effect. Obviously, neither for tax nor for financial accounting should a taxpayer be able to switch back and forth simply to produce the desired tax effect or impact on reported earnings to shareholders, investors, or creditors.

After conducting a physical count of inventory, retailers adjust for "shrinkage." Shrinkage includes undetected theft, breakage, and bookkeeping errors. If a taxpayer takes a physical inventory at year-end, the amount of shrinkage will be known. If the retailer takes his physical inventory at another time, the retailer will need to estimate shrinkage through year-end or not take shrinkage into account until the following year. Section 471(b) allows a taxpayer to estimate inventory shrinkage, as long as the taxpayer subsequently confirms the estimate by a physical count, normally does a physical count of inventories at each location on a regular and consistent basis, and makes proper adjustments to inventories and estimating methods to the extent that the estimates are greater than or less than the actual shrinkage. Congress believed that it was inappropriate to require a physical count of a taxpayer's entire inventory to be taken exactly at year-end. Where retailers do not take a physical inventory at year-end, Congress believed that income will be more clearly reflected if the taxpayer makes a reasonable estimate of the shrinkage occurring through year-end.

§ 74. Some Special Timing Rules—Deferred Compensation, Retirement Savings and Tax Shelters

Special rules that are heavily concerned with timing questions have developed for the taxation of specific kinds of transactions. One example is the set of rules applicable to deferred compensation, one form of which is employee stock options. Options to purchase stock in a corporation at a bargain price—below the market value of the stock—are often given by that corporation to its employees to compensate them, to attract new employees, and to keep old ones. The question then arises whether the employee is to be taxed on income: (i) when he or she receives the option itself, (ii) when he exercises the option and purchases the stock at below the market price, or (iii) when he sells the stock for more than he paid for it.

Some Generalizations. In general, a stock option (other than an Incentive Stock Option or I.S.O., described below), like any other property given to an employee as compensation, will be taxable when received by the employee if it has a readily ascertainable fair market value at that time. When a stock option is involved, the valuation requirement usually means that there must be an active market for the option, since valuation otherwise proves to be too difficult. If not subject to valuation on receipt, the employee is taxed on the difference between the option price and the fair market value of the stock received, when the option is exercised. *See* I.R.C. § 83.

To avoid immediate taxation on the issuance of stock options, or stock itself, to employees as compensation, corporate employers sometimes resort to the technique of issuing restricted options or restricted stock. A restricted option or stock plan is an arrangement under which an employer transfers options or stock subject to restrictions on their exercise or disposition, which restrictions prevent the options or stock from having a readily ascertainable fair market value. For example, such restrictions might provide that the employee must return the property to the employer if she fails to remain in its employ for a period of time, or they might provide a restriction against selling the stock for a period of time.

Section 83 is the provision that generally offers statutory guidance to the taxation of such plans. Section 83 applies whenever *property* (including stock of the employer corporation or of any other corporation, but not I.S.O.s) is transferred to *any person* in connection with the performance of services by the recipient *or by someone else.* For § 83 purposes, "property" does not include cash. *See* Regs. § 1.83–3(c). Under § 83, when the recipient's rights in the property first become transferable or are not subject to a substantial risk of forfeiture, *the person who rendered the services* must recognize income immediately. Thus income will be reportable in the year in which the rights of the person having the beneficial interest in the property are either transferable or no longer are subject to a substantial risk of forfeiture (with a few exceptions)—but the income will be taxed to the person who rendered the services, whether or not he is the actual recipient of the property.

Under § 83(b), the person who performed the services may elect to be taxed in the year of transfer by the employer instead of the year the rights become transferable or free from substantial risk of forfeiture. Whenever the income becomes taxable, the general rule is that the amount of income includable in the income of the person who performed the services is the excess of (a) the fair market value of the property (determined without regard to any restriction other than one which by its terms will never lapse) at the time income first becomes includable, over (b) the amount, if any, paid for the property. The employer will have a deduction in the amount and at the time of inclusion in the income of the person performing the services. *See* I.R.C. § 83(h).

Incentive Stock Options ("I.S.O.s"). Sections 421 and 422 preempt § 83 in the case of an "incentive stock option" or "ISO." *See* I.R.C. § 83(e)(1). No tax consequences attach to either the grant of an I.S.O. by the employer or the exercise of the option by the employee. The employee does not recognize gain, and the employer may take no business expense deduction for tax purposes. I.R.C. § 421(a). Generally, the employee will be taxed at capital gains rates when he or she sells the stock, provided he or she held the stock for at least two years from the date of the option grant and at least one year from the date on which the stock was transferred to the employee. If the employee does not comply with these holding requirements, the gain received on the sale of the stock will be taxed as ordinary income. Only in this latter case may the employer take a business deduction for tax purposes in the year of sale for the difference between the amount realized on sale and the option price. *See* I.R.C. §§ 421(a) and 422(c)(2).

The following conditions must be met for an option to qualify as an incentive stock option:

(1) The grantee must be an employee of the grantor or a related corporation from the date the option is granted until three months before exercise of the option (except for disabled employees, who have 12 months after leaving employment to exercise the option). § 422(a)(2), (c)(6).

(2) The option must be granted under a share-holder-approved plan specifying the employees or class of employees eligible to receive options and the aggregate number of shares that may be issued under the options. § 422(b)(1).

(3) The option must be granted within 10 years from the date the plan is adopted, or the date such plan is approved by the stockholders, which-ever is earlier. *See* § 422(b)(2).

(4) The terms of the option must limit the period during which it may be exercised to within ten years of the date of the option grant. § 422(b)(3).

(5) The option price may not be less than the fair market value of the stock at the time of granting the option. §§ 422(b)(4) and 422(c)(1).

(6) The option may not be transferable other than at death and must be exercisable only by the employee during his or her lifetime. § 422(b)(5).

(7) The employee may not own more than ten percent of the voting power or value of the com-pany (applying the stock ownership attribution rules of § 424(d)), unless the option price is at least 110% of the fair-market value of the stock *and* the option is not exercisable more than five years from the date of the grant. §§ 422(b)(6) and 422(c)(5).

(8) The maximum annual aggregate fair-mar-ket value of an I.S.O. granted to any one employ-ee can not exceed $100,000. § 422(d).

The treatment of stock options for *financial*, as opposed to *tax*, accounting purposes has been a controversial topic. Corporations, especially those in high-technology industries, have opposed expensing of stock options in financial statements because it would significantly reduce their publicly reported profits. The Financial Accounting Standards Board has proposed a rule that would require expensing of options in financial statements beginning December 15, 2004.

Deferred Compensation and Retirement Savings. Pension and profit-sharing plans also have their own timing problems and rules. A set of statutory rules govern the so-called "qualified" pension, profit sharing, stock-bonus, and bond-purchase plans. *See* I.R.C. §§ 401–418E. Basic among these rules is the requirement that the plan not discriminate in favor of employees who are stockholders or officers or who are highly compensated, and that the plan benefit only employees or their beneficiaries. If an employer contributes to a qualified plan that will pay out to employees after retirement, neither the current contributions nor the earnings on the plan trust will be taxable to an employee until he or she begins to receive payments. Nonetheless, the employer may deduct its contributions when made. Moreover, under I.R.C. § 501(a), income received by a qualified plan's fund is not taxed to the fund. These rules amount to a very special combination of tax advantages.

The Employee Retirement Income Security Act of 1974 (E.R.I.S.A.) induced major changes in pension arrangements. The main thrust of the Act was to protect and preserve employee rights in pension plans provided by employers. This problem was attacked through many different devices. First, the Act established mandatory rules for employee participation in the plans, for the vesting of employee rights and their protection, and for the funding of the pension arrangements. Tighter fiduciary standards, based on a "prudent man" standard, were enacted. The Pension Benefit Guaranty Corporation was created to insure plans against failure.

Self-employed persons may enjoy some benefits similar to those available to an employee through corporate pension plans under the so-called Keogh plans (established through the Self–Employed Individuals Tax Retirement Act of 1962), integrated with I.R.C. §§ 401–404. In short, a self-employed taxpayer under a Keogh plan may take a deduction each year for his or her contribution to the plan that year, up to a certain amount. Interest on the contributions is not taxed to the contributor as it accrues. However, the amounts received in retirement are taxed as ordinary income when withdrawn.

The self-employed or employee taxpayer may follow another route to provide himself or herself with funds upon retirement—he may set up an individual retirement account (I.R.A.) or an individual retirement annuity, or he may invest in retirement bonds. These were among the more important changes for individuals (whether self-employed or not) made by ERISA. *See generally* I.R.C. § 219 and

§ 408. An individual who is not covered by an employer-maintained retirement plan may deduct contributions to an individual retirement account (I.R.A.) in an amount up to the lesser of 100% of compensation includable in gross income or $3,000 (in 2004). Contribution limits increase to $5,000 in 2008 and then thereafter are adjusted for inflation. *See* I.R.C. § 219(b). A taxpayer who has attained the age of 50 may make an additional contribution of $500 (in 2004; the amount increases to $1,000 in 2006 and thereafter). *See* I.R.C. § 219(b)(5)(B). Other individuals who are participants in employer plans can make contributions to an I.R.A. within certain limits as well, but they may deduct all, part, or none of the contribution depending on each individual's A.G.I. The amount deductible is reduced proportionately as an individual's A.G.I. rises. For 2004, the deduction is eliminated for single individuals who have A.G.I. above $55,000, married individuals filing a joint return who have A.G.I. above $75,000, and married individuals filing separately who have A.G.I. above $10,000. The income limits for single individuals and married individuals filing jointly will increase each year through 2007. *See* I.R.C. § 219(g). For an individual who is not an active participant in a retirement plan at any time during the taxable year but whose spouse is, the deduction is eliminated for that individual when A.G.I. is above $160,000. *See* I.R.C. § 219(g). Above these A.G.I. levels, no deduction at all is permitted for I.R.A. contributions. The deduction is made from gross income, so the taxpayer may deduct the amount contributed even if he or she does not itemize. See I.R.C. § 62(a)(7). Married couples may compute the deduction under § 219 separately, so long as both receive compensation and otherwise qualify.

The amounts eventually received by an individual will be taxed as ordinary income upon receipt, and withdrawal before the age of 59½ will invoke an additional 10% penalty tax. See I.R.C. § 72(t)(1). The 10–percent early-withdrawal penalty is waived for I.R.A. distributions that taxpayers take to pay for qualified higher-education expenses or for qualified "first-time-homebuyer distributions." See I.R.C. § 72(t)(2). The exemption from the early-withdrawal penalty is available only for the first $10,000 of qualified first-time-homebuyer distributions. I.R.C. § 72(t)(8).

Nonetheless, the tax advantages from this deferral are quite dramatic. Consider Taxpayer T, who is 25 years old. T wishes to save money for her retirement at age 60 and estimates she'll be able to save $3,000 per year. T has two options: (1) Contribute $3,000 after-tax dollars each year to an account in which the interest earned each year is taxable; or (2) Contribute $3,000 pre-tax dollars each year to an I.R.A., in which case neither the contribution nor the interest earned each year will be taxable until the money is withdrawn upon retirement. Assume that the interest rate is constant at 10% and the tax rate is and will continue to be 28%. In option (1), T must earn approximately $4,167 in order to have $3,000 after-tax dollars to contribute.

T is taxed on the interest earned in the account each year. After 35 years, her after-tax account balance will be $464,431. Compare this balance with the result under option (2). Under option (2), after 35 years T's account will have accumulated $894,380 pre-tax dollars. If this balance is then withdrawn and taxed at 28%, T will be left with $643,954. Thus, the deferral of tax on the interest will have allowed T to earn an additional $179,523 (after taxes) for her retirement.[1]

One advantage to a taxpayer in setting up such an I.R.A. account, rather than a Keogh plan, is that the individual need not meet any of the requirements relating to the vesting of benefits, minimum funding, or participation of employees, which must be met to defer taxation and to allow the deductions for Keogh plans.

Roth I.R.A. Section 408A provides for the tax treatment of a "Roth I.R.A." Individuals can contribute up to $3,000 (in 2004) per year (for married individuals, each spouse can contribute $3,000 (in 2004), if both have income and otherwise qualify), provided that the taxpayers have compensation for the year that is at least equal to their contribution. A taxpayer who has attained age 50 may also make an additional $500 contribution (in 2004). The limit on contributions to a Roth I.R.A. is reduced by any contributions to another I.R.A. The maximum annual contribution is phased out for individuals with A.G.I. between $95,000 and $110,000; for joint filers and married individuals filing separate returns, the

1. *See* Appendix to this book.

phaseout occurs for A.G.I. between $150,000 and $160,000. *See* I.R.C. § 408A.

Unlike a contribution to a traditional I.R.A., a contribution to a Roth I.R.A. is *not* deductible. I.R.C. § 408A(c). Taxpayers contribute using after-tax dollars. However, distributions received after age 59½ and more than five years after establishing the Roth I.R.A. are excluded from gross income. I.R.C. § 408A(d). Thus, earnings on the taxpayer's after-tax contributions (*e.g.*, interest or appreciation in a mutual fund) will *never* be taxed. In contrast, with a traditional I.R.A., a taxpayer's contributions are deductible, but accumulations (including principal and interest) are taxable upon distribution. (Non-deductible contributions to a traditional I.R.A. can be withdrawn after age 59½ without tax, but earnings on them will be taxable.)

Returning to the previous example involving Taxpayer T, as was true in option (1) T still must earn $4,167 of income in order to have $3,000 of after-tax income to make a Roth I.R.A. contribution each year. However, each year, the earnings are not taxable, nor are the earnings taxable upon distribution. After 35 years, T will again have $894,380 but owe no taxes on this amount. A traditional I.R.A. would have provided only $643,954 in after-tax dollars. While T must pay taxes in the year in which she earns the income that she uses to make her Roth I.R.A. contribution, she overcomes this detriment because the earnings compound annually tax-free, and she never pays taxes on the earnings even upon taking a distribution. On the other hand, in a traditional I.R.A. the taxpayer also has the annual tax savings from the deduction to save and invest.

Qualified Tuition Programs. Under § 529(a), a qualified tuition program is exempt from tax. A qualified tuition program is a program established and maintained by a State (or instrumentality thereof) or eligible educational institution under which a person may purchase tuition credits or certificates. In addition, a State-run savings program for higher education expenses can be a qualified tuition program. I.R.C. § 529(b). Thus, a taxpayer can prepay the expenses of higher education or save for college on a tax-favored basis through a qualified tuition program. Qualified tuition programs may be used by all taxpayers regardless of income level.

A qualified tuition program is to provide for qualified higher education expenses which generally are defined as tuition, fees, books, supplies, equipment, expenses for a special needs beneficiary, and room and board. I.R.C. § 529(e)(3). Only cash contributions may be made to a qualified tuition program. I.R.C. § 529(b)(2).

Distributions to pay for qualified higher education expenses generally are excluded from gross income so earnings on funds in a qualified tuition program may be used for qualified expenses without being taxed. *See* I.R.C. § 529(c)(3)(B). Excess distributions are included in gross income under the rules in § 72 for annuities and subject to a 10%

additional tax. I.R.C. §§ 529(c)(3)(A), (c)(6); 530(d)(4).

Coverdell Education Savings Accounts. Section 530 has special rules for education savings accounts which generally are savings plans for paying the costs of qualified higher education expenses and qualified elementary and secondary education expenses of a designated beneficiary. Contributions to an education savings account must be made in cash, cannot be made after the beneficiary attains age 18, and cannot exceed $2,000 per year. I.R.C. § 530(b)(1)(A). The $2,000 permissible contribution amount is phased down to zero for taxpayers whose modified A.G.I. (as defined in I.R.C. § 530(c)(2)) is between $95,000 and $110,000 ($190,000 and $220,000 for joint returns). I.R.C. § 530(c). Like § 529 qualified tuition programs, income earned in an education savings account is not taxed and distributions for qualified expenses may be excluded from gross income. I.R.C. § 530(a), (d). Excess distributions generally are taxable under § 72 and subject to a 10% additional tax. I.R.C. § 530(d)(1), (4).

Other Deferral Efforts. Non-qualified compensation or retirement plans can be constructed to defer some tax. For example, an employee and employer may simply agree on a current salary with added amounts to be paid later, perhaps during retirement (low income) years. But such arrangements must be carefully structured to avoid current tax to the employee on theories of "constructive receipt," "economic benefit," or "present value." To avoid these consequences, escrow, trust, or funded arrangements are discouraged. If the employee's rights are forfeitable, the plan will be safer from a tax point of view. More detailed, and authoritative, guidance on these points is offered by Rev.Rul. 60–31, 1960–1 C.B. 174. Unfortunately, the income of any fund under a non-qualified plan is taxed to the fund. Moreover, if the employee's rights are forfeitable, the employer may not take a deduction for his contributions to the plan, since he may not take a deduction until the employee includes an amount attributable to the contribution in his income. I.R.C. § 404(a)(5).

Two examples may illustrate the problems of non-qualified, contractual arrangements to defer compensation. In one, Sugar Ray Robinson contracted to receive 40% of the gate receipts for a title fight, with payments to be made over 4 years. The Tax Court held that he had not constructively received the funds in the first year and hence was not taxable until he received payment. *See* Ray S. Robinson (Tax Court 1965), Acq. In another case, the plan did not succeed. Taxpayers were physicians who formed a medical group partnership that rendered pre-paid medical services to employees of Kaiser. A trust was established for the retirement of taxpayer partners; if a doctor left the partnership before completing 15 years of service or reaching retirement age, his or her interest was forfeitable. The Court held that payments by Kaiser into the trust on behalf of member-patients, as part of the agreement, constituted constructively received earned income to the partners, taxable at the time when made to the trust—rather than when paid out to physicians in retirement. *See* U.S. v. Basye (S.Ct. 1973).

Annuities. Annuities, treated earlier (§ 30, *supra*), are taxed on a sort of deferred basis under I.R.C. § 72. The "recovery exclusion" of I.R.C. § 72 spreads probable gain over all the payment years, rather than allowing a return of capital without tax for several years and then taxing the payments entirely as income. Also, some pension or profit-sharing, life-insurance, and endowment contracts pay out their benefits over a number of years. Such payments are taxed under the annuity rules.

Tax Shelters. Tax shelter investments and activities historically attempted to gain the advantages of leverage (using borrowed money to magnify deductible amounts), conversion (of ordinary income into capital gain or of capital loss into ordinary loss), and deferral (of income, sometimes by acceleration of allowances). Many tax shelters depended upon creating early deductions, sometimes "year-end" items, by pre-paying interest, taxes or other costs, using accelerated depreciation/cost recovery and like techniques, while deferring the realization of income until later. Timing rules have thus thrust upon them the responsibility for preventing undue manipulation or evasion of the annual method of reporting and proper attribution of items of income and allowance to the correct tax year. Over the years, cases and rulings have been addressed particularly to tax shelters in the field of agriculture, motion pictures, and some other fields, often by specialized timing rules, some of which have been mentioned above but many of which are too technical for extensive examination in this book. Anti-shelter timing rules particularly have focused on prepayment of interest, deduction of pre-production expenses (rather than capitalizing them), deferral of income items including advance payments, use of nonrecourse loans, use of sophisticated financial instruments, and freedom to select among various accounting methods. Moreover, the passive-loss limitation rules obstruct the deduction of losses on tax shelters against income from active sources, such as salary or active business income, or from portfolio income. *See* I.R.C. § 469; § 56, *supra.*

§ 75. Realization and Closed Transactions

The requirement of a realization, considered earlier in Chapter II (§ 19, *supra.*) is even more a rule bearing on *when* something is income. In Eisner v. Macomber, the receipt of a stock dividend was held not to be income. *A fortiori,* the mere earning of profits by the corporation—while gain—was not income to Mrs. Macomber, the shareholder. Later, when Mrs. Macomber turned the receipt into cash or otherwise separated the income from the capital, the gain was taxable to her. So, the occurrence of gain, even when accompanied by a receipt of something, is not necessarily income at that time for purposes of Federal income taxation.

Ordinarily, when property is sold the gain from dealing in the property must be included in gross income. I.R.C. § 61(a). Under I.R.C. § 1001(a), to determine the amount of income, a taxpayer must compute the excess of the amount realized, as defined in § 1001(b), over the adjusted basis provided by § 1011, and vice-versa to measure loss. Section 1011 defines basis, by reference to § 1012, as cost— with adjustments under § 1016 for expenditures on the property, depreciation deductions, taxes, etc. If the property were received by gift, § 1015 would apply, and if it were received by bequest, reference to § 1014 would be required.

Sometimes, however, a sale or exchange or other disposition of property does not result in reported income at the time. The doctrines or rules determining that result are not easily labeled but they have to do with "realization" and with the concept of a "closed transaction." For example, if a taxpayer who owns land were to sell it in return for a promise made by the purchaser to pay seller $.60 for every barrel of oil extracted from the land, forever, it is possible that the transaction would not be treated as a closed transaction—for very practical reasons. Suppose that the taxpayer's basis in the land is known to be $100,000. The "amount realized," the other amount necessary for I.R.C. § 1001(a) purposes, cannot easily be determined. If only 100,000 barrels of oil are ever extracted, seller will receive only $60,000 and will have suffered a loss. But if 200,000 barrels gush forth, he will eventually receive $120,000, apparently a gain. It is virtually impossible at the time of the sale to determine (a) whether gain or loss will eventuate and (b) the amount of the gain or loss. So taxpayer will claim that taxation must await later events. As one might expect, the Commissioner of Internal Revenue will not "give in" easily. He will insist that a value *can* be attached to most things, including royalty agreements, that are given as purchase price. But in a case like the one put forward, he may be told by a court that the transaction cannot be treated as a closed one, and taxability must be delayed, a "wait and see" approach. *See* Burnet v. Logan (S.Ct.1931); Inaja Land Co., Ltd. v. Comm. (Tax Court1947). Sometimes the taxpayer and the I.R.S. will reverse roles, the taxpayer contending that the deal is closed (perhaps so he can deduct what he says is a loss) and the I.R.S. stoutly protesting that it is wholly impractical and improper to try to place a value on the amount realized until later.

When a sale transaction is treated as "open," the payments will not be deemed to produce taxable income to the seller until basis has been recovered in full, except that an interest component will be imputed to each payment under I.R.C. § 483(a). Beyond that, gain will be capital gain if the original transaction qualified for capital gain taxation. Loss, if any, also would be taxable as capital or ordinary as determined by the character of the underlying transaction.

Precisely when an event is to be treated as a closed transaction or as a realization of gain or loss is hard to predict. Usually receipt of property (as sales price) is treated as a final sale and a value is somehow placed upon it. On the other hand, when a taxpayer gets his own property back he is usually not taxed even if it is now worth more than when he loaned or leased it or otherwise surrendered possession. But what if both these events are combined? In Helvering v. Bruun (S.Ct.1940), taxpayer leased his land to a tenant for ninety-nine years. The tenant, pursuant to permission given in the lease, tore down the old building and erected a new one. A few years later the tenant defaulted and forfeited the lease. When the owner was returned to possession, the new building had a value of $64,000; the old building had been worth $13,000. The difference, $51,000, the Supreme Court held, was income to the owner. Now, I.R.C. § 109 changes this result; the taxpayer does not recognize income on the improvements, but under § 1019, he does not get a basis increase either. The *Bruun* case remains, however, as an important authority on realization and closed transactions when no statutory rule applies. Some believe it severely undercut the vitality of Eisner v. Macomber, *supra,* and its rule of realization. *See also* Brown v. Comm. (7th Cir.1955) (landlord realized income to the extent that the tenant's account had been credited to reflect improvements made by the tenant).

"Deemed Gain or Loss" and Mark-to-Market Regimes. In recent years Congress has installed and expanded so-called "mark-to-market" rules that compel some taxpayers to include in income, or deduct from income, gain or loss consisting of a change (increase or decrease) in the market value of an asset that has not been sold or disposed of so as

to realize the gain or loss in a conventional sense. For example, under § 475, a dealer in securities must include in inventory at its fair market value any security that is inventory in the hands of the dealer, and as to any security that is not such inventory, the dealer "shall recognize gain or loss as if such security were sold for its fair market value" on the last day of the taxable year, and "any gain or loss shall be taken into account for such taxable year." Proper adjustment is to be made in the amount of gain or loss subsequently realized for gain or loss taken into account under this mark-to-market regime. Exceptions are made for some securities held for investment or as a "hedge." So, even though the dealer has not sold or disposed of a covered security, the dealer will be taxable as if the covered security had been sold for cash at fair market value. In a sense, unrealized appreciation (or loss) will be taxable to (deductible by) the dealer. This movement toward an "accrual" system, like the von-Schanz, Haig & Simons description of income beginning with "a change in net worth," if constitutional, represents a major departure from the historic "realization-based" U.S. income tax system.

A similar rule has been enacted in § 1256, which treats any "section 1256 contract" as having been sold at its fair-market value on the last day of the year and requires that any gain or loss be "taken into account" for the taxable year. A "section 1256 contract" is defined, in § 1256(b), as any regulated futures contract, any foreign currency contract, any non-equity option, any dealer equity option, and any dealer securities futures contact. Obviously, the market in financial products and financial derivatives is requiring special use of the mark-to-market approach, which in theory could be expanded to cover publicly traded stocks and other securities or even real estate and other assets but for the administrative and compliance burdens of proving actual fair-market value changes every year, by appraisals, etc.

In a loose way, "mark-to-market" resembles the income-tax law's approach to original-issue discount (§§ 1271–1275), below-market loans (§ 7872(e)(1)), and market discount bonds (§§ 1276–1278) in requiring recognition of gain or loss different from an amount actually paid or exchanged or even when no amount has been paid or received. "Deemed income" or "constructive realization" or "notional amounts" may be the useful vocabulary.

See also § 1092 ("Straddles"), which limits the amount of realized loss on one or more positions in a straddle to the amount by which it exceeds the *unrecognized* gain with respect to one or more positions that were "offsetting" positions with respect to one or more of the loss positions. So, if a taxpayer buys a "put" (a right to sell stock at a set price) and a "call" (a right to buy at a set price) as to 100 shares of X Corp. stock and sells or exercises one at a loss but has an unrecognized gain in the offsetting position, the loss deduction will be limited by the *unrecognized* gain.

Constructive Sales. Section 1259 mandates "constructive sale" treatment for an "appreciated financial position," meaning a "position" with respect to any stock, debt instrument or partnership interest. It was enacted to combat financial techniques developed by investors and their advisors to end an investor's economic interest, risk of further loss and chance for further gain, in an appreciated asset such as by a short sale (selling borrowed stock) or a "short sale against the box" (a sale of borrowed stock when the seller also owns some shares of that stock which he retains) without actually selling the appreciated property. A constructive sale is defined to include a short sale, an offsetting notional principal contract, a futures or forward contract, etc., each one if it is of the same or substantially identical property.

So, under § 1259, if an investor makes a "constructive sale" of an "appreciated financial position," the investor will be forced to recognize gain, then and there, as if he or she had actually sold the "financial position" to an unrelated third party! So, for example, if an investor who owns 100 shares of X Corp. stock that has appreciated in value enters into a "short sale against the box"—or something similar—he or she will be taxed as if the investor had sold the underlying 100 shares for cash equal to their fair-market value. Upon eventual disposition of the 100 shares actually owned, there will not be a second gain taxed. *See* § 1259(e). In addition, § 1259(f) broadly authorizes the I.R.S. to issue regulations to classify new or different transactions as "constructive sales" if they have the same effect as those enumerated in § 1259.

§ 76. Recognition and Nonrecognition

Even if a realization of gain or loss has occurred, Congress may choose to relieve the taxpayer of the necessity of recognizing and reporting the gain and of paying the tax at that time. Or, a loss otherwise deductible may be denied deductibility until later. Almost always, when recognition is deferred, basis consequences follow.

Nonrecognition of gain has been given in several main areas, and these illustrate one of the chief reasons for nonrecognition treatment. Three main areas of nonrecognition are like-kind exchanges of property, involuntary conversions of property, and reacquisitions of real property.

Like-kind exchanges—§ 1031. One category of nonrecognition transactions covers tax-free exchanges under I.R.C. § 1031. That section provides that neither gain nor loss shall be recognized when property held for productive use in the trade or business of the taxpayer or held for investment is exchanged solely for property of a like kind to be similarly used. (Some specific properties are not covered: stocks and bonds, notes, inventories, etc.) Also, real property in the United States and real property outside the United States are not property of a like kind (§ 1031(h)), nor are livestock of different sexes (§ 1031(e))! Personal property used predominantly within the United States and personal property used predominantly outside the

United States are not property of a like kind. Section 1031(h)(2) defines "predominant use." Regs. § 1.1031(a)–2 contains additional rules for determining whether exchanges of personal property are of a like kind.

Section 1031 is not elective; when it applies, the taxpayer has no choice. Also, sale of property and reinvestment of the proceeds does not qualify for nonrecognition under § 1031. If "boot" (money or non-qualified property) is *received* by the taxpayer, § 1031 does not apply to the "boot", but the taxpayer may *give* money as well as property in the exchange without changing the tax result.

Section 1031(d) contains appropriate basis rules to protect against permanent avoidance (rather than mere deferral) of tax. Again, the reasoning seems evident: let taxpayers make trades that do not close out their investment in that kind of property, without the deterrent of an income tax bill. Don't let them make such trades and deduct their (paper) losses, since the taxpayers are still too much in the same position after the trade as they were before it. *See also* along these lines, I.R.C. § 267 (losses on transactions between related taxpayers). And Cf. I.R.C. § 1091 (losses from wash sales).

To illustrate the nonrecognition rules of § 1031, which exemplify the policies and doctrines of nonrecognition generally, consider the following example. Taxpayer A owns investment property (Greenacres) worth $100,000; his adjusted basis in Greenacres is $60,000. Suppose he exchanges

Greenacres with taxpayer B for Whiteacre, like-kind property, worth $100,000. Taxpayer A has realized $40,000 gain, but that gain will not be recognized by virtue of § 1031(a). In turn, A's basis in Whiteacre will be $60,000. If he later sold Whiteacre for $100,000 cash, he would have to recognize gain in the amount of $40,000 at that time, unless, of course, his basis was increased by other capital expenditures or reduced by allowances per I.R.C. § 1016.

This example, varied slightly, will also illustrate the rules for a partially tax-free transaction. Suppose in the trade A had received Whiteacre and $30,000 in cash. Evidently, Whiteacre was worth only $70,000. Now, A will have to recognize gain to the extent of the property or money other than that permitted to be received without recognition of gain, that is to say, to the extent of "boot" received ($30,000 in the example). A's basis, his unrecovered after-tax dollars, in Whiteacre will be $60,000 ($60,000 basis in Greenacres, less $30,000 cash received, plus $30,000 gain recognized). If he later sells Whiteacre for $70,000 cash, for example, he will then recognize gain of $10,000.

To take up a further complication, suppose A exchanged $100,000 Greenacres (with a basis of $60,000) for Whiteacre (like-kind property) worth $70,000, plus a $20,000 auto, plus $10,000 in cash. Both the auto and cash are "boot," so gain on the disposition of Greenacres ($40,000) will be recognized to the extent of $30,000, the amount of boot received. A's basis in Whiteacre and the auto will be an amount equal to his basis in Greenacres, ($60,-000), decreased in the amount of any money received ($10,000) and increased by the amount of gain recognized ($30,000). As a result, when the smoke has cleared, A, having recognized gain of $30,000 and "cashed out" $10,000, will end up with a total basis of $80,000, $60,000 allocated to Whiteacre and $20,000 to the auto. *See* I.R.C. § 1031(d). (One can think of A as having another $10,000 basis in the cash—which he can spend without recognition of any further gain or loss.) The remaining gain that inhered in Greenacres will be recognized when and if A sells Whiteacre. On this partly taxable and partly tax-free exchange, some gain was recognized. Had loss been realized, it would not have been recognized. The effect of receiving cash, or cash and other boot, would only have been to reduce basis by an amount equal to cash received.

Involuntary conversion—§ 1033. Ordinarily if a fire or storm or condemnation takes a taxpayer's property and as a consequence she receives insurance or some other payment, the "involuntary conversion" is treated as a taxable sale so that gain or loss must be recognized. Section 1033, however, contains a special rule that affords nonrecognition to gain (not loss) on such an involuntary conversion if the taxpayer replaces the property within two years of its loss with other property that is similar or related in service or use. If taxpayer receives cash or unqualified property to boot, he must recognize gain to the extent of this "boot."

Section 1033 declares that gain shall not be recognized (it is not elective) on certain involuntary conversions such as condemnation, destruction of insured property by fire, livestock destroyed by disease, etc. Gain is not to be recognized if the former property is converted into other property directly or by prompt reinvestment of cash. Again, complicated rules accompany the basic section but its *raison d'etre* seems clear: A taxpayer who has been compelled to change his property into other property (or cash to acquire similar property) should not be burdened at that time by a big tax bill on the gains he never wanted to realize. Involuntary realization thus entails (involuntary) nonrecognition. Actually, the nonrecognition is voluntary in a way since it depends on taxpayer's reinvestment in property related in service or use to the converted property.

Section 1033(h) provides a special rule excluding recognition of gain for receipt of insurance proceeds for "unscheduled" personal property in a taxpayer's principal residence that is compulsorily or involuntarily converted as a result of a Presidentially declared disaster. It also treats other insurance proceeds from such a disaster as a common fund for § 1033 replacement purposes. This subsection also extends the replacement period for the property from 2 years to 4 years.

Tax basis in the new property is to be the same as basis in the old one, under I.R.C. § 1033(b), to preserve the taxpayer's position for purposes of future sale, depreciation, etc. If "boot" (cash or other property not reinvested in similar property) is received, gain will be taxed to the extent of the boot, and appropriate basis adjustments made. Loss on involuntary conversions is always recognized.

Other nonrecognition rules. Another nonrecognition rule is that found in I.R.C. § 1038, applicable to a taxpayer who repossesses a piece of real property he formerly sold on an installment basis. Without this statute, the repossessor would have to recognize gain or loss to the extent the fair market value of the property differed from basis, even though he was put back in much the same position he was in before he sold it (apart from payments, if any, made to him before repossession). So, under the nonrecognition rule of § 1038, the original sale is nullified, and the repossession is not treated as a resale of the property back to the original owner. Adjustments are made for prior payments and prior recognition of gain.

In 1997, Congress repealed former I.R.C. § 1034. This section allowed a taxpayer who sold his principal residence at a gain and within two years bought or built a new home to avoid paying tax at the time, but only to the extent that he invested an amount equal to the sales price of the old house in a new one. The taxpayer's basis in the new house was reduced by the amount of the unrecognized gain, so that on later sale of the second house, gain on the first house, as well as on the second one, if any, would have been taxed. This basis rule, resulting from § 1034 "rollovers," will remain important for years to come to compute gain or loss when those houses are sold or exchanged.

Congress replaced the nonrecognition rule of § 1034 by revising § 121. Section 121 now excludes from gross income gain from the sale or exchange of property if the taxpayer had used the property as his principal residence for at least two of the past five years. The exclusion is limited to $250,000 for individuals and $500,000 for spouses filing jointly, provided that they meet the requirements of I.R.C. § 121(b). The exclusion is available for one sale or exchange every two years. It is sometimes available on a prorated basis for occupancy of less than two years. *See* I.R.C. § 121(c).

Congress deemed the old rule to be too complicated, in large part because many taxpayers buy and sell a number of homes over the course of a lifetime (e.g., as their family grows). Thus, taxpayers were required to keep detailed records of transactions and expenditures on home improvements (which increase basis), often for many decades. The new law simplifies taxation of the sale of a principal residence, and provides a potentially huge tax benefit for gains resulting from sales of owner-occupied residences.

See also I.R.C. § 1035 (exchanges of insurance policies); § 1036 (exchanges of stock for stock in the same corporation); § 1041 (interspousal transfers, § 82 *infra*).

All these nonrecognition sections override the usual annual taxing of income. They invariably employ a technique (basis adjustments) designed to result in delayed, but eventual, taxation in another year. Thus, the pattern of nonrecognition rules applicable in transactions where the change in form does not evidence a substantial economic change takes the following shape: gain or loss is not recognized (the transaction is tax-free); the taxpayer retains his old basis, and it is applied to the new property in substitution for the cost basis that otherwise would apply (*see, e.g.,* I.R.C. § 1031(d); § 1033(b)); if property that is not permitted to be received tax-free is received (the unqualified property is called "boot") in an otherwise qualified transaction, gain (but not loss) will be recognized in an amount up to the value of the boot.

Other nonrecognition rules and accompanying basis provisions include I.R.C. § 267. This section provides for nonrecognition of loss on a sale to a family member or other related party. But, the purchaser's basis for computing *loss* is cost rather than seller's basis, so that the loss deduction will be lost altogether. A special basis rule in § 267(d) gives the purchaser credit for seller's basis if the property is eventually sold at a *gain*.

Similarly, I.R.C. § 1091 provides for nonrecognition of loss on a "wash sale"—a sale and repurchase of the same securities within 30 days—with basis equal to that of the original securities. A loss deduction is postponed and may be taken on sale of the second securities.

Note I.R.C. § 1040, providing for limited recognition of gain to an estate if the executor transfers appreciated farm or closely-held business property, valued for estate tax purposes under the "special-use" valuation method of § 2032A, to a "qualified heir" as defined in I.R.C. § 2032A(e)(1).

§ 77. Income Averaging

A distinct departure from the strict annual system of taxing income is the concept of averaging income, allowed until repeal by the 1986 T.R.A. Pre–1986 T.R.A. I.R.C. §§ 1301–1305 allowed a taxpayer to elect to average his income in excess of a certain amount. This system did not literally change the year in which an item was reportable as income or the year in which it was taxed. But the *rate* at which the item was taxed was made to depend not only on the rates and level of income for that year, but also upon the taxpayer's experience over the past four years. The item was (sometimes) taxed *as if* it had been received over a four-year period. Especially for authors, actors, athletes, and other taxpayers who have fluctuating or bunched income and face graduated tax rates that apply on an annual basis, income averaging was most important.

The method employed by the averaging rules was complex, but the concept was not too difficult. In order to qualify, an individual's current taxable income, after some adjustments, had to exceed 140% of his/her average taxable income for the previous three years (the "base period"), and this excess had to exceed $3,000. Averaging was optional; the taxpayer had to elect to average under I.R.C. § 1304(a). Sometimes it was beneficial. It might entail some costs (in addition to the necessity of often difficult calculations) or forgoing some benefits.

In 1986, Congress repealed the general averaging provisions of I.R.C. §§ 1301–1305. The lower, flatter rate structure reduced the need for averaging, so this "simplification of the law" seemed desirable. A return to higher, more graduated rates might produce a call for the return of similar income averaging rules.

A different form of income averaging can be discerned in I.R.C. § 172, which allows net operating losses to be carried forward and backward from the year in which they are sustained to other, gainful years. Thus § 172 permits the averaging of operating gains and losses over a multi-year period.

See also I.R.C. § 170(d) (carryover of excess charitable contributions); § 1212 (capital-loss carrybacks and carryovers); § 39 (unused tax credits).

In addition, some accounting methods and rules achieve a sort of averaging of income. Similarly, rules that permit the deferral or spreading of income to later years in a taxpayer's life when, most likely, his income and therefore his marginal tax rates will be lower also achieve a rough sort of averaging.

§ 78. Other Timing Areas

Other problems, of somewhat lesser importance, exhibit timing aspects. These include capital loss carryovers (§ 1212), charitable contribution carryovers (to each of five years succeeding the contribution year) (§ 170(d)), the requirement that some expenditures be capitalized (§ 263), categorical taxation of quasi-capital gains and losses (§ 1231), depreciation or A.C.R.S. deductions (§§ 167, 168), carryover of unused tax credit carrybacks and carry forwards (§ 39), and others. The annual system remains fundamental, but the exceptions and modifications multiply.

CHAPTER VIII

TO WHOM IS INCOME TAXABLE?

§ 79. Introduction; Income Shifting and Splitting

Prior chapters have dealt with two of the crucial questions an income tax law must answer: What is income and what is deductible? When is income taxed or a deduction allowed? This chapter turns to the third major question, namely: Who is taxable on the income (or who is to be allowed the deduction, or credit or other allowance)? It will survey some basic examples of the problems of shifting and attributing income, as they arise under the Federal Income Tax. It will review both the attempts by taxpayers to shift income (or allowances, such as deductions or credits), and resulting tax liability (or advantage) to one another, and also the attempts of Congress, courts and Internal Revenue Service to attribute income and tax liability so as to prevent undue shifting. In addition, it will witness some of the complexity in taxpayer behavior, revenue administration, and substantive law that results from a few basic characteristics of the U.S. income tax law.

The characteristics that yield incentives for income shifting, and thus create the need for complex

365

attribution rules and administration, are: (1) more or less steeply graduated and multifarious rate schedule(s); (2) annual accounting and determination of tax liability; and (3) designation of the individual (with some exceptions) as the taxpayer whose total income, aggregated for one year (usually), must have the progressive rates, or the various special rates, of the Internal Revenue Code applied against it, and each of whom is entitled to certain exemptions or allowances. Adoption of a proportional and uniform rate (or even lower rates and more gradual progression) would eliminate (or reduce) some of the incentives for income shifting, as would elimination of "per-taxpayer" exemptions or allowances. More widespread income averaging over several tax years also could ameliorate the problem. And selection of the family as the taxable unit would also diminish the frequency of income shifting efforts.

Ordinarily, of course, the question "Who is taxable on the income (or Who is to be allowed the deduction)?" is easily answered; income is taxed to the person who receives it, after earning it by personal services or by virtue of owning property. However, in some instances the question requires more extended analysis, both in terms of rules and policy. One context in which some of these troublesome instances arise is the family, where people often make gifts to each other, where they are economically dependent on each other, and where some people (parents, in the old days at least) exercise some control over the economic and personal lives of others (children). This chapter will take up the question "Who is taxable?" first in the context of intra-family gifts (where the doctrines are rooted), then in community property, and later in connection with divorce, trusts and, briefly, in family businesses. The problem of income attribution often occurs elsewhere in the business context, with affiliated corporations, multiple business entities and inter-company pricing. Some of the most highly developed law has been refined in combat with taxpayers in the business world. *See, e.g.,* I.R.C. § 482 and the Regulations thereunder, Treas. Regs. § 1.482. However, extended treatment of the problem in the business world lies beyond the scope of this chapter, which concentrates on the general world of individual taxpayers.

All sections of the chapter coalesce around the same issue: Who is to be the taxpayer? In principle, the taxpayer or taxable unit for Federal Income Tax purposes is the individual. The individual, not the family or the household or some other unit, must file a return and calculate tax based on his or her economic experience during the year. Some departures from the principle of the individual as the taxpayer are allowed—joint returns for married couples, head-of-household rates for unmarried heads of households, dependency exemptions for family members or others living with the taxpayer and whom he or she supports, attribution of ownership of property from one family member to another, and so on. Nevertheless, these represent departures from the general rule that the individual is the taxable unit. But that rule does not go further and determine *which* individual is to be taxed on income when efforts are made to shift the tax burden from one taxpayer to another.

The fact that the individual is the taxable unit combines with the annual reporting system and the graduated rate scale to motivate some taxpayers to try to have their income taxed to someone else. Their aim is to reduce the total federal income tax on the same amount of income by splitting the income between two returns, shifting part of the income from the higher marginal brackets of one taxpayer to the lower marginal brackets, or exempt brackets, that apply to another individual under the graduated rate system, or to utilize otherwise wasted deductions, exemptions, credits, carryovers, or other allowances.

In order successfully to have his income taxed to taxpayer B, taxpayer A must *at least* arrange for taxpayer B to receive it and keep it. If A and B arrange somehow for B to pay tax on A's income which A receives and keeps, both are committing an outright fraud on the Revenue, and very likely they will be caught and punished. A can arrange for B lawfully to receive and keep the income in a number of ways, including by making a gift of the income, or income-producing property, or services, to B. The various ways in which A can attempt to shift income to B form the subjects of the remaining sections of this chapter.

§ 80. Transfers by Gift; Anticipatory Assignments of Income

As a general matter, if a person (A) makes a gift of his or her services to another person (B), B is not taxable on "income" equal to the cash value of the services, even though B's economic net income increased. Similarly, if A gives property to B, the receipt of that gift property does not constitute income to B; the value of property acquired by gift, bequest, devise or inheritance is excluded from gross income. *See* I.R.C. § 102(a). However, income *from* such property is not excluded from B's gross income, and if the gift is of income from property, the amount of such income is not excluded. I.R.C. § 102(b).

Income-tax shifting by gift is not undertaken for tax reasons *alone,* since it virtually never pays (in the form of taxes saved) to give property away. Inasmuch as the income tax rates never have reached 100 per cent, a U.S. taxpayer can always (with, in some years, a very rare exception involving the charitable contribution deduction) profit by receiving income and paying tax on it, rather than by forgoing the income (and tax burden), or by giving it to another person and escaping the tax bill in the process. However, if taxpayer A would like to give some money or property or services to taxpayer B anyway (for genuinely philanthropic, familial, or other non-tax reasons), A might prefer to give *pre-*tax income to B and let B pay tax on it, rather than receive and pay tax on the income before giving "after-tax dollars" to B.

Tax and non-tax motives have often combined to induce one spouse to make a gift of income or property to another. For example, before husbands and wives were allowed to file joint tax returns at advantageously low rates (and sometimes again in recent years), a married couple whose $100,000 income was earned by the husband alone would pay more tax than would a couple each of whose members earned $50,000. Graduated rates would tax $100,000 in one return more than the aggregate of $50,000 in two returns. Consequently, if the husband in the first couple is the breadwinner, he might attempt to assign half his salary to his wife so that each could file a separate tax return showing $50,000 gross income. If he did so on the eve of the husband's payday, doctrines of "constructive receipt" would probably serve to rule that the entire $100,000 was taxable to the husband, since he virtually received it and gave half to his wife. By turning his back on it as it was about to be paid, he could not escape tax.

But what if he assigned one-half his salary and all other income to his wife years in advance and for the rest of his life? In Lucas v. Earl (S.Ct.1930), the U.S. Supreme Court met such a couple and held the husband taxable on income in 1920 and 1921, notwithstanding his valid 1901 contract assigning one-half his income to his wife for life. Justice Holmes, in a typically terse opinion, stressed that Mr. Earl had earned the income and that the tax law showed an intent to tax income to the taxpayer who earned it. Moreover, he said the statute's import was not to allow the tax to be escaped by "anticipatory arrangements and contracts however skillfully devised to prevent the salary when paid from vesting even for a second in the man who earned it." Resorting to the horticultural analogy, Holmes decreed that the fruits (income) could not be attributed to a tree (taxpayer) different from that on which they grew. (A colleague, Professor B. Barton, calls this doctrine "earnership.") Presumably, these rules would apply equally to a parent-child gift or any other anticipatory assignment of income by the earner to someone else. In Helvering v. Eubank (S.Ct.1940), an assignor of the right to future payment for services *previously* rendered was held taxable on the income; thus control over the future flow of income, present in *Earl,* was not present in *Eubank* and was not deemed essential for judicial re-attribution of the income.

The tax consequences of interspousal income splitting under some states' community-property laws, however, were a different matter. The U.S. Supreme Court ruled in Poe v. Seaborn (S.Ct.1930) that under community-property law, income earned by services rendered by either spouse and income earned by property saved or purchased during marriage all are regarded as owned equally by the husband and the wife. Accordingly, for tax purposes, the Court said, salary, interest on bank deposits, and dividends and profits on sales of real and personal property were reportable one-half by the husband and one-half by the wife, regardless of who earned the income since each owned one-half. Lucas

v. Earl was distinguished. Therefore, spouses in community-property states paid less tax than that paid by common-law property spouses in essentially the same economic position. Similarly, common-law property spouses with separate incomes paid less tax than common-law property spouses who had the same total income but all earned by one's services or property.

As a result of the decision in Poe v. Seaborn, many common-law-property states enacted or planned to enact community-property systems, to place their citizens on a par taxwise with residents of the community property jurisdictions. One state, Oklahoma, went so far as to enact an *optional* community property law. Taxpayers could elect to be governed by community rules if they chose, the thought being that this technique would escape the reach of Lucas v. Earl and improve on Poe v. Seaborn. In Comm. v. Harmon (S.Ct.1944), the Supreme Court held that such an election would not be effective for Federal Income Tax purposes.

Congress, in 1948, enacted joint-tax-return legislation and a set of rates to remove the considerable disparity between tax treatment of married couples in community-property and common-law states, and thereby removed the considerable pressure on the common-law states to adopt community-property systems. By law enacted that year, married couples in all states were given the privilege to split their income, that is to have it taxed on a joint return at a rate equal to that which would apply if each had earned one-half the amount and were taxed on a separate return. They could treat their combined income as if earned one-half by each, with substantial tax savings, particularly in the higher brackets. This legislation removed (nearly) all of the advantages of community property income as to spouses. Today, *see* I.R.C. § 6013 and § 2. Marital status is determined pursuant to I.R.C. § 7703.

The 1948 approach endured until 1969—a married couple was taxed as if it were composed of two single individuals each of whom had one-half the couple's combined income regardless of who earned it or whose investments yielded it. The tax on a joint return was determined by computing the tax at the normal rate on one-half the aggregate taxable income and multiplying that amount by two. Single taxpayers, lacking an income-splitting privilege, paid markedly higher taxes at equal income levels. At some positions in the income scale the single taxpayer paid 42% more tax than the tax on a joint return with equal taxable income. In 1969 Congress retained, but reduced, the disparity between rates imposed on single persons and married couples with the same incomes. This reduction took the form of a new and lower rate schedule for single persons, which took effect beginning in 1971. The single person's tax bill ranged from about 17% to 20% above equal-income married couples, depending on the position in the rate schedule. (A marriage tax "reward" remained for a married couple where one spouse earns significantly more income than the other spouse.)

Strangely enough, an incidental consequence of these rate changes was that, in some income ranges and proportions, a married couple each of whom had income would pay *more* in tax than an unmarried couple with identical incomes but filing separately, the so-called "marriage penalty" or tax on marriage. As a consequence, it often was worthwhile for two single adults, each of whom had earned or investment income, to cohabit without marrying, or otherwise to refrain from marrying, and to file separately.

The 1969 changes and the fact that, under the rate for single persons, married couples filing a joint return often had to pay more tax than did two single persons with the same total income did not go without controversy. The differential in rates was deemed appropriate on the assumption that a married couple has higher living costs than one single person, and thus should pay less tax on equal income, but that the married couple's expenses would fall short of those of two single persons having separate households, and therefore the couple's tax should exceed that of the two separate taxpayers.

The incentives and fairness problems created by the 1969 readjustment led to intensified examination of how to create tax rates that would fairly distribute tax burdens on single and married taxpayers and/or would be "marriage neutral." Soon it became recognized that a marriage-neutral tax rate system cannot be achieved under a progressive tax rate regime, in general, if all equal-income married couples are to have equal tax burdens (regardless of whether one spouse generates all the income or both, in some proportion, generate part of the aggregate household income), and if all equal income households are to be taxed equally (whether consisting of a single person or a couple).[1] A progressive rate schedule can be marriage neutral only if individual connections to earned or investment income continue to control tax burdens even after marriage, rather than making the tax depend on the couple's consolidated income.

Some changes in the relative tax burdens of married taxpayers have been made through changes in the tax allowance for child or dependent care and associated household expenses, by separate head-of-household rates and rules about married taxpayers filing separately. The change from a standard deduction/low income allowance of equal amount to either a single taxpayer or a married couple to different standard deductions for married couples and single persons also altered some of the proportions.

In 1981, in an effort to somewhat alleviate the "marriage tax penalty," one that most seriously affected two-income married couples with relatively equal incomes, Congress enacted I.R.C. § 221, providing a deduction to two-earner married couples filing a joint return. The deduction was equal to 10 percent of the lesser of $30,000 or the qualified earned income of the spouse with the lower qualified earned income (as defined in §§ 61 and 221(b)).

1. Except perhaps with a sophisticated tax-credit device.

Thus, the maximum deduction was $3,000. The deduction was available regardless of whether or not the couple itemized personal deductions. In 1986, Congress repealed this § 221 deduction, partly on the theory that the new lower and less steeply graduated rates would soften the problem, and that repeal of § 221 would simplify the law. In recent legislation, Congress has partially addressed the treatment of married couples for purposes of the 15% bracket and the standard deduction. *See* I.R.C. §§ 1(f)(8); 63(c)(2), (7). Still, the basic dilemmas of taxing single taxpayers who live alone, single taxpayers who live in non-marital liaison, married taxpayers (with and without children), and households with one or two income producers (of earned or of investment kind) in a way that is fair and not distorting of incentives remain unresolved.

Section 66 provides special rules for treatment of community income of married individuals who are living apart for the entire year and who do not file joint returns. Generally, as to earned income, each spouse is taxed only on the income he or she personally earned. *See* I.R.C. § 66.

§ 81. Gifts of Property; Gifts of Income From Property; Gifts of Personal Service Income

Gifts of Appreciated Property. Under familiar principles it is feasible, even easy, to shift taxation on the gain in appreciated property, merely by making a transfer of the property. If a donor owns property for which he paid $100 and it has increased in value to $170, for example, the donor can quite safely and legitimately give the property to almost any donee he chooses and need not fear that the gift transfer itself will entail any tax for the donor. *See* Taft v. Bowers (S.Ct.1929). (Some exceptions will be made for transfers to some recipients, such as to creditors or to those whom the donor is obligated to support, and for some assets, to recapture gain or prior tax allowances. And I.R.C. § 84 contains a special rule that makes the transferor of appreciated property to a political party taxable as if he or she had sold the property and donated the proceeds.) Even if the asset has been used by the donor in business, the making of the gift itself will usually be free of tax to the donor. Neither the withdrawal of a business asset from business use, nor the disposition of that property by gift to another person, will as a general rule be deemed to be a "realization" of the gain so as to give rise to income (or tax) to the owner—as it is in some other income tax systems. Instead, under U.S. concepts, the donee will take over the donor's "basis," which was $100 in the example (plus possibly some gift tax paid), for purposes of computing gain or loss on sale, depreciation, and for all other purposes. *See* I.R.C. § 1015. If and when the donee sells the property for $170, the donee will have $70 gain, taxable at that time. Under U.S. law, this is an entirely lawful and proper way to shift taxation of the gain in appreciated property to a donee.

Deductible loss, however, cannot be shifted in this way. If the property was purchased for $100 and has decreased in value to $85, for the purpose of determining *loss* the donee must take the lesser of fair market value ($85) or donor's basis ($100) as the donee's basis. *See* I.R.C. § 1015(a). Hence, if the donee sells the property for $85, he will have neither taxable gain nor deductible loss. The potential loss deduction will have disappeared; no deduction will be available to anyone. Perhaps the policy justification for allowing gain and tax burden to be shifted is that the donee will be in a more liquid position than the donor when the gain is realized by sale; a similar policy does not support shifting losses between taxpayers. Cf. I.R.C. § 267 (loss disallowance in related-party transactions).

The rule for inheritances and bequests (gifts made by transfer at death) is somewhat different from the rule for lifetime gifts. The donee of appreciated (or depreciated) property takes the fair market value of that property at the date of death (or as of an alternate valuation date) as his or her basis, regardless of the basis of the donor. *See* I.R.C. § 1014(a). Again, the reason for not taxing gain at death may be a concern over lack of liquidity. And the decedent's old basis is not carried over after death because of the heavy administrative burdens involved in tracing the decedent's basis. So potentially taxable gain escapes tax altogether, and potentially deductible loss disappears without a deduction, under "fresh-start" basis.

These rules for death transfers create strong income-tax-motivated incentives for an elderly taxpayer to sell property that has decreased in value below his basis, in order to realize and deduct the loss, and to retain property that has risen in value in order to avoid realizing the gain, and to give his or her heirs an elevated basis—equal to fair market value—at death. Gift property with gain inhering in it can often be donated to a low-bracket (or tax-exempt) person and the gain transferred to that person; loss property is better sold, if the loss will be deductible by the high-bracket original owner.

In 2001, Congress enacted I.R.C. § 1022 which is scheduled to apply to property acquired from a decedent dying after December 31, 2009, when the estate tax is scheduled to be repealed. Under § 1022 property acquired from a decedent will be treated as transferred by gift and take a basis equal to the lesser of the decedent's adjusted basis or the property's value at the decedent's death. I.R.C. 1022(a). The basis rule in § 1022 is subject to an exception that generally allows a $1.3 million upward adjustment in the basis of property transferred to anyone and a $3 million upward adjustment in the basis of property left to a spouse.

Gifts of Income From Property. An important consideration in shifting income tax is the income *from*, in addition to the appreciation *in*, property. To shift income from property, and the tax on it, to someone else, U.S. taxpayers have resorted to gifts of property and to gifts of the income from property, among other arrangements. If a donor gives property to a donee and that property generates income in the hands of the donee, the income generally will be taxed to the donee. The broad rule ("ownership") declares that income from property is to be taxed to the owner of the property. Consequently, income earned by the property while it was owned by the donor is taxed to him; income earned after ownership of the property has been shifted to the donee will be taxed to the donee. [Similar rules exist for sales of property. *See, e.g.,* the rules for dividends on corporate stock that has been sold. Treas.Regs. § 1.61–9(c).] The making of the gift itself has not been treated as a realization of income to the donor, and the donee excludes the value of the gift property from his income under I.R.C. § 102.

The general rule that income from property is taxed to the owner of the property ("ownership") becomes more difficult to apply, or less satisfactory in result, in two troublesome kinds of situations. The first is when a taxpayer, whose property has "earned" income that is about to be paid to him, makes a gift of the property on the eve of receiving the income, so that the income is then actually paid to the donee. In this situation, the income was earned by the donor's property—while it was in his hands—but is paid on the donee's property and paid to the donee. Who should be taxed on that income? A doctrine of "constructive receipt" and a rule against "anticipatory assignment of income" have evolved to make the donor taxable in some of these borderline instances.

The second troublesome situation is one in which the donor gives not property itself in the usual sense of capital or an income-producing asset, but rather he or she carves out an interest and gives the donee a right to the income from property and retains ownership of that income-producing property itself. A more extreme example may be seen when the donor never owned that property but merely owned the right to its income, which he then gave to the donee. When the donee actually receives the income, should the donor or the donee be taxable? The answer to this question depends on complex variables, which the following passages will review.

By way of illustration of the two trouble spots— gift on eve of receipt and gift of income only— consider the celebrated *Horst* case. There, a father who owned negotiable corporate bonds detached some of their negotiable interest coupons shortly before the coupons' due date and delivered the coupons as a gift to his son who, in the same year, collected them at their maturity. This fact situation presented the court with two major tax questions— was the father or the son to be taxed on the interest, and if the father were to be taxable, was his income realized when the son collected it or when the father gave the coupons to the son? The U.S. Supreme Court held that the father, not the son, was taxable on the interest, much as if he had collected it, paid the tax, and given it (tax-free) to his son. Helvering v. Horst (S.Ct.1940). The Court did not use "constructive receipt" language in explaining its decision. Instead, the Court said that the father had "realized" the income when he commanded its payment to another, his son. He could not escape taxation by procuring payment to another, whether as a gift or in payment of a debt or by any other arrangement. "The power to dispose of income is the equivalent of ownership of it," the Court said, again asserting that the "fruit" could not be attributed to a different "tree" from that on which it grew. Since the interest was collected by the son in the same tax year in which the father made the gift, the Court did not have to decide the "When is it income?" question. The Court's "realization" language, however, suggested that the time of income to the father was the time of gift, not the time the son collected the interest.

The Commissioner took the Court at its word about "realization" and about how a taxpayer enjoys non-material satisfactions by making a gift to a charity or to his children. Accordingly, he tried to tax a farmer who gave his farm products to charity as having realized income by and at the time of the gift. Similarly, he asserted that a gift of farm products to the farmer's son was also the occasion for taxing the donor on the gain.

After several rebuffs in court, the Commissioner has retreated from these aggressive assertions of the realization doctrine. *See, e.g.,* Rev.Rul. 55–138, 1955–1 C.B. 223 (farm or manufactured products to charity); Rev.Rul. 55–531, 1955–2 C.B. 520 (farm or manufactured products to children); Rev.Rul. 55–410, 1955–1 C.B. 297 (appreciated property to charity). Perhaps these results can be explained by equating these examples with cases on gifts of property (subject to the rule of Taft v. Bowers), rather than gifts of income as in *Horst,* since these farm and manufactured items do not constitute fixed and almost inevitable, matured income by themselves and without further action. In any event, the realization doctrine has not, at least as to gifts of income from property, been carried so far as some of the language in the *Horst* case might suggest.

The general notion of taxing income from property to the taxpayer who owns it has not proven sufficient as a rule of taxation any more than the connotative analogy of fruit and tree. For example, in another leading case, Edward was the owner of a life interest in a trust established by his father, William. In other words (and to simplify the actual trust disposition), Edward was entitled to all the income from the property in the trust established by William, his father, for so long as Edward should live. Edward, the income beneficiary, then made irrevocable gifts to his children of specified dollar interests in his own income interest. For example, one gift provided that Edward's daughter Lucy would receive $9,000 in each calendar year thereafter, in other words so long as the life interest of Edward would last. The question presented was whether the income received in future years by Lucy and her siblings would be taxed to them or to Edward, their father. The court held that Lucy, not the father, would be taxable. *See* Blair v. Comm. (S.Ct.1937). Fruit-tree analogies cannot easily predict that outcome and, of course, neither Edward nor Lucy "earned" the income, either by rendering personal services or by owning and leasing, loaning or otherwise investing property. The trust property, the corpus or capital or principal, was not "owned" by Edward or Lucy. The Court's language was "property" language nonetheless. It held that the valid assignments had transferred to Lucy and her siblings, as "owners," specified beneficial ownership interests in the trust, that Edward had been the owner of an "equitable interest" in the corpus of the property, and he transferred that interest to his children. Evidently, then, income from "property" is to be taxed to the owner of the property. The Court simply must search for and discover "the property." Compare and contrast Harrison v. Schaffner (S.Ct.1941) (income beneficiary of trust assigned specific dollar amounts from trust income to her children, to be paid out of trust income for the next year; income held taxable to donor). Also compare Comm. v. P.G. Lake, Inc. (S.Ct.1958).

While the maxim that "the owner of property is to be taxed on its income" may underlie the law, it does not prove to be a workable and self-sufficient legal rule, partly because some hard questions remain about what is "property." Evidently the negotiable interest coupons in *Horst* were not property, but rather were the income from it. Yet calves raised for sale and given to a Y.M.C.A. and sold by the donor for the donee are "property," and the donor will escape tax on the gain. *See* Campbell v. Prothro (5th Cir.1954). While one might think that a lease itself could be assigned and would be treated as a transfer of "property," that result is not clear. Compare Iber v. U.S. (7th Cir.1969) with Lum v. Comm. (3d Cir.1945) and U.S. v. Shafto (4th Cir.

1957). Other "property" situations have involved assignments of claims, patent royalties, working interests in oil property, shares of stock, prizes and other receipts. Special statutory rules govern some categories: *see* I.R.C. § 691 (income in respect of decedents); Regs. § 1.61–9(c) (dividends on stock sold); § 453B (disposition of installment obligations); § 704(e) (family partnerships); § 1366(e) (family group shareholders and employees of S corporation); § 83 (property transferred in connection with the performance of services).

Shifting Property and Personal Service Income. In the assignment-of-income-by-gift areas that are not covered by explicit statutory law (or the statutory rules on trusts), reliable general statements are risky. Exactly when it is that one taxpayer rather than another will be deemed to have such a relationship to a particular receipt that it will be attributed to the first, rather than the second, taxpayer, for tax purposes depends on a number of variables. Generally speaking, income earned by personal effort will be taxed to the one rendering the services, and it cannot easily escape tax by anticipatory (much less subsequent) assignment to another. This general rule reaches statutory dignity in one place: I.R.C. § 73 states that amounts received in respect of the services of a child shall be included in the child's gross income, not the parents', even if the child does not receive them. Similarly, all expenses attributable to such amounts shall be treated as paid or incurred by the child. So, when a famous baseball player named Richie Allen, while still a

minor, signed a contract to play professional baseball and tried to arrange for part of his bonus for
signing to be paid and taxed to his mother, the Tax
Court and Third Circuit Court of Appeals taxed the
entire bonus to the player. Richard A. Allen (Tax
Court 1968).

When property other than cash is transferred by
a person for whom services were performed to any
other person, § 83 will govern and, under it, the
service provider, not the recipient of the property,
will be taxed.

Some artists, entertainers and athletes offer their
services to charitable organizations and such to
channel to an exempt organization income that
normally would be that of the individual artist.
Often the tax aim is to avoid percentage limitations
on the deduction of charitable contributions under
I.R.C. § 170. If the income from an evening's performance, for example, were taxed to the performer,
and he or she contributed it to the charity, the
taxpayer could not offset income to the extent the
deductions were not allowed by § 170. If the charity
itself promotes this event, and a performer or artist
contributes or loans services or property for use in
this event, the contributor will not realize taxable
income. G.C.M. 27026, 1951–2 C.B. 7; Rev.Rul. 68–
503, 1968–2 C.B. 44. But if the private promoter or
performer merely designates a certain day or regular performance as a charity performance and turns
the net proceeds over to charity, the proceeds will
be taxable to the promoter or performer. *See* Regs.

§ 1.61–2(c); Rev.Rul. 71, 1953–1 C.B. 18; Rev.Rul. 58–235, 1959–1 C.B. 26.

Just as the notion that income from property is to be taxed to the owner of the property does not prove to be self-executing, and just as "fruit-tree" metaphors don't serve to predict the outcome of cases very well, so it is hard to be content with a sweeping statement that income from personal efforts is taxable to the person who rendered those services. To be sure, that notion underlies Lucas v. Earl, *supra,* where a breadwinner was taxed on earned income he had assigned to his wife, and which she actually received as owner. Other cases, too, have blocked attempts to escape from taxation by assigning personal service income after it was earned, as well as in advance of earning it (as in *Earl*). *See, e.g.,* Helvering v. Eubank (S.Ct.1940) (renewal commissions on taxpayer's sales of life insurance were assigned to his wife); Wilkinson v. U.S. (Ct.Cl.1962) (an interest in contingent fee contract assigned by lawyer was given to charity). *See also* I.R.C. § 83(a), for a statutory rule of "earner-ship."

However, some instances involve a taxpayer's personal efforts that have produced a tangible or intangible piece of property, such as a painting or a patent, copyright, royalty agreement, or the like. When the creator of such property transfers it to a donee, who in turn collects the proceeds, the creator may succeed in escaping the tax. *See, e.g.,* Heim v. Fitzpatrick (2d Cir.1959); Rev.Rul. 54–599, 1954–2 C.B. 52; Wodehouse v. Comm. (4th Cir.1949). The authorities in these instances have treated the facts as if they involved a transfer of income-producing property rather than an assignment of income earned by personal services. Other courts have not been so willing to use this pigeon-hole approach or have employed it with contrary results. *See, e.g.,* Strauss v. Comm. (2d Cir.1948); Wodehouse v. Comm. (2d Cir.1949). At best, the law in this area must be admitted to be equivocal. Nonetheless, some nagging truth remains in the initial generalization—that income from personal efforts should and (usually) will be taxed to the one earner who rendered those services.

Also, generally speaking, the owner of "property" (such as stock or land or a truck) will be taxed on income from the property. So, by giving such *property* to his child or anyone else, a taxpayer can manage to avoid tax on future income. But, what if he gives just the rights to the *income* (rents, dividends, interest) from the property to the donee? Or, what if he gives the donee a right only to income and only for a few years? Much may depend on the imminence of the receipts, their certainty, the substantiality and the value of the rights given away compared to the rights and value retained, the evasionary flavor of the arrangement, whether the donor has retained or otherwise possesses material control over the economic interest transferred to the donee, and other such factors. An exceedingly important factor is whether the transfer was a gift or for consideration in money or money's worth. For example, if the son in *Horst* had paid the father for the interest coupons (which payments would have been income to the father), the father would not have been taxable again when the son collected the interest income.

The approach of the *Horst* case and the doctrines of "realization" and, perhaps, "constructive receipt" are most likely to arise when property is transferred immediately before a payment is about to be made of income it has already earned. *See, e.g.,* Friedman v. Comm. (6th Cir.1965) (donor of endowment policies taxable on appreciation when he "gave" them to charity sixteen days before maturity). Similarly, the courts and tax administrators will invoke such doctrines in connection with transfers of property when much of its value is due to personal services or efforts of the transferor and when the donee can collect the income without sustaining any remaining investment risk or any activity on his part. *See, e.g.,* Wilkinson v. U.S. (Ct.Cl.1962); *but see* contrary authorities cited above. A taxpayer may not make an assignment of income already earned and about to be received without a very high risk of taxation to him. *See, e.g.,* Austin v. Comm. (6th Cir.1947); Doyle v. Comm. (4th Cir.1945); Stephen S. Townsend (Tax Court 1962). The exact extent and limits of these risks, however, stoutly defy precise delineation. Further clarification may be possible by reference to the trust rules (*infra,* §§ 85–90) and to the following sections on property settlements, alimony, etc.

The potential for shifting income from property by parents to children was significantly restricted by enactment of the so-called "kiddie tax" in I.R.C. § 1(g). Specifically, the net *unearned* income of a child under age 14 (in excess of $1,000) is taxed *to the child* at the rates applicable if it were the parents' income. The tax basically is calculated by determining what the parents' tax would have been if the child's net unearned income were added to the parents' taxable income. *See* I.R.C. § 1(g).

Altogether it would appear that income from property can be shifted much more readily than income from services (except for services rendered in kind, the imputed income from which, shifted from performer to recipient, goes untaxed to either). But property consists of after-tax income, in most instances, and hence the apparent disparity between the sets of principles about shifting service income and property income can at least partly be reconciled by viewing both as designed to block shifting pre-tax income in ways that would undermine the graduated rate structure of the income tax.

§ 82. Divisions of Property and Property Settlements

When co-owners of property have occasion to divide up a piece of jointly-owned land or some other asset, they would not ordinarily expect the event to produce immediate income tax consequences. After all, they have not "sold" anything, and each probably feels he or she has not "exchanged or otherwise disposed" of his property. However, it is true that each has exchanged an undivided one-half interest in the whole asset for an undivided ownership in one-half of the property.

If the property has appreciated in value, will gain be taxable upon the division in the U.S.? The answer is that it will not be, as the law stands, in the situation involving a division of property between co-owners. Rev. Rul. 55–77, 1955–1 C.B. 339.

A similar problem arises when a divorce or separation gives rise to a property settlement and, for example, one spouse becomes the sole owner of an asset formerly held jointly or in community by both. Or, one may surrender an asset to the other to satisfy an order of the court. Will division or transfer of property in connection with divorce or separation occasion the recognition of gain or loss? The answer now, by virtue of § 1041, is in the negative. The background of this section is given next, followed by a description of its new rule.

For many years, the most authoritative pronouncement on the subject of property settlements was U.S. v. Davis (S.Ct.1962). The Court there held that a spouse (there the husband) did realize taxable gain when he transferred appreciated property (DuPont stock) to his former wife pursuant to a property settlement agreement executed before the divorce. Under Delaware state property law, the property transferred was the husband's own property, subject only to statutory marital rights of the wife. He therefore found himself in the position of transferring his appreciated property in satisfaction of his wife's right, on divorce, to a share of his property. There remained only the matter of valuing the rights she surrendered (which the Court did by equating them with the fair market value of what the husband gave up in the arm's-length settlement) and comparing that value with his "basis" in the property, to determine his gain. Interestingly enough, the Court said that the wife's basis in the property received would be its fair market value, although she evidently would not be taxable on receiving the property in exchange for the surrender of her marital rights. *See* Rev.Rul. 67–221, 1967–2 C.B. 63, to the same effect.

The Court in *Davis* distinguished the situation there—transfer of property by a taxpayer in satisfaction of a claim against him and thus realizing gain or loss—from a non-taxable division of community property half of which is owned by each spouse before the divorce and from similar non-taxable divisions among joint tenants or other co-owners. *See also* Rev.Rul. 74–347, 1974–2 C.B. 26; Pulliam v. Comm. (10th Cir.1964). In at least some of these situations, the issue of realization and *when* income is taxable affects the question *who* is taxable. For in *Davis,* if the appreciation were not taxable to the husband when his wife took the property, she probably would have been the one to be taxable when she sold it. If the division of community property or other co-owned property is not treated as a taxable event at the time (and it will not be), each owner will take a pro-rata share of the original unified basis and each will be taxable on his one-half or other fraction of the gain (or loss) when and if he sells his half of the property.

Enactment of § 1041 brought about a significant change in the law of property settlements. Section 1041, a nonrecognition rule, reversed the pre-existing law on the transfer of property incident to divorce. Section 1041(a) states that no gain or loss shall be recognized on a transfer of property from an individual to a spouse, or a former spouse, *if* the transfer is incident to a divorce. The transfer is treated as a gift; accordingly, the basis of the property in the hands of the transferee will be the adjusted basis of the transferor. *See* § 1041(b). Note: This rule is not exactly the same as the general basis rule for gifts under § 1015(a), which requires that the lower of the donor's basis or fair market value be taken as basis by the donee for purposes of determining the amount of a loss.

The Code also provides that a transfer is "incident to a divorce" if it occurs within one year after the cessation of the marriage or is "related to the cessation of the marriage." § 1041(c).

As a result of the enactment of § 1041, the rule of *Davis* has been legislatively overruled. And, under § 1041, sales between happily married spouses are covered, as well as property settlements or other sales related to divorce; there cannot be a sale with normal recognition of gain or loss and basis consequences between spouses during marriage or between former spouses for at least one year after the cessation of the marriage.

§ 83. Alimony; Spousal or Child Support

A "Whose income is it?" problem is presented when a divorced spouse pays alimony, child support or other amounts to his or her former marital partner. If alimony is paid by former husband to former wife, will he be taxed when he earns it? Can he deduct his payment to her? Will she be taxed when she receives it? Will it be treated as a gift analogous to a property division or settlement?

The Internal Revenue Code does not leave these questions to the courts: I.R.C. § 71 spells out a rule under which a wife (if she is the "recipient spouse") who receives alimony or separate maintenance in periodic payments, as statutorily defined, will be taxable, but payments fixed as support for minor children will not be taxable when received by her. Corresponding to the treatment of the recipient spouse in I.R.C. § 71, § 215 affords a deduction to the husband (if he is the payor spouse) for payments taxable to the wife under § 71. And § 62(a)(10) allows the deduction to be taken from gross income, to enable the taxpayer whose itemized deductions do not exceed the standard deduction (the amount of income exempt from tax) to get the full benefit of the deduction. The result then is to tax alimony to her and child support payments to him (by disallowance of a deduction for the child support payments). Section 682 correlates with the treatment in §§ 71 and 215 to exclude from the husband's income, and include in the wife's, amounts paid to her by a trust established by him for her benefit as part of the divorce or separate maintenance arrangements.[2]

The I.R.C. § 71(a) treatment is not given to child support, to some installment payments of a principal sum, or to proceeds of a property settlement in general; section 71 applies only to those payments that are viewed by the tax law as arising out of the duty of support owed by the payor spouse to the recipient spouse as a consequence of the marital relationship; that is, § 71 applies only to alimony or separate maintenance payments.

An alimony (or separate maintenance) payment is defined to mean any payment in cash if: (i) such payment is received by a spouse under a divorce or separation instrument, (ii) the instrument does not designate such payment as payment not includable in gross income, (iii) in cases of spouses legally separated under a decree of divorce or separate maintenance, the payee and payor spouses are not members of the same household, and (iv) such payments are to stop at the death of the payee spouse. I.R.C. § 71(b). The child support payments may entitle the payor spouse to claim the children as dependents for purposes of the dependency exemption, under § 152, but § 152(e) imposes a presumption that the parent having custody is entitled to the exemption unless certain requirements of § 152(e)(2)–(4) are met.

2. The terms "husband" and "wife" as used in I.R.C. § 71 and other sections may be interchanged as required by circumstances and authorized by I.R.C. § 7701(a)(17).

In order to ensure that spousal support payments deducted are not a disguised property settlement, a six-year minimum term and recapture rule was introduced in the 1984 T.R.A. and replaced with a three-year recapture rule in 1986. This rule provides for the recapture of excess amounts that have been treated as alimony if, for example, annual payments drop off significantly after a short time, implying that they were installment payments of a lump sum (property settlement or accelerated payments of an agreed amount) rather than long-term support. This phenomenon is called "excess frontloading of alimony payments." *See* § 71(f). The excess amount is specifically defined as the sum of the first post-separation year excess amount and the second post-separation year excess amount. The first post-separation year excess amount is basically the excess of the first post-separation year payment over the sum of the average of the second (reduced by the second year excess amount) and third post-separation year payments plus $15,000. Likewise, the second post-separation year excess amount is the excess of the second (post-separation) year payment over the sum of the third year payment and $15,000.

§ 84. Income in Respect of a Decedent

When a taxpayer dies, the question arises whether income earned before death, but paid after death, should be taxed in a final individual tax return filed on the decedent's behalf for the partial tax year before death, or taxed to the estate (a separate taxable entity) in its own income tax return, or taxed to someone else. Such income could consist of wages, fees, bonuses, royalties, interest, accounts receivable, or partnership income, among others. If all such income were taxed in the deceased's return, as if accrued at death, it might "bunch" income and thus inflate tax liability.

Section 691 was enacted to allocate such income (income not actually received by a cash-method decedent or accrued by an accrual-method decedent before death) to the decedent's estate or to other actual recipients of the income. Income is reported either by the estate or by that person who obtained the right to receive the income—as a beneficiary through the estate or otherwise—depending on who received the income and how the right to receive it was acquired. *See* I.R.C. § 691(a)(1). The income retains, in that recipient's hands, the character (as ordinary income, capital gain, exempt income, etc.) it would have had if received by the deceased taxpayer. I.R.C. § 691(a)(3). The recipient to whom such income is taxed may also enjoy the deductions and credits for those items that are related to the income. I.R.C. § 691(b). If the estate is taxed, it will be entitled to take the deductions. Similarly, estate tax payable on income in respect of a decedent may be deducted by the estate or other recipient, as the case may be. I.R.C. § 691(c).

If property has been sold but the proceeds are not payable until after death, these proceeds are treated as income in respect of a decedent and governed by § 691. Income in respect of a decedent, however, does not receive a basis of its fair market value at the date of the decedent's death. I.R.C. § 1014(c). Unfortunately, neither § 1014(c) nor § 691 defines "income in respect of a decedent," but a definition is given in Regs. § 1.691(a)–1(b).

§ 85. Estates and Trusts—Introduction

The common-law trust has suggested itself as a vehicle for intrafamily property transfers to split or shift income, because it involves the creation of another (artificial) legal "person" or taxpayer whose income will begin to be taxed in the bottom rate brackets. Use of the trust raises a question whether income from trust property is to be taxed to the donor, the beneficiaries, the trust itself, or to someone else. Likewise, the presence of an estate (of a decedent), being administered after the death of a taxpayer, raises income-attribution problems of much the same sort. As for the question of whether parents can escape their higher marginal rates by placing property in trust for minor children, the "kiddie tax" of I.R.C. § 1(g) will often tax the child at the parents' higher rate.

The U.S. Federal income taxation of trusts and estates is a large and sometimes immensely complicated subject. For present purposes, it must be reduced to an outline of simple principles.

Generally speaking, in the U.S. a trust or estate is formally treated as a separate taxpayer. *See generally* I.R.C. § 641. Special tax rates and narrow "brackets" contained in I.R.C. § 1(e) are applicable to the trust or estate, as are most of the general principles of "What is income?", "When is income taxable?", "What is deductible?", etc. Because of possible deductions, however, the trust often does not pay the tax, but immediately or ultimately shifts that burden to the beneficiaries of the trust, under a kind of "flow-through" tax regime.

The statute requires a trust to include in its income any income it receives, whether that income is to be paid out currently to a beneficiary, accumulated for later distribution, or either (at the discretion of the trustee or some other person). Much the same deductions may be taken as are allowed to an individual taxpayer. Special provisions substitute for the usual personal exemption, and the standard deduction may not be taken, so deductions must be itemized. In the case of an estate, some deductions may be taken either on the estate's income tax return or as deductions against the estate tax. I.R.C. § 642(g). As will be seen later, estates and trusts are allowed an additional deduction for amounts they distribute to their beneficiaries, up to the distributable net income of the trust—which is more or less equal to the trust's taxable income. Thus the trust, and the estate in most instances, will prove to be a rather transparent taxpayer, a conduit through which income passes with a deduction offsetting some or all of the gross income reported by the trust if the trust distributes all its income currently. If the trust does not distribute all its income, the undistributed income is taxed to the trust, at least until distribution at a later time, and for an estate the tax is permanent. Such a trust becomes a separate taxpayer, at least for a time. (For more on this, *see* §§ 88–90, *infra*.)

As a separate taxpayer, the trust or estate presents itself as a possible tax-saving (by income-splitting) device. If a person who owns income-producing property can arrange to have some of that property put in trust, and if the income from it is taxable not to him in his marginal brackets but to the trust in lower brackets, perhaps with additional exemptions, tax can be saved. If the trust provides for the benefit of the grantor himself, he may be seeking to escape tax on income that he still intends to devote to his own benefit. If the trust is for others, it may present tax-saving ways of giving to family members or others so that they, not the donor, will be taxable on the income. So, several "Whose income is it?" questions present themselves. Will trust income be taxed to the grantor (settlor) of the trust, to the trust itself, to the beneficiaries of the trust, or possibly to someone else altogether? Can a person by parting with his property for a while, by putting it in trust, escape income tax on income from the property and still get back the property or the income or both, or at least give the income to others as pre-tax, not after-tax, dollars? Can the separate estate of a deceased taxpayer be used after his death to reduce the tax bill otherwise owing on his income?

Sections 641–668 of the Code provide general (and sometimes highly complex and technical) rules for answering these questions. Sections 671–677 deal with the so-called "grantor trusts," trusts whose income arguably is taxable to the grantor, the person who established the trust. Section 678 deals with the so-called *Mallinckrodt* trust, named after the leading case, where the question is whether someone other than the grantor or trust or beneficiaries will be taxable. Section 679 deals with the taxation of foreign trusts having one or more U.S. beneficiaries. And §§ 651–668 pertain to trusts whose income is either to be taxed to the beneficiaries or to the trust, the so-called "simple" or "complex" rules for non-grantor trusts.

§ 86. Grantor Trusts

If a taxpayer places income-producing property in trust and retains so much control and dominion over the property and income that he is virtually still its owner, he will be taxed on the income of the trust whether or not he receives it. This rule, amounting to one of "constructive ownership," stems from the leading case of Helvering v. Clifford (S.Ct.1940). There, a husband established a five-year irrevocable trust for the benefit of his wife. The trust would terminate on the earlier date of the death of the grantor or of his wife. On termination the corpus would return to the grantor, but any accumulated, undistributed income or investment gain was to go to the wife. The husband-grantor was trustee and not only held broad administrative powers over the trust property, but he also enjoyed absolute discretion in deciding whether to pay over income to his wife-beneficiary or retain it in the trust. The Supreme Court held that the grantor was to be taxed as the owner of the corpus because of all the facts and circumstances—especially the short duration, retention of control over the corpus and the fact that his wife was the beneficiary. All in all, the grantor retained too many of the incidents of ownership and that bundle of rights and benefits that amount to "property." The statutory authority relied on was nothing more than the forerunner of present I.R.C. § 61(a), which merely states that "gross income means all income from whatever source derived," a rule that does not seem to speak to the issue of *who* must pay tax on the income.

In an earlier case, the grantor of a revocable trust was held taxable, since his power to revoke gave him such a relationship to the income earned by trust property that he was appropriately taxable on it. *See* Corliss v. Bowers (S.Ct.1930). By exercising the power to revoke, he could get the property back at any time and terminate the interest of the income beneficiary. Other cases taxed grantors who in other ways kept too many strings on the income they "gave away."

To help settle the confusion that *Clifford* and other cases had introduced, the Internal Revenue Service promulgated regulations, informally called the *Clifford* Regulations, spelling out some guidelines. Those guidelines have now been elevated to statutory law, supported by Regulations of their own, in I.R.C. §§ 671–677. Some of these rules were modified by the 1986 T.R.A., which made the use of "grantor trusts" less often attractive, particularly by closing an "after–10–years" safe harbor formerly found in § 673(a).

Under the statutory scheme, several main themes appear, though exceptions and qualifications surround them all. The main themes stem from the notion—found in the gift-of-property cases—that income from property is to be taxed to the owner of the property. When property was placed in trust, special rules of "ownership" for tax purposes had to be developed. Generally speaking, it may be said that the income of a trust will be attributed and taxable to the grantor if, and so long as: he (the grantor) holds a power to revoke the trust and revest the corpus in himself (I.R.C. § 676); he retains a reversionary interest having a value in excess of 5% of the trust property (§ 673); the income of the trust or the corpus may inure to the benefit of the grantor by distribution to himself or his spouse, by accumulation for future distribution to either of them, or by payment of life insurance premiums on the lives of either one of them (I.R.C. § 677); the income, in the discretion of another person, may be applied or distributed for the support of a beneficiary whom the grantor is legally obligated to support, *but only* to the extent such income is so applied (I.R.C. § 677(b)); the beneficial enjoyment of the corpus or income is subject to a power of disposition in the grantor or a non-adverse party (I.R.C. § 674); or, the grantor retains excessive administrative powers (I.R.C. § 675). Each of these statutory rules has exceptions and conditions and must be consulted carefully to understand the law. Furthermore, under § 672 the grantor will be taxed on the strength of any of these retained powers whether it can be exercised by him alone, by someone else who does not have an interest in the trust substantially adverse to the grantor's, or only by the grantor and a non-adverse party acting together. In other words, the grantor must give up almost all strings on the property and on the income. If he does not give them up, he will be taxed on trust income whether or not he actually receives it. Formerly the grantor could escape these consequences if he gave up the strings for at least 10 years; this safe harbor was repealed in 1986.

Section 671 states that §§ 671–677 preempt the field; consequently section 61 cannot now be used by the authorities to reach a *Clifford*-like result.

If §§ 671–677 make a grantor taxable as owner, the trust will be disregarded in computing his income; neither the trust nor any of the beneficiaries will be taxable on the income. If they actually get it, I.R.C. § 102 (excluding from income property received by gift or bequest) will protect them from income tax on the receipt, if it is a gift.

As mentioned above, another way in which the Code makes use of the trust device less effective for income splitting is the "kiddie tax" in I.R.C. § 1(g).

§ 87. Mallinckrodt Trusts—Income Taxable to a Third Person

The *Clifford* rules of constructive ownership and income attribution were later applied not only to grantors who retained too much control, but to some other persons who were given powers equivalent to those which, if retained by the grantor, would make him taxable. Now, I.R.C. § 678 declares that a person other than the grantor will be treated as the substantial owner of any portion of a trust with respect to which he holds a power to vest corpus in himself or has released such a power but retained such control that under §§ 671–677 a grantor in such a position would be taxed as owner. So, if A sets up a trust for B and gives *B* a power to vest the corpus in himself, plus other powers of the §§ 671–677 variety, and A retains no control, and B releases his power to revest but retains a §§ 671–677 power, B (not A, nor the trust or any of its beneficiaries) will be taxable on the trust income.

§ 88. Non-grantor Trusts

If a trust survives I.R.C. §§ 671–678, the income from the trust property must then be taxed either to the trust or to its beneficiaries. Rules for determining which of them shall be taxed, when, on how much, and as what kind of income are contained in I.R.C. §§ 651–668. These rules base themselves on the premises (i) that the trust is a separate taxpayer and (ii) that it is a conduit through which income can pass untaxed and unchanged in character until it reaches actual beneficiaries. I.R.C. §§ 652(b), 661(b), 662(b). These rules are designed to counter the moves of taxpayers who seek to manipulate their affairs to gain unfair tax advantages. The rules are also designed to further the philosophy of

I.R.C. § 102—gift property received in trust, just as if received outright, shall not be taxable to the recipient; income on gift property (or a gift of income only) shall be taxable to the recipient—if not to the grantor.

To accomplish these aims, the trust sections allow a deduction to a trust for income it receives and immediately pays out to the beneficiaries, up to distributable net income (D.N.I.)—about the same as otherwise taxable income—for that year. I.R.C. §§ 651, 661. The trust's deduction offsets its income, and to this extent no tax is payable by the trust. Thus the income is taxed just once (up to D.N.I.) and is taxed to the beneficiaries, not the trust. I.R.C. §§ 652, 662. Later, when the trust terminates and distributes corpus to the remainderman, that corpus will not be taxable to him. Thus § 102's theory works here too—the remainderman has received property (corpus) as a gift or bequest excludable from his gross income by I.R.C. § 102. Distributable net income, defined in I.R.C. § 643(a), serves several technical purposes, all of which flow from the purpose of I.R.C. § 102(a) and (b) to separate *property* received by gift or bequest (tax free) from *income* on such property (taxable) or income alone received by gift or bequest (taxable). Technically, D.N.I. forms a ceiling on the amount of the trust's additional deduction for distributed income and a ceiling on the amount taxable as income to the beneficiary. It also insures that income will be treated as the same in form to the beneficiary as to the trust.

However, if a trust accumulates some of its income, the trust will be taxable on that income at that time. I.R.C. §§ 661 and 662. Later, when the accumulated and previously taxed income is distributed, it will be taxed again to the beneficiaries (§ 666), but they will be able to subtract the taxes paid by the trust in determining their tax. *See* § 667. Under this rule, however, the beneficiary cannot offset the excess tax previously paid by the trust against his or her tax liability from *other* income. When the dust has settled, the trust's income—except for some capital gains—will have been taxed to the beneficiaries and at their rates, not the trust's.

The rate structure applicable to non-grantor trusts also reduces their income-splitting utility. In 2004, only the first $1,500 of taxable income is taxed at 15% and any excess over $7,500 is taxed at 35%. *See* I.R.C. §§ 1(e), (i)(2).

These simple results are not always perfectly obtained and in any event are implemented by some of the most complex legislation in the code. So-called simple trusts, those required to pay out all income (and only income) currently, and having no charitable beneficiaries, are governed by I.R.C. §§ 651–652. All other trusts are called complex trusts—in them income can be accumulated to be paid out later, corpus can be distributed currently, or there are charitable beneficiaries in the picture. Code Sections 661–668 apply to such trusts and to estates, which are taxable under the complex trust rules. Rules called the "tier system," the "throwback rule" and the "separate-share rule" are just part of the armament of this legislation and are too intricate to permit detailed coverage here. They are illustrated in the example below, however, and are also briefly explained. (*See* §§ 89–90, *infra.*) All address themselves to the problem of correctly identifying who should be taxed, on what, when, and how.

§ 89. Simple Trusts Illustrated

A few simple (and over-simplified) examples will help illustrate the skeleton of the statute and how it works. Suppose A sets up a trust by transferring $200,000 in cash that T, the trustee, is to keep in the bank. Income (suppose 5% interest yields $10,000 per year) is to be paid out each year to B, the beneficiary, for 15 years, the term of the trust. At the expiration of the trust's term, corpus will be distributed to B. This is a "simple trust" since all income must be paid out each year. If we ignore trustee's fees and other complicating details, the tax picture will be very simple. The trust will have $10,000 income each year. Under § 651 it will be allowed a special deduction of $10,000 for income required to be distributed currently. Under § 652, that same amount ($10,000) will be taxable to B in the year she receives it, at her marginal rates, or her parents' marginal rate if she is a minor under age 14 and subject to the "kiddie tax" rate rule of § 1(g). The trust is a conduit both as to amount of income and its character. For example, if the interest were paid on municipal bonds rather than a bank account, it would be tax free to B by virtue of I.R.C. § 103.

Now suppose that the trustee were required to pay out all current income but was allowed to pay it to either B or C or to both, in such proportions as he saw fit. The tax result would be much the same. The trust has income of $10,000, and a deduction of $10,000 under § 651, and each beneficiary will have income in the amount he or she actually receives. (If B or C were dependents of the grantor, of course, there might be a possibility that the trust would be a grantor trust and its income taxable to A, under § 677—so assume B and C are not dependent on A). This too is a simple trust, governed by I.R.C. §§ 651–652 (and by §§ 641–643, as are all trusts and estates). It can disregard the more convoluted rules of §§ 661–668, designed for complex trusts. Thus, a trust may be a simple trust even if the trustee has discretion to determine who shall receive the income. If he also has power to distribute corpus, the trust will be a simple trust only in any year in which he does not distribute corpus; when he exercises the power, the trust will be a complex trust. Further examples are given in the Regulations. Regs. § 1.652(c)–4.

§ 90. Complex Trusts Illustrated

The complex trust rules[3] grew in order to preserve the philosophy of I.R.C. § 102 in the context of complicated trusts when a trustee is given the

3. The Regulations use "complex trust" as a term to describe trusts subject to § 661. *See* Regs. § 1.661(a)–1.

power to accumulate income and make a delayed distribution later or is empowered to distribute corpus currently among beneficiaries. Rules were needed to separate, as to each recipient, amounts that were income (and thus taxable) from amounts that were corpus or "property" and hence excludable under § 102.

At the same time, taxpayers could not be allowed to shift their tax burdens to trusts while remaining in essentially the same economic position as other taxpayers bearing a heavier burden. So, to separate distributions of income from distributions of capital and to prevent tax shifting or splitting or postponement, the complex trust tax rules were developed to focus on how beneficiaries of such trusts should be taxed.

The complex trust (or estate) is taxed much like a simple trust. It receives a special deduction for amounts required to be distributed currently and any other amounts actually paid out, up to Distributable Net Income (D.N.I.). Moreover, amounts actually distributed by a complex trust will be taxable as income to the beneficiaries, up to D.N.I., whether in fact made out of current income, accumulated income or corpus. So, the complex trust rules override any tracing or earmarking by the trustee of the source from which funds were taken to make up a current distribution. Current D.N.I. is the mandatory ceiling on the trust's deduction and the measure of income to the beneficiaries who receive distributions. Other rules of priority, the two-tier system, the separate-share rule and the throwback rule further serve to implement this approach.

To illustrate the complex trust rules, again consider A's trust for B, who is the only beneficiary. (*See* § 89, *supra.*) However, suppose that T, the trustee, is not only required to distribute all income, but also is empowered to invade corpus for B's benefit. Suppose also that trust income during the first year is $10,000 but T actually pays out $15,000 to B. We know that the extra $5,000 must have come from corpus, under T's power to invade. The tax picture will reflect that fact. The trust will have income of $10,000 and a deduction under § 661 of $10,000—not $15,000. B, the beneficiary, will be taxable on $10,000 under § 662(a). If B is a minor under age 14, the kiddie tax of § 1(g) will apply. She will receive the additional $5,000 tax free. Why should she? Because it is a gift of property to her, which she would have been entitled to receive tax-free if given outright, under § 102(a). The same result should, and does, obtain when the property is given by invading the trust corpus.

Now suppose that the trustee in the first year of the trust was not required to pay out all income and that he did not have a power to invade corpus (principal). Further, suppose that in year 1, T paid out $5,000 to B and accumulated the other $5,000 pursuant to a power given to him in the trust instrument, under which he could accumulate income and distribute the accumulated income in a later year, and must distribute it to B by the end of the trust. In year 1, the trust had income of $10,000 and a deduction of $5,000. The beneficiary was taxable on the $5,000 she received and that is all, under § 662(a). The trust therefore was taxable on the $5,000 it retained; its special deduction for amounts distributed amounted to only $5,000 of the trust's income. While the tax will be computed under § 1(e), for ease of illustration, let us suppose the trust paid $1,000 in tax on that earned but undistributed income.

Further, suppose the next year, the trust earned $10,000 as usual. But the trustee distributed $14,000 to B. Evidently he distributed the current income and some of the money retained (after taxes) from year 1. (He *may* have gotten the additional $4,000 by some other means; it does not matter.) The trust in year 2 has income of $10,000 and a deduction of $10,000 since it distributed all its income. I.R.C. § 661. The beneficiary, B, will be taxable as follows. Of the $14,000 she received, B will be taxable to the extent of the trust's current income, namely $10,000, under § 662(a). Under the throwback rule, I.R.C. §§ 666–667, B will also be taxed on the $4,000 received in year 2, which will be deemed to have come as a result of accumulating received but undistributed income of $5,000 in year 1. The actual payment to her of $4,000 will be "grossed up" to $5,000 to include the tax of $1,000 paid by the trust. I.R.C. § 666(b). That is, B will be treated as having received $5,000 ($4,000 cash plus tax prepayment of $1,000 for a total of $5,000). Her tax will be determined on $5,000 income by the use of a complex averaging method to be summarized below. To some extent B will be taxed as if the money had been distributed to her in year 1. Suppose the beneficiary's tax when so computed amounts to $1,500, with or without the kiddie tax of § 1(g). She will then receive an offset against her tax on that distribution in the amount of the tax paid by the trust, namely $1,000. I.R.C. § 667(b). That payment by the trust, at its rates, will be treated as if it were a prepayment of her tax obligation computed at her rates. Again, the trust ultimately will serve as a conduit even when distributions of income are delayed to later years.

The computation of the beneficiary's tax in the event of an accumulation distribution, and the offset to which she becomes entitled, must be made under the intricate rules of I.R.C. §§ 666–667. They contain a so-called throwback rule which, loosely speaking, throws back an accumulation distribution (for tax purposes) to prior years and taxes it somewhat as if made when the income was accumulated by the trust.

The Throwback Rule. The throwback rule, involved in the example given above, addresses itself to the problem of delayed distributions. It does so by the following technique. If, in a given year, the trust distributes more than its current D.N.I., the law wants to inquire whether this excess comes from income received by the trust in prior years and accumulated, not distributed, or whether it comes from some other source. For if income has been accumulated earlier and taxed to the trust, upon later distribution it should be taxed to the beneficiaries and at their rates. If it is taxed to the trust and only to the trust, an unacceptable shifting of tax burden will have occurred. So, when current distributions exceed current D.N.I., the excess is thrown back to the earliest preceding year in which income was accumulated and treated as if distributed then for purposes of taxability up to D.N.I. This process is repeated for the year after that and the year after that and so on until all of the distribution is covered by D.N.I. (and hence taxable to beneficiaries) or until no more D.N.I. can be found. The mechanics of this process can become quite complicated and will not be described in full detail here. The purpose and effect is simple—to test any distribution against current D.N.I. and, if that is not enough, against historical or left-over D.N.I. from prior years. The reason is simply to detect the income component of any distribution and to treat it as income, not as a tax-free gift or bequest of property.

Although the throwback rule in some ways taxes the beneficiaries as if the trust had distributed the income earlier, no interest is charged on the "deferred tax."

To compute the tax for a year of an accumulation distribution, the beneficiary looks back at her taxable income for the five years immediately preceding the year of the distribution, disregarding the years of the highest and lowest taxable income. She then divides the amount distributed ("grossed up" by the tax paid by the trust with respect to that distribution) by the number of years of accumulation and adds this amount to the taxable amount of the remaining three years. Finally, the beneficiary computes the average increase in tax for those three years, the tax that the additional amounts would have generated to her, and multiplies this average by the number of years of accumulation. *See* example in Regs. § 1.666(c)–2A. The amount of tax on the distribution is the excess of this amount over the taxes paid by the trust on this income. *See* § 667(b). No refund of any excess tax paid by the trust is authorized. I.R.C. § 666(e).

Under the throwback rule, the beneficiaries do not—in form—get a credit against their taxes for the taxes paid by the trust; instead, the beneficiaries are entitled to subtract, or offset, these taxes only in determining the partial tax imposed by § 667(a)(2). *See* § 667(b). As a result, a beneficiary cannot offset the excess tax previously paid by the trust against his or her tax liability from other income.

In the case of an accumulation distribution, sums accumulated before a beneficiary is born or before the beneficiary reaches age 21 are excluded. *See* § 665(b). However, a beneficiary may take advantage of this rule only with regard to the accumulation distribution of no more than two trusts. There is a monetary limit on the application of the throwback rule; under the statute, the throwback rule does not apply to accumulation distributions of less than $1,000 per year. *See* § 667(c).

The tier system. Now come greater complications. They have to do not with accumulation distributions, but with distributions from corpus, not income. Assume that two beneficiaries, B and C, are back in the picture. Also assume T has a power to invade corpus, but only for B's benefit. T is required to distribute all income currently to B or C or both in such proportions as T determines. In the first year, when the trust has $10,000 income, T pays $5,000 to C and $10,000 to B. How will B and C be taxed? (The trust will have no tax to pay since its special deduction of $10,000 fully will offset its income.) Under the intricate tier system, C will be taxed on $5,000 income and B will be taxed on $5,000 income and B will receive $5,000 tax-free (as corpus).

The tier system is a way of establishing priorities or constructive rules about whether a trust beneficiary receives income or corpus. The first tier consists of payments of amounts which the trust is required to distribute currently. All such amounts, up to the amount of D.N.I., are taxable as income to those beneficiaries who are entitled to receive them and do receive them. If these first tier payments do not exhaust D.N.I., the excess D.N.I. will make second tier distributions (namely, all other distributions) partially or fully taxable. In any event, the current taxable income of the trust as D.N.I. must be taxed to beneficiaries up to the amounts distributed that year. A distribution is thus conclusively presumed to come out of current trust income, if there is any, no matter where the trustee actually got it or paid it from.

In the foregoing example, C is a first-tier beneficiary only. *See* I.R.C. § 662(a)(1). He is entitled to
receive income but not corpus. B is both a first tier
beneficiary [and as such she received $5,000 in-
come, *see* I.R.C. § 662(a)(1)] and a second tier beneficiary [as such she received $5,000 of other
amounts, namely corpus, *see* I.R.C. § 662(a)(2)].

If in year 2, T had paid $5,000 to C and $10,000
to B, not by invading corpus but because T accumulated $5,000 income in a prior year, the tax result
would be different. Both B and C would be second
tier beneficiaries in this example, since both evidently are entitled to receive accumulated income
saved up in prior years. Accordingly, since two-
thirds of the total amount distributed was current
income, C will have $3,333.34 income plus $1,666.66
accumulated income; B will have $6,666.67 income
and $3,333.33 accumulated income. Each will be
entitled to a pro-rata portion of offset for the tax
paid earlier by the trust ($1,000) when it received
and accumulated the income.

If the trust for B and C were set up as two
separate trusts or as one trust with two separate
shares, the so-called separate share rule of I.R.C.
§ 663(c) would avoid spreading the total D.N.I. over
the two beneficiaries under the two-tier system.
Also, if a so-called "non-periodic distribution" is
made by a trust or estate, it will be exempted from
the tier system and treated as a direct gift or
bequest of property under I.R.C. § 663(a)(1).

In conclusion, the complex trust rules have been shaped by their purposes, which are to block attempts by high-income-tax-bracket taxpayers to shift their tax burden to low-tax-bracket trusts and to prevent such taxpayers and trusts from shifting the tax burden from high-tax-rate years to lower-rate years by delaying distributions of income or invading corpus rather than by distributing income. At the same time, the complex trust rules have sought to preserve the distinction between capital (property) and taxable income along the lines of the gift exclusion in I.R.C. § 102. Likewise, the complex trust rules have sought to avoid imposing a "double tax" on trust income—once to the trust and again to the beneficiary—and thus to preserve the "conduit" conception of a trust. To accomplish these ends, doctrines such as the throwback rule, which stands in the way of a trust distributing income every other year and thus splitting the taxation of trust income between the trust and beneficiary, had to be used. Such doctrines then were elevated to statutory stature in the faint hope that if nearly every fact situation were anticipated and provided for, the rules could execute themselves and minimize administrative and courtroom disputes or uncertainty. Perhaps this very elaborateness and intricacy of rules accounts for the fact that taxpayers' lawyers and I.R.S. agents alike are often said to disregard much of the statutory law and to settle on taxation of complex trusts on a rough-hewn logical and sensible basis not necessarily identical to that compelled by the statute.

§ 91. Family Partnerships, Other Business Arrangements, and Income Splitting

Another area of taxpayer behavior that involves income shifting and problems of income attribution, and which has been subjected to specific legislative rules, is the formation and operation of family partnerships. The family partnership affords a tax-shifting and tax-saving opportunity because high-bracket family members (such as parents) can take into partnership their lower-bracket relatives (children, for example) and attempt to have at least part of the income from the partnership taxed to the low-bracket children, rather than the higher-bracket parents. In other words, the high-bracket parents may be attempting to shift pre-tax income, from the personal services or the capital (or both) involved in the family partnership, from themselves to their children, or to other relatives, or even to unrelated friends.

In general, if two parents are actively rendering services in a business, perhaps a partnership between the two of them, and if capital owned by the parents is also devoted to the production of income in the business, all the income from the business will be taxed to the partners, whether or not distributed, when earned. This is the general rule of partnership taxation; partnerships, unlike corporations, are not treated as separate taxable entities. Nonetheless, the partnership may employ persons, even the partners themselves, and pay salaries to them with a deduction from partnership gross income for the salary expenses. Such salaries are then taxable to the employees, of course. If the two equal partners are also equal employees, all the net profits of the business will be taxable to them, either in their capacity as partners or as employees. If they undercompensate themselves as employees, partnership income will grow and be taxable to them as partners and vice versa.

If the parents, whose income is taxed in relatively high brackets, take their two children into partnership with them, so that each of the four partners is a 25% partner, and entitled to that much of the income and the capital of the partnership, some income attributable to the partnership capital, and to the efforts of the adults who are active in the business, if their salaries do not fully compensate them for their services, would be shifted to the children. Such a result would seem to be consistent with the cases on gifts of property, to the extent the partnership income resulted from capital owned by the parents and given to the children, by taking them into partnership. The result would be inconsistent with the cases that prevent the shifting of personal service income from the tax return of the person who performs the services to his or her donee.

In § 704(e) of the I.R.C., Congress has enacted some specific rules that are designed to prevent the shifting of income in the family partnership in ways that would not be permitted outside the partnership context. Section 704(e)(1) provides that a person shall be recognized as a partner if he owns a capital interest in the partnership in which capital is a material income-producing factor, whether or not such interest was derived by purchase or gift from any other person. In other words, even if the children's capital interest in the partnership comes to them by gift from their parents, they can be partners by virtue of owning such capital interest.

This leaves the question of how the income of the partnership resulting from the personal efforts of the parents should be taxable, and that question is answered by § 704(e)(2). That section states that in the case of a partnership interest created by gift, the distributive share of the donee under the partnership agreement shall be taxable to the donee as part of his or her gross income, except to the extent that such share is determined without allowance of reasonable compensation for services rendered to the partnership by the donor, and except to the extent that the portion of such share attributable to donated capital is proportionately greater than the share of the donor attributable to the donor's capital. Therefore, so long as the partnership adequately compensates the parents for their services rendered to the partnership, the remaining profits of the partnership can be divided among the four partners, and the children's shares will be includable in their gross incomes, even though the capital that produced that income was obtained by them in the form of gifts from their parents. The portion of the partnership income that the children receive as attributable to donated capital must meet the second condition of the statute in that it must not be proportionately greater than the share of the donor that is attributable to the donor's capital.

As the end result, the parents cannot refrain from compensating themselves adequately for their services and attempt to have the benefits of those services taxable to the children. But they can shift the income from the portion of their capital interests in the partnership that they choose to give to the children, much as donors can shift the income on any property by making a gift of that property to donees. However, the income splitting available under § 704(e) may prove of less advantage due to the kiddie tax rate rule of § 1(g), as well as lower, flatter tax rates.

In general, in a pure service partnership, no shifting of income will be permitted, inasmuch as it would amount to an attempted assignment of earned income through the vehicle of a partnership. In contrast, when capital serves as a material income-producing factor, and a bona-fide partnership has been formed [*see* Comm. v. Culbertson (S.Ct. 1949)] income may be split, even among family members. *See* I.R.C. § 704(e). Such splitting remains possible even if the capital interest of some partners was obtained by gift from another partner, but reasonable allowance for services must be made so that service income is not shifted in the guise of capital income.

By way of comparison, it is worth noting that shifting of income of the kind that § 704(e) prevents in the partnership context can often be achieved by use of a (family) corporation, though not so readily in an "S Corporation," due to § 1366(e), a stricter counterpart of § 704(e) and § 482. *See* below. That is to say, the parents could incorporate their business and give stock to their children, remain employed by the business, and cause the corporation to under-compensate them for their services as employees and managers, with the result that the income from such under-compensation would be shared by the children as well as the parents, in the form of dividends or an increase in the net worth of the corporation.

While this result seems anomalous, when viewed against the background of the partnership rules, some explanation may be found in the different tax regime applicable to corporations in the United States. Corporate income is taxed first when realized by the corporation, and then again to the shareholders when distributed to them as a dividend (reduced by the corporate tax paid earlier). This is the so-called "classical system"; there is no integration of the two taxes although dividends are taxed at a preferential 15% tax rate to individual shareholders. *See* I.R.C. § 1(h)(11). Also, the corporate tax rates are set at somewhat different levels and are graduated somewhat differently. In addition, the corporate earnings are taxed to the shareholders only when actually distributed, not earlier (when earned) as in the case of a partnership. Thus, incorporation may produce a higher tax burden, if profits are distributed currently and thus invoke the shareholder tax on dividends as well as the corporate tax on corporate income; or a lower tax burden, if corporate earnings are to be taxed only to the corporation (possibly at lower, or higher, rates) and not to be distributed for a long time, or to be converted into some lower taxed form of income, such as long-term capital gain; or indefinitely to escape tax for still longer through corporate reorganizations and other tax-free transactions; or permanently to escape tax by virtue of the fresh-start-basis rule for bequests.

Section 704(e) does not apply to the family corporation, and there is no analogous statutory rule that applies in the regular corporate context. Parents can make their children shareholders, by gift or otherwise, and can provide valuable services to the corporation while taking less than fair market value compensation for those services, and thus, at least in part, shift the pre-tax value of the services not fully compensated to the children. But *see* § 1(g). On audit, the I.R.S. might insist that some dividends paid to the parents be recast as wages, subject to FICA tax, etc., and might argue for reallocation of income from children to parents on non-statutory grounds. [Income shifting potential also can be exploited by using a "Subchapter–S corporation," a corporate form taxable generally as a partnership, but to which § 704(e) does not apply. *But see* § 1366(e), described below, and § 1(g).] This may or may not be in accord with Congressional purpose, as expressed by the different rates applicable to corporations, and the Code's separate-entity treatment of corporations. Evidently it is not a problem of such prominence, or dissonance with corporate tax policy, as to invite Congressional attention, at least as of now.

Still another income-shifting device often used in a family setting is a sale and leaseback arrangement or a gift and leaseback. To illustrate, a mother who is a dentist and who owns the building in which her dental offices (and perhaps a few other tenants) are located might convey that building to a trust (or guardianship). Suppose the conveyance is to a trustee for the benefit of her two children, and the trustee immediately leases the building back to the dentist. She now seeks to convert her own rent payment (presumably derived from her fees for dental services) and those of other tenants into income taxable to the children. If the transaction were a sale and leaseback, the trust might use its income in part to pay off a loan incurred to finance its purchase of the building from the dentist. The Internal Revenue Service has taken the position that the rental paid by the dentist may not be deducted, in some of these situations, because the transaction lacks business purpose and consists merely of a device to assign income to a lower-bracket taxpayer. The Service has met with some courtroom success and some failure, with many variations on the basic fact situation. *See, e.g.,* Wiles v. Comm. (5th Cir.1974); Mathews v. Comm. (5th Cir.1975); Van Zandt v. Comm. (5th Cir.1965); Skemp v. Comm. (7th Cir.1948); Alden Oakes (Tax Court 1965) non acq.; Audano v. U.S. (5th Cir. 1970); Perry v. U.S. (4th Cir.1975). *See also* I.R.C.

§ 1(g), the kiddie tax, which will discourage some of the sale/leaseback ideas.

A trust may be a shareholder in a Subchapter–S corporation. Not only may a grantor trust be a qualified shareholder of a Subchapter–S corporation, but also qualified are § 678 trusts and a new type of trust, the "qualified Subchapter–S trust," in which a beneficiary elects to be treated as the owner of Sub–S stock held by the trust. In more recent years, other trusts and persons have been permitted to be "S Corporation" shareholders. *See* I.R.C. § 1361(a)–(d).

Under I.R.C. § 1366(e), if any individual who is a member of the family [within the meaning of § 704(e)(3)] of one or more shareholders of a Subchapter–S corporation renders services for, or furnishes capital to, the corporation without receiving reasonable compensation therefor, the I.R.S. can make such adjustments "in the items taken into account" by such individual and such shareholders as may be necessary in order to reflect the value of such services or capital.

CHAPTER IX

HOW IS INCOME TAXABLE?

DISPOSITIONS OF PROPERTY; CAPITAL
GAINS AND LOSSES; TAX–PREFERENCE
INCOME; SPECIAL TAX RATES
AND THEIR INTERACTIONS

§ 92. Introduction

Asking *how* income is taxable is largely another
way of asking at *what rate* it is taxable. Tax rates
are applied to a tax base to compute actual tax
liability. How an expense or loss is deducted presents yet another rate question, since a deduction
from income taxed at a high rate reduces the actual
tax paid more than does a deduction from income
taxed at a lower rate. Likewise, a deduction of part
of an expenditure or loss reduces tax less than a
deduction allowed in full. Among others, §§ 1–5 and
11 of the Internal Revenue Code specify rates of tax
to be applied to taxable income. Surprisingly perhaps, these rate schedules are not the only provisions that determine the rate of tax payable. Personal and dependency exemptions, as in I.R.C.
§ 151, affect the amount of tax paid on a given level
of income. And phaseouts, cutbacks, and limitations
on deductions for higher income taxpayers, like
those in §§ 67 and 68, affect the marginal rate at

427

which income is taxed. In some sense, all deductions and exclusions and credits (and other allowances) affect tax payable as a function of *gross* income, but these are rather remote "How is it taxable" questions.

A few very concrete tax rate specifications have been made elsewhere in the Code. One is the alternative minimum tax, which came into the Code in 1969 as a minimum tax on tax preference income. *See* I.R.C. §§ 53–59. Another is the special tax rate generally applicable to dividends from domestic corporations. *See* I.R.C. § 1(h). These sections will be discussed later in this chapter, §§ 106, 108, *infra.* Some special rates interact, by their terms or in practical tax planning. An exceedingly important rate rule is the special rate applicable to capital gains. This "How is it taxable" question will be taken up first and will occupy most of this Chapter IX.

Throughout most of the history of income taxation in the U.S., a distinction has been drawn between the rate of taxation on "ordinary income" (or ordinary loss) and "capital gain" (or capital loss). "Capital gain" refers to the income from certain transactions in some assets, called capital assets, or from other transactions that Congress has said should be taxed as capital gain. Similarly, capital losses are losses sustained on capital assets or other losses that Congress has decided to treat as if they were capital losses. The most common form of capital gain or loss transaction is a sale for cash of an asset, such as a share of stock or a parcel of land.

Historically, preferential rate treatment was afforded to capital gain. For example, before the 1986 T.R.A., a deduction equal to 60% of the amount of the long-term capital gains was allowed. This deduction, by reducing the amount of gain that had to be included in income by 60%, reduced the rate of tax on the entire gain to 40% of the rate otherwise to be borne.

Although Congress repealed the preferential treatment for long-term gain in the 1986 Act, it retained most of the pre-existing provisions for capital gains and losses. In 1990, these provisions became relevant again when Congress increased the maximum rate for ordinary income to 31% but capped the rate for capital gains at 28%. As of 2004, the maximum rate for most capital gains is 15 percent, while ordinary income can be taxed at a rate as high as 35%. *See* I.R.C. § 1(a) & (h). The taxation of capital gains has also become much more complex. *See* the detailed discussion *infra* in § 95. Thus, because the Code still differentiates between capital gain and ordinary income, a particular taxpayer's gain must be characterized as either capital gain or ordinary income. Both the taxpayer and the I.R.S. will care if the taxpayer is eligible for a lower rate of tax on capital gain. This characterization also is relevant because otherwise-deductible capital losses (of taxpayers other than corporations) continue to be allowed to individual taxpayers only to the extent of capital gain plus $3,000 (of ordinary income) each year. *See* I.R.C. § 1211(b). Because of this limitation, taxpayers usually will prefer characterization of their losses as ordinary losses rather than as capital losses, unless they have ample capital gains against which to offset their losses.

Also, § 1202 excludes from gross income 50% of the gain from qualified small-business stock held more than five years. A small business is defined, in general, as a corporation with aggregate gross assets not exceeding $50,000,000. *See* § 1202(d). This exclusion from income produces the equivalent of a rate reduction for this particular form of capital gain. [In addition, § 1045 allows an individual taxpayer who sells qualified small-business stock held for more than six months to avoid recognizing gain from the sale to the extent that he uses the proceeds to purchase other qualified small-business stock within 60 days of the sale. I.R.C. § 1045(a).] The § 1202 exclusion remains available when the taxpayer sells the replacement property.

Consequently, attention must be given to sales and exchanges of property in general and to the capital gain and loss questions they may present. Later, other capital transactions and events treated like capital transactions will be discussed.

§ 93. Sales of Property

When a taxpayer sells or exchanges property in a given year for more than he or she paid for the property plus what he or she has "put into it" by additions or improvements, the receipt of the purchase price produces a *realization* of gain. I.R.C. § 1001(c) goes on to say that gain or loss on the "sale or exchange" of property, determined under

I.R.C. § 1001, shall be *recognized* except as otherwise provided (by the nonrecognition sections such as §§ 1031–1038, etc.). (As to nonrecognition, *see* § 76, *supra.*) Section 1001(a) defines gain from the "sale or other disposition" of property as the excess of the amount realized therefrom over the adjusted basis provided in § 1011 for determining gain; and defines loss as the excess of adjusted basis over the amount realized. "Amount realized" is defined in § 1001(b) as a sum of any money received plus the fair market value of the property (other than money) received. "Adjusted basis" is determined under § 1011, which explicitly refers to §§ 1012 and 1016.

Section 1012 decrees that the "basis" of property shall be its cost, except as otherwise provided. Some of the other provisions include § 1015, which sets the basis of gifts (where basis for determining gain on subsequent sale by the donee is the donor's basis, and the basis for determining loss is the fair market value of the property at the time of the gift if such value falls short of the donor's basis), and § 1014 as to bequests of decedents (where basis is fair market value at death, "fresh-start basis"). The basis determined under these rules often is also adjusted for gift or estate tax paid on the transfer. In the case of a decedent dying after December 31, 2009, § 1022 provides that property acquired from the decedent will take a modified-carryover basis with an allowance for certain basis increases.

"Cost" usually means the price paid by taxpayer when he purchased the property, and it includes liabilities of the seller that the taxpayer assumed.

Basis in property held subject to a mortgage that does not exceed fair market value, even if without personal liability, includes the entire property (not merely the net equity), for purposes of depreciation or computing gain or loss on sale or other disposition. *See* Crane v. Comm. (S.Ct.1947); Parker v. Delaney (1st Cir.1950). So, basis is cost, no matter how financed. It also can mean "tax cost," the amount taxed to the purchaser as income when he received the property, for example if he received it as pay for services or in a taxable exchange.

Section 1016, in turn, sets the guidelines for adjusting basis from the starting point of historic cost. For example, adjustments are made (upward) for capital expenditures on the property and (downward) for depreciation or A.C.R.S. and amortization deductions allowable. Other special basis adjustments are provided for particular events.

Although a taxpayer generally is allowed full basis for the cost of property even if it was purchased with borrowed funds or on credit, and deductible loss will generally be allowed up to (but not in excess of) basis, losses from some investments or activities will be allowed only to the extent of the assets taxpayer has "at risk." *See* I.R.C. § 465. Amounts "at risk" include amounts of cash and the adjusted basis of other property actually contributed by the taxpayer and amounts borrowed for which he or she will personally be liable. The term "at risk" does not cover funds borrowed on "nonrecourse" liability, that for which the taxpayer does not have personal liability and for which he has not pledged other property as security.

The allowance of otherwise deductible losses will also be limited by I.R.C. § 469, which limits the deductibility of a loss incurred in passive activities to the extent of gain from such activities—not from active or portfolio income.

Sometimes a question arises whether a "sale or other disposition" has taken place. By way of illustration, a lease is not a sale or other disposition (unless it really amounted to a sale in disguise), and placing a mortgage on property does not dispose of it even if the amount of the loan exceeded the owner's basis and he was not personally liable to repay the loan (in which event the lender could look only to the property for repayment). Collection of the amount due on a promissory note has been held not to be a sale of the note, although in principle it is possible to sell a note. But *see* § 1271 (amounts received on retirement of any debt instrument considered as received in exchange therefor). Settlement of a judgment (by accepting payment) is not, in principle, a "sale"; it is not a "transfer of property" by which "one person acquires a property in the thing sold and the other parts with it for a valuable consideration." *See* Galvin Hudson (Tax Court 1953). According to the Supreme Court, an exchange of property is a "disposition of property" only if the exchanged properties are "materially different" each from the other. *See* Cottage Savings Association v. Comm. (S.Ct.1991).

Sale and leaseback transactions have sparked controversy with somewhat mixed results. In one leading case, taxpayers sold property at a loss, for cash, and leased it back for 30 years and three days. The court allowed deduction of a realized loss on the transfer and concluded that more than a change merely in form of ownership had occurred; also, the court held, it was a sale, not an exchange for like-kind property, but for a lesser interest. *See* Jordan Marsh Co. v. Comm. (2d Cir.1959). Had the lease extended 99 years the result might well have differed. The I.R.S. does not follow *Jordan Marsh. See* Rev.Rul. 60–43, 1960–1 C.B. 687. *See also* Frank Lyon Co. v. U. S. (S.Ct.1978) (held: sale and lease-back, not mere loan by lessor to lessee). Unlike these possibly borderline cases, most transactions do not raise doubt about their finality or character for tax purposes.

The statutory rules for determining gain or loss on sale or other disposition of property may be seen in application to a simple fact situation. If taxpayer A buys Blackacre for $100,000 in Year 1 and sells it for $150,000 in Year 5, his income will be the amount realized ($150,000) less the basis ($100,-000—cost) or $50,000. If A bought Blackacre for $100,000 in Year 1 and built a house on it in Year 2 at a cost of $220,000, his adjusted basis would be $320,000. If he sold both for $390,000 in Year 5 the sale would give A recognizable income of $70,000. If the house had been rental property and taxpayer A had been allowed $34,000 depreciation (or A.C.R.S.) deductions from Year 2 to the date of sale, A's basis would be cost ($100,000 + $220,000 = $320,000) minus the § 1016 adjustment for depreciation ($320,000–$34,000 = $286,000). On sale for $390,000, recognizable income would be $104,000.

The terms "basis" and "amount realized" deserve further elaboration. Basis is, of course, cost as stated in § 1012. To remove any doubt, cost means actual historic cost, not replacement cost. *See* Hinckley v. Comm. (8th Cir.1969). The cost of property may have to be allocated among its component parts, to determine gain or loss if part alone is sold, for depreciation or A.C.R.S. allowances and for other reasons. So, if A buys a factory building, land on which it stands, and machines and equipment in the building for a lump-sum price, it will become necessary to determine how much of the total price A paid separately for the land, building and machinery. If an arm's-length contract with the seller to A breaks down the aggregate price, that ascription very likely will be used. *See* I.R.C. § 1060(a). If not, or if none is made, the total price will be attributed to the parts, probably by using the "residual" method whereby each asset is assigned a basis equal to its fair market value and any extra amount paid (the residual) is deemed an amount paid for goodwill or going concern value of the business. *See generally,* Regs. §§ 1.1060–1, 1.338–6. Allocating cost among parts of a cohesive or unified property may be required, as in Rev.Rul. 68–291, 1968–1 C.B. 351 (involving payments for an easement), or may prove impossible, as in Inaja Land Co., Ltd. v. Comm. (Tax Court 1947) (Acq.), in which case payments for an easement were treated as return of capital until total basis was reduced to zero, and only after that would be treated as income.

If purchaser pays cash and takes out or assumes a mortgage when buying Blackacre, the principal amount of the mortgage will be treated as part of cost, as will other capital expenditures to make the purchase. But *see* I.R.C. § 465 (limiting loss deductions to amount "at risk" in most activities). If the taxpayer acquires the property in a non-taxable transaction such as a tax-free exchange of properties, he will take a "substituted basis" in the property he acquires, a basis equal to his basis in the property he surrendered, rather than a basis stepped up by the taxability of a transaction on which gain is recognized. If some gain is recognized on an otherwise tax-free transaction, the substituted basis will be stepped up by the amount of the gain recognized and on which tax then is paid. The Regulations §§ 1.1012–1 & 1.1012–2 give further information. If the taxpayer acquired the property by gift he or she might have a carryover basis, the same basis carried over from the donor, or fair market value if lower and if the taxpayer hopes to deduct a loss. *See* I.R.C. § 1015. If taxpayer acquired the property by bequest, he or she will generally have a basis equal to the fair-market value of the property at the date of the decedent's death. *See* I.R.C. § 1014. Property acquired from a decedent dying after December 31, 2009, will take a modified-carryover basis with an allowance for certain basis increases. Adjustments to basis are described in § 1016 and its accompanying Regulations. *See* Regs. §§ 1.1016–1, 1.1016–2, 1.1016–3(a)(1), 1.1016–5, 1.1016–6 & 1.1016–10.

"Amount realized" includes the full price received for property, whether the price be paid in money or in property other than money. The amount realized by a seller of property includes the assumption of a mortgage or a mortgage subject to which the property is taken by the buyer, and it can include the satisfaction of a claim or the discharge of an obligation. Cf. Crane v. Comm. (S.Ct.1947); U.S. v. Davis (S.Ct.1962); Comm. v. Tufts (S.Ct. 1983). The fair market value of property is a question of fact. In rare and exceptional cases, but only then, property may be considered to have no ascertainable fair market value, and the transaction then is held "open" until the value can be established. *See* Reg. § 1.1001–1; Burnet v. Logan (S.Ct.1931); Comm. v. Kann's Estate (3rd Cir.1949). *And see* § 75, *supra*. Some expenses incurred in selling property are subtracted in determining the amount realized, Regs. § 1.263(a)–2(e), and some carrying charges that have not been deducted, and other costs such as those for research and development, are added to basis. *See* Regs. § 1.1016–2, § 1.1016–5(j). When property is transferred to satisfy a claim against the transferor, the amount of the claim that is satisfied will be the "amount realized." If the amount or value of that claim is uncertain, the value of the property that was accepted in satisfaction in an arm's-length trade can serve to place a value on the claim to determine the "amount realized." *See, e.g.*, U.S. v. Davis (S.Ct.1962). The apparent "amount realized" may be reduced if some of the cash payments, for example, must be treated as imputed interest. *See* I.R.C. § 483.

Realization of income and an "amount realized" can occur when the taxpayer "sheds a liability." For example, if he or she is personally liable for a debt, relief from that obligation constitutes income. It is much as if an employer paid an employee's monthly home mortgage payment to the bank instead of giving money to the employee to make the payment. *See*, e.g., Old Colony Trust Co. v. Comm. (S.Ct. 1929) (taxing as income an employer's payment of an employee's income taxes); and *see* U.S. v. Kirby Lumber Co., § 18, *supra*. Such discharge-of-indebtedness income resembles, but should be differentiated from, the income that can arise from shedding a liability in connection with a transfer of property subject to that liability, since I.R.C. § 108 will apply only to the former. *See* Spartan Petroleum Co. v. U.S. (D.C.S.C.1977).

If the taxpayer is not personally liable, but owns property securing a nonrecourse debt, a transfer of the property subject to the debt, or with the debt assumed, produces income to the former owner. *See*, *e.g.*, Crane v. Comm. (S.Ct.1947) (taxpayer disposed of property mortgaged to secure a loan on which the taxpayer was not personally liable). To see the appropriateness of this approach, imagine a taxpayer who paid $10,000 for "Sea-acres," then watched its fair market value climb to $100,000, borrowed $80,000 without recourse but by mortgaging Sea-acres as security, and finally walked away from the property. Surely in this case taxpayer would be deemed to have income of $70,000 (amount realized less basis). Similarly, if taxpayer conveyed Sea-acres to her child or to a charity, either of which took this land subject to the debt, with no remaining liability to taxpayer, income would be realized. A similar result has been reached when a taxpayer borrowed money on his appreciated property, without personal liability, in order to pay the gift taxes that were imposed when he then conveyed the property to a trust that took it subject to the liability and took over that liability, leaving taxpayer free and clear. It was much as if he sold it to the trust, or to a third party, and used the proceeds to pay gift taxes (or for any other purpose). *See* Diedrich v. Comm. (S.Ct.1982); Johnson v. Comm. (6th Cir.1974). *But see* § 108(c), which excludes from income discharge of qualified real property business indebtedness, as defined in § 108(c)(3).

Even if the nonrecourse indebtedness exceeds the property's value, the "amount realized" includes the full amount of the debt assumed by the buyer or "shed" by the seller. *See* Comm. v. Tufts (S.Ct. 1983). *See also* Regs. § 1.1001–2(b), which states that the fair market value of property securing a nonrecourse liability is irrelevant to a determination of amount realized on its disposition.

Although I.R.C. §§ 1001(a) and 1011(a) require a "sale or other disposition" and § 1001(c) refers to a "sale or exchange," the Regulations say that even if property is not sold or otherwise disposed of, gain is realized if the sum of all amounts received that are required by § 1016 and other sections to be applied against the basis exceeds such basis, because I.R.C. § 61 includes income "from whatever source derived." On the other hand, a loss is not ordinarily sustained prior to the sale or other disposition of the property, since until then the taxpayer may still recover or recoup his adjusted basis. *See* Regs. § 1.1001–1(c).

When a taxpayer, perhaps just once in his lifetime, sells a piece of property such as his house or some shares of stock, and if the purchase price exceeds what the taxpayer-seller paid for the property, he seems to have realized gain and thus "income." Not all tax systems or taxpayers would instantly agree, however. Some would say that the sales price was a capital payment to the seller, or a mere change in form of the investment asset from land or stock into cash. They would go on to add that the sales price is not part of that regular flow of receipts akin to salary or interest or dividends on which a person can live, and which he can treat as part of his profit, separate from his investment, savings, or capital. Moreover, they might say that any apparent gain is likely due to inflation or accidents of the market; to reinvest an amount necessary to throw off income at the same rate, an amount equal to the full sales price of the property sold will have to be paid. So, the argument goes, "capital gain" is not income at all and, even if it is, it should not be taxed when lumped in one year under a graduated rate schedule designed to tax an annual flow of income or profits. Some tax systems have accepted these arguments and have excluded capital gains entirely from income tax. Others have taxed them just like any other income item. A third technique, historically adopted in the U.S. Income Tax, is to tax capital gains as income, but as a special kind of income and at special rates.

The U.S. income tax generally has applied a preferential rate to certain capital gains income. The original purpose of this preferential rate was to encourage taxpayers freely to sell their investments, by removing the lock-in effect of a high ordinary income tax bill, and thus more efficiently to allocate resources throughout the economy. Other possible justifications included encouraging private saving and investment, relieving the burden of progressive rates on bunched income (a kind of averaging), adjusting for illusory income from inflation, compensating for a perceived double tax on, or other discrimination against, savings (versus consumption), and compromising the polar views that capital gains are, or are not, income. Much of the impetus for special rates of tax on capital gains stems from the realization rule, which makes gain taxable not when it accrues in the form of unrealized appreciation, but when the property is sold or disposed of, and the progressive rate schedule for ordinary income, which affects the tax on "bunched income."

Any possible purity of reasoning or technique concerning capital gains has been lost in the welter of rules and special provisions Congress loaded onto the basic capital gains statutes. Moreover, the preferential rate of tax on capital gains brought about a huge volume of litigation and administration and a correspondingly large quantity of doctrine.

Gains and losses from the sale, exchange, or other disposition of property are computed in nominal monetary values—that is, in dollars and cents—regardless of the actual buying power or "real" value of the property or of the dollars and cents. Basis is historic cost, in dollars, regardless of inflation. Basis is not indexed to reflect the current (at time of sale) value of the dollars invested earlier. No indexation of basis, in other words, is provided for—or allowed.

As a separate point from the indexation of *basis*, no indexation in *rates* applicable to the gain or loss was provided for or allowed, until general rate indexing was enacted and first scheduled to take effect in 1985. Now, an automatic "cost of living" adjustment is made annually in the rate schedule to tax more of the gain, measured in dollars, at a lower rate because the value of the dollar has shrunk due to inflation and the gain has been inflated in such a way as to rise higher into the graduated rate brackets than gain of equal real value rose in prior years, or vice versa.

Traditional failure to index was thought by some to provide a justification for taxing long-term capital gain at a preferential rate. Since some of the nominal gain is inflationary and due to general price level increases, rather than real, it should go untaxed. Consistent with that argument, at one time the capital gains preference excluded a portion of the gain from income. Now a lower set of rates on all the (long-term) capital gain is the mechanism. *See* I.R.C. § 1(h). But this adjustment will work only roughly, and only in times of inflation (rather than deflation) and probably only by coincidence would it produce an effect equal to that of indexing.

To index the Code fully for inflation, both adjustments would have to be installed—indexation of basis and indexation of rates on gain. The failure to do so may in part be offset by another, counteracting, failure of the Code, namely to charge or to tax imputed interest on gain that has accrued earlier but goes untaxed until the time of realization and recognition. The deferral of tax has worked to the taxpayer's advantage and may be reflected in the values gained on sale, but the gain is taxed only then and (possibly) at a preferential rate; ordinary income has been converted to capital gains.

Basis is not indexed, and interest is not imputed on gain accrued prior to disposition. Thus, with respect to capital gains, the addition of indexing of rates may generate some benefit for the taxpayer or, at least, some better correspondence to economic reality.

§ 94. Capital Gains and Losses—Introduction

For most of the history of the Federal Income Tax, gains from the sale or exchange of property have been taxable at lower than ordinary income rates if they were long-term capital gains. Deductible losses from such transactions also have been given special (generally unfavorable) treatment. The form of the preference for long-term capital gains (*e.g.*, an exclusion of part of the gain or application of a lower rate) has varied over time. Beginning in 2003, a maximum rate of 15 percent applied to most long-term capital gains, and even lower rates sometimes apply. (Details are discussed in § 95, *infra.*) This ceiling uses the pre-existing Code rules and definitions to implement the differential in rate. Also, the distinction between capital gain/loss and ordinary gain/loss matters for some purposes even when the tax *rate* on both kinds of gain remains the same.

Not all gains and losses from transactions in property are capital gains or losses. To establish favorable capital gain treatment, the facts must show that the gain was derived from: (a) a *capital* asset (*see* I.R.C. § 1221) or its equivalent (*e.g.*, I.R.C. § 1231), (b) that was *sold or exchanged* (*see* I.R.C. § 1222) or the equivalent (*see* I.R.C. § 166(d)(1)(B)), (c) after being *held* by the taxpayer for more than one year, or any other requisite holding period (*see* I.R.C. §§ 1222 and 1223), or should be treated as having been held by him for such time (by substituting or tacking on the holding period of someone or something else, *see* I.R.C. § 1223), and (d) that the gain is not disqualified from capital gain treatment by *common-law* (judicial, non-statutory) tests. If gain was *realized* and if no *nonrecognition* section applies, the gain will be categorized as capital gain if it meets these tests. Also, some other items of gain that do not meet these tests will be taxed as capital gains simply because Congress says in so many words that they should be taxed that way.

As to losses, if they are *realized,* and if they are *deductible,* and if they are to be *recognized,* they will be deductible as capital losses (*see* I.R.C. §§ 1211–1212) *if* they meet the foregoing tests. Also, some other losses that do not meet these tests will nonetheless be deductible as capital losses simply because Congress says so.

Under present law, I.R.C. § 64 defines "ordinary income" to include any gain from the sale or exchange of property that is neither a capital asset nor property described in § 1231(b), and commands to treat as such gain any gain from the sale of property that is treated or considered, under other provisions of the Code, as "ordinary income."

Section 65 defines "ordinary loss" to include any loss from the sale or exchange of property that is not a capital asset. Any loss from the sale or exchange of property which is treated or considered as "ordinary loss" likewise is to be treated as loss from the sale or exchange of property that is not a capital asset.

Thus, capital gains and losses (and other items to be treated as if they were capital gains or losses) are separated into those called short-term and long-term gains or losses. The basic dividing line between short-term and long-term capital gains and losses is one year. *See* I.R.C. §§ 1222 and 1223. At different times, Congress has either shortened or lengthened the required holding period (e.g., it has been six and 18 months). By and large, net short-term capital gains are taxable as ordinary income; only long-term capital gains receive favorable treatment.

To determine the *net* capital gains and losses, deductible long-term capital losses must first be subtracted from long-term gains, and short-term losses must first be subtracted from short-term gains. Then net *short*-term losses or gains and net *long*-term losses or gains must be netted against each other to compute the tax correctly on the various forms of income. In this process, short-term capital gains—otherwise taxed at ordinary income rates—may be offset by short-term losses or (perhaps surprisingly) by net *long*-term losses, if any. *See* I.R.C. § 1222 for the definitions of short and long-term capital gains and other important terms.

§ 95. The Mechanics of Capital Gains Rates

To illustrate the process of separately taxing long-term capital gains and losses, suppose Taxpayer A in Year 1 received a salary of $40,000. He also realized long-term capital gain of $8,000 by selling stock he had owned for several years, and a long-term capital loss of $4,000 on other stock. On selling some land he had just bought three months before, he enjoyed short-term capital gain of $1,000, and he suffered a short-term capital loss of $500 on selling a bond. Assuming all his gains are includable in gross income and that all his losses are deductible, he should go about computing his tax as follows. By netting his long-term transactions (in stock), he sees that he has a *net* long-term capital gain of $4,000 ($8,000 minus $4,000). By netting his short-term transactions (in land and the bond), he determines that he has a *net* short-term capital gain of $500 ($1,000 minus $500). His net short-term capital gain of $500 must simply be added to his $40,000 salary in computing taxable income, since it is to be taxed at the same rates as his salary (ordinary income). His net long-term capital gain ($4,000) also must be included in gross income. But it is eligible to be taxed at a rate lower than the rate that would apply if that $4,000 were "ordinary income." The maximum rate that will apply will be 15% or less.

If a taxpayer has a net capital gain (*i.e.*, an excess of net long-term capital gain over net short-term capital loss–*see* I.R.C. § 1222(11)), special rates will be applied to the gain under § 1(h). The rate that applies depends upon the source of the gain. The most widely applicable rates currently are 28%, 25%, and 15%.

28 Percent Rate. The 28% rate applies to gains from the sale of "collectibles," which are defined in § 408(m) as including works of art, rugs and antiques, metals or gems, stamps, coins, alcoholic beverages, and other tangible personal property specified by the I.R.S. The 28% rate also applies to gain under § 1202. Section 1202 provides a 50% exclusion for gain from the sale or exchange of qualified small business stock held for more than five years.

25 Percent Rate. A special 25% rate applies to some capital gains on the sale of depreciable real estate (§ 1250 property). This rate is discussed in detail within the discussion of § 1250 in § 104, *infra.*

15 Percent Rate. A 15% rate generally applies to net capital gain that is not in either the 28% or 25% categories. Thus, long-term capital gains from sales of stock, investments, and other capital assets are generally taxed at a 15% rate.

Special capital gains rates may also apply to taxpayers with low amounts of taxable income. For example, if a taxpayer's other income is low enough to make it so the taxpayer's marginal tax rate is 10% or 15%, capital gain in higher rate categories (*e.g.*, 28% or 25%) may take advantage of any room left in the lower brackets. Also, a special 5% rate (0% after 2007) is available for the portion of any gain that falls into the 10% or 15% bracket because the taxpayer has low income, if the gain would have been a 15% gain if it had been recognized by a higher bracket (25% or greater) taxpayer.

§ 96. Mechanics of Capital Losses

Not all losses incurred on the sale or exchange of capital assets are allowed as deductions. Capital losses, like ordinary losses, can be deducted only if they meet the terms of I.R.C. § 165 as to *deductibility*. I.R.C. § 165(f) goes on to state that losses from the sale or exchange of capital assets shall be *allowed* only to the extent allowed in I.R.C. §§ 1211 and 1212.

Pursuant to those rules; deductible capital losses are deductible from capital gains in the netting process—long-term losses first subtracted from long-term gains and short-term losses subtracted first from short-term gains. If there are net short-term losses and net long-term gains, or vice versa, the net figures are again netted or offset against each other, so that net long-term losses reduce or eliminate net short-term gains and vice versa. If, after all capital gains have been erased, the end result is that net deductible capital losses remain unused, they (whether net short-term or long-term) may also be deducted from ordinary income by individual taxpayers but only to a limited extent— up to $3,000. I.R.C. § 1211(b)(1).

If taxpayer has both a net long-term loss and a net short-term loss, he must add up the two losses and deduct the sum from ordinary income, but only up to $3,000. *See* I.R.C. § 1211(b). Under § 1212(b), an individual taxpayer is obliged to use up the short-term loss first against the ordinary income up to $3,000 (rather than first using up the long-term loss), for purposes of ascertaining a capital-loss carryover to the following year. Some other "netting" of gains and losses, and limits on such netting, are entailed for special categories of § 1(h) assets, as the definitions in § 1(h) require.

"Rate" of Deduction of Capital Losses. The basic rule for deducting a short-term or long-term capital loss is that it must be used to offset capital gain in the same category ("short-term" or "long-term"), to arrive at amounts called net short-term capital gain (or loss) and net long-term capital gain (or loss). These two quantities must then be netted to arrive at "net capital gain" used in § 1(h) and related amounts.

Because special rates potentially apply to different components of net capital gain, some ordering rules are necessary to determine how losses in different categories are used to offset gains recognized in different categories. *See* § 95, *supra.* The rules are embedded in § 1(h). Those rules provide losses within a category (*e.g.*, 28%, 25% or 15%) are first used to reduce gains in the same category. Next any net loss in a category may then be used to reduce any gains left in other rate categories, starting with the highest rates first. To illustrate these rules, assume a taxpayer has a 28% collectibles gain of $5,000, a 28% collectibles loss of $3,000, and a 15% gain of $10,000. In that case, the $3,000 loss would be used to reduce the $5,000 gain leaving the taxpayer with a net $2,000 28% collectibles gain and a $10,000 15% gain. If the 28% collectibles loss had been $8,000, it would first offset the $5,000 28% collectibles gain and then the net $3,000 loss would reduce the $10,000 15% gain to $7,000. As a final example, if a taxpayer had a $5,000 28% collectibles gain, a $10,000 25% gain from real estate, and a $7,000 short-term capital loss, the short-term capital loss would first offset the 28% gain and then offset $2,000 of the 25% gain. A system favoring taxpayers!

§ 97.   Capital Loss Carryovers

Net deductible capital losses, whether short-term or long-term, that remain after offsetting capital gains and ordinary income within the limits of § 1211, may be carried forward to subsequent tax years and deducted then until they are eventually exhausted. *See* I.R.C. § 1212(b). When carried forward, each loss retains its original character as short-term or long-term capital loss, as the case may be, and is subject to the same rules of deductibility in the later years. Any long-term capital loss carryover is treated as being in the 28% category for purposes of netting gains and losses and calculating capital gains rates.

On the gain side, taxpayers like their income to qualify as long-term capital gain. If it cannot, they prefer short-term capital gain to ordinary income, since short-term or sometimes even long-term losses offset the short-term gain free of the limits that apply to capital losses when offsetting ordinary income. And it is better to be able to use long-term losses against short-term gains than against long-term gains, so taxpayers often attempt to time their losses and gains in order to gain maximum benefit from the losses. Finally, because capital losses can be carried forward but not backward by individual taxpayers, it is better for them to sustain excess capital losses in the year before, rather than the year after, large short-term or even long-term capital gains. *See generally* § 1212(b).

The net result of all these rules may be recast in terms of maxims for tax planning. Generally speaking, deductible ordinary losses provide greater tax relief than any kind of deductible capital loss, since ordinary losses are deductible against all income, even that income which is taxed at the highest rates. In turn, short-term capital losses usually save more in taxes than do long-term losses, because the short-term losses can offset short-term capital gains that otherwise will be taxed at ordinary income rates. Long-term losses also can offset short-term gains, but only to the extent long-term losses exceeded long-term gains. So taxpayers usually like their losses to qualify as ordinary losses; if the losses can not qualify as ordinary, taxpayers like them to be short-term rather than long-term capital losses.

To summarize, on the gain side, long-term capital gain obviously is more advantageous than short-term capital gain because most long-term capital gain is taxed at a rate no higher than 15%, while short-term capital gain and ordinary income can be taxed at a rate as high as 35%. The distinction between capital gain (long- or short-term) and ordinary income is still relevant in determining the amount of a deductible capital loss, either long-term or short-term, that will be allowed to be deducted from ordinary income—up to the limit ($3,000). *See* § 1211. Capital losses are fully deductible up to, and to the extent of, capital gain, as a general matter.

The characterization of gain as long- or short-term capital gain also is important in determining the amount of a charitable contribution deduction under § 170(e). Section 170(e) restricts the deduction to the adjusted basis of the property in the case of a donation of appreciated property, if *ordinary* gain or *short*-term capital gain (rather than long-term capital gain) would have been realized *if* the property had been sold instead. *See* § 170(e)(1)(A). But, property which would have produced *long*-term capital gain, if sold, is allowed a full deduction when it is donated to a public charity whose purpose is directly related thereto. *See* I.R.C. §§ 170(e)(1)(A) and (B).

§ 98.   What Is a Capital Asset?

The statute defines capital assets in § 1221(a) as "property" *other than*: (1) stock in trade, inventory, or property held primarily for sale to customers in the ordinary course of taxpayer's trade or business; (2) depreciable or real property used in the trade or business; (3) letters, memoranda, or a copyright or other composition produced by the taxpayer or given to him by the creator; (4) accounts or notes receivable for services rendered or from the sale of property described in (1) above; (5) U.S. publications received at a discount; (6) any commodities derivative financial instrument held by a dealer in such property; (7) any hedging transaction clearly identified as such; and (8) supplies regularly used or consumed in the trade or business. As we shall see, this very inclusive definition of "capital asset"—all property except that excepted—does not exhaust the class of property whose sale will give rise to gain or loss that will be given capital gain or loss treatment. (*See, e.g.,* the quasi-capital asset rules of I.R.C. § 1231.) Nor does the § 1221 definition insure that sale or exchange of property fitting that description will produce capital gain. *See* "Common Law Tests," § 99 *infra,* and the recapture rules of I.R.C. §§ 1239, 1245, 1250, etc. Nevertheless, § 1221 is the keystone.

The statutory exceptions from the category of capital assets obviously cover many items whose sale at a profit produce the kind of income that should be taxed just as are salaries, interest, dividends, and other items of "ordinary income." Some of the terms in I.R.C. § 1221 have given rise to much litigation, perhaps in part because so much tax liability can hinge on whether an item fits an exception in § 1221 or not. The regulations and cases provide some guidelines. One of the most important questions was what "primarily" means in the phrase "primarily for sale to customers." In a case dealing with I.R.C. § 1221, the Supreme Court held that "primarily" means "principally" or "of first importance," not just "substantially" or "essentially." *See* Malat v. Riddell (S.Ct.1966). When the taxpayer holds an asset for dual purposes—to rent or to sell, whichever becomes most profitable—he generally gets capital treatment since he did not hold it *primarily* for sale to customers.

In general under this meaning of "primarily for sale to customers," the cases have given an investor or even a trader (versus a "dealer") in stocks and securities capital gain treatment when he sells his securities at a gain. He is not deemed to hold them primarily for sale to customers, but rather to hold them primarily for investment income. Only if he is a *dealer,* performs an underwriting function, or buys in one market (wholesale, in large lots) and resells in another (retail, in small quantities to many small buyers) will he fit the first exception to the capital asset definition. In contrast, only an investor (not a trader and not a dealer) in land will be given capital gain/loss treatment. *And see* I.R.C. § 1237 (real property subdivided for sale not necessarily excluded from capital treatment); § 1236 (gain by a dealer in securities rarely capital). The trader-dealer distinction is submerged, so that if a taxpayer buys land and subdivides it or repeatedly sells it (intact) to customers, or if he advertises and frequently engages in trader-like purchases and sales, his land will fail to qualify as a capital asset.

Troublesome cases arise when a taxpayer either changes his or her state of mind about property he holds or changes his behavior with respect to it. For example, a taxpayer who holds land or securities as an investment may decide to hold them for sale to customers without evidencing his change of mind by overt behavior. Or, he may liquidate his investment by selling off the stock or land to a number of buyers, rather than to a single buyer, without really having changed the nature of that investment at all.

Faced with ambiguous facts or facts suggesting a change of purpose, the courts have groped for grounds to decide whether gain or loss on sale should be given capital or ordinary tax treatment. In doing so, the courts have focused on the taxpayer's original purpose in acquiring the property, the number, timing and pattern of sales, the activity of the taxpayer with regard to the property sold, whether his personal efforts produced or materially increased the value of the property, whether the payment substitutes for a flow of ordinary income and whether the inventory exception of § 1221(a)(1) is at issue. The cases are not wholly consistent, and general statements about which factors will be determinative are not reliable. However, the Supreme Court held in Arkansas Best Corp. v. Comm. (S.Ct.1988) that the taxpayer's motivation in purchasing an asset is irrelevant to the question of whether the property is a § 1221 capital asset, unless the issue is whether the property should fall under the § 1221(a)(1) inventory exclusion for property held primarily for sale to customers in the ordinary course of trade or business. Thus, a holding company's sale of stock it held in a bank was a sale of a capital asset because stock falls within the broad definition of § 1221. The taxpayer's claim that it originally acquired the stock for business purposes to save its reputation (by providing needed capital to the bank in which it already held stock) was irrelevant.

Different kinds of assets and different business contexts or taxpayers seem to have received different treatment at times, although no principled justification for the differences has been articulated and a factual inquiry constitutes the focus of each case. As noted, investors and traders in securities usually get capital treatment. There seems to be a greater tendency to apply ordinary treatment to sellers of real property. Owners of property that sometimes is leased and sometimes (or eventually) sold have won some cases and lost some. Owners of income interests (such as life estates or leaseholds or contractual rights) often are taxed on ordinary income on sale. Authors, artists, and actors are given ordinary income treatment by I.R.C. § 1221(a)(3). In contrast, special and favorable treatment is given to inventors by I.R.C. § 1235 under which a patent holder who sells or licenses all substantial rights to a patent in return for a lump sum or even for royalties paid periodically and in proportion to use or sales of the patented item will receive long-term capital gain treatment, even if his efforts created the "property." *See* I.R.C. §§ 1235(a) & (b).

Another controversy flowing from the definitional language in I.R.C. § 1221(a)(2) is whether a particular piece of property is "used" in the trade or business. Even if this property is not actively involved in the business, it will qualify as so "used" if it was acquired or is held for such purposes and is "devoted" to the business. Still another definitional problem is whether a gain-seeking activity is an "investment" or a "trade or business." Generally speaking, if this taxpayer is actively engaged, as manager or overseer of something even as passive as an apartment house, "trade or business" treatment will result. If he merely collects profits such as dividends or interest, or even perhaps if he passively collects or accepts rents, the "investment" label will be applied.

When the properties of a going business are sold, each asset separately will be treated as a capital asset or not depending on its individual nature. *See, e.g.,* Williams v. McGowan (2d Cir.1945). Therefore, if a lump-sum purchase price is paid, it must be allocated among the assets to determine gain or loss and capital or ordinary treatment separately for each. So the inventory, accounts receivable and a covenant not to compete will not give rise to capital gain; the fixtures and plant will not be capital assets (but may get capital asset treatment under I.R.C. § 1231); goodwill will yield capital gain or loss, etc.

Section 1060 provides special allocation rules to be used to allocate the purchase price in certain asset acquisitions, such as the purchase of a going business, for § 197, and other, purposes. *See* I.R.C. § 1060.

Section 1221's definition of capital asset is in terms of "property." Not every payment related to property is for a purchase of property (viz. rent, dividends, payment for cancellation of a lease as in Hort v. Comm. (S.Ct.1941), or release from an exclusive purchase contract, *see* Comm. v. Pittston Co. (2d Cir.1958)). Nor is every payment for something given up a payment for "property." For example, payments for invading the taxpayer's right of privacy, and compensation for requisitioning the use of taxpayer's business properties during wartime, have been held not to be payments for "property."

§ 99. Non-statutory Exclusion From Capital Asset Treatment; Common Law Tests

The statute expresses its rules for capital gain or loss treatment in terms of the kind of asset sold or exchanged (*see* § 1221). Sometimes § 1221 describes that asset not in the abstract but rather in terms of its relation to the taxpayer in his particular line of business or economic life. To illustrate, § 1221(a)(1) excludes "property held by the taxpayer primarily for sale to customers in the ordinary course of his trade or business." These descriptions have given rise to much litigation, some of it turning on factual questions and some on issues of law, because the tax differential between ordinary income or deduction and capital gain or loss treatment has been so momentous. Many cases have considered whether a particular piece of property was held for one purpose or another by the taxpayer or was used by him in his business or not, and so on. In some of these cases, assets that would be capital assets in the hands of other taxpayers have been held to fall within an exclusion from the definition of capital asset for the taxpayer involved, and vice versa. In doubtful or borderline cases when gain is at issue, the taxpayer usually argues that the property was a capital asset. When a loss was sustained, he stoutly denies that a capital asset was involved.

In deciding these cases on the meaning of "capital asset," the courts have been known to rise above mere conceptualism and the pigeonholing process of labels and facts. The courts have stepped back far enough to ask whether the income or loss in question was of the kind Congress meant to tax at capital-gain rates or not. Policy analysis and a functional approach have appeared. Increasingly, the authorities have inquired: Whatever the usual label that would be applied to such an asset in the hands of this kind of taxpayer, is it to be treated as a capital asset for purposes of applying the limits on taxing or deducting capital gains or losses? In the life of this taxpayer, do the transactions in question produce the kind of economic gain or loss that is comparable to ordinary income taxed as such to other taxpayers, or not?

In using this intelligent approach, the courts have sometimes seemed to say that the issue is not just whether the asset fits a statutory pigeonhole. Rather, the courts sometimes seem to say, at the risk of putting it too strongly, if this asset or transaction does not seem clearly to fit one statutory category or another, the question is should it be treated as capital or ordinary? To put it another way, the question is whether the transaction was so closely related to the taxpayer's regular income-producing activities as to require equivalent tax treatment as ordinary income or loss rather than capital treatment. Thus, the courts have engrafted a common-law non-statutory and functional test for capital treatment onto the statutory definitions of § 1221 et seq. However, later the U.S. Supreme Court retreated from this position, as will be explained below, after the background has been set forth.

The leading example of this former judicial approach is the well-known case entitled Corn Products Refining Co. v. Comm. (S.Ct.1955). There, a manufacturer of products made from grain corn sought to insure that it would have a reliable supply of raw corn not only by storing millions of bushels of corn but also by buying corn futures. (A corn future is a contract or option enabling the holder to buy corn or take delivery at a future time at a price set earlier.) If the company needed corn when the futures came due, it would take delivery. If not and if no shortage appeared imminent, the taxpayer would sell the futures, sometimes at a loss and sometimes at a gain. In general, corn future contracts would be non-capital assets in the hands of a dealer who held them primarily for sale to customers. To an investor or trader, who bought and sold them for speculative profits, they would be capital assets. To Corn Products Company, the Supreme Court held, the futures were not capital assets and hence the profits and losses must be treated as ordinary income and ordinary losses or expenses of doing business. The futures constituted an integral part of taxpayer's manufacturing business as viewed by the lower courts. The Supreme Court said that, although the futures did not fit the literal language of (the precursor of) § 1221, Congress intended the profits and losses arising from the everyday operation of a business to be considered as ordinary income or loss. The category of "capital assets" was to be narrowly applied and its exclusions broadly interpreted, since capital treatment is an exception from the normal tax requirements of the Code.

However, in a later case, Arkansas Best Corp. v. Comm. (S.Ct.1988), the Supreme Court repudiated the *Corn Products* doctrine. It said that *Corn Products* simply stands for the proposition that hedging transactions that are an integral part of a business' inventory system fall within the inventory exclusion of § 1221(a)(1). The Court held that additional bank stock purchased by Arkansas Best in order to avert sanctions by regulatory authorities (including a possible closing of the bank) was a capital asset because it did not fall into one of the § 1221 exclusions. The Court stated that, in general, the taxpayer's motivation or purpose in purchasing an asset is irrelevant for the definition of "capital asset" in § 1221 and that the only exceptions to classification of assets as capital assets are those listed in § 1221. A strong reading of *Arkansas Best* would say that there is no *non-statutory* exception to the definition of a capital asset. There remains, however, the matter of interpreting and applying the statutory exceptions. The taxation of hedging transactions, like those in *Corn Products*, is now specifically addressed in § 1221(a)(7), § 1221(b)(2), and Regs. § 1.1221–2.

In another well-known case, the taxpayer and Commissioner stood on opposite sides of the same fence. Taxpayer had bought U.S. bonds to deposit as security for completion of a contract with the Finnish government. When they were released on completion of his performance, he sold them, at a loss. Accordingly taxpayer argued that the bonds were ordinary assets in his hands and the losses were fully deductible. The Second Circuit agreed and likened the loss to an expense of paying a premium for an indemnity or performance bond. No investment was intended, the court observed. *See* Comm. v. The Bagley & Sewall Co. (2d Cir.1955). As a "rule of law," the doctrine of *Corn Products* could be invoked by taxpayer as well as the Treasury.

Other cases sustained this approach. In Comm. v. P.G. Lake (S.Ct.1958), the Supreme Court held that amounts received by taxpayers in return for an assignment of oil and sulphur payment rights were taxable as ordinary income. Similarly, in Hort v. Comm. (S.Ct.1941), amounts paid by a lessee to a lessor for release from burdensome lease obligations were held taxable as ordinary income, in lieu of rent, rather than as payments for the sale of a leasehold property.

Another factor predominated in Arrowsmith v. Comm. (S.Ct.1952)—the relationship to events in prior years. There, amounts paid out by taxpayers in a later year were given capital loss treatment because they were closely related to amounts received in prior years as capital gains. Again, logic, policy and equity overcame strict categorical reasoning. *See* also Mitchell v. Comm. (6th Cir.1970) (corporate officer's repayment to corporation deductible only as capital loss, not business expense, because of transactional relationship to prior capital gain).

All in all, the cases adumbrate several notions beyond the statutory language. Among those notions are: whether the receipt or expenditure is a substitute for an ordinary income or expense item; whether it is related to items taxed in prior years in a way that implies particular treatment in the later year; whether the lump receipt (or payment) is merely an anticipation of, or substitute for, ordinary income or expenditures; whether there is a functional equivalence (for capital versus ordinary purposes) between the transaction at issue and another one whose character is fixed; and whether a quality of "sham" or tax evasion permeates the facts. No single statement can encapsulate these disparate ideas, but a good lawyer can project them to still different fact settings.

§ 100. Sale or Exchange

The terms "sale or exchange" used in § 1222, and thus fed into operative sections of the Code, are not defined in the Code and are not always easily applied. Collection of a judgment, purchased by taxpayer from the original plaintiff, has been held not to qualify as a sale or exchange. *See, e.g.*, Galvin Hudson (Tax Court 1953). Retirement, collection or settlement of a debt does not meet the sale-or-exchange requirement. *See* Fairbanks v. U.S. (S.Ct. 1939). (In this instance failure to meet the sale requirement kept out of capital gains preference the "imputed interest" of the creditor's gain.) Obviously a sale or exchange does not occur when a taxpayer receives dividends or rent or cashes in the interest coupon on a bond. Sale of stock before it goes "ex-dividend" will be treated as a sale, even though part of the price includes payment for the right to an expected but as yet undeclared dividend. Sale of a lessor's rights in a lease is likely to give rise to ordinary income, on grounds resembling the anticipatory-assignment-of-income theory in the gift cases, which presented the question "Who is taxable?" The logic is that when the lessor assigns his rights to rent payments, the payment made to him substitutes for rent that would be taxed as ordinary income. The anticipatory receipt should be taxed the same way. Some extreme fact situations may permit a contrary result.

Sales or exchanges usually are found to occur in the event of foreclosure, condemnation, transfer of property subject to a mortgage without personal liability, and transfer of property in satisfaction of a claim against the debtor. Some inconsistencies may be found among decisions on whether releasing, terminating or rescinding a contract in return for a payment is a sale or exchange and likewise among decisions on a copyright or patent holder's transfer with a retained royalty interest. A sale or exchange is not present upon making a gift, collecting an amount owing on a note, or when investment property such as a stock, bond, note or even land evidently becomes worthless. However, some special statutory provisions specifically declare that otherwise doubtful transactions are, or shall be treated as, sales or exchanges. *See, e.g.,* § 166(d)(1)(B); § 165(g)(1), 165(h).

For these purposes, a sale should be differentiated from a consignment for sale and from an agreement to sell. But a sale may be made for payment to be made in installments. Under the notorious *Clay Brown* decision, "sale" is to be taken in its usual meaning of a transfer for a fixed price in money or its equivalent; it need not involve complex determinations of risk shifting, financial responsibility of the buyer, substantial down payment or purchase price to come from other earnings of the assets sold. Comm. v. Clay B. Brown (S.Ct.1965). Nevertheless, a sham transaction or one that lacks the qualities of a sale as usually understood will be challenged by the I.R.S. *See, e.g.,* Rev.Rul. 66–153, 1966–1 C.B. 187.

One of the most difficult transactions to categorize as a sale or not is the lease of equipment or other property accompanied by an option to purchase. Such an arrangement will be treated as a lease unless all the facts and circumstances, especially the option price, timing and other terms, indicate that the option almost surely will be exercised, in which event the deal will receive treatment as a sale for a purchase price to be paid in installments. *See, e.g.,* Estate of Starr v. Comm. (9th Cir.1959); Rev.Rul. 55–540, 1955–2 C.B. 39; Rev. Proc. 2001–28, 2001–1 C.B. 1156. Some of this difficulty was eliminated at times when there were statutory provisions for lease classification, but those rules were repealed. Thus only the non-statutory rules now govern whether a transaction amounts to a "lease" or a "sale." (*See* § 46, *supra*.)

Occasionally it happens that an amount is received or paid by a taxpayer in one year as part of or related to a transaction that involved a sale or exchange in a prior year. In that event, the year of receipt or restoration does not witness a "sale or exchange"; nevertheless, the prior year's event will cause the payment or recovery to be taxed as if it involved a sale or exchange in the current year—if the current events are truly part of, or integrally related to, the prior year's sale or exchange. For example, in the celebrated case of Arrowsmith v. Comm. (S.Ct.1952), the taxpayers had received amounts in an early year as capital gain on the liquidation (treated as a sale or exchange) of their corporation. In a later year, they were required to pay back some of the properties they had received, and the Supreme Court held that they could deduct the repayment only as a capital loss, not as an ordinary loss, because it was an integral part of the earlier sale or exchange. (In such a situation, I.R.C. § 1341 would give the taxpayer a choice whether to deduct the capital loss in the year he made repayment or to reduce his tax in that year by the amount his tax was increased in the earlier year of receipt.)

In some instances, Congress has chosen to specify that a particular transaction will be treated as a sale or exchange whether or not that result would have been reached under general principles. *See, e.g.,* I.R.C. § 1241 (cancellation of lease or distributor's agreement), § 165(g) (worthless securities), § 165(h) (personal casualty gains and losses when gains exceed losses), § 166(d) (non-business bad debts), § 1231 (involuntary conversions). Sometimes Congress has done the opposite—specified that a transaction will not be treated as a sale or exchange. *See, e.g.,* § 1253 (transfers of franchises, trademarks, and trade names).

§ 101. The Holding Period

The holding period requirement for long-term capital treatment lies embedded in the definitions of I.R.C. § 1222, the rules contained in § 1223, and their use in operative code sections such as §§ 1(h), 1212, etc. The rule is applied strictly and technically, without regard to intent or motive of the taxpayer. In computing the holding period, the day of acquisition is excluded and the day of disposition is included. *See* Rev.Rul. 66–7, 1966–1 C.B. 188. If a taxpayer holds a number of fungible pieces of property (such as shares of stock) that were acquired at different times, and if he cannot show which items were sold, he can and must use a first-in, first-out rule for purposes of determining holding period and for determining basis as well. (In some instances, gain or loss from mutual fund shares may be determined by an "average basis" method.)

I.R.C. § 1223 gives the holding requirements further meaning for special transactions in which the holding period for an asset sold by taxpayer A is to be determined by adding the period for which (a) the same taxpayer held another asset or (b) the period for which a different taxpayer held the asset sold by taxpayer A. These are the nonrecognition, carry-over-of-basis or substitution-of-basis transactions, such as those under I.R.C. § 1031, discussed *supra,* § 76. If A's asset sold has the basis of other property for which it was exchanged by A, it similarly shall have the other property's holding period in A's hands. *See* I.R.C. § 1223(1) (substituted or carry-over holding period). And, if A's property sold has the basis that taxpayer B had in the same property (for example if B gave the property to A and A sells it at a gain—§ 1015), then B's holding period shall be tacked on to A's for long-term capital gain or loss determinations. *See* I.R.C. § 1223(2); Regs. § 1.1223–1 (tacking holding period). If A receives property from a decedent and takes a basis equal to the property's fair market value at the time of the decedent's death under § 1014, the property is deemed to have a long-term holding period if it is sold or disposed of within one year of the decedent's death. I.R.C. § 1223(11).

Different holding periods have been used in the Code in its earlier history. At present, one year is used to mark the line dividing long-term from short-term capital gain or loss. *See* I.R.C. § 1222; and *see* § 1223. The required holding period has been six or eighteen months at earlier times.

The holding-period requirement has to do with distinguishing between speculation gains and investment gains. The one-year period, in particular, serves to separate gains that have accrued wholly in one tax year from those possibly accruing over a longer period and hence being "bunched" in one annual accounting period by the rule of realization and subjected to progressive rates.

§ 102. Patents, Copyrights and Other Special Assets

Under I.R.C. § 1235(a), capital asset treatment is accorded inventors in a way that authors, not able to get such treatment (*see* § 1221(3)), must envy. They can get capital-gain treatment on sale of (all substantial rights to) a patent with a price that is contingent on sales or profits of the licensee, payments that are much like royalties. Special treatment is declared for other properties or transactions in other sections: § 1233 (short sales); § 1234 (options); § 1236 (dealers in securities); § 1237 (real property subdivided for sale); §§ 1238–1260 (various items, some soon to be discussed). Especially important is I.R.C. § 1244, which allows holders of shares of stock in small businesses that comply with the rules of § 1244 and thereby issue "§ 1244 stock" to obtain ordinary loss deductibility (rather than capital loss treatment) if the stock should become worthless or be sold at a loss.

§ 103. Quasi–Capital Assets—I.R.C. § 1231

Some kinds of property that § 1221 excludes from capital asset treatment may nevertheless receive capital treatment upon sale or exchange or other disposition by virtue of § 1231 [and parallel provisions such as I.R.C. §§ 1233, 1235; *see also* capital treatment for losses on worthless securities under § 165(g) and bad debts under § 166(d)(2)(B)]. In contrast, some sales or exchanges of what might appear to be capital assets are partly or wholly denied capital treatment by such provisions as I.R.C. §§ 1236, 1239, 1244, 1245, 1250, 1253, etc.

One of the most important provisions that allows a taxpayer to treat assets that are not § 1221 capital assets much as if they were capital assets is I.R.C. § 1231. This section picks up a broad group of properties that § 1221(a)(2) excludes from the capital asset definition, namely property used in the trade or business. [The precise definition of § 1231 property is given in I.R.C. § 1231(b). Note that the definition of § 1231 property is not related to recovery property eligible for A.C.R.S. deductions, but rather to I.R.C. § 167 depreciable property—probably because § 167 adopts § 168 as granting a "reasonable allowance."] However, § 1231 does not simply restore such assets to capital status. A much more complicated effect is produced. To sum it up loosely, § 1231 (taken alone) gives long-term capital gain and loss treatment to gains and losses on sales (and some involuntary conversions—destruction, theft or seizure, requisition or condemnation, or threat or imminence thereof) of § 1231 assets if, and only if, such gains exceed such losses during the year. If § 1231 losses exceed such gains, both gains and losses are ordinary. In actuality, gain or loss on each § 1231 asset must be computed by comparing its adjusted basis with the amount realized on its sale or exchange, etc. Then the taxpayer must set off the losses on § 1231 assets against gains on such assets. If the net result is gain, then each of the individual asset transactions is deemed to have yielded capital gain or loss as the case may be. If the net result is a loss, none of the asset transactions is given capital treatment, so each is deemed to have produced ordinary income or ordinary loss. Heads, taxpayer wins; tails, Commissioner loses. However, a taxpayer who stops thinking when he has concluded that § 1231 will give him capital gain treatment may be surprised to find that I.R.C. § 1245 or § 1250 (both recapturing some depreciation at ordinary income rates) or some other section has changed the result. *See* § 104, *infra*.

See also the separate netting processes for personal casualty losses and gains in I.R.C. §§ 165(h)(2)(B) and (h)(3)(A).

The reasons and role of I.R.C. § 1231 go back to the time of the enactment of its forerunner in 1942. At that time, the § 1231 predecessor was applicable to industrial equipment, factories, rental properties and assets such as ships. Such properties were sometimes lost by taxpayers due to enemy submarine action or other military attack, or through requisition of war production assets by the government for its use. Wartime inflation and peaking income tax rates and excess profits taxes placed a heavy tax burden on taxpayers whose low-basis property was involuntarily "sold" and who were compensated by insurance, condemnation award or other payment. So a tax "break" in the form of capital gain treatment of such "gains" was introduced. Soon that tax relief was extended to other involuntary conversions, to other insured losses and even to voluntary sales (some of which were not so voluntary, when made under threat of condemnation, the draft, or other wartime pressures).

Since losses on such transactions sometimes reflected inadequate depreciation allowances in earlier years or worked a hardship in other ways, tax relief in the form of deductibility as "ordinary" losses recommended itself. Finally, the net effect of such transactions during the year was used to determine whether the final result should be favorable tax on the gains or favorable deductibility of the losses; in either event, one was to wash out the other to the extent of the smaller of the two.

So, § 1231 produces what has been well-termed a hotchpot (or hodge-podge) of gains and losses. Gains in § 1231 transactions are lumped together with § 1231 losses, and the excess of one over the other determines the treatment of both. Both must then be fed into the taxpayer's computation along with his "pure" capital gains and losses and with his "pure" ordinary income or deductible losses.

Section 1231 contains terms, such as "sale or exchange" and "held by the taxpayers primarily for sale to customers in the ordinary course of business," that have produced controversy just as those terms have done when used in §§ 1221, 1222 and 1223. Largely the same meaning is given to them in § 1231, since it is designed to correlate with the prior rules. *See, e.g.,* Hollywood Baseball Ass'n v.

Comm. (9th Cir.1970). Note that § 1231(b) excludes from § 1231 treatment all property that is inventory or property held primarily for sale to customers. Such property cannot receive capital asset treatment either (*see* § 1221), and thus will yield ordinary gain and loss on sale.

In some instances, a taxpayer may not care whether the asset he has sold is called a capital asset (under § 1221) or a quasi-capital asset (under § 1231) because, in isolation, its sale will yield capital gain treatment. But, if the sale were to produce a loss, or if other § 1231 transactions in quasi-capital assets occurred that same year, his sale would produce different tax treatment under § 1221 from that which it might be given under § 1231. So a taxpayer probably will attempt to characterize his asset as "used in the trade or business" in order to obtain ordinary loss treatment in the event of an overall loss. (There is no difference between § 1231 and § 1221 treatment when there is an overall gain.) The taxpayer also may seek to delay or accelerate the timing of a quasi-capital-asset transaction to avoid or fit into the § 1231 netting process in a given year.

In addition to sales or exchanges, some other transactions season the § 1231 goulash. Not only are involuntary conversions of § 1231 assets and capital assets to be tossed in, but a special netting of some involuntary conversions (those by casualty or theft) must be made; if such losses exceed such gains, both are removed from § 1231 treatment— and will be given such treatment as the Code otherwise determines. *See* I.R.C. § 1231(a)(4)(C). That treatment means ordinary gain and loss treatment, since no sale or exchange has occurred to satisfy the capital gain and loss rules. The net result is to treat the net loss as an ordinary loss. *See* Regs. § 1.1231–1(e)(3). If such gains exceed losses, both will be added to the general § 1231 netting along with gains and losses from voluntary sales of § 1231 assets, etc., so that their taxability and deductibility will ultimately depend on the outcome of the entire § 1231 netting process.

The recapture rule of § 1231(c) prevents the taxpayer from exploiting § 1231 by making all losses occur in one year and all gains in another year, producing ordinary loss treatment for the losses and long-term capital gain treatment for the gains. Under § 1231(c), if the losses are taken in an earlier year, gain in later years will be treated as ordinary to the extent of the earlier losses. This is achieved by allowing the gain to be treated as capital gain only to the extent that it exceeds the non-recaptured net § 1231 losses, as defined in § 1231(c)(4).

Section 1231 by its terms applies only to recognized gains and losses; hence nonrecognition sections such as §§ 267, 1031–1033, and 1091 will keep a gain or loss out of the hotchpot even if realized, until it is recognized. *See* Regs. § 1.1231–1(d).

§ 104. Recapture of Depreciation and Other Allowances

Section 1231 does not operate without exceptions, however. The recapture-of-depreciation sections, here referring to §§ 1245 and 1250, restrict the benefits offered by § 1231. These sections, to summarize them broadly, require that a taxpayer who (at a gain) sells or otherwise disposes of real or personal property of a character subject to an allowance for depreciation, accelerated cost recovery or amortization must recognize such gain at once (notwithstanding most nonrecognition rules) and must treat some or all of the gain as ordinary income. Thus §§ 1245 and 1250 override many other statutory and judicial rules, not only rules for capital treatment but also some rules for nonrecognition of gain. Sections 1245 and 1250 do not apply to losses.

Note that powerful § 1239 also recaptures as ordinary income *all* gain recognized on a sale or exchange of property between related persons if, in the hands of the transferee, the property is of a character subject to the allowance for depreciation provided in § 167. I.R.C. § 1239(a). The purpose of § 1239 is to block *repeated* depreciation and conversion of ordinary income to capital gain by affiliated or related taxpayers.

The recapture rules of § 1245 for depreciable personal and other property [not including a building or its structural components, so long as it is tangible property and otherwise fits the description in § 1245(a)(3)(B)], and of § 1250 for depreciable real property,` other than § 1245 property (*see* § 1250(c)), differ from each other in detail but have a common philosophy. Their purpose is to recapture from the taxpayer a correct amount of the tax benefit he has gained through depreciation or

A.C.R.S. deductions allowed in prior years if he "recaptures" that economic depreciation or cost recovery by selling the property at a profit.

Suppose, for example, a taxpayer owns a piece of equipment that he uses in his trade or business. Assume that he paid $30,000 for it originally, and therefore that amount became his cost basis under § 1012. During the years he has owned the machine, he has been allowed and has taken a total of $10,000 in depreciation or A.C.R.S. deductions. As a consequence, his adjusted basis in the machine, for purposes of determining gain or loss, is $20,000— cost basis adjusted as prescribed by § 1011 and § 1016. Also assume, for purposes of illustration, that taxpayer's marginal rate of taxation on his ordinary income during the years he held the machine was, say, 35%. Since the depreciation deductions (totaling $10,000) were all taken from gross income to arrive at taxable income, the $10,000 deductions saved him approximately $3,500 in tax over the years. The $10,000 deductions allowed him to receive tax-free $10,000 in ordinary income that otherwise would have been taxed at the 35% rate— a total of $3,500 in tax was saved.

If taxpayer sells his machine for $20,000 he will realize neither gain nor loss on sale. His prior depreciation or cost recovery deductions will have served their purpose—to take account of the $10,000 cost he incurred in the form of a capital expenditure for an income-producing machine that he eventually sold for $10,000 less than he paid for it. He is treated like a taxpayer who paid $10,000 to rent such a machine for those years, with the rental deducted from gross income as a cost of doing business. If he is able to sell the machine for only $18,000, a loss deduction of $2,000 in the year of sale, deductible as an ordinary loss under § 1231 if no other § 1231 transaction occurs that year, will set him right.

Suppose, however, that the taxpayer ultimately sells the machine for $27,000. If only § 1231 applied and if no other § 1231 transaction occurred, he would have gain of $7,000 (*see* §§ 1001–1002), but that gain would be taxed as capital gain. Under present law, he would benefit by the 15% rate ceiling on long-term capital gain. Consider closely, however, what would be occurring. The taxpayer took $10,000 in depreciation that, presumably, allowed him to receive $10,000 of ordinary income tax-free, and he benefited $3,500 from deducting that $10,000 as depreciation (35% × $10,000 = $3,500). As it turned out, the depreciation or A.C.R.S. allowances were excessive, because it appears that the market value of the machine did not fall as much as everyone anticipated. Taxpayer's basis was reduced by the $10,000 allowed, which increases his gain on sale by $7,000, but that gain would be taxed as *capital gain,* at a maximum rate of 15%, for a tax bill of only $1,050 ($7,000 × 15%). He enjoyed a tax benefit earlier of $3,500 on depreciation that, as things turned out, he did not have to suffer as a cost, yet only part of that tax saving ($1,050) would be returned to the government under § 1231 (and § 1(h)). He would be receiving an unearned, tax-free gift of $2,450 from the government. To be sure, he suffered a net cost of $3,000 (unregained depreciation), so he should get an eventual benefit of $1,050 (35% × $3,000), but not $2,450. Section 1245 remedies this problem.

Section 1245 sets out to recapture taxpayer's full tax benefit from some allowances [including depreciation (§ 167); A.C.R.S. (§§ 168, 179); amortization of goodwill and other intangibles (*see* § 197(f)(7)); and the 50% reduction in basis required when taking a § 38 general business credit (§ 50(c))] that exceed actual price deterioration. It does so simply by declaring, with a few exceptions, that if § 1245 property, which generally includes personal property on which A.C.R.S. deductions were taken (or simply could have been taken—"allowable deductions"), is sold at a gain, the amount of the gain attributable to the above allowances shall be treated as gain from the sale or exchange of property that is neither a capital asset nor a § 1231 asset—in short, as ordinary income. Section 1245 employs the concept of "recomputed basis," which (generally) amounts to adjusted basis plus depreciation, A.C.R.S. and expensing deductions that the taxpayer either took or was entitled to take, and the § 50(c) basis reduction or amortization deductions taken since § 1245 became effective in 1962. Gain up to recomputed basis is ordinary income. The rest, if any, is capital gain or § 1231 gain, as the nature of the asset requires. (Exceptions are made for gifts, bequests, some tax-free transactions, like-kind exchanges, involuntary conversions, etc.)

Returning to the previous example, the recomputed basis is $30,000—the $20,000 adjusted basis plus the $10,000 in depreciation deductions the taxpayer enjoyed. Under § 1245, the taxpayer is required to report as ordinary income the amount by which the *lower* of (a) *recomputed basis* ($30,000), or (b) the *amount realized* ($27,000), exceeds the adjusted basis ($20,000). Thus, the taxpayer must report as ordinary income $7,000—the difference between $27,000 and $20,000. At 35% that gain will produce a tax of $2,450, recapturing all but $1,050 of his $3,500 benefit from depreciation of $10,000, namely, recapturing all of the benefit of deducting $7,000 (the amount he regained on sale).

Now suppose instead that the taxpayer sells the machine for $33,000. The recomputed basis still will be $30,000. The first $10,000 of gain will be ordinary income ($30,000–$20,000), but the last $3,000 will be taxed as a capital or § 1231 hotchpot gain. This outcome makes sense: the taxpayer has sold the machine for $3,000 more than he paid for it, so he certainly has realized a capital (or § 1231 hotchpot) gain. Therefore, once the tax law has recovered all of the taxpayer's depreciation deductions—which overstated the depreciation on his machine—it will allow him to enjoy his capital or § 1231 hotchpot gain.

Since § 1245 overrides nonrecognition sections (except where it explicitly refrains from doing so) it can produce recognition of gain when otherwise there would be none. [Note: § 1245 says "is disposed of," not "sold or exchanged." But § 1245(b) exempts some dispositions, such as gifts and bequests and some nonrecognition transactions, from this broad mandatory rule of recognition.] And then it applies ordinary income treatment to the gain so recognized.

While § 1245 generally applies to personal property, it also applies to *some* (specified) depreciable or amortizable real property. But, it does not apply to a building or its structural components. *See* I.R.C. § 1245(a)(3)(B). Buildings and most depreciable real property are relegated to the tender mercies of § 1250.

Section 1250 makes a similar but lesser attempt to recapture depreciation in the event *depreciable* real property (but not § 1245 property) is disposed of. Roughly speaking, § 1250 recaptures only that portion of gain on the disposition of § 1250 property [defined in § 1250(c)] held more than one year that is attributable to prior depreciation deductions *in excess of* those that would have been taken on the straight-line method of depreciation.

If the § 1250 property was acquired after 1986, and if the taxpayer's holding period exceeds one year, there usually will be no recapture. Since all buildings placed in service after 1986 must be depreciated on the straight-line method, there will be no "additional depreciation." *See* I.R.C. § 168(b)(3). Actually, § 1250 recovers the "applicable percentage" of the lower of the additional depreciation or the gain. For most § 1250 property, the applicable percentage is 100%. However, for certain types of low-income housing, the applicable percentage is 100% minus one percentage point for each full month the property was held beyond 100 full months. As to methods of depreciation, *see* § 44 in Chapter IV *supra*.

Even after 1986, if § 1250 property is held *less than* one year, *all* depreciation (for that period), even straight-line depreciation, will constitute "additional depreciation" and be "recaptured" under § 1250(a)(1). *See* § 1250(b)(1).

Thus, ordinary income rates apply only to the lesser of (the applicable percentage of) *excess* depreciation (over straight line) or gain realized. So, gain that returns what turned out to be "overgenerous" straight line depreciation deductions on § 167/ § 168 property or gain in excess of that (*e.g.* if sales price exceeds original cost basis) will be gain on the sale of depreciable real property. Because the straight-line method is required after 1986 for all non-residential real property, residential rental property and property as to which taxpayer elects to have straight-line recovery under § 168(b)(5), all gain on disposition of such property will be capital gain, and there will be no recapture by § 1250. (*But see* § 1(h) for possible taxation at the 25–percent rate, as discussed in more detail below.) As such, it will be gain on the sale of a capital or § 1231 asset. If it is gain on sale of a § 1231 asset, the gain will be thrown into the § 1231 hotchpot. However, § 1(h)(1)(D) will apply a *special* 25% capital-gain rate to such "unrecaptured § 1250 gain."

A special 25% capital-gain rate applies for some capital gain on the sale or exchange of § 1250 property. As explained above, § 1250 recaptures gain on sale of § 1250 property as ordinary income to the extent of the *excess* of accelerated depreciation over straight-line depreciation, and § 1250 also recaptures as ordinary income all gain up to the amount of all depreciation deductions (even straight-line) for property held for under one year. Next, under § 1(h), to the extent that depreciation has been taken on the § 1250 property, and *except for* gain recaptured by § 1250 or § 1231(c), the gain will be taxed at a maximum rate of 25 percent. This latter gain is called "unrecaptured § 1250 gain." *See* I.R.C. § 1(h)(1)(D) and § 1(h)(6). Stated differently, the portion of the gain attributable to depreciation that ordinarily would have been taxed as capital gain or § 1231 gain—the amount of straight-line (but not "additional") depreciation—is taxed at a flat, fixed rate of 25 percent. Accelerated depreciation and first-year depreciation are subject to recapture by § 1250 as ordinary income. The remainder of the long-term capital gain (due to market factors or inflation) is subject to the new, favorable rates (such as 15%) for long-term capital gain.

For example, Mr. and Mrs. X own a piece of rental property that they bought several years ago for $100,000. Up to the date of sale, they have properly taken $15,000 in straight-line depreciation deductions, so the property's adjusted basis in their hands is now $85,000. They sell the property in

2004 for $150,000, realizing a $65,000 long-term capital gain. Assuming the couple is in the 35%–percent tax bracket, $15,000 of their gain—the amount of depreciation they claimed—will be taxed at 25 percent. See § 1(h)(1)(D). The rest of the gain, $50,000, will be subject to tax at 15 percent. If they had taken accelerated depreciation (under former A.C.R.S. rules), section 1250 would recapture *that* amount as ordinary income to them. Hence "unrecaptured § 1250 gain" means gain *up to* depreciation allowable but *not* reconverted to ordinary income by § 1250's normal recapture process, or by § 1231(c), etc.

Returning to Mr. and Mrs. X, now suppose that they had properly taken $23,000 in depreciation deductions (this amount, $23,000, exceeds the amount that they would have been allowed by straight-line depreciation ($15,000) by $8,000). The adjusted basis of their property in 2004 would be $77,000. With a sale price of $150,000, their gain would be $73,000. The gain breaks down as follows. First, section 1250 recaptures the excess of total depreciation deductions taken ($23,000) over allowable straight-line depreciation ($15,000). This excess is $8,000. Section 1250 taxes this excess as ordinary income. The next $15,000 of gain is "unrecaptured § 1250 gain"—gain *up to* depreciation allowed but *not* reconverted to ordinary income by § 1250's normal recapture process, or by § 1231(c). Put another way, "allowable" depreciation was $23,000; § 1250 recaptured $8,000 of the depreciation as ordinary income, so $15,000 of depreciation was "allowable" but *not* recaptured. This $15,000 of gain ("unrecaptured § 1250 gain") will be taxed at 25 percent under § 1(h). The remaining $50,000 of gain will be taxed as long-term capital gain (at the 15% rate, since Mr. and Mrs. X are in the 35% tax bracket).

Like § 1245, § 1250 overrides the general nonrecognition rules, with specified exceptions. Like § 1245, it applies only to sales at a gain, not to losses. Allowances and special rules are made for low income housing, rehabilitation expenditures and substantial improvements to property. A number of technical qualifications arm § 1250's weapon and must be consulted before attempting to apply § 1250 in practice.

The Code also contains other, less important recapture rules. To help prevent taxpayers from converting farm expenses that have been deducted from ordinary income into capital gain, I.R.C. § 1252 applies a recapture rule on the sale of farm property. Section 1254 recaptures some intangible drilling and development costs of oil and gas property.

Under important I.R.C. § 1239, if taxpayer sells or exchanges property that will be depreciable in the hands of a transferee who is an entity such as a corporation 50% of whose stock is owned by him or his spouse, or if a sale takes place between two commonly controlled corporations (owned directly or indirectly by the same taxpayer), gain recognized may not receive capital asset or quasi-capital asset treatment; it will be taxed as ordinary income.

Gain from sale of some other special assets is covered by various Code sections in the §§ 1245–1250, 1252–1260 range.

Finally, recapture of another special tax allowance, the § 38 "general business credit," including the (former) investment credit, is imposed when property on which such a credit was allowed (§ 38 property) is disposed of before the end of its estimated useful life. I.R.C. § 50(a). Section 50(a)(1) allows a taxpayer some credit for each year § 38 business-credit property is held.

Like the depreciation deduction, the deduction for interest interacts closely with the preferential rate applicable to long-term capital gains. Section 163(d) disallows a deduction for interest on investment indebtedness to the extent such interest exceeds the taxpayer's net investment income. Since no offset of the excess investment interest is allowed against ordinary income, the section attempts to restrict the translation of ordinary deductions for gain-producing expenses into income taxed at preferential long-term capital gain rates, a conversion sought by some high-bracket ordinary income people who borrowed to make investments and used the interest deduction to "shelter" their ordinary income from tax.

Section 163(d) also reduces opportunities to take a current deduction for an expense that produces income later, such that the tax is deferred. *Conver-*

sion and *deferral,* often magnified by *leverage,* the use of borrowed money in making an investment, are prime objectives of tax shelters. Against techniques devised to achieve these objectives are arrayed, in addition to § 163(d), recapture rules such as those in §§ 1239, 1245 and 1250, "at risk" rules of § 465, passive loss limitation rules of § 469, accounting rules such as § 447, ceilings or disallowance of deductions as in § 280A, limitations on amounts allowable to the basis of assets quickly depreciated as in § 1056, and (to be described in § 108, *infra*) the alternative minimum tax. Many interact with the rules about capital gains and losses, in their effect on tax-shelter and other investments targeted at preferential rates on income, when those rates are available. Much of the complexity of the law and its administration and compliance can be traced to the decision to allow long-term capital gains to be taxed at a preferential rate.

§ 105. Delayed Recognition of Capital Gain or Loss

Rules of nonrecognition, treated at § 76 *supra,* have largely been disregarded in this chapter, which deals mainly with *how* (not *when*) income is taxed, or *how* losses, costs, and expenditures are deductible in connection with sales of property. The question of how income is taxed (or how a deduction is allowed) can arise, of course, only if and when the gain or loss is recognized. If the item is not to be recognized, the "how?" question cannot then arise.

Nevertheless, a word or two about nonrecognition must be said at this point, since nonrecognition rules often apply to transactions in property, the capital gains playground. They apply when a direct or ultimate exchange of properties is deemed to leave the taxpayer in an investment situation so largely unchanged as to warrant postponement of tax. Nonrecognition rules always aim to postpone, not to eliminate, the tax consequences. Events, however, may lead to reduction or elimination of tax. For example, a taxpayer whose gain on an exchange of property was not recognized later may die while owning the new property in which his unrecovered investment is that which he had in the first property. A stepped-up basis under I.R.C. § 1014 will be obtained at his death, and the gain or loss on the first investment—on which tax or an allowance was deferred—will never be taken into account, nor will gain or loss on the second investment.

Reduction of tax also may occur, for example, when § 1250 property or a capital asset or a § 1231 asset is exchanged without recognition (as under § 1031 or § 1033) and held to be disposed of later in a taxable sale when the holding period has become sufficient to reduce recapture or the rate of tax applied. The indexation of tax rates may also reduce taxes that have been deferred. The effect will presumably be greater the longer the tax is deferred and the higher the rate of inflation.

Deferral alone, of course, usually proves valuable because of the time-value of money. Postponing payment of tax allows the taxpayer to invest the postponed tax at interest or otherwise use it to generate income in the interim.

Even when some nonrecognition rule applies, its nonrecognition may be overridden by some recapture or dominating rule requiring recognition "notwithstanding any other provision of this subtitle." *See, e.g.,* I.R.C. §§ 1245(a) and 1250(a). These overriding recognition rules contain some exceptions of their own, as for gifts, transfers at death, and specified tax-free transactions. *See* I.R.C. §§ 1245(b) and 1250(d).

If gain or loss goes unrecognized on a property exchange, the consequence will be a substitution or other adjustment of basis to preserve taxpayer's record of unrecovered investment, which at some later time is to be taken into account. If the gain or loss that went unrecognized would have been capital gain, the question arises whether, when it ultimately is recognized (on sale of the second investment), it will retain its character as capital rather than ordinary. The answer is "not necessarily." Later events may transmute the gain or loss from capital to ordinary. For example, if taxpayer holds investment property whose sale would produce capital gain and instead of selling it exchanges it tax-free for a second property of like kind, it is possible that when he sells the second property that second property will have lost its character as a capital asset. To illustrate, that result might occur if taxpayer, some time after the tax-free exchange, turned his investment property to a new use, by using it in his trade or business (thus perhaps fitting it into the § 1231 quasi-capital-asset category) or by holding it for sale to customers in the ordinary course of his business. If so, all the gain in selling the second asset will be § 1231 hotchpot gain or ordinary income, as the case may be. This transformation resembles the change that could have occurred if he had altered the character of his first property from investment to § 1231 or inventory property and then sold it. But the consequence of changing the second property is to alter the characterization of his gain on the first as well as on the second property, since taxation of gain on the first was delayed and became inherent in the second.

§ 106. Dividends

Corporate income paid out to shareholders as dividends is subjected to two taxes. First, the corporation must pay tax on its taxable income under the rates in § 11. When the corporation's net profits are paid out to its shareholders as dividends, the shareholders must include the dividends in taxable income and pay a second tax. In contrast, if a corporation borrows capital, the interest it pays on the borrowed funds will be deductible and reduce its taxable income. The tax distinction between corporate equity (double tax) and corporate debt (one tax paid by the recipient of the interest) has long been a feature of corporate taxation in the United States. However, income earned by partnerships and other pass-through entities (*e.g.*, Subchapter S corporations) is taxed directly to the investors and therefore is subject to only one level of tax.

In 2003, Congress became concerned about the economic distortions produced by the tax incentives for corporations to finance using debt rather than equity, and encouraging corporations to retain and accumulate earnings instead of paying dividends. To alleviate the tax burden on dividends, I.R.C. § 1(h)(11) provides that "qualified dividend income" is to be taxed as net capital gain and at a maximum tax rate of 15%. Like net capital gain, taxpayers in the 10% and 15% brackets may be taxed at a 5% rate (0% after 2007).

Section 1(h) defines qualified dividend income as dividends received from (a) domestic corporations, and (b) certain foreign corporations, including those incorporated in a U.S. possession, eligible for the benefits of a treaty with the U.S. that the I.R.S. determines is satisfactory and includes an exchange of information program, or readily tradeable on an established U.S. securities market. If a shareholder does not hold a share of stock for more than 60 days during the 120–day period beginning 60 days before the ex-dividend date, dividends on the stock are not eligible for the lower rates. The preferential tax treatment for dividends is scheduled to terminate ("sunset") after December 31, 2008, unless revived.

§ 107. Individual Tax Rates

The graduated tax rates applicable to the ordinary income of individual taxpayers and trusts and estates are set forth in I.R.C. §§ 1–3, together with certain definitions of categories. Single persons, heads of households, married taxpayers filing joint returns and surviving spouses are separately categorized, and this filing status determines the levels of taxable income subject to the tax rates, which range from 10% to 35%. The lowest rate-dividing line (the dollar figure that divides the 10% bracket from the 15% bracket) is lowest for single persons and highest for married persons filing a joint return, with heads of households at an intermediate level. Two single taxpayers with separate incomes will pay less tax than will a married couple who file a joint return with the same total income, in some income ranges and proportions. Sometimes the reverse is true, creating a "marriage reward." *See* § 80, *supra,* for more detailed description of rates and comparative tax burdens on married and single taxpayers.

Rates of tax actually paid by taxpayers are a function not only of the nominal rates contained in the rate schedules but also of exemptions, standard deductions, and other allowances. Even a proportional or flat rate schedule can produce a tax that is progressive with income if some amounts of income are exempt (*i.e.*, taxed at a zero rate). For example, a flat rate of 25% applied to all income above $5,000 yields a harvest of 12½% on an income totaling $10,000 (25% × $5,000 *taxable* income = $1,250); 16.6% on total income of $15,000; 18.75% on total income of $20,000; and so on. Thus to understand the rates of tax, in some senses of the phrase, requires knowledge of exemption levels, as well as other allowances.

The standard deduction specified is a flat $3,000 for single persons, $4,400 for heads of households, $5,000 for married persons filing joint returns and surviving spouses, and $2,500 for married persons filing separate returns. All have changed, in time, and will continue to change, inasmuch as they are adjusted for inflation (or may legislatively be expanded or contracted). The standard deduction amounts are modified to address concerns about the treatment of married taxpayers compared to single taxpayers. *See* I.R.C. § 63(c)(2), (7). (To illustrate, the 2004 tax year amounts corresponding to those given above are: $4,850; $7,150; $9,700 and $4,850.)

Eligible taxpayers may take the refundable earned income credit, which is described in detail above in § 64, *supra.*

Lower- and middle-income taxpayers aged 65 and over may take the § 22 "credit for the elderly and permanently and totally disabled." The credit is computed at the rate of 15% of a *base amount* of $5,000 for a single individual or a joint return if only one spouse is qualified, or $7,500 for a married couple filing a joint return where both spouses are qualified, or a maximum credit of $750 ($1,125 for a married couple filing a joint return). The *base amount* is still further reduced by Social Security (payroll tax) payments and is also reduced by one-half of adjusted gross income in excess of $7,500 ($10,000 for a married couple). Thus, even without

Social Security payments, no credit is available if adjusted gross income exceeds $17,500 ($25,000 if married).

Purely by way of comparison, Federal Income Tax on corporations as of 2004 is levied at the rate of 15% on the first $50,000 of corporate income, 25% on income over $50,000 but not over $75,000, 34% on corporate income above $75,000 but not over $10,000,000, and 35% on amounts over $10,000,000. Section 11(b) also provides for surcharges on high-income corporations (with a special surtax of 5% on income over $100,000, but only up to a surtax amount of $11,750). Since distributions of corporate income after tax, as dividends, are not deductible by the corporation and constitute income to the share-holders, corporate earnings have two toll gates to cross before ending up in the hands of human beings, unlike earnings of a proprietorship or partnership. However, dividends are taxed at a maximum rate of 15% under § 1(h)(11). *See* § 106, *supra.*

§ 108.   The Alternative Minimum Tax

The Tax Reform Act of 1969 introduced a tax on a quantity called "tax preference" income or "items of tax preference." In addition, the 1986 T.R.A. requires some "adjustments" to be made in computing the base figure, "alternative minimum taxable income." *See* I.R.C. §§ 56–59 and § 35, *supra,* this text. The items covered by this tax measure income that otherwise would be taxed but for a tax preference, such as some amortization, accelerated depreciation, depletion or even some allowed deductions. The "adjustments" of I.R.C. § 56 now recompute taxable income by altering the amount of some deductions, such as those for depreciation, net operating losses, miscellaneous itemized deductions, medical expenses, taxes, interest, and the standard deduction.

Some of the tax preference items listed in § 57 are certain tax-exempt interest, intangible drilling costs, and depletion. Examples of items that need to be adjusted to derive an alternative taxable income in § 56 are itemized deductions (miscellaneous itemized deductions, medical expenses, interest deductions and standard deductions), net operating loss deductions and research and experimental expenditure deductions. Once again, tax preference items will be added back to taxable income, whereas the tax adjustment items will recompute the deductions already taken, thereby readjusting taxable income.

The minimum tax is based on the philosophy that a taxpayer who receives significant amounts of economic income should not be able to avoid all—or "too much"—tax liability through applicable exclusions, deductions and other allowances. Congress and the public were moved to act in part by the revelation that some very high income individuals paid no federal income tax at all because of allowances, preferences or "loopholes"—tax-favored income or special deductions. Everyone, it was thought, should have to pay some significant amount of tax on his or her economic income.

The alternative minimum tax has a two-tiered rate structure for individuals: 26% of the "taxable excess" up to $175,000 above the exemption amount (defined in § 55(d)) and 28% of the "taxable excess" above $175,000. *See* I.R.C. § 55.

The base of the § 55 tax is "alternative minimum taxable income," defined generally in § 55(b) as taxable income plus tax preferences (listed in I.R.C. § 57) and recomputed by the adjustments specified in I.R.C. § 56. The final amount is subject to an exemption (in 2004, $40,250 for single taxpayers, $58,000 for married taxpayers filing jointly, $29,000 for married taxpayers filing separately, and $22,500 for estates and trusts). *See* I.R.C. § 55(d). The tax is then payable only to the extent that it exceeds the regular income tax owed.

APPENDIX

TIME–VALUE OF MONEY, DEFERRAL, COMPOUND INTEREST AND INDIVIDUAL RETIREMENT ACCOUNTS

To see how money invested at a positive rate of return can increase very greatly and how early saving in a person's lifetime can be especially beneficial, particularly so if it's tax preferred, consider these two individuals. One of them, Alice, opens an I.R.A. at age 22 and begins contributing $2,000 to it each year. For illustrative purposes, suppose the account earns 12% per year in interest. Her contribution each year is deductible, and the interest earned in the account is not included in her income. She contributes for six years and then stops; she never contributes another penny, but instead just lets the account remain—earning 12% interest each year until she reaches age 65, when the balance will be the amount shown.

The second person, Barclay, doesn't start saving until later. He opens his account at age 28, just when Alice stops contributing. Barclay then has to contribute $2,000 each year for almost the rest of his working life to match the fund (of as-yet untaxed dollars) in Alice's account. At age 60, Barclay's account will for the first time equal Alice's.

Look how much each person has accumulated. Even assuming the withdrawal by each will be taxed, suppose at 40%, look how much each will have left for retirement. The amounts would be less if the rate of interest credited were lower or if the account were not tax-favored and some of each year's interest had to be withdrawn to pay tax on the total amount of interest credited. But the principle remains the same, and the increase in the balance in the account in each case is impressive.

TIME VALUE OF MONEY—COMPOUND INTEREST AT 12%, TAX–FREE IN AN I.R.A.

	Alice (deposits $12,000 over 6 years)		Barclay (deposits $74,000 over 37 years)	
Age	Deposit	Balance in Account at End of Year	Deposit	Balance in Account at End of Year
22	$2,000	$ 2,240	0	0
23	2,000	4,749	0	0
24	2,000	7,559	0	0
25	2,000	10,706	0	0
26	2,000	14,230	0	0
27	2,000	18,178	0	0
28	0	20,359	$2,000	$ 2,240
29	0	22,803	2,000	4,749
30	0	25,539	2,000	7,559
31	0	28,603	2,000	10,706
32	0	32,036	2,000	14,230
33	0	35,880	2,000	18,178
34	0	40,186	2,000	22,599
35	0	45,008	2,000	27,551
36	0	50,409	2,000	33,097
37	0	56,458	2,000	39,309
38	0	63,233	2,000	46,266
39	0	70,821	2,000	54,058
40	0	79,320	2,000	62,785
41	0	88,838	2,000	72,559

	Alice (deposits $12,000 over 6 years)		Barclay (deposits $74,000 over 37 years)	
Age	Deposit	Balance in Account at End of Year	Deposit	Balance in Account at End of Year
42	0	99,499	2,000	83,507
43	0	111,438	2,000	95,767
44	0	124,811	2,000	109,499
45	0	139,788	2,000	124,879
46	0	156,563	2,000	142,105
47	0	175,351	2,000	161,397
48	0	196,393	2,000	183,005
49	0	219,960	2,000	207,206
50	0	246,355	2,000	234,310
51	0	275,917	2,000	264,668
52	0	309,028	2,000	298,668
53	0	346,111	2,000	336,748
54	0	387,644	2,000	379,398
55	0	434,161	2,000	427,166
56	0	486,261	2,000	480,665
57	0	544,612	2,000	540,585
58	0	609,966	2,000	607,695
59	0	683,162	2,000	682,859
60	0	765,141	2,000	767,042
61	0	856,958	2,000	861,327
62	0	959,793	2,000	966,926
63	0	1,074,968	2,000	1,085,197
64	0	1,203,964	2,000	1,217,661
65	0	1,348,440	0	1,363,780

*

INDEX

References are to Sections of this book

DEFERRED PAYMENT METHOD OF ACCOUNTING
See "Accounting, Methods"

DEPENDENCY EXEMPTIONS, § 63

DEPENDENT
   See also "Dependency Exemptions"
Credit for expenses in caring for, § 57
Exemption for employer-paid expenses, § 34

DEPLETION ALLOWANCES, § 47
Cost depletion, § 47
General, § 47
Gross income, percentage of, § 47
Natural deposits, minerals, etc., § 47
Percentage depletion, § 47

DEPRECIATION, § 7, § 44
Accelerated Cost Recovery System, § 44
Accelerated depreciation, § 44
Amortization, § 44
Asset depreciation range system, § 44
Assets depreciable, § 44
Basis, § 44
Basis adjustments, § 44
Cost, historic vs. replacement, § 44, § 93
Deduction, introduction, § 44
Expensing, § 44
First year, additional depreciation, § 44
Guidelines, § 44
Recapture, § 104
Recovery property, § 44
Salvage value, § 44
Unrecaptured § 1250 gain, § 95
Useful life, § 44
   Guidelines, § 44

DISABILITY PAYMENTS, FORMER EXCLUSION FOR, § 31

DISCHARGE OF DEBT
Income, § 18
Solvency of debtor as affecting, § 18

DISCOUNTING
Original issue discount, § 50
To present value, of money, § 11

DISPOSITION OF PROPERTY, HOW TAXED, § 92, § 93

PRIZES AND AWARDS
Statutory exclusion, § 27

PROFIT RELATED DEDUCTIONS
See "Deductions"

PROFIT SHARING
See "Pension and Profit Sharing Plans"

PROGRESSIVE RATES
See "Rates"

PROPERTY
Basis, *see* "Basis," this index
Capital assets, § 98
    See "Capital Assets"
Dispositions of, how taxed, § 92
Gains and losses on sale or disposition of, § 92
Imputed income from ownership of, § 20
Income from, as gift, § 26
Patents, copyrights, etc., § 98, § 102
Primarily held for sale to customers, § 98
Recovery property, § 44
Sale of, § 92
Settlements, § 82
    Alimony distinguished, § 83
    As taxable events, § 82
    Gain or loss recognized, § 82
Transfers,
    In connection with services, § 74
    Incident to divorce, § 82
Income taxable to whom, § 79

PROPORTIONAL RATES
See "Rates"

PUBLIC POLICY, LIMIT ON DEDUCTIONS, § 9

PUNITIVE DAMAGES
As income, § 16, § 31

RATES
Applied to taxable income, § 7
Capital gains, § 93, § 95
Corporate income tax, § 4
Effective rate, § 8
Graduated rates, § 8
Head of household, § 107

†